2-50

D1639536

The Royal Shakespeare Company

The Royal Shakespeare Company

The Peter Hall Years

by

DAVID ADDENBROOKE

With a foreword by
PETER HALL
and afterword by
TREVOR NUNN

WILLIAM KIMBER · LONDON

First published in 1974 by
WILLIAM KIMBER & CO. LIMITED
Godolphin House, 22a Queen Anne's Gate,
London, SW1H 9AE

© David Addenbrooke, 1974
SBN 7183 0103 X

Typeset by
Specialised Offset Services Ltd., Liverpool
and printed in Great Britain by
W.J. Mackay & Co. Ltd., Chatham

For Vivienne

'. . . . *O brave new world,*
that has such people in't!'

Contents

Part I

The Development of The Royal Shakespeare Company over the years 1960-8

Part II

Personal Interviews

Part III

Appendices

List of Illustrations

Table of Abbreviations

ADC (Theatre, Cambridge)	Amateur Dramatic Club
ATV (UK)	Associated Television
BBC	The British Broadcasting Corporation
CBS (USA)	The Columbia Broadcasting System
DALTA	The Dramatic and Lyric Theatres Association
LAMDA	The London Academy of Music and Dramatic Art
NBC (USA)	The National Broadcasting Company
OUDS	The Oxford University Dramatic Society
RADA	The Royal Academy of Dramatic Art
RSC (RSC)	The Royal Shakespeare Company
RST (RST)	The Royal Shakespeare Theatre
SMT (SMT)	The Shakespeare Memorial Theatre
TGR (TGR)	Theatregoround

Foreword
by Peter Hall

This book began its career as a thesis submitted for the Degree of Master of Philosophy in the School of Literature at the University of Warwick in April 1972. The submission was successful.

David Addenbrooke kindly sent me a copy the following month. I began reading it gloomily: I dislike considering my past — particularly when there is something to be done about the present. But I soon found myself reading the book avidly.

I suppose it was partly the pleasure of vanity. Here was a book in which I seemed to be the principal figure. Yet I could not recognize myself — I never can, in books or in interviews. The antics of this stranger who occasionally reminds me of someone I know slightly were interesting, if sometimes maddening.

But the book's factual accuracy (two years of research, all references substantiated) forced me to recreate the tumult of the early years of the RSC. I felt again the pleasures and the pains, not nostalgically, but concretely. Readers without my special advantages may be unmoved, but I hope not.

I believe in the impossibility of history. How can anyone recreate the past accurately? It wasn't actually *like* this — not to me anyway. My remembered experiences at the RSC are not the same as Peggy Ashcroft's or Peter Brook's or John Barton's, although we all lived through the same events. Actuality has as many faces as there are people. Then if you add to this Hydra, the faults and indulgences of memory, what chance is there of capturing reality?

But there is a good story here, the facts are true, and their interpreter is gracious and generous. I am flattered. But I cannot introduce the book in any considered way. I take up enough of its pages without adding more. I can make one statement:

It is pleasing that a theatre company's organization and growth, rather than its productions, should be thought worthy of this amount of study. Trevor Nunn has said that a company is built upon a series of 'relationships'. In that sense, it is a metaphor of society at large.

The only point in putting on a play is to develop these relationships. Good communication within a group makes actors and directors better at their tasks than they knew they could be. And a good performance makes a good audience; it is more responsive and intelligent than its individual members. And if we of the theatre don't achieve this, it is preferable to leave the play on the book-shelf in the hope that someone will take it down and read it from time to time.

This volume is the story of the struggles of a group of people to make that communication more general in their theatres. . . .

Peter Hall
1973

Introduction

The spectacular growth of the Royal Shakespeare Company under the direction of Peter Hall is one of the most remarkable achievements in the history of the modern British theatre. The years 1960 to 1968 marked the development of a series of artistic and administrative policies at Stratford-upon-Avon and in London, which have greatly influenced the basic framework of many subsequent theatrical organizations in this country and abroad. Since 1960 the production output of the company has been enormous in volume, variety and quality, and the initials 'RSC' have become an international synonym for the best in British theatre.

Peter Hall's ideas for the formation of a permanent ensemble company at Stratford were by no means new or unique, but under his direction the RSC was the first major company to succeed in implementing such ideas on a large scale in Britain. When Hall began his revolution at Stratford a commercial star system dominated the British theatre; earlier ensemble schemes had collapsed or been severely modified through lack of financial support; the National Theatre was still a subject for debate and controversy; and the notion of a large state subsidy for the theatre was still a somewhat embryonic concept. Finance was the key factor, and in the determination to make his ideas work Hall set out to create an organization with one primary objective in mind — the attainment of a substantial government subsidy. He believed that only through financial support from public funds could his ensemble grow up under purely artistic conditions, and, to achieve this goal, the RSC embarked on a development scheme of immense proportions. The scheme also involved immense risks, and the first three crucial years of the company's growth necessitated continual compromise between artistic ideal and economic necessity.

The National Theatre was created in 1962, and in the following year Peter Hall's company was also granted government subsidy. It might well be said that the early years of the RSC paved the way for the National Theatre, as Hall's organization was certainly the first to formulate and successfully operate under the policies and precedents which have been followed by the National and later subsidized theatres. Between 1960 and 1963, the RSC exemplified what could be achieved when a company and its artists were freed from the accepted 'commercial' and 'success' pressures of the theatrical profession. The company which Hall created in 1960 was, in many ways, the beginning of a movement which spread throughout Britain during the sixties: now, subsidized theatre is an accepted fact-of-life, and most provincial cities have at least one theatre under local or state subsidy.

The production work of the RSC has been widely praised, criticized, discussed and written about, and over the Hall years the sum total of the company's presentations amounts to a very considerable achievement. A less widely publicized but no less impressive achievement is the internal growth of the organization since 1960, and it is this latter subject — the development of the RSC structure under Peter Hall — which is the major concern of this work. RSC productions are discussed and referred to throughout these chapters, but these productions have been considered mainly in relation to the creation of the overall company structure. A full discussion of the RSC's production output is a complete subject in itself.

To compress the record of a company like the RSC into a single work demands an intensely selective approach in which, of necessity, certain minor details must be touched on only briefly or omitted altogether. There are also many elements in the composition of any theatre company which simply defy formalisation. Trevor Nunn, who succeeded Peter Hall, has stated that the organization which he controls is built upon a series of 'relationships': like any artistic enterprise, there is much in the day-to-day working of the RSC which depends solely on personality, mood, time, place, prevailing conditions — and a vast assortment of intangible factors. These factors cannot be forced into any neat category, and can never be satisfactorily spelled out.

The aim of this book is to present an overall view of the

Peter Hall

Shakespeare Memorial Theatre (*c.* 1895)

Royal Shakespeare Theatre

historical development, structure and operation of a major theatrical organization, and to give some insight into the policies, ideals and personalities which influenced and controlled its creation.

This work had its beginnings in a post-graduate degree thesis at the University of Warwick. I would like to express my thanks to Professor G.K. Hunter for his initial faith in the project, and for his constant advice and encouragement over a two-year period.

The Shakespeare Centre Library, Stratford-upon-Avon, has provided much of the reference material used during my research, and I would like to thank Mrs Marguerite Darvill and Miss Eileen Robinson for their many kindnesses, assistance and constructive suggestions.

I am most grateful to the Directorate, Acting Company and Administrative Staff of the Royal Shakespeare Company for devoting considerable time to interviews and conversations which have been of the utmost importance to my work. I would also like to express my gratitude to the RSC Management for allowing me unrestricted access to the Stratford theatre, and the opportunity to observe its artistic and administrative operation during the 1971 season. In particular I would like to thank Trevor Nunn, David Brierley, Maurice Daniels, Ann Robinson, Tony Church, John Goodwin and his Staff in the Publicity and Publications Department.

John Trewin's kindness in supplying me with information from his biography of Peter Brook a year before its publication, and his continued assistance with the location of reference material and sources, has been greatly appreciated. In this context, Dr. Gareth Lloyd Evans of the University of Birmingham has also been of assistance, and his recollections of the RSC's work over the sixties have been of considerable interest. I have also been much helped by Derek Longhurst through his reading and checking of the completed manuscript.

Finally, I would like to thank Peter Hall for giving his time to talk with me about his career in the theatre and his years at Stratford. In a sense, it is Peter Hall who has provided much of the inspiration for this project: what began as a very strong interest in the development of the RSC under his direction, has since grown to incorporate a sincere admiration for the man and a firm belief in the artistic principles for which he stands.

David Addenbrooke
Perth, Western Australia
1973

Part I

The Development of the
Royal Shakespeare Company
over the years 1960-8

1. The Background Years
1946 - 1959

When I first came to Stratford in 1945 every conceivable value was buried in deadly sentimentality and complacent worthiness — a traditionalism approved largely by town, scholar and Press. It needed the boldness of a very extraordinary old gentleman, Sir Barry Jackson, to throw all this out of the window and so make a true search for values possible once more.

Peter Brook, *The Empty Space*.

When Shakespeare died in 1616, play acting was forbidden in Stratford-upon-Avon.[1] The Borough Council actually paid to prevent the King's Players from performing in the town in 1622. As these players held a Royal Licence to perform wherever they thought fit, the Council were in a quandary: the actors had been members of Shakespeare's own company and they wished to perform plays in his own town. How the Council prevented what would have been Stratford's first Shakespeare Festival is still preserved in the Borough Chamberlain's accounts of 1622: 'To the King's Players for not playing in the Hall six shillings'.[2]

Shakespeare's anniversary was first publicly celebrated at Stratford in 1769, but at that time his plays were not performed. Instead there were banquets, dances, oratorios, fireworks and horseracing, all originated and organized by the greatest Shakespeare actor of the day, David Garrick. The principal events took place in an octagonal building measuring nearly seventy feet in diameter, erected on the Bancroft, the stretch of grass in front of the present theatre. The celebrations lasted for three days.

In December 1827, a theatre opened on the site of the Great Garden of New Place, the property that Shakespeare had purchased on his return from London. This theatre was a complete financial failure, despite the appearances there of such celebrated actors as Edmund and Charles Kean, W.C. Macready and Charles

Dillon. The building became a public ballroom in 1842 and reverted to a theatre in 1869, but again without success. It was finally demolished in 1872, the site once more becoming the lawn of New Place garden. In 1864 a temporary building was erected in Southern Lane. It was twelve-sided, 152 feet in diameter and constructed 'of timber on foundations of masonry, with galleries, orchestra and stage and lighted by gas'.[3] Here the tercentenary of Shakespeare's birth was celebrated for twelve days. There were banquets, balls and pageants, but six of Shakespeare's plays were also presented. This was the first celebration to bear any resemblance to later Shakespeare Festivals.

Charles Edward Flower (1830-1892), a prominent Stratford brewer, had long visualized the town as a centre of pilgrimage for Shakespeare devotees, with a major theatre of its own where the plays might be presented in ideal surroundings. In 1874 he inaugurated a scheme for building a theatre by presenting a two-acre site on the banks of the Avon. On 23rd April 1879, the first Shakespeare Festival opened; Barry Sullivan (one of the leading classical actors of the day) and Helen Faucit played *Much Ado About Nothing.* From that time, Festivals were held for a few weeks every year.[4]

In 1886, Frank R. Benson gave his first season as Festival Director at Stratford, beginning an historic association which lasted for nearly thirty five years — broken only by Osmund Tearle's Company from 1889 to 1890 and Ben Greet's Company in the season of 1895. Benson had been 'discovered' by Ellen Terry and Henry Irving when they attended an OUDS performance and with his directorate began a time when the world began to notice Stratford, audiences increased, and the theatre prospered. Between Stratford seasons Benson and his company would tour England, returning to Stratford with an additional play in the repertoire. This new play was invariably performed on 23rd April, Shakespeare's birthday, and so the Birthday Play tradition began. During the first world war the Memorial Theatre was closed in 1917 and 1918, but Benson returned in 1919, confining that year's Festival to presentations of scenes from the plays. Frank Benson's long association with Stratford ended in 1920.[5]

The first Shakespeare Memorial Theatre was burnt to the ground on 6th March 1926. The cause of the fire was unknown and only the theatre museum and library escaped the flames. The world was shocked by the disaster, but not Bernard Shaw:

'I am extremely glad to hear the news. Stratford-upon-Avon is to be congratulated upon the fire ... it will be a tremendous advantage to have a proper modern building.'[6]

For the next six years the Shakespeare Festival was held in the hastily converted Stratford Picture House, while the Chairman of the Memorial Theatre Board of Governors, Mr (later Sir) Archibald Flower, directed a world-wide campaign for funds to rebuild. Nearly a quarter of a million pounds was subscribed to the rebuilding fund and in 1929 the foundation stone was laid for a new £200,000 Shakespeare Memorial Theatre — the building which stands today.

The theatre opened on 23rd April 1932 with a performance of *King Henry IV:* Part One was given in the afternoon and Part Two at night. The theatre accommodated 1,000 people as opposed to the old theatre's 800 capacity, and possessed a rolling stage which enabled many scene changes without holding up the action of the play. W. Bridges Adams was Festival Director at the time of rebuilding (a position he had held since 1920). On his resignation in 1934, Ben Iden Payne succeeded him, to be followed by Milton Rosmer in 1943.

Robert Atkins came to Stratford to direct the 1944 Festival with a long list of Shakespeare achievements to his credit. The four columns that stand to his name in *Who's Who in the Theatre* are full of Shakespeare roles. He had taken his own company twice to Egypt; he had played at the Old Vic; he had produced plays at the Open Air Theatre for ten years; he had been Director of the British Empire Shakespeare Society in 1927. Atkins was fully aware of the difficulties of staging Shakespeare and he came to a Memorial Theatre that was not noted for excellence of presentation — though there were occasional performances of distinction. Notable was an outstanding *King Lear*, directed by Komsiarjevsky in 1936 (with Randall Ayrton in the title role). An intensely selective production relying on lighting effects for impact, this *Lear* was a pre-echo of later selectivity under Hall and Brook — and highly unconventional in terms of thirties staging ideas.

To bridge the gap that had always yawned between players and audience, he had the stage platform extended out over the orchestra pit, and in his productions he frequently set the action outside the proscenium arch — a technique which added much to intimacy in performance. Atkins also placed great emphasis on the spoken word, and addressing the Stratford-upon-Avon Rotary Club on 30th August 1945, he said:

'The most important aspect in producing the plays of Shakespeare is that the spoken word should be heard distinctly. To me this is fundamental. I would like to leave behind me the memory of a Shakespeare play spoken as beautifully as human beings can speak . . . that will be my masterpiece.'[7]

Yet despite the admirable work done by Atkins to improve standards and introduce change, the Memorial Theatre in 1945 was still largely governed by parish-pump policies. The national press all but ignored its productions; actors considered Stratford as exile — 'the actor's way to the tomb'; the theatre administration was unwieldy; the Festival Director was burdened with more responsibility than one man could handle: for in addition to his duties as overall Director of the Festival, he was also responsible for the production of all the plays — often eight in one season.

Sir Barry Jackson took over the direction of the Stratford Festival in the Spring of 1946. Since his building of the famous Birmingham Repertory Theatre in 1913, Jackson had become a unique figure in the British theatre and achieved a world-wide reputation as a man of vision, experiment and culture. Apart from long and successful work at Birmingham[8] where he had presented some five hundred plays and operas, he was, for ten years, responsible for many outstanding productions in the West End of London. He had also created the Malvern Festival which he had directed for nine years from 1929. On his appointment as Festival Director at Stratford, Sir Barry wrote for *Theatre World*:

'Tradition should never be outraged by radical change, but neither should it encourage the stereotyped. . . . Stratford has ceased to be parochial or even national; it is international. By the standards set, every incentive will be given to the world to make its pilgrimage . . . to continue and to recreate Shakespeare's perfection at Stratford is my sincere aim.'[9]

Jackson began the 1946 season with a series of innovations which were designed to free the Director from the responsibility of staging and supervising all productions himself. He engaged a separate producer for each play to be presented, in the hope that this would 'lend individuality and infuse vitality in maintaining tradition'. It was hoped that this policy would deal a death-blow at the stereotyped: 'the unhappy issue of one producer over-burdened with eight plays in one season'.

It was decided to open the season with only three plays and to add one new play each third week until the repertoire was complete. Previous Festivals had the entire programme ready for presentation by the opening date, which meant that there were eight (or more) plays in production at once. Sir Barry felt that staggered presentation would allow more adequate rehearsal time, and would also 'add healthy labour to all concerned'. Lack of time for rehearsal had been the prime cause of the overall mediocrity of previous Festivals, and Directors since Bridges Adams had com-plained of it. Under Jackson's new system, the actors would rehearse and play throughout the entire season. It was further intended that the plays presented later in the season would form the nucleus of the following season's repertoire, thus resulting in a continuity of effort.

Sir Barry's overall policy also called for the eventual formation of a permanent company of artists under long-term contract. 'The attitude of "play a season, finish, begin again" must be killed.'[10] From his earliest days in Birmingham Sir Barry had fostered and encouraged youth: 'he preferred ardour and loyalty to the often wayward mannerisms of the famous'. He saw the team spirit as the underlying principle which would govern the company and his first year at Stratford saw the emphasis placed very heavily on youth and new talent — and the rejection of repeated suggestions that West End stars be engaged to 'draw the public'. Some critics recognized the validity of this policy:

'Teamwork is, in the long run, more important than stars, whose acting may often tend to be over-individualistic. It is sounder policy to build up a team who know each other and can learn to work together . . . that is how stars are made!'[11]

It is interesting to note that these Jackson decisions — some extremely unpopular and much criticized at the time — are

definite pre-echoes of early Royal Shakespeare Company pronouncements and policies (1960-1963), and still form the basis of
present day RSC company structure. Barry Jackson was, in some
ways, the architect and forerunner of the policy which governs the
present Royal Shakespeare Theatre.

Among the eight producers engaged for the 1946 season was a
young man of twenty, who had enjoyed considerable success in his
early work for OUDS, and later as a producer under Sir Barry at
the Birmingham Rep. As part of his long-avowed youth policy
Jackson invited him to Stratford to produce *Love's Labour's Lost*.
His name was Peter Brook.[1 2]

At the same time a young actor, also from the Birmingham
Rep, joined the Stratford company. His name — Paul Scofield.

The Recorder noted this combination at the end of the 1947
season:

'Peter Brook and Paul Scofield are the outstanding names to
remember. During the next decade both will probably
become households words in the world of the theatre.'[1 3]

Yet, in contrast, Norman Marshall in *The Other Theatre* wrote:

'It is Stratford's plain duty to give us the best Shakespearian
acting in England, and no amount of conscientious teamwork
will compensate for the absence from Stratford of . . .' [and
here follows a list of some twenty eminent actors].[1 4]

Marshall endorsed Jackson's plan for a permanent company, but
with the proviso that 'great stars be engaged' to ensure quality of
performance and public response. The real success of Jackson's
policy to look for talent rather than reputation may best be
judged by examining the records of the Birmingham Repertory
Theatre: Laurence Olivier, Peggy Ashcroft, Greer Garson, Cedric
Hardwicke, Peter Brook, Paul Scofield, Stewart Granger, Eric‑
Porter . . . these and many other now-famous names worked at the
Birmingham Rep before they were ever heard of in London.

Plays inseparably associated with Jackson and the Birmingham
Rep include *The Apple Cart, Back to Methuselah, Hamlet* (in
modern dress), *1066 and All That, The Barretts of Wimpole
Street*, and Rutland Boughton's opera *The Immortal Hour*.[1 5]
Above all else Jackson wanted a company consisting of players,
producers and technicians whose hearts were in their job. He was

in favour of a fully self-contained theatre along repertory lines, by 1947 the bulk of the scenery and costumes were being made on the premises at Stratford by theatre workpeople.

In fairness it must be said that Robert Atkins had previously tried to introduce some of these changes. He had attempted to stagger programmes and increase rehearsal time, but was hampered by the very nature of his position. Atkins was only in control of the Festival; the actual theatre had a General Manager with autonomous powers. In 1947 Jackson assumed the absolute Directorship of the Memorial Theatre. From the time of his appointment he had insisted that the six-month Shakespeare season and the Winter season of touring plays should develop under one head. He felt that this was imperative if the theatre was to develop into the creative institution with the long-term policy that he envisaged. Since Jackson's time, the theatre has remained under the absolute control of the Director, responsible for the artistic and administrative direction and answerable only to the Governors.

Among Jackson's other innovations at Stratford was the general improvement in working conditions. He increased salaries, and re-decorated the theatre backstage to make surroundings more attractive. During his directorate the wardrobe and costume storage facilities were greatly enlarged and systematized; scenery storage facilities were extended; the theatre workshops were enlarged and completely re-fitted. In addition, he began to build up the highly trained technical staff that would be a necessity for a creative and smooth-running organization.

But innovations are costly, and the 1946 season resulted in a nett loss to the theatre of £13,385, mainly due to higher salaries, a bigger company, and increased production costs. It was also estimated that the theatre would show a loss on the forthcoming 1947 season – and possibly on the 1948. In 1944, Fordham Flower as Chairman of the Governors had said: 'May it never be said that the tinkle of silver and the rustle of notes in the box office deafened the Governors' ears'. Yet at the end of 1946 there was considerable criticism from a section of the Governors when a loss was announced. There were others who were far-sighted enough to see ahead:

'Sir Barry Jackson is sticking to a policy of enhancing the

prestige of the Festival — even though it has meant a heavy financial loss on its first year of application . . . but he has made going to the Memorial Theatre an exciting adventure. He has recruited a youthful company which, though devoid of stars, shines out unquestionably as a milky way of enthusiasm.'[16]

'Sir Barry obviously views the Memorial Theatre's function as something higher than that of a provincial showplace concerned primarily with takings.'[17]

And another comment, more meaningful when one looks back from the heavily subsidized seventies:

'A great artist is a unique personality; an autocrat and an aristocrat within his sphere. It is the privilege — often the exacting and exasperating privilege — of others to provide him with the means to realize his genius in action. . . . Patronage of the arts in an increasingly egalitarian society is passing from the wealthy individual to corporate bodies and public authorities. If they are to get the best, they must be prepared — like their individual predecessors — to 'lose' money in a spirit of faith and high endeavour. Those handling public money may find this exceedingly difficult unless they have the stimulus of an enlightened public opinion.'[18]

However, despite the severe criticism of his artistic policy and financial losses, Jackson had altered the general critical attitude towards Stratford, and with it, the attitude of a wider public. From 1946 Stratford grew sharply in fashion and began to rival the Old Vic as 'the acknowledged centre of Shakespearian acting that has no equal'. By 1957, Philip Hope Wallace could write: ' . . . apart from Bayreuth it [Stratford] must be the most successful artistic/commercial enterprise in the world.'

The 1946 Festival opened with *The Tempest*, produced by Eric Crozier, and was followed on 23rd April by *Cymbeline* (Nugent Monck); 26th April *Love's Labour's Lost* (Peter Brook); 10th May, *Macbeth* (Michael MacOwan); 31st May, *As You Like It* (H.M. Prentice); 21st June, *Henry V* (Dorothy Green); 12th July, Marlowe's *Dr. Faustus* (Walter Hudd); and 23rd August, *Measure for Measure* (Frank McMullen). The company was predominantly youthful, none had ever played at Stratford, and over fifty per cent were demobbed artists. As an 'academic gesture' Sir Barry had invited George Rylands to come to Stratford to produce *Dr Faustus* (this proved impossible, and Walter Hudd took the production), and in August, Frank McMullen arrived from the Yale University Drama Department to produce *Measure for Measure*.

Peter Brook's *Love's Labour's Lost* was the most successful production of the 1946 season. John Trewin recalled it: 'The first two had been very ordinary. *The Tempest* was a frightful flop and *Cymbeline* was just so-so. Then Brook came in with *Love's Labour's* which was completely different — utterly different! I'd been going to Stratford since 1929 and it was quite the most staggering first night I remember. Apart from anything else, the stage *looked* so beautiful.'[19]

In 1947, following the policy that some of the artistic capital from one Festival should be carried over to the next, the productions of *Dr. Faustus, Love's Labour's Lost, Measure for Measure* and *The Tempest* were repeated. At the end of the season, the Theatre Governors again announced a loss, and in January 1948 Sir Barry announced that he would resign at the expiration of his three year contract. What actually prompted Sir Barry's resignation was not made clear at the time, although it was supposed that a general dissatisfaction (among a section of the Governors) with the financial situation had much to do with it. *Illustrated* reported in April 1948:

'At their last meeting the Executive Council of the Board of Governors thanked Sir Barry for the good work he had done, and informed him that they had decided not to renew his contract at the end of the year's season. In plain English, the Director had been sacked!'

Tom English, Sir Barry's private secretary, corroborates this,[20] and John Trewin claims that Jackson's departure was 'an unpublished sacrifice to an insistence on youth'.[21] If this is so then it was Sir Barry's own policy which finally defeated him. It is significant to note that for the 1948 season, presumably under pressure, Jackson changed his youth policy in favour of one of stars. The press reacted favourably: a 'wealth of talent' from the London stage was engaged to lead the company; Robert Helpmann, Diana Wynyard, Esmond Knight, Ena Burrill, Godfrey Tearle, and two young discoveries, Claire Bloom and Anthony Quayle.

In June 1948, Anthony Quayle was appointed Director of the Memorial Theatre. Ruth Ellis wrote in the *Stratford Herald*:

'The time has not yet come to assess the benefits of Sir Barry Jackson's directorate. . . . Not least among Sir Barry's achievements at Stratford has been his introduction of gifted young men, and this is stressed by the announcement that one of them is to succeed him. . . .'[22]

And T.C. Kemp, writing for the *Birmingham Post* said:

'The director's job at Stratford is no sinecure. It is a task for inventive young men with ideas, and none but the finical will complain if enthusiasm occasionally outruns discretion. But the distinction between spurious force and true power, between extraneous trimming and inherent grace, between the crudely sensational and the exquisitely dramatic – this distinction, I say, should be drawn at Stratford with fastidious artistry.'[23]

The Times reported:

'Mr Quayle has not yet had time to acquire the international prestige of his predecessor, but as an actor and producer he has already done things which suggest imagination, youthful energy, and independence of mind.'[24]

Anthony Quayle was thirty-four years old when he became Director at Stratford. He had been an actor for seventeen years (RADA trained); had played a variety of Shakespeare roles, and had acted in America and on the Continent. During the war he served with distinction in the army, and after the war he returned to acting, playing in seasons at the Criterion, the Lyric (Hammersmith), New Theatre and the Stratford Memorial. He also tried his hand at producing and writing.[25]

Quayle announced his policy for Stratford as 'foreign and domestic'; in addition to maintaining Stratford standards he wished to take the Memorial Theatre Company on tours of the Dominions and the United States, and one of his first moves as Director was to organize an Australian tour immediately following the 1949 Stratford season. This season played over a longer period than usual (March to September) to an audience of over 250,000 people. The Australian tour which followed was an artistic and financial success, and Australian audiences totalled over 200,000.

Following the success of this tour, the Governors (at the Annual Meeting in 1950) discussed the possibility of forming two companies — one to tour 'permanently' overseas.[26]

Quayle contended that the Stratford public had changed its character since the days when a Festival filled a small theatre for a very short time. In those days a large repertoire was performed — and the public made up almost entirely of Shakespeare lovers who had come primarily to see his works in his home town. Quayle felt that the public of 1950 were primarily interested in good theatre, and not in Shakespeare for his own sake. His answer was in a large company, led by distinguished actors, playing a small repertoire so that every play could be produced up to a polished West End standard. Audience demand was well in excess of the number of seats available, and the national press acclaimed 1950 as the most successful Festival ever. *The Scotsman* dissented from the general praise: ' . . . it is an audience in which the indiscriminate probably outnumber the judicious.'[27]

Under Quayle the number of plays presented in a season was cut to five, and the first nights were much more widely spaced. It was felt that a better standard would be the result of more money and more rehearsal time for each production, and this policy of five productions a season continued throughout the fifties. Eric Johns, writing for *The Stage*, said:

'By restricting the number of plays in any one season to five, each one can be rehearsed thoroughly for a month. From the very first day the rehearsal room is blacked out so that the company works under stage lighting conditions. They capture the atmosphere of the play at the outset, which means there is no violent transition when the play leaves the rehearsal room for the stage.[28]

Quayle did not entirely agree with Sir Barry Jackson's scheme for a permanent company, and actively engaged in a star policy throughout his directorate:

'A wholly permanent company is neither desirable, nor, with the English theatre system as it is, practicable. A certain degree of continuity is the aim . . . I have never discovered, either at Stratford or in the London theatre, any "system" or policy of engaging stars. Certainly a "star name" is good box office, and let it not be forgotten that all theatre is show business — even when it is concerned with the Higher Drama.'[29]

At the conclusion of the 1950 Festival the Memorial Theatre was closed for extensive renovations and extensions. These renovations were to be completed before March 1951, and were designed to make the Memorial Theatre 'one of the best equipped, not only in Britain, but in the world'. The stage had always been a 'problem' for directors and designers, as had bad acoustics, audience 'blind' spots and inadequate seating arrangements. Quayle, writing for *Illustrated* in April 1949 said:

> 'Our stage is so constructed that there is a curious lack of intimacy between actor and audience, and Shakespeare's plays depend on intimacy . . . the whole building is badly planned . . . the dressing rooms are badly placed and too small . . . access to the stage is difficult. . . .'

And C.B. Purdom, in *Drama*, March 1949:

> 'Nothing more destructive of drama than the picture-stage was ever invented . . . the Memorial Theatre could do nothing better than to show the way by installing a new stage. At Stratford the stage is cut off from the audience — it is a room on its own — separated, except for the fourth wall gap, from all contact with the room occupied by the audience.'

Rather than undertake any major structural changes to the stage, Quayle set out to reconstruct the auditorium, and one of the major alterations was a re-modelling of the dress circle so that it became slightly curved in towards the stage. Wing sections with open boxes were then added to the side walls, to help to overcome the feeling of remoteness between gallery and stage. The seating capacity was increased by 150 to 1350 seats, added at the front of the stalls to further diminish the gap between stage and auditorium; a new wing was added down the river side of the building, containing sixteen new dressing rooms and a new Green Room; a new theatre lighting switchboard was installed at the back of the dress circle, thus enabling the lighting operator to see the action of a play as it progressed (this was a revolutionary development in 1950). The auditorium seating was completely renewed and the interior was repainted. The theatre re-opened on 24th March for the 1951 Festival of Britain season, and the productions were Shakespeare's History Cycle — from *Richard II*

Photo Angus McBean, © RSC

Top: Peter Brook's production of *Titus Andronicus* at Stratford in 1955, with Laurence Olivier as Titus Andronicus, Vivien Leigh as Lavinia and Alan Webb as Marcus Andronicus. *Bottom:* Richard Burton as Prince Hal, Alan Badel as Poins and Anthony Quayle as Falstaff in *Henry IV, Part 1,* at Stratford in 1951, directed by Anthony Quayle and John Kidd.

Photo Angus McBean, © RSC

Peter Hall's production at Stratford in 1956, with Geraldine McEwan as The Princess of France and Basil Hoskins as The King of Navarre.

James Bailey's design for Rosaline in Pet Hall's production.

LOVE'S LABOUR'S LOST

Peter Brook's production at Stratford in 1946 with Ruth Lodge as Rosaline and David King-Wood as Berowne.

to *Henry V.* Theatre records show that these Histories had last been performed as a cycle at Stratford by Sir Frank Benson's company in 1905.

Anthony Quayle planned the productions on the contention that the four plays had been conceived as 'one great play', with *Henry V* as the climax to the whole and *Richard II* as a kind of prologue to the main action. Indeed there was literary precedent for this line of thought,[30] and Quayle said:

'Many of the characters live and develop through several of the plays; it is not only that literary and dramatic ideas reverberate backwards and forwards through the four texts; it is what appear to be puzzling psychological inconsistencies when the plays are treated singly, disappear when they are considered as a whole.'[31]

To present the Histories successfully, Quayle realized that several things were needed; a continuing director who could fit the four productions into his conception; a permanent setting which would remain unchanged throughout and give unity of place; and a set of actors who could carry, from play to play, those roles which overlap. Quayle himself, assisted by John Kidd, directed *Richard II, Henry IV, Part One*, and *Henry V*. Michael Redgrave (who also played Richard II and Hotspur) directed *Henry IV, Part Two*. Tanya Moiseiwitsch designed a permanent setting, suggesting an Elizabethan theatre in its central gallery which spanned a wide gateway. The setting was embellished as occasion demanded with various props or hangings to suggest different times and places, and a throne was placed downstage right (by the proscenium arch) as a permanent fixture throughout. The political business of the plays was centred around it, and as there was no curtain, the throne was the first thing which was gradually illuminated to mark the beginning of each play. The setting provided three main acting areas and a large variety of entrances, which allowed the action of the plays to move in an uninterrupted flow. Moiseiwitsch also designed costumes for the cycle — brilliantly heraldic to contrast with the necessary austerity of the setting.[32]

In 1952, Ralph Richardson and Margaret Leighton led the company. Kenneth Tynan wrote: 'I am told that Stratford opinion regards this as having been a mediocre season . . . [but] the safest introduction to the best in English theatre is still, for my money, the 2.10 from Paddington (change at Leamington for the shrine)'.[33] In May of that year it was announced that two companies would be formed in 1953; one to play an eight-month season at Stratford and the other to tour Australia and New Zealand. In the same month it was announced that Glen Byam Shaw, an ex-Director of the Old Vic Theatre, had been appointed as co-Director of the Memorial Theatre with Anthony Quayle. While Quayle led the touring company on the thirty-four week Australian tour, Shaw was to take charge of the Stratford season.

Glen Byam Shaw was an actor of wide experience and a producer with a reputation for clear, vigorous work. As an actor he played, between 1923 and 1940, a great many roles in London, also visiting New York and touring South Africa. Between 1947 and 1952 he was Director of the Old Vic Theatre School and Theatre Centre, and resigned from this post following a policy clash with the Governors. Anthony Quayle immediately invited him to Stratford. *Plays and Players* wrote of Shaw:

> 'The production of a play for him, is like a business undertaking; something to be run with scrupulous care and attention to the most minute detail. He remains the most competent of our Shakespearian producers; never indulging in eccentricities or forcing his interpretation on the work of the author.'[34]

During the 1952 season, Anthony Quayle laid down a three-year plan for the Memorial Theatre, in which his declared foreign policy played a prominent role. He said:

> 'The duty of a great institution like the Memorial Theatre is clear; it must not be content only to strive for the highest standard of work at Stratford, but it must send that work overseas to every corner of the world. In pursuit of that policy, the Governors and Directors of the theatre have formed a plan which, over the next three years, will both maintain the Stratford season and will also send companies to Australia, New Zealand, Canada, the United States, and the Continent . . . the impulse which drove the old Elizabethans outwards was one of intense nationalism; the impulse we new Elizabethans must achieve is of practical internationalism.'[35]

Some years later, Fordham Flower as Chairman of Governors wrote in the Memorial Theatre Illustrated Programme for 1959:

'Top standard Shakespeare in repertory is fiendishly expensive. Unless we stretch the life of one or more of our productions after the season's end, a total of about £60,000 worth of scenery and costumes are written off, to mention the material assets alone. So by exporting our best work overseas we are not just spreading Stratford's name. It is an economic necessity!'

Quayle took three plays on the 1953 Australasian tour, and immediately following the Stratford season, Glen Byam Shaw took the 'home' company to London for six weeks, and then on a touring season to Holland, Belgium and France. At the conclusion of the 1953 season it was announced that the Memorial Theatre would send a company on a twenty-six week tour of the United States and Canada in 1954.

For the 1954 Stratford season, in what appeared to be a reversal of declared star policy, the accent was placed on youth and a move was made away from star casting. Quayle and Harry Andrews led the Stratford company, supported by a long list of comparatively unknown names. Quayle stated that it was time to give major roles to young actors and actresses who had developed within the company 'in the hope and belief that these names will become household words'.[36] Somewhat 'prophetically', *The Birmingham Gazette* wrote:

'The real stars will be the men behind the scenes ... the directors of the plays. Audiences will be paying simply to see a Shakespeare Memorial Theatre production, not a particular actor in a particular play.'[37]

And T.C. Kemp wrote in the *Birmingham Post*:

' ... I have no idea how far this move has been dictated by [economic] necessity.'[38]

The reasons behind this change of policy would not appear to have been financial. The Australian tour was reported as a box office success, and at the annual Board of Governors meeting in 1954, Lord Iliffe as President, announced that over 360,000 people had seen the 1953 Stratford season, and that box office takings had amounted to £179,512. The 1954 'youth' season was not a critical success, and in May of that year it was announced that the proposed tour of the United States and Canada had been cancelled. No official reason was given, but it was generally assumed by the national press that the cancellation was the result of a season which had no star names to offer the American public.

In January 1955 the programme for the coming season was announced; there were two companies planned — one at Stratford and one touring. The Stratford company was to be headed by Laurence Olivier and Vivien Leigh (both appearing professionally at Stratford for the first time[39]) and the other company was to be headed by John Gielgud and Peggy Ashcroft. This company planned to tour in Austria, Switzerland, Germany, Holland, Denmark and Norway; then returning to play seasons in London, Edinburgh, Glasgow, Manchester, Liverpool and finally Stratford after the home company had completed their season. Ruth Ellis wrote in the *Stratford Herald*:

> 'The Memorial Theatre's plans for 1955 are boldly ambitious
> to a startling degree. . . .'[40]

Peter Brook's production of Shakespeare's early Senecan tragedy *Titus Andronicus* was, without doubt, the major production of the 1955 season. The play had long been considered unactable, and had never been staged at the Memorial Theatre.[41] The authorship was considered dubious in some academic circles, and the content of the play too horrific for public presentation. Its physical horror of mutilation, rape and cannibalism, although relished by a Tudor audience with a taste for gruesome incident, was thought to be too grotesquely excessive for a modern audience to accept.[42]

Undoubtedly the presence of the Oliviers at Stratford had much to do with the overall success of the 1955 season. Although *Titus* was the outstanding production, *King Lear*, George Devine's tour production with Gielgud as Lear, (set in starkly abstract decor by Japanese designer Isamu Noguchi), and Glen Byam Shaw's production of *Macbeth* with Olivier in the title role, also received considerable critical attention. 1956 was a less ambitious year, and activities were concentrated at Stratford. A new director was engaged to direct *Love's Labour's Lost*:

> 'Still only twentyfive, Peter Hall is one of the most
> considerable personalities in the theatre today; with ideas
> that are as definite as his work is distinguished, and with
> integrity to match the breadth of his imagination. He should
> continue to enliven the theatre scene for many years to
> come.'[43]

Peter Hall came from a background of Cambridge (where he had a record of successful stage productions) followed by productions at Windsor, Oxford, Worthing, and a series of outstanding presentations as Director of the Arts Theatre in London. It is interesting to note that his first Stratford production, *Love's Labour's Lost*, had last been produced ten years earlier by Peter Brook — as his Stratford debut.[44]

In July 1956, Anthony Quayle resigned as Co-Director of the Memorial Theatre, and the Governors announced that Glen Byam Shaw would continue as sole Director. No major change in policy was announced during Shaw's directorate; there was some discussion during the 1956 season about the possible formation of a permanent company but Shaw felt that such a company would have to offer actors contracts of at least five years' duration:

'Mr Shaw believes that the very finest actors are needed to do justice to the finest plays Shakespeare wrote. Shakespeare calls for stars that sound the trumpets and make the air in the theatre vibrate — players such as Ashcroft, Gielgud, Olivier and Redgrave. They made history at Stratford in the post-war years and their performances will be discussed for generations. Stars of their magnitude would never join a permanent company in these days when actors have to rely on films, television and overseas tours. . . .'[45]

And Anthony Quayle, echoing an earlier statement, said:

'To have a permanent company at the Memorial Theatre is undesirable and impossible. Undesirable, because no young actor should work in only one author's plays. Impossible, because great stars, essential to a first class performance, cannot be expected to live permanently away from the West End — the centre of British theatre life.'[46]

Certainly, as the English Theatre was structured in the fifties, a permanent company at Stratford would have been extremely difficult to organize and to maintain. A permanent company would have entailed the financial responsibility for keeping a large company of actors together and fully employed over twelve months of the year. Touring was a possibility during the Winter Seasons at the Memorial Theatre, but the only viable answer was a second London theatre for the company. It is now known that both Anthony Quayle and Glen Byam Shaw were anxious to acquire a 'London base' where Shakespeare Memorial Theatre productions could be shown. It has been reported that they were, at one stage, negotiating for a lease on the Royal Court Theatre — subsequently taken over and now operated by the English Stage Company. It is interesting to note that in April 1925, Sir Barry Jackson (as Director of the Birmingham Repertory Theatre) announced that he had acquired a lease on the Kingsway Theatre in London, and that successful Birmingham Rep productions would be transferred.

Between the years 1956 and 1959 the Memorial Theatre continued its star policy and there were further overseas tours. Brook's production of *Titus Andronicus* toured five European countries in 1957, and in 1958 the company, led by Michael Redgrave, visited the Soviet Union for four weeks. In October 1959, it was announced that the NBC Television network in the United States would film Peter Hall's production of *A Midsummer Night's Dream* — taking a Memorial Theatre production to an estimated audience of forty million viewers in the United States. Also during this period, and following Brook's successful production of *Titus Andronicus* there was a reawakening of interest in the less frequently staged plays: Peter Hall produced *Cymbeline* in 1957, and in 1958, Tony Richardson, the young director who had become prominent through his productions of *Look Back in Anger* and *The Entertainer*,[47] produced *Pericles* at Stratford.

On 24th August 1956, *The Tribune* carried a long article on the future of the Memorial Theatre:

'Whatever critics may think of the 1957 season, it will be as popular as the last six or seven. Nothing can now destroy the enormous institutional popularity that the Shakespeare Memorial Theatre has built up since the war, and yet there is room for improvement within the obvious limits of Stratford policy . . . there is a need for a common acting style . . . an unmistakable Stratford style, which will set the Shakespearian standard for the 1960's. A standard cannot be imposed upon players in the space of a few weeks' rehearsal. A miscellany of directors in a hard working season of repertory cannot develop the ensemble playing which must be the seed and flower of a new style. What is needed is a satellite studio-school; a workshop open all year round, where both novices and veterans would have time and opportunity to apply and develop the lessons of the repertoire. Much would depend of course, on the man in charge.'

In October 1958, Glen Byam Shaw announced that he did not wish to continue as Memorial Theatre Director after the 1959 season. He had privately informed the Governors of this decision some twelve months earlier, as he believed that the theatre directorship should not be held too long by any one man.

Speaking at Stratford Civic Reception for the 1959 company on 15th March 1959, he said: 'After eight years a fresh impetus is needed, and a man with a new vision for the future. I have no doubt that that man is Peter Hall.'

Peter Hall was appointed Director-designate of the Memorial Theatre on 14th November 1958 — his appointment as Director to take effect on 1st January 1960. He made a statement for the press on 15th November:

'A tradition has been built up at Stratford over the past twelve years, and this is something that I would like to pick up and maintain. Of course any change in the directorship of a theatre must carry with it certain changes in policy . . . [and] probably my personality will be stamped on these changes.'[48]

2. Peter Hall

In spite of my whirlwind entry into the profession, I had little talent as a beginner. I don't know how much I have now, but I know my craft. I have been taught it by over sixty major productions and a dozen years of experience and mistakes. But you cannot rest on your laurels in the theatre; all that matters is what you are doing *now*. I throw away the past, whether it be programmes or press cuttings (I have none) or the memory of success.

Peter Hall, 'Theatre for Me',
The Sunday Telegraph, July 1966

In the summer of 1952, a 'somewhat shy' undergraduate named Peter Hall made his début as a theatre director with what was later described as a 'quite expert' production of Anouilh's *Point of Departure* at the ADC Theatre, Cambridge. In 1973, at the age of forty-two, Peter Hall's name is internationally famous. He has already held two of the most influential and coveted positions in world theatre: he founded and directed the Royal Shakespeare Company over a period of nine years, and was later appointed Director-designate of the Royal Opera House, Covent Garden — a position which he subsequently chose to relinquish. In 1972 it was announced that he would succeed Sir Laurence Olivier as Director of the National Theatre of Great Britain in 1974. In effect, this appointment places Hall in the most prestigious position in the English speaking theatre world.

Over a working life of twenty years, through exceptional talent, and a capacity for unrelenting work, Hall has established himself as a totally unique figure in the arts — combining the roles of director-producer of theatre, films and opera, impresario, and business administrator with brilliant success. It was this combination of talents which enabled him to take complete control of the Memorial Theatre at the age of twenty-nine, and over the period of his directorate turn the RSC into the most successful

theatre venture in Britain and the largest acting company in the
world: 'Despite the constellation of talents he has attracted since
he took over in 1960, it all orbits around him. The Royal
Shakespeare Company story is the Peter Hall story.'[1]

Peter Reginald Frederick Hall was born in Bury St. Edmunds,
Suffolk, on 22nd November 1930, the only child of Reginald Hall
and his wife Grace. His paternal grandfather was a vermin-
exterminator (rat-catcher was considered indelicate at the turn of
the century) and his maternal grandfather was a house-painter.
Reginald Hall was employed as a county station master, and
Peter's earliest childhood images were of the railway and of the
Suffolk countryside:

> 'I rode the shunting engine, played the ukelele to the driver
> and fireman and tramped for miles with an old gamekeeper in
> the woods. Theatre was an occasional local pantomime or an
> inspiring visit from a travelling puppet theatre at school. It
> was seductive but distant. East Anglia then existed in a slow
> post-Victorian melancholy, with lace curtains in the front
> parlour ("Let us keep ourselves to ourselves", said my
> family). The land was never very far away.'[2]

The Hall family was large, close, affectionate and non-intellectual:
'My father with a school certificate was the best educated, but the
family did not have the normal working-class distrust of books'.[3]
To be a 'six-pound a week man' was believed to be the ultimate
standard of success, and none of the family were in this category.
A love of music played a strong part in the family life, but there
was no theatre background or interest. At the age of seven, Peter
was given a model railway station: this he transformed into a
model theatre and equipped with a clockwork powered curtain:

> 'I was much cared for and spoilt, the only child in the large
> hot family. I know I was ungrateful, but the affection
> oppressed me. I was restless early. My parents, wonderful
> understanding people, encouraged my instinct to escape. The
> way out was books. I read voraciously, and was encouraged
> to learn, learn, learn. . . . I was already uneasy with home, the
> close-knit family life, and hideously precocious and "dif-
> ferent" . . .'[4]

In 1939, the Hall family moved to Cambridge, and Reginald Hall went on relief as a travelling station master deputising for sickness or vacancy. Peter was not happy at the change of environment and felt out of place in his new surroundings. As a child, and while at school, he did not make friends easily. Even today, he numbers his real friends at 'about half-a-dozen':

> 'All my life I have felt ridiculous and likely to be mocked .... Inside I was untouchable. Outside, I was worried, insecure. Unless I organized. I always bossed other children about. Unless they hit me. Then I avoided them.'[5]

At Cambridge he worked for a County Council Scholarship, and was awarded a place at the Perse School: 'Five of us poor boys were taken in to this grand school, and so that none of us should forget our non-paying status we were called minor scholars.'[6] When he was eight, Peter started learning the piano, and later became a good pianist and organist, 'a passable flautist and a hopeless clarinet player'. By the time he arrived in Cambridge, his ambition was to be an orchestral conductor: ' . . . his mother wanted him to be a concert pianist: she wanted him to have an "artistic career". There was something respectable about a concert pianist. . . .'[7]

His early interest in music began to open the arts to him — music first and then theatre. During the war years, Cambridge was very much culturally alive: Gielgud's first war-time *Hamlet* was presented at the Arts Theatre, the Sadler's Wells Opera performed Mozart's Requiem in King's College Chapel, and there were continuous productions from the Marlowe Society — 'One shilling to stand at the back on Mondays — half the week's pocket money gone!' There were also numerous visits to London for theatre, music and art galleries — using the free rail-travel passes provided for Mr Hall and his family:

> 'I was a misfit in my school, a misfit in my town, and a misfit in my family. So my love of the arts was partly neurotic: they gave me security. . . . By the time I was fourteen my ambition was clear. Those visits to London and to the theatre of the war years — Olivier and Richardson at the New, Gielgud and Ashcroft at the Haymarket — determined me. I wanted to be a theatre director.'[8]

As a Cambridge schoolboy, Hall cycled to Stratford to see plays at the Memorial Theatre, and pitched a tent on the Municipal

Camping Ground: 'My first indelible Stratford memory is Peter Brook's *Love's Labour's Lost* in 1946. He was twenty-one and already a great director. I was very jealous.'[9] At this time, the fifteen-year old Hall stood on the Bancroft in front of the Memorial Theatre and said, 'One day I'll run that theatre!' It has been suggested that this sounds like the opening sequence of a movie to be called The Peter Hall Story — but the anecdote *is* factual.

While at school in Cambridge, his interest in the theatre was developed to include acting, and he played Hamlet in a final-year school production. John Tanfield, Senior History Master at the Perse School, and producer of the play, said of Hall's performance: 'He had an incredibly vivid awareness of the part, and the dramatic element involved. I was amazed by his maturity and imagination.'[10] The 'Drama Critic' for *The Pelican* (Perse School Magazine) of 1949 commented: ' . . . we felt with new force the full horror of the experience that's come to the Prince, of a brave and goodly world defiled and rotting . . .'. Hall finished his schooldays as Head Boy at the Perse and won a Cambridge scholarship to St. Catharine's, but prior to taking up this scholarship he was called up for National Service in the RAF. As a sergeant in the Education Corps he was posted to Germany to teach business management and economics at a 'sugar-plum Schloss': his teaching qualifications consisted of 'some economics' — taken as a subsidiary subject for his Higher School Certificate:

'I learned a great deal about economics that year. Mostly from my pupils. . . . I also learned two other techniques: how to persuade people to like what they naturally resist, and the wisdom of admitting my ignorance. The perception of any group is extremely fast: an audience is much more intelligent than its individual members. So actor, teacher or director must never lie. He will get caught out.'[11]

In Germany, Hall did some acting for an RAF drama group: ' . . . my friends applauded and the sergeants in my mess sniggered. I was rather a success!'[12] He also saw a tremendous variety of musical, opera and theatre performances, and it was in Germany that he first observed the concept of State subsidized arts in operation: 'Very poor though the Germans were . . . although there wasn't enough to eat and drink, they still had their theatres and opera houses!'[13] His observations in Germany undoubtedly influenced his later thinking.

On his discharge from National Service he returned to Cambridge to begin studies: he had also 'decided' his future, and reversed his long-held intention to become a theatre director: according to Tony Church, 'He had been seriously considering a career as a teacher. He was engaged to be married to a girl he met in the RAF, and he had a "settled life" as a teacher and a married man in front of him.'[14]

During his first two years at Cambridge, Hall concentrated on his academic work — he read English in both parts of the Tripos — and in the course of his studies he met and worked with scholars who greatly influenced his intellectual development — and subsequent choice of career:

'One half of our teaching (the side I was on) was emotional appreciation, fine drawn poetasting. The other half was quite simply Dr. Leavis. His analysis was concrete, unsentimental and unfailingly perceptive. Although he clearly hated the theatre, his lectures taught me the meaning of poetry, and a great deal about the social responsibility of the arts. It was George Rylands who taught me the structure of a line of Shakespeare; and T.R. Henn, how to appreciate the ambiguity of a metaphor.'[15]

His political consciousness also developed at university, although he played no active part in university political life: 'I joined no political party . . . nor have I since. But I was, and remain, a socialist. . . .'[16] During his first two years as an undergraduate, Hall took minor roles in various productions for the Marlowe Society, and, during his first term of studies, he put his name down to do a production at the ADC theatre at the beginning of his final year — some two years later. He had no definite ideas about this production, no financial backing, and was very much a theatrical 'nobody' at the time. His booking of the ADC theatre was 'instinctive rather than rational'.[17] The theatre life of the university in 1951 was led by John Barton (who had been a Cambridge undergraduate for two years prior to Hall's arrival), and it was under the direction of Barton or George Rylands that Hall made his early appearances as an undergraduate actor. Plays he appeared in included the John Barton production of *Julius Caesar* (in reconstructed Elizabethan pronunciation — with the Arts Theatre converted to resemble the Globe Playhouse), George Rylands' production of *Romeo and Juliet* in 1952, in which Hall played Tybalt to John Barton's Mercutio, and Michael (now Lord) Birkett's production of *Cyrano de Bergerac* in which he played De Guiche.

Tony Church, who appeared with (and for) Hall in many Cambridge productions, spoke of his career as an undergraduate actor: 'He would probably say (now) that he was a very bad actor. He wasn't bad, he was very competent. He was an "accurate" actor, but not in any way exceptional. Actually, he didn't have a great deal of personality on stage, but he *was* a sound undergraduate performer.'[18]

At the end of the summer term in his second year at Cambridge, Hall began setting up his first production — to be presented at the ADC Theatre:

'The ADC Committee were surprised to find that their theatre was let to the hopeless Hall. I remember their secretary, John Barton, being rightly unimpressed with my production ideas. I borrowed £40 from two generous and trusting schoolmasters and hastened forward with no knowledge and no experience. The result — a heavily romantic staging of Anouilh's *Point of Departure* — was no miracle, but it wasn't bad.'[19]

He directed seven more university productions in his final year: 'Suddenly, every production in that year was by Peter Hall . . . we worked virtually a three-weekly "repertory" right through our final year at Cambridge.'[20] *Point of Departure* was followed by John Whiting's *Saint's Day, Uncle Vanya*, a play by John Barton called *Winterlude*, Anouilh's *Antigone*, Whiting's *A Penny for a Song*, and Pirandello's *Henry IV*. This year also marked a turning point in Hall's personal development: he neglected his academic work, and became fully committed to the idea of a career in the professional theatre: 'It was madness, and everybody told me so. I would have to tell anybody the same.'[21]

Tony Church remembers Hall's final year, and the changes in his life: 'He seemed to 'swing into gear', and the man emerged from a chrysalis that he had deliberately enclosed himself in . . . it was an extraordinary sight. The confidence that grew from production to production and the ease of social contact. Peter had been a very shy man — and still basically is of course. He has *learned* how to be a public man.'[22]

It is interesting to note that many of the people who were associated with Hall in Cambridge theatre life, later joined him at Stratford when he became Director of the RSC. John Barton joined him as Assistant Director of the Memorial Theatre in 1960. Hall later said:

'As university students our theatrical interests were very different, although we frequently overlapped. I was mostly concerned with modern drama ... and Barton was the Shakespearian. Even in those days Barton dreamed of a definitive production of the *Henry VI*'s ... I was fascinated and intrigued by his dreams, but I never thought that it would concern me as a director.'[23]

Tony Church joined the Stratford company in 1960 (as a contract actor), Peter Wood came to direct *The Winter's Tale* and David Jones later joined the company as a director. Raymond Leppard (who worked with Hall at Cambridge) became Music Adviser to the company, and Guy Woolfenden, the present Music Director of the RSC, is a Cambridge graduate.

Much of Hall's outside working life has also been bound up with Cambridge associations: Lord Birkett produced Hall's film of *A Midsummer Night's Dream* for the RSC, and has been involved with Hall and the company through other film work. Hall's chosen successor at the RSC, Trevor Nunn, is also a Cambridge graduate who studied under Leavis.

In the final stages of Hall's Cambridge career, Alec Clunes, then Manager of the Arts Theatre in London saw his Cambridge production of Pirandello's *Henry IV*, and invited Hall and his company to bring it to London for a two-week season at the Arts. This was in August 1953. The following month — and as a direct result of the *Henry IV* London season — Hall was offered his first professional engagement, to direct Somerset Maugham's *The Letter* at the Theatre Royal, Windsor. The Windsor engagement was followed by weekly repertory work at Worthing, a series of productions of Shakespeare for The Elizabethan Theatre Company, a production of Lorca's *Blood Wedding* at the London

Arts Theatre and a brief season as Director of Productions at the
Oxford Playhouse.

His work at Oxford and with The Elizabethan Theatre
Company also has Cambridge associations. The Elizabethan
Theatre Company grew from a group called The Oxford and
Cambridge Players, formed by Colin George (Oxford) and John
Barton (Cambridge) to tour Shakespeare productions on the
number-two touring circuit.[24] This group later became associated
with the management of the Oxford Playhouse for a period, and it
was for the Elizabethan Theatre Company at Oxford that Hall did
much of his early Shakespearian work. In a little over a year after
leaving Cambridge, Hall had directed fifteen stage productions,
and by the end of that first year 'out', his career as a theatre
director was assured:

> 'The way was not hard for a university man. The procession,
> led by Peter Brook, was in full progress. I joined the
> column — as did Peter Wood, Tony Richardson, Ken Tynan,
> Bill Gaskill, Michael Elliot, Toby Robertson. . . . All of us, on
> enthusiasm, bluff, and the quick perception encouraged by
> the universities, persuaded managements that we could direct
> long before we possibly could. We learnt by doing it.'[25]

In January 1954, Hall was appointed Assistant Director of the
Arts Theatre in London, and in January 1955 he was made
Director of the theatre. It was here that he directed the
now-famous British premiere of Samuel Beckett's *Waiting for
Godot* in 1955. It was this production which pushed Peter Hall
into the front ranks of English theatre directors. The first night of
Waiting for Godot was as much a theatrical revolution as the
opening of Tony Richardson's production of *Look Back in Anger*
at the Royal Court a year later. Tony Church said: '. . . all the old
ideas of what theatre was about were smashed to pieces . . . it was
an enormous step in the dark for Peter to do it.'[26]

Peter Woodthorpe, who played Estragon in the original production, told me about Hall's direction and the play's impact: 'We
arrived for the first rehearsal, and I remember Peter Hall saying:
"I'm not sure what this play means: I cannot pretend! I don't
understand it, but I think it may be highly significant. I think it's
probably a great work . . . we will explore — I have no scheme or

plan"... When it first opened it was booed... and the critics were very savage about it the next day. It was only when the Sunday papers came out that Hobson and Tynan changed the whole character of theatrical opinion.'[27]

Other Hall productions at the Arts included *Mourning Becomes Electra, The Waltz of the Toreadors*, Ionesco's *The Lesson*, and *South* — a play about the American Civil War by Julian Green. John Trewin saw this production:

> 'I called it later a "delighted fury of atmospherics"... While listening and watching, I felt again that Hall was a director who could hardly be bound to the simple statement. My programme bears the scrawled note, "Atmosphere!": it has been the word for Peter Hall throughout his record. We can sometimes make too much of a director's part: it is unfair to play and players. But, now and then, one appears who can seal any work with his own personality... on the stage I associate a Hall production with heat and tension: thunder is never very far away.'[28]

In 1956, Hall was invited to direct at the Shakespeare Memorial Theatre, and his first Stratford production of *Love's Labour's Lost* was followed by *Cymbeline* in 1957, *Twelfth Night* in 1958, and *A Midsummer Night's Dream*[29] and *Coriolanus* in 1959. Between 1955 and 1959, he also directed for various West End managements; and resigning from his post at the Arts Theatre, he formed his own production company, The International Playwrights Theatre, 1957. Due to lack of adequate financial backing this company did only two productions — Tennessee Williams' *Camino Real* at the Phoenix Theatre in April 1957 and Anouilh's *Traveller Without Luggage* in 1958 — but it did signal a definite attempt by Hall to form an ensemble company. He firmly believed that the ensemble principle and the freedom to work without commercial pressures was the ideal; Tony Church recalled student ambitions at Cambridge: 'Peter and I had sat down and talked for long periods about what we wanted to do in the theatre.... Peter very much wanted to see an ensemble company working in this country under state subsidy. In fact, this is the way we all felt... this was the "revolution" that we all wanted to see.'[30]

He directed *The Moon and Sixpence* — an opera based on the Somerset Maugham story — at Sadler's Wells in May 1957; the first

Peter Hall and John Barton's production of *Troilus and Cressida* at Stratford in 1960. *Centre:* Derek Godfrey as Hector; behind (not wearing cloak) Patrick Allen as Achilles.

David Warner as Henry VI, Donald Sinden as the Duke of York, and Brewster Mason as the Earl of Warwick in *Edward IV*, from *The Wars of the Roses* trilogy, directed by Peter Hall with John Barton and Frank Evans at Stratford in 1963.

Eric Porter as Shylock in Clifford Williams' production of *The Merchant of Venice* at Stratford in 1965.

opera ever to be commissioned by The Sadler's Wells Trust, and
the first that Hall had directed. In November 1957, he staged his
first Broadway production — *The Rope Dancer* at New York's
Cort Theatre — and on returning to England, directed productions
including *Cat On a Hot Tin Roof, Brouhaha* (with Peter Sellers),
Shadow of Heroes, Madame De . . ., A Traveller Without Luggage
and *The Wrong Side of the Park* for various London managements.
In November 1958, he was named as Director-designate of the
Memorial Theatre at Stratford. During his 1956 West End
production of *Gigi*, he met the French actress and dancer Leslie
Caron, who was appearing in the title-role. Peter Hall and Leslie
Caron were married in 1956.

On his appointment as Director of the Memorial Theatre, and in
the following early years of the RSC, when he introduced his new
policies and innovations, Peter Hall's name became increasingly
well known, both in England and overseas. Over the years that he
was in control at Stratford, the amount of publicity that he
generated — both personal and for his company — was enormous.

John Goodwin, the RSC's Head of Publicity and Publications,
attributed the extent of RSC publicity in the sixties to Hall's
personality more than to any other single factor: 'Peter Hall was
always very open with the Press. He likes to tell people what he's
doing. Theatre, he thinks, if it's alive, must be fairly noisy. He
never *sought* publicity. But he believes intentions should be
declared. It needs a certain amount of daring to do that.'[31]

Hall later spoke to me about his public image and personal
publicity while Director of the RSC: 'In the fight to establish the
company and to get the money for the company, we *had* to be in
the newspaper every day of the week if possible! I think one has
to be reasonably cynical about public relations. There's so many
demands upon the public's attention, that unless there is a very
clear image to "put over" — a company, a theatre, a play . . . a
leader of the company — then you haven't got much hope of
getting it through!'[32]

The man who directs an enterprise — and particularly a theatre
enterprise — the size of the RSC is unlikely to be popular with all,
and Hall has frequently admitted that he enjoys power: 'I get a
secret pleasure from complaining that the buck has to stop with
me. . . .'[33] Closely related to this was his artistic fascination with

politics — and more particularly power-politics, the uses and misuses of power within a political context and the various manoeuvrings and double-dealings of the political machine. In particular, *The Wars of the Roses* and *Hamlet* were designed as studies in power politics; in both cases relating the historical text and situations to modern political and social parallels.

As the extent of his personal influence grew, so too there grew up pockets of pro-Hall and anti-Hall feeling, both within the RSC and through the theatre world in general. Peter Hall has been variously labelled 'a born schemer', 'power mad', 'bloody-minded', 'utterly ruthless', and 'a self-confessed megalomaniac'; he has been compared to Iago, Machiavelli and Genghis Khan. In 1967, *Nova Magazine* published an article on the RSC, in which various actors, directors and theatre personalities talked about the company — and about working for Peter Hall.[34] A cross-section of these views on Hall read:

'... the man of the most vision and daring the English Theatre has produced in my time. *Dame Peggy Ashcroft*
I do wish he'd stop pretending to be so bloody nice and simple, when he's really very complicated and ambitious and a dictator ... *Glenda Jackson*
Peter uses you. He's quite straightforward about it. You benefit, he benefits. No sentiment! *Diana Rigg*
A brilliant administrator, a very good director and basically, unfortunately, a bloody nice bloke. It would be much easier if I hated his guts! *Roy Dotrice*
... like a super brother ... *Dorothy Tutin*
We all have this love-hate relationship with him. *Clifford Williams*'

Clifford Williams later elaborated on this statement to me: 'One becomes very attached to Peter, and one likes to be "in the sun". If you suspected there was a shadow falling on you, then you got very hurt about it. This perhaps explains the "hate" side of that remark. ... I do think that I would expect to find that phrase (love-hate) used by any associate of anyone who was in office — and powerfully in office — for that amount of time.'[35]
Despite the differences of opinion about Hall, his personal

charm and quality of attraction are recognized by almost all who speak of him. Even within the most informal conversation, there is an indefinable air of charisma which seems to surround him, and that is not something which he consciously projects — it simply exists.

Ian Richardson, who was recruited from the Birmingham Repertory Theatre, and acted with the RSC throughout the period of Hall's directorate, recognized this: 'He surrounds himself with a kind of "glamour" which is very unobtrusive. . . . And he is a born leader of men.'[36]

John Kane, who joined the RSC in 1964, echoed Richardson: 'Peter Hall has a "star quality" off-stage . . . he "hypnotizes" you actually . . . he could sweet-talk the birds off the trees. He really is amazing. A superb diplomat. You realize (in retrospect) that he's probably diddled you, but you don't care about it — because he did it so *beautifully*!'[37]

Hall himself said of his role at the RSC: 'You could call it a dictatorship checked and criticized!'[38] He did, however, try to run the RSC along democratic lines as much as possible: he was advised on all matters by his co-Directors and by a planning committee. But, if necessary, it was Hall who had the last word on choice of plays, casting and sets. He made himself personally responsible for the overall quality of all RSC productions: 'I see each production about a fortnight before the opening. If I think it's going to be a disaster I have three choices: cancel it, sack the director for another, or take over rehearsals myself.'[39]

While in control of the RSC, Hall also saw each actor once a year to tell him what he thought of the year's work: 'If I think he's no good I say so . . . that's better than saying, "You're bloody marvellous but we've got nothing for you next year!"'[40] Characteristically, he saw his own rapid rise in the theatre profession, his gaining the powerful position as Director of the RSC, and the bouts of adverse criticism which the holding of this position and power entailed, in extremely realistic terms: 'I have been lucky in my friends and often lucky in my enemies, for opposition is a necessary part of creation. There is no profession more generous than the theatre to developing talent. Seniority does not count.'[41] In a recent interview Hall looked back on his years at Stratford and talked about his 'love of power':

'I'm not as ambitious as I have made out . . . or as others have made me out to be! . . . I was ambitious in the Stratford years for something that I'm not ambitious for now. If you get the chance at the age of twenty nine to have a lot of power — and to try to realize a dream in the theatre — then you do perhaps fall in love with power. And I think I did. But I'm not in love with it any more . . . But that's because I'm forty-one now, and different I suppose. One changes. I still enjoy power. I *love* committees! I love meeting what seem insuperable odds . . . I don't like power when it means that you've got to fire somebody, or take a production away from a director, or take a part away from an actor. . . .'[42]

Hall's capacity for hard and sustained work has been widely reported. It was said that he frequently worked a seventeen-hour day during his first four years at Stratford, and certainly his production output since 1954 would suggest an excessively overloaded work schedule. He was asked — by Peter Lewis for *Nova* — why he worked so hard:

'I don't know. It isn't for money. It's not for the name in the papers. I've just got a mind that wants to be doing ten things at once. I like working. I have given up any sort of recreation apart from half an hour's Mozart or Haydn on the piano about three times a week. . . .'[43]

In 1963, the complicated mechanism that drives him collapsed. In May, an official theatre press statement announced that he was ill, and that the Stratford productions of *The Wars of the Roses* (beginning rehearsal at the time) would be postponed until August. In actual fact, Hall had been told he must rest completely for at least six months. During early 1963, the pressures on him were immense: the security and future of the RSC were still extremely uncertain (following the financial crisis of 1962) and there were innumerable problems involved in the editing, planning, casting and rehearsing *The Wars of the Roses*. In addition, Hall's marriage to Leslie Caron was on the verge of breaking up. This combination of personal strain, professional uncertainty and extreme overwork resulted in his collapse: 'I went down with deep depression and loss of faith in my talents. The doctors say that I am suffering from a "classic anxiety condition" — whatever that means!'[44] Characteristically, he defied his doctors' advice and was

back in the theatre working on *The Wars of the Roses* within three
weeks of his breakdown: 'The thing I learned was that you can
work through anything, any agony. I didn't want to walk into that
theatre. I didn't want to see those plays. But I found that if there's
a totally self-absorbing job you can do, you can go on doing it
however you're feeling. . . .'[45]

The Wars of the Roses was an extraordinary success. In June
1963, Hall was created CBE in the Birthday Honours List, and at
the end of that year, his work on *The Wars of the Roses* won him
the London Theatre Critics' Award for the Best Director. Dame
Peggy Ashcroft and David Warner also won acting awards for their
roles in the production. In early 1964, Hall's first marriage was
dissolved, and in October 1965 he married Jaqueline Taylor — his
former assistant. In March 1966, it was announced that the
University of Warwick had appointed him as Associate Professor
of Drama — the first Arts appointment of its kind in Britain.[46]

Between 1960 and 1968, Peter Hall was personally responsible
for directing fourteen stage productions for the RSC. In addition
to this work he also directed two operas for Covent Garden, and
made his first film — *Work is a Four Letter Word* (based on Henry
Livings's stage play *Eh?*) — in 1967. Following this film, Hall
became progressively more interested in the cinema:
'What is exciting and terrifying about the cinema, is that once
you've got it, you've got it. There's nothing you can change.
All right, you can do a lot in the cutting room: you can
juxtapose one image against another ... you can also
eliminate. But you can't really change what you've actually
shot. . . . In the theatre you can go back and see your play
again after six months of a season, and say to your actors:
"Come on, let's kick it about a bit: I want to change that
scene because it's not working . . .".'[47]
In 1968 he directed the RSC film of *A Midsummer Night's Dream*
based on his 1959 stage production at Stratford, and in the
following year his third film, *Three Into Two Won't Go*, scripted
by Edna O'Brien from a novel by Andrea Newman. Hall was
involved in a row with the American production company backing
this film: they insisted on the later addition of certain sequences
(for television presentation) not directed or approved by Hall, and

he retaliated by insisting that his name be removed from the credits. None of Hall's first three films were critical successes, but his fourth, *Perfect Friday* (released in 1971), was on the whole well received: '. . . I'm only just getting to a point where I know by instinct where the camera ought to be, in the same way that I know how to move an actor about the stage in a play. . . . It took some time in the theatre before I felt at ease, and I think it's taken me about the same length of time in the cinema. . . .'[48]

As well as a fascination with film making, Hall has developed a 'reasonable competence' as a practising musician, and a high degree of knowledge about music and musical forms, most notably opera. In speeches and recorded interviews, it is immediately recognizable that he uses frequent musical analogies when describing the 'texture' of a play, and actors who have worked with him say that music is the key to – and an integral part of – his working approach to a dramatic text: '. . . he has a superb ear – a really remarkable ear for the "music" of theatre work . . . for the rhythms and music of his work. . . .'[49] His early interest in the actual *speaking* of a Shakespeare text at Stratford is only one indication of this musical awareness, and some critics have seen the Hall/Pinter theatre relationship as another case of music and drama as a joint art: 'When Gareth Lloyd Evans wrote for *The Guardian* about the pre-London run of *Old Times*, he described Hall as Beecham to Pinter's Mozart. The capsule fits, not just because Hall has become the first exponent of Pinter but also because Pinter's use of silence has as much in common with music as with drama.'[50] During the sixties, Hall ventured into the production of opera, with the staging of a highly controversial *Moses and Aaron* at Covent Garden in 1965,[51] and a production of *The Magic Flute* in 1966. In 1969 it was announced that he had been appointed co-Director of the Royal Opera House, and together with conductor Colin Davis, would take up the appointment in September 1971. Since that announcement, Hall has directed three operas at Covent Garden – Sir Michael Tippett's new opera *The Knot Garden* (1970), Tchaikovsky's *Eugene Onegin*, and Wagner's *Tristan and Isolde* (1971).

It was stated that Hall and Davis 'intend to introduce new composers in an attempt to find a more diversified audience. They will try to make the classic repertoire, particularly Mozart, Wagner and Verdi, as relevant to today as Shakespeare is. . . .'[52]

It was widely assumed (and feared in some musical circles) that Hall intended to revolutionize the Opera House in the same way that he had tackled the theatre at Stratford, and that he would turn the production of opera into something as dynamic and forward-looking as the works of the RSC. He certainly stated that one of his primary aims at Covent Garden would be to improve the level of acting and to apply principles of direction to the staging of productions. John Bury, former RSC Head of Design, joined him at Covent Garden, and it was assumed that the same innovations would be carried through into the field of opera design. Hall soon discovered that the ensemble principles and creative processes applied in rehearsal at Stratford were not readily transferable to production at the Royal Opera House:

> 'The difficulties are greater in opera. Here time is shorter and there is an accepted tradition of being given the moves . . . Opera singers are not more inflexible or difficult than actors. Rather the reverse. Tell a singer to do something and he will do it. I suppose it is the discipline of years of obeying the man with the stick. But a singer is sometimes reluctant to transmute a suggestion into his own terms.'[53]

Critical reception of the production of *The Knot Garden* was good. It was a new and somewhat theatrical opera: ' . . . a triumphant example of musical theatre concerning itself with genuinely human values.'[54] *Eugene Onegin* and *Tristan and Isolde* were also successful in critical terms, although some critics dissented:

> 'Peter Hall's production, more accomplished though it in many ways is to any that Wagner has received at Covent Garden since the war, finally fails. . . . There are other details in the production which make me wonder whether Peter Hall fully understands the work . . . the spectacle of Tristan's entrails gushing out of his stricken body after he has deliriously torn off his bandages reveals an approach more akin to Elizabethan melodrama than Schopenhauerian other-worldliness.'[55]

John Bury spoke to me about working at Covent Garden: 'One is tending to feel at the moment that the Opera House is a pretty immovable beast, and although you may set out to do battle with it, it has a way of winning. It's so bound by tradition — and probably rightly so.[56]

On 7th July, 1971, it was announced in the Press that Hall had decided not to take up his appointment as co-Director of the Royal Opera House, and that he would not continue with a scheduled production of *The Marriage of Figaro* planned for the following season at Covent Garden. He gave his reasons for this decision:

> 'It was a mistake on my part to accept it. It is no-one's fault but my own. It was really over-optimistic for me to think I could do there what I wanted to do in the time available . . . it would mean that there would be no more Pinter, no films, no more theatre. I would find it a bit imprisoning to work only at Covent Garden and no theatre.'[57]

Kenneth Pearson commented on Hall's resignation:

> '. . . the artistic tensions between the Covent Garden board, led by Lord Drogheda, and its directorate (Peter Hall and Colin Davis) were destructive. Hall and Davies wanted to move the Opera House towards a twentieth century commitment: a group activity in which drama and music were equally deeply rooted. That would have called for more experiment, longer rehearsals, greater involvement on the part of top rank singers. Drogheda loved the high capacity box-office returns and respected the jet-set stars who flew in to keep them buoyant . . . the two ambitions were incompatible.'[58]

Despite his interest in music and opera, and his fascination with the techniques of the cinema, Peter Hall is fundamentally a man of the dramatic theatre. He is also a realist and a superb politician. He evidently came to the conclusion that to effect the changes he wished at the Royal Opera House would have cost him too much. Speaking to me several months after his resignation, he said: 'I don't believe that an opera house which does fine productions which only have an audience for six or eight performances is really justifying its subsidy. The audiences at Covent Garden are about twenty thousand opera buffs who go to everything . . . and often go to everything two or three times. The ordinary public can't get in, so the ordinary public don't go.' . . . I think this is nonsense. I think that if the opera was able to create a proper ensemble of stars (or people who become stars.) . . . then it would be able to have performances of its productions at a serious level twenty or thirty times. . . . The chief reason I left the Opera House was that having gone through months of work on a production — and achieved it in some measure with a cast — when it comes back [into the repertory] it's with a different cast, with maybe eight days rehearsal. If we did this in the theatre we'd be booed off the stage. . . . As I discovered that I could not change it, I thought it wasn't profitable to remain there.'[5 9]

Since relinquishing control of the RSC, Hall has continued his association with Harold Pinter: he directed *Landscape* and *Silence* for the RSC in 1969. Following the highly successful Aldwych opening of *Old Times*, he re-directed the play for managements in the United States and Europe. He directed a commercial production of Peter Shaffer's play *The Battle of Shrivings* in London during 1970, and the UK's premiere of Edward Albee's new play *All Over* for the RSC in January 1972. Before then, he directed three acclaimed Glyndebourne operas: *La Calisto* (1970 revived 1971), *Il Rittorno d'Ulisse in Patria* (1972), and *The Marriage of Figaro* (1973). His much publicised US production of *Via Galactica* — a musical scored by *Hair* composer Galt McDermot — was a critical disaster, and closed after only four nights on Broadway. Late in 1972, Hall began filming Pinter's *The Homecoming*, and this film is due for commercial release during 1974. Also in 1974 he will make a film, *Akenfield*, shot over four seasons in the Suffolk countryside and using local people rather than professional actors.

The work programme outlined above makes one thing about Peter Hall evident: he is able to work on a series of projects with a pace and energy that would break most people. He lives his life at tension point and admits to working at his best under extreme pressure. If there is no existing pressure — he will create it.

Peter Hall's conversation in interview, and indeed his general sphere of reference when talking about the theatre, returns repeatedly to Stratford and the organization he created there. He is still a member of the RSC, as a Consultant Director, in which capacity he is involved with the scheme for the Barbican Theatre — the RSC's proposed new London home — which he initiated in 1965. The Royal Shakespeare Company will undoubtedly always be a strong interest and influence in his life. Trevor Nunn, the present RSC Artistic Director, said of Hall: 'I've been massively influenced by him. It would be impossible for me to disguise that Peter Hall has been one of the most major influences in my life.'[60]

It will be interesting to observe the developing relationship between the RSC and the National Theatre after Hall becomes the National's Director: effectively Hall's new appointment will mean that Britain's two major theatrical organizations are, in some senses, influenced by the figure of Peter Hall, and by his philosophy of theatre.

Although Hall's National appointment came as no surprise when announced, his career did appear to be non-directional for some months following his resignation from Covent Garden. Several major projects were announced: a production of a musical spectacular, *Great Harry*, for the Bernard Delfont management; the possibility of his directing the inaugural production at the new Sydney Opera House in Australia; a production of *The Seagull* for the RSC; the possible production of his own film script *Huntsman* (adapted from the H.E. Bates short story).

None of these reported projects came to fruition, and towards the end of 1971 and in early 1972 rumours began to gain momentum. It was reported with increasing frequency that Hall would accept (or had already accepted) the Directorate of the National Theatre. The appointment was formally announced in March 1972, and caused little stir as Hall was the logical choice for the job. The extent of change he will introduce at the National is still unknown. Certainly his overall outlook and philosophy of theatre has altered since he created the RSC.

Some indication of Hall's programme for the National was given at a press conference on 13th March 1973. It was announced that he would join the National as co-Director from 1st April 1973, and assume full directorial responsibility from the beginning of November. As the two main auditoriums of the new National Theatre building (plus a smaller studio theatre) will require the company to produce a much greater volume of work than in the past, it was announced that a group of Associate Directors would join Hall and Olivier in the company's planning. John Dexter and Michael Blakemore, (already Associate Directors of the National) will be joined by Jonathan Miller, Harold Pinter and John Schlesinger. These Directors will begin building up a bank of productions which will be first seen at the Old Vic in 1974, and transfer to the new building when it opens in early 1975. It was further announced that John Bury would join the National Theatre as Head of Design, and that Kenneth Tynan, Head of the National's Literary Department since its inception, would end his association with the company during the 1973/4 season.

Though still a young man Peter Hall has a unique record of achievement behind him. Where does one 'move' when one has virtually done it all at an early age? Hall replied to his question before the announcement of his National appointment:

'I don't know. I think I will have to write some more: whether it's a sort of boring theoretical book about the theatre (which I'm afraid I shall write!) or perhaps film scripts . . . But these are only actually subsidiaries to what I *know* I shall have to do sooner or later — which is to run a theatre company again.'[6] [1]

3. The `Crucial` Years
1960 - 1963

The plan was radical and creative . . . before the structure
was ready he opened his grand project: suddenly the vast
company, the immense repertoire, the constant output, the
excitement, the disasters, the strain all came into existence.
. . . He was trying to create a living organism, where
flexible imaginative conditions were related to flexible
imaginative individuals in key positions. The new traditions
of the new company were intelligence, youth and skill. . . .
> Peter Brook, 'Peter Hall by Peter Brook',
> *RSC Annual Report*, 1968

In 1959, while still Director-designate of the Memorial Theatre,
Peter Hall made it clear that the formation of a 'near permanent'
company would be his primary objective at Stratford. He believed
that Shakespeare, more than any other dramatist, needed a
'style' — a tradition and unity of direction and acting — and he felt
that only a permanent company could provide the necessary
resources and conditions to make the development of a style
possible:

'If I were taking over a Continental theatre this great heritage
would be tangible. There would be a number of leading
actors associated with the theatre; a more or less permanent
company; a series of famous productions still in the
repertory. All this would produce a style . . . at Stratford, at
the end of each season the productions normally vanish and
the company is broken up. My heritage is made up of ghosts
and legends . . . I hope to create a style which is recognizable
as Stratford's own, and to reinterpret the plays in terms of
that style. To do this I shall need a company that remains
basically, though not entirely the same. . . . My plans are very
ambitious, and next year is only the beginning. . . .'[1]

Hall believed that a company structure — a group of actors,
directors and designers working together with shared assumptions

— would unconsciously develop a company style, which would come from the choice of repertoire and the way in which the company, as a whole, approached what a play should 'say' on stage.

His first policy statement as Director went to the national press on 14th January 1960. It was, broadly speaking, a four-point plan, enclosed in a scheme for the acquisition of a second theatre, in London, to be used as a city outlet for selected Stratford productions and also for the presentation of modern plays. Hall felt that actors needed both classical and modern work, and that no company could develop properly if restricted to serving only one author.

The major point in his plan was the formation, as soon as possible, of a permanent company at Stratford: '. . . a fairly loose nucleus of actors who regarded this company as their permanent home, although they may go away from time to time in order to benefit from working in films and television.'[2] Other points included an immediate concentration on improving the standard of verse speaking; a newly designed stage at Stratford; and occasional seasons of Shakespeare at Stratford — each intended to convey a different Shakespeare theme.

Emphasis was placed on verse speaking from the outset, as Hall wished to have a company with the idea of acting 'based on the word first and the Method second'. He felt that modern actors had spent much of their time at drama schools learning to play a meaning 'underneath' the text, instead of learning to illuminate the meaning of the text itself: 'There is a common belief that if an actor is "true" in the Stanislavsky sense, he will be led instinctively to the form of the verse. I don't believe this. An intelligent understanding of the form and expression of the text is as much the raw material of your creation as knowing the name of the character you are playing. We want to tell you about ends of lines, about alliteration, about rhyme, about the form of the verse, the nature of verse, and verse speaking as a craft. We want you to think about these things in rehearsal in creative terms.'[3]

In January 1960, Hall appointed John Barton, who at this time was Lay Dean of King's College, Cambridge, and an authority on Elizabethan speech and drama, as Assistant Director of the Memorial Theatre. Barton was deputed to give special attention to the training of the company in the art of verse speaking, and Hall indicated that facilities would be extended at a later date to include a scheme for more comprehensive training in Shakepeare acting. It was stressed that any training should be a natural outcome of productions rather than a formal theatre school, and for the 1960 season rehearsal periods were extended to allow for this.

Hall felt that the staging and setting of Shakespeare was still largely dependent on a Victorian tradition. Productions either had tons of realistic scenery, or were mounted in a self-consciously progressive way on a bare, wooden 'Elizabethan' stage. Prior to the opening of the 1960 season, Hall re-designed the Stratford stage to accommodate his new style of staging: 'a style in which visual effects would remain secondary to the speaking actor'.[4] Three renaissance arches, forming a false proscenium, were introduced to form a permanent setting for the season. The actual stage was re-shaped further out over the orchestra pit, and this extension incorporated a hand-operated revolve which spanned the width of the proscenium opening. The stage was raked, and the apron was cut away at both sides to allow two rows of angled seats to be added at the front of the stalls. The new stage apron extended 14 feet into the auditorium and was intended to bring the players into closer contact with the audience than had ever before been possible at Stratford. Hall declared that he wished to use the stage as a 'platform for the imagination': 'A stage should be very frankly a stage — and not just an illusionist's bag of tricks.'[5]

On 8th March 1960, a second major policy statement was released to the press. It was announced that an agreement had been made between the Shakespeare Memorial Theatre and Mr Prince Littler, Chairman and Managing Director of Associated Theatre Properties (London) Ltd., guaranteeing a London theatre for the Stratford-upon-Avon company for five years from December 1960. The theatre would probably be the Aldwych, but should this not be available the Stratford company would be provided with another comparable theatre.

Hall intended that Stratford's London branch should present an all-the-year-round programme of modern plays, Shakespeare and other classics, and that important foreign companies should be invited to appear occasionally at this theatre. But the emphasis in London would not be on Shakespeare, which would be given, as usual, at Stratford from April to December each year. Hall hoped that this dual-theatre policy would enable him to offer actors varied and continuous work. The initial plan was to build up a semi-permanent ensemble of at least thirty players, on contracts lasting a minimum of three years, though the actors would be free to spend a third of that time working elsewhere if they wished.

It was also announced that the Memorial Theatre was commissioning a number of plays from modern dramatists — including Robert Bolt, Peter Shaffer, John Arden, and John Whiting — the idea being to encourage young playwrights to make ' . . . free and epic use of the theatre, and not to be worried if their theme needs large casts'.[6]

A replica of the re-designed Stratford stage was to be constructed at the London theatre, and it was announced that the company would present their first West End season in December 1960 — a repertoire consisting of a new play by a British author, one Shakespeare production from Stratford, and a further play to be decided. A production of Anouilh's *Becket* was also planned.[7]

On 19th July 1960, it was announced that London's Aldwych Theatre would definitely be the Memorial Theatre's West End branch, and that a three-year agreement had been signed. At the same time the Governors announced that a grant of £5,000 a year for three years had been given to the Memorial Theatre by the Calouste Gulbenkian Foundation, a Trust that exists to support, amongst other things, the Arts in any country in the world. This grant was given to help meet the costs of the long-term contract system on which Hall wished to base his company structure. Until this time the Memorial Theatre had been completely self-supporting and was in receipt of no grant or subsidy from any government or private agency.

The existence of long-term contracts was officially announced on 16th October 1960. Sixteen actors and actresses had been engaged on a contract that was unique in the history of the English theatre, and some twenty more actors were to be signed up on this long-term basis.[8] The contract gave the Stratford management first call on the actors' services for three years, but also allowed them the right to work elsewhere — for other managements and in films and television. Mr Hugh Jenkins of Equity, the Actors' Union, stated:

'We welcome the satisfactory conclusion of this revolutionary scheme. It introduces a long-term element into the employment of actors without seriously inhibiting their freedom . . . the contract also allows the right to holidays with pay for the first time in the West End theatre.'[9]

Peter Hall said:

'For our first contract artists I have secured players at all levels. Dame Peggy Ashcroft and Max Adrian add enormous experience to superb talent, and Dorothy Tutin is in the top rank of our established younger actresses. I think that Peter O'Toole, Richard Johnson, Ian Bannen and Eric Porter are perhaps the most brilliantly promising of any young actors in this country. . . . Eventually I want to engage about thirty five artists on this long-term contract. They will provide the possibility of real ensemble work. At the same time we will continue to invite many other players, including stars, to act for us on the normal short-term arrangements. By April next year we will have a total of about ninety actors employed in Stratford and London.'[10]

From his pool of actors, Hall hoped to draw two complete companies — one for Stratford and the other for London — the players to be interchangeable. He hoped that it would eventually be possible for ' . . . an actor to play Shakespeare in Stratford on Monday and John Whiting in London on Tuesday'.[11] His overall plan for the company was ambitious — and costly. The basis of Hall's early financial policy was the eventual goal of a permanent Government subsidy for the Memorial Theatre, and he felt that the best way to attract the support he needed was to create a continual sense of drama and energy surrounding the company's activities. He calculated that if the volume and quality of his company's work was sufficiently outstanding, officialdom could not afford to ignore it: 'He calculated daringly, yet wisely, that unless his grand project was realised completely, the theatre would inevitably stagnate, and so it was better to spend the last penny today than save something for a future that would not be worth inheriting . . . a great deal of exciting and costly activity was the first constant on which he relied. . . .'[12]

Peter Brook, directing *King Lear* in the Danish snow.

The Devils directed by Peter Wood at the Aldwych in 1961. This photograph, taken after the casting had changed, shows Patrick Wymark as Father Barre and Virginia McKenna as Sister Jeanne.

The Board of Governors led by Sir Fordham Flower supported Hall's plan:

'In 1959 the Governors had a clear choice. It was either to continue with Shakespeare at Stratford, finding it increasingly difficult to maintain standards, but showing a small profit which in turn would start to run down. Or of leaving this semi-commercial status, changing to top gear, and going all out for a place among the five or six great Art theatres of the world. We were ripe for this change and the Governors made it . . . the change meant a complete alteration in our attitudes . . . we were suddenly asked to forget accepted commercial notions and realise that, in the new world we had chosen, a large annual deficit was a part of life.'[13]

And Peter Hall, speaking to the company in 1963, declared:

'We're not running this company to make money. We try to lose as little as possible, but we believe that the company we are trying to create is impossible to run on a commercial basis. We cannot be activated by the profit principle.'[14]

In November 1960, Hall announced that he had completed a ticket deal (sometimes called a 'library deal') with Peter Cadbury, Managing Director of Keith Prowse Ltd., the largest theatre ticket agency in Britain. The deal guaranteed the purchase of tickets valued at £250,000 for the Memorial Theatre's Aldwych season in 1960/61 — and was the largest deal of its kind ever completed in Britain. The agreement meant that the agency had undertaken to buy the stated value of tickets from the theatre, thus assuming all risk and responsibility, whether the tickets were sold or not. This deal removed some of the financial risk from the company's first London season, although Hall still estimated a loss of between £20,000 and £40,000 on the company's combined operations over the first two years.[15]

On 20th March 1961, it was formally announced that, by command of Her Majesty the Queen, the Shakespeare Memorial Theatre would henceforth be known as the Royal Shakespeare Theatre, and the company as the Royal Shakespeare Company. Since the granting of a Royal Charter by George V in 1925, the theatre had operated under the official patronage of the Sovereign, and the 1961 change was in name only. It was generally felt that

'Memorial' Theatre was not sufficiently expressive of the new, forward-looking company image that Hall wished to project, and was not in keeping with the role in which he wished to see the new RSC.

From 1961, all RSC press releases and theatre programmes began to carry the following statement: 'Incorporated under Royal Charter, with the Queen as Patron, it [the RSC] virtually belongs to the Nation. . . .' A National Theatre in Britain had been a subject of discussion for years. During 1961 there were many who felt, and publicly expressed the fact, that a 'National Theatre' was already in existence — in the Royal Shakespeare Company. 1961 was the year in which the whole National Theatre question again came into official prominence. Under the National Theatre Act of 1949 the Government had approved, in principle, a scheme for the setting up of a National Theatre, and had also approved the granting of £1 million towards the building costs. The basis of the original scheme was, broadly speaking, a form of merger between the Old Vic Theatre, the Shakespeare Memorial Theatre and Sadler's Wells — the 'combine' to operate under the name of a National Theatre. On 13th July 1951, a foundation stone was laid on a site on the South Bank of the Thames and throughout the fifties, innumerable conferences were held (in conjunction with the Arts Council) on the question of how this National Theatre combine would operate.

Nothing of a definite nature was ever decided or achieved, and the scheme remained a question for debate and theatrical controversy. On 13th July 1961, the Government, under considerable pressure to do so, announced that it was already to release the £1 million already approved for the National Theatre scheme, and the London County Council announced that it would also contribute an estimated £1,300,000 towards the building costs. All that was now required was an agreement between the three theatre companies in question.

This announcement caused considerable problems for Peter Hall, as it came only months after an earlier Government announcement that it was *not* yet prepared to build a National Theatre, but would make a substantial subsidy to the RSC and other theatre organizations instead. On the strength of this promise, Hall had acquired a short lease on the Arts Theatre in

London – to be used as an experimental wing of the two major theatres, and to present new plays and new theatre ideas. He intended to open a season of modern plays there early in 1962. The Government's change-of-mind on the National Theatre question left Hall with three theatres – two of which were on lease – vast expenses in overhead and production costs, a growing company of actors, and no subsidy. Speaking in November 1961, he said:

'These are dangerous times for us ... we must watch this situation very closely.'[1 6]

In March 1962, despite the lack of a subsidy, Hall opened his second London theatre project at the Arts, with a season of modern plays designed to run for a month each. This 'Play-a-Month' scheme was intended to 'introduce new authors, producers and leading players to the public'. At the same time, Hall announced that he had reached an agreement with the BBC under which two plays from the company's repertoire would be filmed or telerecorded each year, and then televised after their withdrawal from the live theatre repertory.

On 7th March 1962, the Board of Governors announced that the RSC had decided to withdraw from the Joint Council of the National Theatre – and from the National Theatre project. The official reasons given were 'constitutional difficulties' and the fear that Stratford traditions would be lost. Certainly the 1962 scheme was totally unacceptable to the RSC, and Hall announced his intention of continuing with existing policy and commitments in the hope of Government assistance. He estimated he would require a subsidy of £88,000 to complete the projects he had begun. When the National Theatre plans were finally agreed in July 1962, it was announced that the National Theatre Board would receive a grant of £40,000 towards the running costs of the project. The Royal Shakespeare Company was not mentioned.

The four months from July to November 1962 were extremely uncertain for the company. Without sufficient funds there was no possibility of continuing with the projects begun in London, and the Arts Theatre experiment was forced to close after only six months of operation. Hall realized that there was a strong possibility that he would also be forced to close the Aldwych and return all company activities to Stratford, and the RSC began a massive, and desperate, press campaign to win public support:

'To make any plans for next year is difficult. That is why we are trying to get some assurance that the sum we have needed for so long might turn itself into hard cash. We shall not get anything until next April, if we get anything at all. . . . Next year is vague. The day the Aldwych closes the company will stop. The long-term contracts will be liquidated and the whole policy will be no more. . . .'[17]

Several influential national newspapers took up the fight on the RSC's behalf:

'The Royal Shakespeare Company's future is apparently in danger. Under the direction of Peter Hall this company has begun to establish a unique organization, providing writers, actors and artists with a continuity and purpose that the anarchy of commercial show business can never hope to offer. The Stratford Governors, it is reported, have been waiting for over a year for Whitehall's reply to their appeal for aid, but this has been postponed because of the muddle and indecision over the National Theatre. . . It is hard to believe that the Arts Council can stand by and see such a remarkable and successful venture being extinguished for the lack of State alms, which are now being given freely to all kinds of unsuccessful,' unexciting and uncreative establishments.'[18]

In November 1962, the Treasury, through the Arts Council, promised the Royal Shakespeare Company a grant of £47,000 for the financial year 1963/64. This was half the amount that Hall had asked for and it allowed no margin for increasing actors' salaries, continuing with the experimental work begun at the Arts, or improving the company's training methods. It did, however, enable the Aldwych project to continue operating, and it did establish the precedent that Hall had hoped for — that of a Government subsidy for his company. Nevertheless, the initial grant received by the RSC was still considerably lower than that received by other theatres of comparable size and standing. Hall made it clear that this grant had merely 'plugged the gap', and that he would not relax in his efforts to get much greater support from public funds: 'The signs are that while 1962 was the first of our crucial years, it is unlikely to be the last. . . .'[19]

Although financial problems and theatre politics dominated the first three years of Peter Hall's Directorate, these were also the years in which his project took on a definite shape and identity, and the RSC began to achieve recognition as one of the most imaginative and creative artistic enterprises in Britain. In early 1960, the press was encouraging:

'After a spell of hectic, and sometimes opportunist work in recent seasons, when brilliance and exhibitionism were not always far enough apart, there are now signs of a settled artistic policy. As Peter Hall is careful to point out, such objectives as the formation of a style cannot be brought about in a single production or a single season.'[20]

T.C. Worsley wrote in the *Financial Times*:

'. . . with Mr Peter Hall's appointment as director, a new era begins. It may well be a great era too — the auspices are excellent. But it will be different.[21]

During the 1960 and 1961 seasons, critics began noting a 'freshness of approach' and 'rare and surprising developments in the individual' and although there were a certain amount of consistently adverse criticism, it was generally felt that Hall's training methods, concentration on verse speaking, and ideas of ensemble playing were beginning to show dividends. The actors appeared to accept the company principle readily, ' . . . perhaps because we have, as a nation, elevated the team spirit to mythical heights',[22] and the new company placed a heavy emphasis on youth — young directors working with young actors. Ian Richardson said: 'In the early stages of his Directorate he gathered around him many old colleagues . . . all relatively youthful men . . . and recruited actors like myself, simply because we were young. The thing I noticed most during my first year with the RSC was the youth of the company.'[23] Gareth Lloyd Evans wrote in the *Manchester Guardian*, 31st March 1960:

'One has the sense that the 1960 season is already contained within a bigger time scale and meaning and that, in some ways, it is only the beginning of an unfolding whose final dimensions may well stretch beyond the confines of this theatre . . . the company seems happy. It is heartening, if unnerving, to hear actors argue over their pie and bitter about rhythm and end-stopping. . . .'

In 1962, Peter Hall made two appointments that were to have a considerable influence on the immediate and future development of the company. On 8th February he appointed Michel St. Denis as General Artistic Adviser to the company, and on 11th April he invited Peter Brook to join him in the Directorate. This meant, in effect, that the Royal Shakespeare Company was to be directed by a triumvirate — Hall, Brook and St. Denis. A theatre press statement said:

> 'The triumvirate will share collectively the responsibility for the company's entire artistic quality and administration in both Stratford and London, with Peter Hall having responsibility to Governors.'[24]

Peter Hall, writing in *Crucial Years*, spoke of the reasons for the triumvirate, and how he hoped it would influence the company:

> 'In early 1962, my anxiety was great. I had always known that I could not direct alone an enterprise as large and active as ours. But by April Michel St. Denis and Peter Brook had agreed to join me. Their presence strengthened us beyond measure, for in addition to guiding the general policy, they will be responsible for two other vital activities. The strength of a company lies in its artistic security. Yet this can be a prison to an actor unless he is constantly liberated by training and experiment. The Studio that Michel St. Denis has already started will train the young, develop the experienced, and privately try out new forms of staging. Peter Brook is to direct public productions experimenting in new writing and new forms — an extension of our short lived work at the Arts.'[25]

Michel St. Denis was born in France in 1897, and as a young man became an actor under his uncle, Jaques Copeau, at the Vieux-Colombier Theatre in Paris. In 1930, he formed his own acting group, the Compagnie des Quinze, which toured Europe and England for several seasons. St. Denis later came to live in London, where he founded, with John Gielgud and Tyrone Guthrie, the London Theatre Studio, and he also organized the Old Vic Theatre School. His career outside England included the establishment of the Théâtre de l'Est in Strasbourg, and he was, for ten years, the director of its combined theatre school and performing companies. He was later named Artistic Councillor to the Comédie Française

and Inspector General of the French Theatre. In the later years of
his life he was invited to America by the Rockefeller Foundation
to study American theatre needs, and he spent nearly two years
visiting almost every theatre enterprise in the U.S.A. He was also
invited to become Artistic Adviser to Canada's bi-lingual National
School of Dramatic Art, and co-Director of the Drama Division of
the Julliard School at the Lincoln Center in New York. He led the
International Theatre Institute conferences on theatre problems in
Venice, Helsinki, Prague and New York, and was recognized
throughout the world as one of the century's great men of the
theatre.[26]

Peter Hall hoped that his presence at Stratford would infuse the
company with some elements of the European tradition of
theatre, and in 1962, St. Denis founded the RSC Actor's Studio,
intended to function as a workshop for the entire company —
actors, directors, playwrights, designers, and technicians. Within
this studio, the company was to examine all the various problems
relating to the working of the theatre, and the project called for
the holding of almost continuous classes and individual tuition in
speech, improvisation, singing, movement, dance, fencing, acrobatics, wrestling, and mask work. St. Denis also intended that the
Studio should stage occasional experimental productions in
private, at which new methods could be tried and experiments in
casting made: 'In the Studio we all had a chance to re-explore the
entire nature of our own personalities and our profession. It was
therapeutic.'[27] St. Denis, writing about the Studio in *Crucial
Years*, said:

> '. . . a re-examination of the nature of Shakespearian poetry,
> of its style, of its direct power to reveal reality in modern
> terms, is an urgent need if the interpretation of Shakespeare
> is to be brought up to date . . .'[28]

St. Denis saw the Studio as an instrument of this re-examination,
and its function to evolve ways and means, and to conduct the
necessary experiments. It also had the more practical purpose of
training the actors' technical abilities and their creative imagination.

However, apart from founding and setting up the Studio, the
long-term influence of Michel St. Denis on the Royal Shakespeare
Company as a whole was severely limited by his ill-health.

Yet there were some young actors who still feel the influence of St. Denis in their work. The RSC's initial Studio plan also consisted of taking a group of very young actors straight from drama school, allowing them to be trained under St. Denis, and then assimilating them into the company: John Kane was one of these first Studio 'pupils': 'There were ten of us . . . and we all worked with Michel St. Denis . . . I remember him doing the most superb work with masks; he was an old man at this stage, and I watched him put on a young man's mask — and he was sixteen years old! It was absolutely incredible! . . . Although he was very dogmatic in his views, he gave us a tremendous grounding in approaching various authors. Every Friday he would talk about someone in particular — Beckett, Brecht, Stanislavsky; and he had *met* all these people at one time or another. It was an incredible experience to talk to this man. . . . Like Peter Brook in many ways, he was *so* demanding . . . in the same way as Peter rejects everything but that which is "right" and "truthful", so Michel St. Denis did this too . . . I will never forget the debt I owe to him. . . .'[29]

In 1946, at the age of twenty, Peter Brook was already being acclaimed a genius and a brilliant innovator by theatre critics and audiences. In 1971, these descriptions are still being applied to the man who, over a career of some twenty five years in the theatre, films and opera, has been possibly the most controversial, the most exciting, the most influential, and certainly the most talked-about director in the English theatre: 'A Brook production is always newsworthy. It may be slammed or extolled, but it is never ignored.[30] His appointment to the Stratford Directorate in 1962 had far-reaching effects on the stylistic development of the RSC, and indeed, next to Peter Hall, it is Brook who must share responsibility for the shape of the organization which Trevor Nunn inherited in 1968. Between 1962 and 1968 the names Peter Hall, Peter Brook, and Royal Shakespeare Company became synonymous.

Peter Stephen Paul Brook was born in London in 1925 of White Russian parents — his mother a Doctor of Science and his father a wealthy Pharmaceutical Manufacturer. Neither of his parents had any theatre background, although as a child Brook was fascinated by the theatre, and at the age of seven he presented a four-hour *Hamlet* on a toy stage.[31] His early education was varied — 'I went to half a dozen schools where I quarrelled, fought and made trouble'[32] — and in 1942 he went up to Oxford to read English. During his first term at Oxford, Brook directed an undergraduate production of *Dr. Faustus* at London's Torch Theatre, and in 1943 he made his first film, Sterne's *Sentimental Journey*, again with an undergraduate cast. On leaving Oxford in 1944, Brook worked with a film studio in London, making propaganda and commercial films, and in 1945 he presented Cocteau's *Infernal Machine* at the Chanticleer Theatre in South Kensington. Notices for this production were good, and led to other offers of stage work. He produced for the Kew Theatre and was invited by ENSA (an entertainments for the Services organization) to produce *Pygmalion*. William Armstrong, a producer who had been invited to direct *Man and Superman* at the Birmingham Repertory Theatre but had been obliged to cancel, saw Brook's *Pygmalion* during a run-through at Drury Lane: 'Armstrong, impressed by the production, wired Sir Barry Jackson at Birmingham suggesting Brook as a substitute producer.'[33] Brook went to Birmingham in the August of 1945 to produce *Man and Superman*, and there he met Paul Scofield — a leading young member of the Birmingham company — who played Tanner in *Man and Superman* and the Bastard in Brook's subsequent production of *King John*. John Trewin saw this production: 'I happened to see this production quite by accident — I was on my way back from Liverpool — and it was truly fantastic: quite in the Brook manner — and he was still only twenty. I was with *The Observer* then, and I wrote a long piece about it. It was so incredibly alive! So unlike the routine Shakespeare of those days.'[34]

When Sir Barry Jackson took over as Director of the Memorial Theatre in 1946, he invited Brook to produce *Love's Labour's Lost*. This production was an outstanding personal success for Brook, and after a period of work for London managements, he returned to Stratford in 1947 to produce *Romeo and Juliet*. He decided to treat the production with stark simplicity, and announced that he saw the play in terms of 'open spaces, in which scenery and decoration could easily become an irrelevance'. The critics did not agree:

> 'The settings created an architectural isolation suggesting an anachronistic air-raid. . . . Shakespeare's poetry submerged under a peevish impatience. . . .[35]
>
> While nobody minds the brilliant Mr Brook bedevilling lesser plays, I suggest he might be more modest with master-pieces.'[36]

For an audience used to a fully-furnished stage and elaborate settings, this production must have come as something of a shock. Brook set the play in a bare orange arena, and lit fiercely with strong white lighting. He cut the text drastically, employed a variety of stage tricks that were completely new to Shakespeare production, and used suggestive rather than realistic staging techniques throughout. 'What Brook thought was essentially 1947, was in fact essentially 1965!'[37]

His early Stratford productions established Brook in the front rank of directors, and in 1949, at the age of twenty four, he became Director of Productions at Covent Garden. Here he produced a number of operas with success, the most notable being his production of *Salome* designed by Salvadore Dali. He continued to be fascinated by films, and in 1952 he directed a film of *The Beggar's Opera* with Sir Laurence Olivier, followed four years later by a much-praised *Moderato Cantabile*. He directed stage productions in Europe, England and America, and continued to direct occasionally at Stratford throughout the fifties. For the 1955 Stratford season, he directed Laurence Olivier in *Titus Andronicus*, and this production became the most controversial presentation of the year. An unpopular and unevenly written play, *Titus Andronicus* had rarely been performed, and never before at Stratford: potential producers were scared off by the play's lack of credibility and sheer excess of horror. Brook gave his reasons for wishing to direct it:

> 'It is not so much a piece of Grand Guignol as an austere and grim Roman tragedy – horrifying indeed, but with a real primitive strength, and achieving at times even a barbaric dignity . . . *Titus* has some superbly written passages of immense power and vivid beauty, as well as an extremely exciting plot.'[38]

Brook made cuts in the text, removing or re-arranging many of the 'unactable' or 'unspeakable' lines. He designed his own settings of vast columns, racks, cages and naked torches — a series of selective effects designed to heighten the sense of the ominous. He directed for speed in performance, and used formal patterns of moving figures, contrasted with motionless tableaux. Horrors were suggested rather than portrayed realistically — symbolic scarlet ribbons around the wrist and hands suggested Lavinia's physical mutilation. Brook also composed a special score of musique concrète to accompany the action — plucked strings, single drum beats and eerie throbbing sounds:

'Peter Brook . . . has squeezed every drop of brutality out of the drama, but hardly a drop of gore . . . on paper this hideous tale of revenge is not so much a play as a dramatised abattoir; an orgy of horror for horror's sake. On the stage, Mr Brook discovers an unsuspected dramatic meaning.'[39]

Kenneth Tynan, in an article written during a later season of *Titus Andronicus* in London, found certain similarities in approach between Brook and Stratford's newest young director, Peter Hall:

'Having closely compared Peter Brook's production of *Titus Andronicus* with Peter Hall's production of *Cymbeline*, I am persuaded that these two young directors should at once go into partnership. I have even worked out business cards for them:— "Hall and Brook Ltd., the Home of Lost Theatrical Causes . . .' The present examples of Hallage and Brookery come unmistakably from the same firm. In each case the director has imposed on a bloodstained, uneven play, a unifying conception of his own.'[40]

In 1962, Brook completed another film, William Golding's *Lord of the Flies*, and in the late Autumn he came to Stratford to direct Paul Scofield in *King Lear*. Brook had not worked at Stratford since 1955, and *Lear* was his first production for the new Royal Shakespeare Company — the beginning of his working association with Peter Hall: 'Unlike many shooting stars, Brook has never flopped into an official rut. But as one of the governing triumvirate of the Royal Shakespeare Company he has found a niche — and freedom to range.'[41]

Peter Hall's first Stratford season in 1960 made it evident that there had been a definite change in theatre policy. It was not just a group of five plays by Shakespeare, but a selection of plays planned as an organic sequence — designed to trace the 'development, range and paradox of Shakespearian Comedy.'[42] The intention was an attempt to span Shakespeare's creative growth from the early romantic comedies like *Two Gentlemen of Verona* and *Twelfth Night*, through the near-farce of *The Taming of the Shrew*, to the 'hard, ironic comedy of the middle period' in *Troilus and Cressida*, and finally to *The Winter's Tale*, 'where the sombre beginnings have given way to a world of pastoral, and the malaise in the characters has been resolved.'[43] Hall also intended that there should be some homogeneity in the way the productions were staged, and all the directors at Stratford in 1960 (with the exception of Michael Langham) had been known to Hall since his Cambridge days, and could be expected, in some ways, to share his vision of the theatre.

In December 1960, the company opened the Aldwych project with a production of Webster's *The Duchess of Malfi*: '... the first London performance of a national repertory company ... which will rank eventually with the Comédie Française, the Berliner Ensemble and the Moscow Arts Theatre.'[44] In early 1961, the first London season continued with productions of John Whiting's *The Devils* (the first of the company's commissioned plays), *Ondine*, and a presentation devised by John Barton called *The Hollow Crown*, a programme of music, speeches, letters, and other writings by and about the Kings and Queens of England.[45]

For his second season as director, Hall departed from the principle of linking plays together with a common theme. The 1961 Stratford season was centred on a quartet of Shakespeare's tragedies — *Hamlet, Richard III, Romeo and Juliet* and *Othello* — and the programme was completed by two of the major comedies — *Much Ado About Nothing* and *As You Like It*. It was announced that a second company would appear in works by other dramatists 'old and new' at the Aldwych.

Together the two companies totalled nearly 100 actors, and during the year they staged twelve productions, covering plays not only by Shakespeare, but also Webster, Giraudoux, John Whiting, Anhouilh and Chekhov. Dame Peggy Ashcroft, Vanessa Redgrave, Dorothy Tutin and Ian Bannen led the permanent company, and several star names were engaged for the season: Franco Zeffirelli, the Italian film and opera director, was invited to produce *Othello*, and Dame Edith Evans, Sir John Gielgud and Christopher Plummer joined the company.

However, despite a first-rate cast list and a programme of widely varied theatre, 1961 — except for *As You Like It*, with Vanessa Redgrave much acclaimed as Rosalind — was a bad year critically for the RSC: the production with the highest expectation was most damned by the critics. Of Zeffirelli's *Othello* with John Gielgud, Tynan wrote:

'Not since the heyday of Charles Kean ... has more been asked of an English stage staff in a classical production ... Given the use of Zeffirelli's decor, a respectable opera company could send two productions out on tour and still have enough over for the Verdi *Otello*! ... Gielgud himself is quite simply over parted. ...'[46]

The *Hamlet* production was chiefly noted (or notorious) for its device of having the Prince speak his 'rogue and peasant slave' soliloquy sitting in a cabin trunk: 'Vengeance, vengeance! he cried, shutting himself in it, and he was not alone in his demand.'[47] Bernard Levin wrote:

'... [1961] showed the strain of keeping two companies going ... [but] ... they set no limits to their possible achievement; their programme is incomparable in its range; even their flops are spectacular and gigantic.'[48]

The 1962 season, planned and executed in the midst of the company's worst financial crisis, was the most ambitious programme of productions ever attempted by a Stratford company — before or since. Over a period of twelve months, the company staged a total of twenty four productions; the public bought 708,400 tickets at Stratford, the Aldwych, the Arts, and on tour; and the combined box offices netted a total of £495,890. In fact, in 1962, the Royal Shakespeare Company operated on a bigger scale than any other theatre company in the world, employing a total of nearly 500 people — including actors, administrative, stage and production, technical and front-of-house staff.[49]

'Theatre-goers were blessed in 1962 with a substantial blueprint for the National Theatre in the varied activities of the Royal Shakespeare Company: no less than twenty four

productions, playing to audiences, which for the type of
plays involved, were massive . . . nor has Peter Hall's regime
showed any tendency to ossify into an Establishment — the
spirit remains youthful, pragmatic and forward-looking.'[50]

The Stratford season presented four new productions and two
revivals from the 1961 season, and the Aldwych continued with a
programme of modern plays and Shakespeare. At the Arts
Theatre, the Play-a-Month project staged seven productions,
ranging from new plays like David Rudkin's *Afore Night Come*
and Giles Cooper's *Everything in the Garden*, to Middleton's
Jacobean classic *Women Beware Women*. The considerable and
varied output of the 1962 season did much to further the
development of the company as an ensemble, and it was the high
degree of ensemble playing achieved which made possible the
proposals for the 1963 seasons — in many ways the end product
and result of Hall's master-plan and work with the company since
1960.

The 1963 season was announced as including a history
sequence, directed by Peter Hall, to be called *The Wars of the
Roses*. It was an adaptation, in three parts, of Shakespeare's
Henry VI plays and *Richard III*. The productions were planned as
a continuous sequence, and Hall intended that they should
occasionally be presented in the course of a single day, with *Henry
VI* in the morning, *Edward IV* (a 'new' play) in the afternoon, and
Richard III at night. John Barton collaborated on the textual
adaptation of the plays, and Hall admitted that the cycle,
' . . . perpetrates the ultimate literary heresy: Shakespeare cut,
rewritten and rearranged. Characters have been deleted and
compressed, speeches reapportioned, and one whole scene has
been invented.'[51] No project of this scale had been undertaken at
Stratford since Anthony Quayle's production of the second
tetralogy of history plays in 1951, and the *Henry VI* plays had
rarely been seen in their complete form in the British theatre.[52]
Hall gave his reasons for wishing to direct *The Wars of the Roses*:

> 'There's a certain verbal similarity in the quality of the
> writing, except Shakespeare is better as he gets going. . . . The
> unity of the principle was why I wanted to do them at all. I
> wanted to show something about the nature of the political
> animal in power. The justifications used for ambition haven't

really changed much in four hundred years. The terms have changed. Instead of saying "I do this in the name of St. George" or "the common weal", or "the populace" or "God", we now say, "in the public interest", "the commonwealth", "the man in the street" — all those things. . . . But the nature of power, and the irony of power, and the corruption of power, which is a cliché, was what I was concerned with showing. And that is a large part of those plays. That is why I wanted to do them, and that particular impulse affected the way they looked, the way they were edited, the way they were staged, the way they sounded.'[53]

John Barton's 'rewriting' of Shakespeare's text and creation of pastiche Elizabethan verse to bridge the gaps in the plot line, was criticized by some scholars, on the grounds that the company was moving into territory as questionable as Nahum Tate's adaptation of *King Lear* or Shaw's alternative fifth act for *Cymbeline*. Barton defended his adaptation on the grounds that much of the original text, particularly parts of *Henry VI*, was 'Elizabethan hack-work, dry of imagery and vigour, and different in kind as well as quality from the remainder'. He believed that Shakespeare's own revision of the texts was 'fitful, pragmatic and hasty', in the style of a working Elizabethan playwright writing for the needs of a performing company. Barton stated that he wished the Royal Shakespeare Company adaptation to be looked at, not as an attempt to improve Shakespeare — but simply as a further stage of revision on the 'only partly revised originals'.[54] The 1963 programmes further stated:

'Though it is our conviction that mature Shakespeare cannot be monkeyed with — even cutting is perilous — we are sure that these early plays produced in an unadapted form would not show to a modern audience the force of their political and human meaning. We believe and hope that we have not changed Shakespeare's main intentions.'[55]

The Wars of the Roses was the realization of three years of company work: the product of Hall's early plans to develop an ensemble company of actors, directors and technicians who could work together in pursuit of a common aim. Within a commercial structure, a project like *The Wars of the Roses* would have been virtually impossible to stage, as the cycle demanded a unity of

approach in conception and execution, time and care in prepa-
ration, and staging with attention to detail and visual unity. *The
Wars of the Roses* measured the success of Hall's declared aim in
1959 — to create a style of acting and staging that was recognizable as 'Stratford's', and to reinterpret the plays in terms of that
style.[56]

Although the Histories dominated 1963, the Stratford
programme also included productions of *The Tempest, Julius
Caesar* and *The Comedy of Errors*, and the Aldwych staged two
modern plays, *The Physicists* (directed by Peter Brook), and *The
Representative.* There was also a revival of Hall's 1959 production
of *A Midsummer Night's Dream* and a production of *The Beggar's
Opera.*

During 1963, it was announced that the 1964 season — the year
of Shakespeare's 400th anniversary — the history plays from
Richard II to *Henry V* would be added to the *Wars of the Roses*
cycle, and that the company would present Shakespeare's entire
History Cycle; all the history plays that follow one another
chronologically, dramatizing a span of more than a hundred years
of English history. At the conclusion of the 1963 *Wars of the
Roses* productions, Bernard Levin wrote:

> 'It is over, the ninety years of merciless struggle for power
> that followed the division of the House of Plantagenet. And
> over too, is the monumental production by Mr Peter Hall of
> the four plays of Shakespeare (compressed into three) that
> tell the bloody story . . . one of the mightiest stage projects
> of our time, whose final third last night was carried through
> to the end with the same bloodstained power, the same
> attention to the verse and depth of the characters who speak
> it, that characterized the first two thirds. . . .
>
> Mr Hall and his company, in the ten-hours traffic of their
> stage, have not only given us a production to remember all
> our lives; what they have done above all is to demonstrate
> that great drama, interpreted by men of imagination and
> understanding, has a power and a reality that can make us
> forget entirely that we are in a theatre.'[57]

4. The Royal Shakespeare Company
1960-1968

The title Royal Shakespeare Company helps us. Somebody once said to me, 'It's got everything in it except God!' And it *is* a good commercial title, but it also has an enormous danger. It makes us sound antique, square, institutional, conservative, traditional. . . . We are none of these things. We want to run a popular theatre. We don't want to be an institution supported by middle-class expense accounts. We want to be socially as well as artistically open. We want to get people who have never been to the theatre — and particularly the young — to see our plays. . . .

Peter Hall, to the Company, January 1963.

The years 1960 to 1963 were the 'crucial years' in the development of Peter Hall's ideas — for the Royal Shakespeare Company. These were the years in which he had to establish the entirely new company principle at Stratford; to create a new style of production and staging — and subsequently a new breed of Shakespeare actor;[1] to introduce his dual-theatre policy — and with it many changes in the concept of management; and finally, to effect a complete and overall change in the Theatre's financial policy and thinking.

This financial aspect was perhaps the most crucial, for without the backing of Sir Fordham Flower and the Stratford Governors in 1960 and their constant support through the crisis period of 1962, Peter Hall's revolution in the British theatre would not have been possible. State support for his scheme came, Hall achieved his goal of a subsidized permanent company at Stratford and in London, and by 1964 he could say:

'We can look forward to comparative stability. Our grants [of £96,000 for 1964-65] are near at hand and we have been recognized nationally as a company which must be supported, not only for next year, but for all time. At the moment *Comedy of Errors* and *King Lear* are going round the world, having the most extraordinary season of any theatre company abroad in our time. We have been present-ing *The Wars of the Roses* at the Aldwych independently of the world tour. . . . The fact that we can do productions like these at one time is proof of the strength, solidarity and purpose built up in this organization. . . .'[2]

Hall realized that the major financial battle was virtually won and that the next years could be devoted to consolidation and exploration of new theatre territory, but he also realized the increasing dangers of complacency within the organization. Speak-ing privately to the company he warned of this: 'I think that we have been somewhat over-praised! Something started to emerge, was seen, and was inflated. We now have a grant. We will now be judged as a company, as an institution, as something with a style . . . our artistic objectives must be to increase the imaginative life of the company and the actual creative work. . . .'[3]

Hall also recognized that change was necessary — and inevit-able — within the company structure:

'. . . however unified a company may be, it is not automatic-ally stable. If you are lucky enough to create it, it immediately begins to disintegrate . . . a company, like friendship, must be constantly repaired. These must be give and take on both sides, management and actor. Why shouldn't an actor want more money or fame? . . . the re-building is constant.'[4]

The three-year contract system introduced in 1960 created, within the company, new stars who had been developed and recognized by the RSC. Having achieved this recognition they naturally wished to take greater advantage of the outside money-earning. potential their new status offered. Realizing that the company could not retain these people — even under the fairly liberal terms offered by three-year contracts — Hall, in 1965, instituted an RSC Associate Artists scheme. This was a system by which these new star players could take fullest advantage of commercial oppor-tunities and still 'belong' to the RSC organization.

Maurice Daniels, RSC Planning Controller, explained the Associate Artists system: 'Instead of trying to hang on to actors by asking them to sign another contract, Peter offered an "open contract" to those we wanted as "Associate Artists". . . . The open contract was a "relationship" between the Director and the actor. Associate Artists agreed to let the management know before they accepted any outside work — particularly theatre — and then allow the RSC management the option to offer them something else. However neither actor nor management was bound by this. It was a gentleman's agreement. . . .'[5]

At the same time the three-year contract system for company players was amended to compensate for mistakes made when it was first introduced. The first RSC contracts allowed the actor time off to work elsewhere, and the RSC paid the actor no salary during these periods. Should the RSC management decide not to cast an available actor, he was then paid three-quarters of his normal playing salary. The second version of the three-year contract, introduced in 1965,[6] was a play-as-cast contract. Maurice Daniels explained: 'Under the initial contracts actors had the right to reject any part offered. The new contracts were more specific. Play-as-cast meant that the actor undertook to accept the line of parts allocated to him . . . But the director of the theatre still continued to discuss parts with each contract artist, who was of course free to raise any strong objections.[7] Associate Artists' salaries were decided by negotiation, but it is reported that these were rarely above the highest company grading.

By the mid-sixties, an RSC house-style of producing, acting and speaking had become evident; ' . . . the new, cool, intellectual, rather formed, rather witty (in the eighteenth century sense) style of speaking Shakespeare which we adopt, which concentrates more on meaning than it does on emotion . . .'.[8] and a definite company image began to form around the organization. The Royal Shakespeare Company developed a reputation for innovation, experiment and daring; ' . . . the Hovercraft to the National Theatre's Rolls Royce: the National mounting beautifully engineered productions . . . the RSC trying to find a new means of locomotion altogether . . .'[9]. Certainly by the mid-sixties, the RSC had become the pace-setters for Shakespeare production in Britain; ' . . . for good or ill! What Hall did today, Northampton and Nottingham did tomorrow'.[10] The company's presentations of Shakespeare and modern drama at Stratford, in London and on tour, provided some of the most controversial theatre of the decade. The RSC was seen as a democratic, no-nonsense institution with a very decidedly left-wing outlook, perhaps to a large extent the result of Hall's own political pre-occupations and thought. Gareth Lloyd Evans said: 'Hall instinctively had a socialistic attitude towards theatre . . . [and] this is what happened to the actor. He was "socialized" . . . In an odd sort of way, the Hall regime was an emblem of what's been happening in England. The more socialism we had in the sixties the less "glamour" was in existence. . . .'[11]

Hall, reported in *The Stratford Herald*, said:

'Shakespeare is our main task, but we cannot keep his plays alive unless we are truly in the market-place of Now. We must be expert in the past, but alive to the present . . . I am a radical, and I could not work in the theatre if I were not. The theatre must question everything and disturb its audience.

. . . At this theatre you will not get comprehensive lists of the world's classics: you will get classics that are relevant to now, and also modern works.'[12]

The RSC's declared policy — stated in all programmes during 1964 and 1965 — was to express plays in terms of immediacy for a modern audience and to make the production of Shakespeare, ' . . . an experience that reverberates with the thoughts and feelings of today'.[13] Peter Hall's presentation of *The Wars of the Roses* was conceived in terms of modern political parallels, and the text was adapted to suit the conditions and terms of the production. His *Hamlet* in 1965 was a primary example of the sucess of the RSC's attempt to speak directly to the generation of today, and indeed this production generated an unprecedented emotional response from its predominantly youthful audience.[14] Inevitably this policy led to charges that the RSC was dealing in 'pop-Shakespeare', and critics like Gareth Lloyd Evans were outspoken in condemning the RSC's 'Now Policy' and Hall's 'philosophy of the present tense':[15]

' . . . the form of adaptation nurtured by the Royal Shakespeare Theatre may set a standard which could map the course of Shakespeare productions for decades to come. In hands less skilful than those of the Royal Shakespeare Theatre the adaptation, and the resultant behaviourism which is its main flaw, would become unbearable. . . . Already there are many people who believe Shakespeare wrote a play called *Edward IV*. It is only a short step from this to a situation in which people might never have the opportunity to recognize or to experience the innate reality of plays called *Hamlet*. . . .'[16]

Hall frequently stated that he was searching for a new audience and that he wished to break down the social barriers which existed in the theatre. When the 'crucial years' were over and the company principle properly established, the RSC embarked on several projects designed specifically to increase the range of its audience, and to take productions 'out' to entirely new audiences. In 1964 a club — named the RSC Club — was set up by the company. Peter Hall, writing in the Club introductory pamphlet, said:

> 'A theatre's life is dependent not only on the size but on the quality of its audience. We want to nourish and encourage ours. There is no "catch". We don't have many empty seats in the year. But we do want to help those who care about theatre. . . .'

The RSC Club offered members reduced prices for special preview performances and ordinary scheduled performances at both theatres, and also priority booking facilities. In addition to this, the Club offered a regular supply of literature on the RC and theatre in general, and a special programme of talks, discussions and exhibitions involving members of the company. In June 1964, the Club's newspaper, *Flourish*, was issued to members for the first time. It was announced that *Flourish* would be published monthly and it was aimed to make it a popular newspaper dealing with all aspects of theatre activity. An editorial in the first issue stated:

> 'This first issue of *Flourish* plays its part in an attempt to build up a new relationship between our company's work and the public. A great deal of mystique and knowingness surrounds theatregoing . . . we hope to explain clearly and boldly what we are doing. . . .'[17]

By 1967 the RSC Club claimed a membership of 40,000, and in that year the Club split into two branches — one handling London audiences and the other Stratford audiences. *Flourish* — by then issued on a quarterly basis — was distributed to all members, and was also on sale to the general public at both theatres. Between 1968 and 1971 *Flourish* was issued on an occasional basis, with an average of two editions a year. It is now issued five or six times a year in a smaller format.

In March 1965, an activity called Actors Commando, sponsored by the RSC Club, prepared a number of mobile performances devised specially for playing in canteens, halls and social clubs at lunch hours or after work. The scheme was staffed by a group of four young actors from the company, and the performances were of thirty-minutes duration, made up of excerpts from Shakespeare, modern plays and other selected writings. The scheme — the first in Hall's bid to 'forge a new audience' — aimed to 'introduce the world of theatre in a painless way, in the belief that thirty minutes of actual performance is worth thirty hours of explanation, exhortation or recommendation about the theatre'.[18]

Actors Commando took mobile shows out from Stratford during the Spring and Summer of 1965. In September 1965, it was announced that a group of actors from the RSC, under the direction of Michael Kustow, would give a show-on-wheels to London audiences. The first Theatregoround performances took place in the East End and Lambeth areas. Two or three times a week, six actors, using a portable stage and a handful of props, staged performances in schools, youth clubs, canteens, evening institutes, Town Halls and housing estates — in fact anywhere that a group of people could gather to form an audience:

'Theatregoround is a ninety-minute tour de force anthology recital, from *Lysistrata* to *The Birthday Party*, loosely schematized and played mainly for laughs, proceeding on the assumption that if the audience won't come to the theatre, then the theatre must come to its audience. . . .'[19]

Early Theatregoround performances were financed by two private donations and a grant from the Gulbenkian Foundation, but later TGR[20] projects were backed by the RSC as an official company venture. The actors were paid no special fees for performing in Theatregoround, and they also appeared with the company at Stratford and in London as part of their normal duties. The RSC stated that it saw Theatregoround as a practical gesture towards attracting all sections of the community to the theatre — to create an appetite for theatre among those not normally exposed to it. Michael Kustow said:

'... a friend suggested that I call the programme "Shake-speare Mate". The perils of being cultural missionaries! And yet, this is precisely what we are trying *not* to be. All we want to show is that the theatre, given the right conditions, can become accessible to all.'[21]

And the Theatregoround hand-out programme stated:

'Why don't the dockers, the busmen, the families from the housing estates come to the theatre today? A barrier of snobbishness has walled them off from the theatre, bad education has turned Shakespeare into a dusty textbook. ... We believe the theatre belongs to everyone, and that it can offer an experience which all the TV channels and wide screens and long-play records cannot equal. ... And that is why we're here tonight.'[22]

As a further move in his search for a new audience, Hall wished to build a new theatre containing a 'high proportion of low-priced seats': a theatre which could show RSC productions at 'popular prices'. In July 1963, it was announced that Sir Basil Spence, the architect of Coventry Cathedral, would design a new £800,000 theatre for the RSC, to be situated in the Notting Hill Gate area of London. This theatre – to have a seating capacity of 1600 – was to be shared with the Ballet Rambert, and would replace the Aldwych as the RSC's London home. A £1 million building fund was launched in 1963, but by early 1965 only £100,000 had been provided.

In December 1964, the City of London announced that it intended to incorporate an Arts Centre, including a theatre, in the vast redevelopment plan for the City's Barbican area, north of Cheapside. Several theatre companies indicated interest in this new centre, but in February 1965 it was announced that the RSC had been chosen to occupy the proposed theatre. The City of London's agreement with the RSC envisaged building a theatre at a cost of £1,250,000 in the centre of the Barbican development. To diversify its attractions, the City stipulated that the RSC could, for two months of the year, sub-let the building to the Ballet Rambert. The costs of running this theatre were estimated (in 1965) at £90,000 p.a., and the City of London agreed to meet half this sum. Peter Hall and John Bury were to collaborate with the architects on the auditorium and stage design,[23] the seating capacity was to be between 1400 and 1500 with more than half of these seats at popular prices, and it was hoped that the building would be completed and occupied by 1970. The latest estimated completion date is 1978. Peter Hall said in 1965:

> 'The selection of the RSC to occupy the new theatre planned for the City of London will be the most important thing to happen to Stratford-upon-Avon since the first theatre was built there. This will mark the summit of all the progress that we have made during the past five years . . . we will have a London branch which will be of better size and more economical to run. We will also be able to have enough cheap seats to satisfy the demands of the new young audience that we have been able to cultivate. . . '[24]

In addition to the new moves in search of a wider audience, the Royal Shakespeare Theatre's Summer School on Shakespeare continued its activities in catering for the regular or more involved theatre-goer. The Summer School was founded in 1948, and has since been held annually under the auspices of the Theatre. Originally designed for teachers of English in schools, its membership has widened to include all who have an amateur or professional interest in the theatre and in Shakespeare. The course, held in Stratford during August, provides members with the opportunity to hear 'critical and scholarly opinions about Shakespeare and also to learn something about the practical problems involved in presenting his plays on the stage'.[25] Lectures and seminars are held, and speakers include scholars, critics, actors, directors and various other people connected with the theatre. Until 1961, the Summer School was directed by John Garrett, and then until 1970 by John Wilders. The 1971 Summer School was directed by Stanley Wells of the University of Birmingham.

In 1964, the RSC's Publicity and Publications Department began to present a new RSC look to the public. Throughout the fifties, the Memorial Theatre, in conjunction with Reinhardt, the publisher, had produced a three-yearly book, with many photographs on the Memorial Theatre's productions.[26] In addition there was a yearly special programme — an elaborate Vogue type of presentation, printed in colour and very much pictorially orientated. Because these programmes had to be produced before the season started, the amount of information and pictures provided on late-season productions was practically negligible, and even for early productions there was, as a matter of policy, little or no information on what the plays were about or what the directors' ideas were. Throughout the fifties and early sixties the theatre published these special programmes, and also a standard four-page cast list for each production.

In 1964, the RSC introduced a new format – and new concept – in theatre programmes. The old ideas were dropped, and instead an elaborate programme was published for each production, containing pictures, background information, director's viewpoint and other material on the production, together with a cast list and general information about the RSC and its activities. In addition, the theatre issued a cast list for each production entirely free. John Goodwin, the RSC's Head of Publicity and Publications, said: 'The thing that we are rather proud of is that we started the idea of having free cast lists, so that you didn't need to pay just to know who was playing what. And alongside them, for those who wanted it, was a programme that was more substantial than those normally got in theatres. This idea was copied by the National and subsequently by other theatres . . . .'[27] R.B. Marriot, writing in *The Stage*, commented:

'It has always been part of the policy of the Aldwych/ Stratford on Avon companies to explain their aims and work to the public as much as possible. The programme notes and more elaborate booklets are models of what this kind of thing should be. Informative without being condescending: lively and readable for their own sake. . . .'[28]

The three-yearly Reinhardt publications were also dropped in 1964, and during the later sixties the RSC relied more on day-to-day press releases, *Flourish* and their new programmes to present the theatre and its work. On certain occasions, the Publicity and Publications Department published pamphlets to illustrate a particular aspect of the company's activities or to clarify a particular point. These were occasionally issued about the financial or artistic situation, and also on productions or experiments.[29] John Goodwin commented on the ideas behind the new policy: 'The attitude of the company now is slightly against the endless recording of past productions – what people said about

"Then". It is much more a case of illuminating what's "Now". This feeling was particularly strong in Peter Hall's day.'[30]

Although the RSC's financial situation was relatively secured by the state grant in 1962, there were periods of fluctuation throughout the sixties, and, in common with all other similar organizations, the RSC always needed and spent more money than was available at the time. There was a secondary financial crisis in 1963, when the Governors announced that, despite the existing grant, the RSC still showed a nett operating loss of £38,000, a deficit that was being made up from the company's rapidly dwindling surplus-funds account.[31]

The 'surplus funds' in this account were largely the result of foreign tours made during the fifties. When Peter Hall took over at Stratford this account stood at approximately £100,000,— and it was the knowledge of the existence of these funds that encouraged Hall in his pursuit of Government subsidy. Yet both Hall and the Governors were well aware that the surplus was not inexhaustible. In 1964 the company lost £45,000, and the Arts Council stated that the grant for 1964/65 would be increased to £88,000. In 1965 a loss of £65,000 was shown, and the Governors announced that this amount would completely exhaust the company's surplus funds.

In December 1965, aware that his company could no longer carry the burden of financial loss, Hall announced that the RSC would immediately cut its acting staff by one third, stage repeat productions at Stratford in 1966 (because it could not afford to stage new ones), and drop its touring policy altogether. Hall's financial squeeze of 1965/66 showed results in a greatly increased Arts Council grant — £152,000 for 1966/67 — and in November 1966, Hall announced that the squeeze was over and that the programme for 1967 would be the most comprehensive yet undertaken. The acting staff would be raised to full strength; there would be six new Shakespeare productions at Stratford; the RSC would undertake a December tour of the Soviet Union and a 'home' regional tour; and an agreement had been reached with an American company to make colour films of selected RSC productions. However, 1966, which led to this, had been an extremely bad year for the company: there was general despondency among the actors at the prospect of a year of revivals, and company morale was at its lowest ebb.

Looking back on his Stratford years, Peter Hall saw 1966 as the year of his biggest 'mistake': 'In 1966, the Arts Council and Lord Goodman said: "There's no more money — you can't have an increase!" And we did a season of revivals . . . in order to try and mark time. You *can't* mark time in the theatre. That was my biggest mistake. . . . I just saw it as a never ending battle for subsidy. I thought it would go on for ever. In those days I disliked Lord Goodman more than I can say: he seemed to me the "villain" of my scenario! He was putting us up against the wall and seeing what we were made of. And I made the mistake of compromising when I should *not* have compromised. I should have announced a season of new productions.'[32]

In 1964, John Harrison, Director of the Birmingham Repertory Theatre, wrote about theatre finance and state subsidy in *The Stage*:

> 'We must separate theatre once and for all in the governing mind from the commercial cookies of life, and place it squarely alongside the good things which nobody minds collectively paying for: universities, libraries, art galleries, swimming pools, orchestras. Encouragement of the art of living in this day and age has to be a community venture. Producing "important" theatre can only cost more as the years go on. It is as well that the national and municipal accounts should realize this, and realize too that the building, though packed to the doors, will never show a trading profit. The "profit" is their enrichment of the life of the community, along with the libraries, the art galleries, the playing fields. . . .'[33]

By 1967, the RSC's grant had become 'sufficient' to enable them to carry out their policies effectively, and to realize many of Hall's ambitions and aims for his company. The RSC's grants increased yearly since 1967, and for the year 1970/71 stood at £236,450.[34] But, of course, 'sufficient' is a relative term, and any member of the company questioned about the RSC's financial situation today will say, 'The grant from the Arts' Council is woefully inadequate'[35], or words to that effect. It would seem that producing 'important' theatre *is* likely to cost more as the years go on.

The years 1963 to 1968 saw a progressive widening of the RSC's scope of activity and sphere of influence in Britain. These years also saw Peter Hall's company — through touring, television, films and promotion of Peter Daubeny's World Theatre Seasons — achieve a vast international reputation as one of the world's great theatre companies: 'The RSC is, if anything, better known abroad than it is in this country. It has a very, very big reputation abroad....'[36] In Autumn 1962, the RSC began a policy of touring Britain with some of the principal productions from both theatres. Peter Hall explained his 'internal' touring policy to the company:

'We must tour. We are immoral if we don't. Our two centres in London and the Midlands have a large audience, but we can increase this audience. There is also a practical reason. No backbencher is going to support our claim for public money if his constituents can't see the plays. And I think he's right! We must make our tours an exciting part of our work....'[37]

Between 1960 and 1968, the RSC took productions to nearly every major city in Britain, and also played at the Edinburgh Festival in 1962. In the later sixties, these tours were frequently used as pre-London runs, to test audience and critical reaction to new productions. Theatregoround productions also toured independently of the parent company. From 1960 to 1970, the RSC toured internationally with a total of sixteen productions,. visiting France, Holland, Finland, Italy, Switzerland, the United States, Canada, Japan and Australia. Many of these countries were toured on several occasions. Most regional touring was done with assistance from the Arts Council, and international touring often at the request of (and with financial backing from) the British Council. However, some RSC foreign tours, particularly to the United States and Canada, have not needed subsidy.[38]

In June 1964, it was announced that the RSC/BBC-TV contract of 1962 would be renewed for a further three years. Under the new contract, the BBC agreed to record seven RSC productions drawn from the repertoire at Stratford and the Aldwych. *The Wars of the Roses* was the first production to be televised under the renewed contract. Altogether. the BBC screened six RSC productions over the years 1962 to 1968: *The Cherry Orchard* was shown in April 1962, *As You Like It* (March 1963), *The Comedy of*

Errors (January 1964), *The Wars of the Roses* (April 1965), *Days in the Trees* (1967) and *All's Well that Ends Well* (June 1968).[39] On signing the renewed contract, Sydney Newman, BBC Head of Drama, said:

> 'Our association in the past has been so fruitful, we are delighted. The unique achievements of the Royal Shakespeare Company interpreted before our cameras, will make it possible for people all over the world to see their work. It will bring credit to us all. . . .'[40]

The televising of *The Wars of the Roses* was a mammoth operation. Twelve tons of outside broadcast equipment was brought to the Stratford theatre, and to give the eight cameras plenty of tracking area, the stage was lengthened by 40 ft. and thirteen rows of seats were removed. The stage also had to be strengthened to take the weight of a large crane-camera; over two hundred extra lamps were brought in to supplement the theatre's lighting equipment; and the circle bar of the theatre was transformed into a control gallery, with monitors and a complete control desk. The TV version, recorded in November 1964, took over five weeks to complete, and was directed for BBC-TV by Robin Midgley and Michael Hayes. Peter Hall and John Barton 'watched' the production on behalf of the RSC. Barton spoke about the TV version: '*Richard III* was done first, and I thought it was the least good. Then came *Henry VI* and then *Edward IV*. I think *Edward* is without doubt the best of the three: we and the television directors had got to know each other's language, and had found a style. But it all comes back to the basic problem of how to film Shakespeare . . . I doubt (and I think Peter doubts)· whether it's possible to translate Shakespeare into another medium with total success.'[41]

The Wars of the Roses was broadcast over three consecutive weeks on BBC-1 in April/May 1965, and later went to other television networks overseas: it was screened by the ABC network in Australia in 1966 and was also shown in the USA and Canada.[42]

In November 1966, the RSC announced that they had entered into a long-term agreement to make colour films of Shakespeare plays with CBS (the American TV network), and a British film production company, Filmways Incorporated. For the purpose of film-making under this agreement, the RSC also set up a company called Royal Shakespeare Enterprises Limited — totally the nominee of the Royal Shakespeare Company, and with a directorate comprising the Finance Committee of the RSC, Peter Hall and Lord Birkett. The agreement called, initially, for two plays to be filmed during 1967/68, and a third during 1968/69. The first three films were announced as Peter Brook's production of *King Lear* and Peter Hall's production of *A Midsummer Night's Dream* and *Macbeth*, and the RSC were to have complete control over all filming. Hall's *A Midsummer Night's Dream* was the first, and only, film to be completed under this agreement. Much of the location shooting was done around the Stratford area during 1968, and the film was released commercially in 1969. It was also shown on the CBS television network in America during 1969.

David Brierley, RSC General Manager, spoke of the RSC's involvement with this film: '*The Dream* only was made under this agreement, and unhappily made, in the sense that financially it got out of hand. . . . It went way over budget . . . added to which, it has to be said, that in some ways it wasn't a frightfully good film either, and the other two films never got made.'[43]

Brook's *King Lear* was in fact completed under a separate commercial agreement in 1969, and released in Britain in 1971. The RSC was not involved in either the financing or distribution of this film — although they do claim it as an RSC credit on the grounds that it had its genesis in an RSC production, and used an RSC director and cast. In the same sense, the RSC claim Brook's film of *Marat-Sade* (made under an independent agreement in 1966) and his film of *US* (re-titled *Tell Me Lies*) made in 1967. The proposed *Macbeth*, to be based on Hall's 1967 Stratford production, was dropped entirely, owing to Paul Scofield's disinclination to recreate the role on film. Thus, in the legal and contractual sense, *A Midsummer Night's Dream* was the only film actually 'made' by the RSC, and Royal Shakespeare Enterprises Limited now exists solely to administer the residual affairs of this film.[44] David Brierley spoke to me about the RSC's future in films and television: 'In ordinary television there is little money to be made. I think we could make money from video-cassettes in due course . . . But it's a long way ahead. . . . There has been a sort of quietness recently about films and television, but they are very, very far from being a dead issue!'[45]

In February 1964, the RSC productions of *King Lear* and *The Comedy of Errors* began a sixteen-week tour of Europe and America, arranged as part of the Shakespeare 400th anniversary celebrations. To complement this tour, Hall announced that a three-month 'World Theatre Season' would be staged at the Aldwych: seven of Europe's greatest theatre companies — The Comédie Française, The Schiller Theatre, Peppino de Filippo's Italian Theatre, The Abbey Theatre, The Polish Contemporary Theatre, The Greek Art Theatre and The Moscow Art Theatre — would be brought to London to present representative works from their repertoires. The first World Theatre Season was sponsored jointly by the RSC and The Sunday Telegraph and directed by Peter Daubeny — a noted impresario who had, since 1951, been bringing artists and companies of international repute to London. Peter Hall, speaking of the first season, said:

'This exchange is planned to honour William Shakespeare. Politically it should draw our countries together: artistically it should provide capital that can be used in the future.'[46]

Peter Daubeny's first season was an enormous success, as a consequence World Theatre Seasons with international companies have been staged yearly at the Aldwych since 1964. In 1966, it was announced that the RSC had taken over management of these seasons. Peter Daubeny was appointed a Consultant Director to the RSC, a position which enabled him to expand his duties as Artistic Director of the World Theatre Seasons and also associated him permanently with the RSC organization.[47] In 1966 he said:

'The World Theatre Season makes the world of drama expand its boundaries. It is the aggregate of world culture . . . it is a world which can re-fashion thought and standards and vision in the theatre. In turn it becomes an unfailing source of new creation in Britain.'[48]

The RSC's relationship with the National Theatre gradually settled down following the 'withdrawal crisis' of 1962. The National opened on 22nd October 1963 with a production of *Hamlet*, (directed by Laurence Olivier, with Peter O'Toole in the title role), and during the mid-sixties the two companies began to operate on a basis of friendly rivalry. However, only in 1971 did the RSC receive an identical Arts Council grant, and the National operates on a far greater total subsidy. Kenneth Tynan, appointed as

Literary Manager of the National, recognized this disparity:

'There are many other serious legitimate theatres in Britain ... the National Theatre gets more money than any of the others ... I should like them [the RSC] to be able to compete with us on equal terms, because artistic competition usually makes for better art. ... The National Theatre and the Royal Shakespeare Theatre should be able to live side by side in the same kind of relationship which exists between the Comédie Française and Jean-Louis Barrault's Théâtre de France.'[49]

In 1964, it was announced that a co-ordinating committee had been set up between the two companies, to discuss matters of mutual interest such as repertory, touring and contracts, and that this committee would meet on a regular basis. During one of the many early financial crises at the RSC, the National Theatre came out publicly in favour of greater financial support for Peter Hall's organization: 'The National Theatre Board has passed a resolution saying that it would "view with dismay any curtailment in the activities of the Royal Shakespeare Company".'[50] Certainly the two companies functioned on different levels. The National was more concerned with presenting a varied repertoire of the world's classics while the RSC (by its very name) was based in the production of Shakespeare. The RSC also tended to be more adventurous in the presentation of controversial modern works.

Throughout the sixties, the RSC's reputation for experiment and daring rested mainly on its productions of modern plays at the Aldwych and the Arts, and also with experiments like the 1964 *Theatre of Cruelty* season at LAMDA — which led to works like the *Marat-Sade* and *US* entering the company's repertoire. Many modern and controversial plays were given their first performance by the RSC and Peter Hall was never reluctant to promote an exciting or challenging work on the grounds that some members of his audience might find it offensive. Gareth Lloyd Evans saw this attitude as opportunism rather than artistic vision: 'At the end of the fifties we were at the beginning of what we now have in full flood. Permissiveness — in everything, and particularly in the theatre ... part of a growing movement which had already been latched on to by people like Hall and Brook ... because there's no

Top: Paul Scofield as Lear in Peter Brook's production at Stratford in 1962. Alan Webb as Gloucester, and Brian Murray as Edgar. *Bottom: Afore Night Come*, directed by Clifford Williams, part of the RSC's experimental season at the Arts Theatre in 1962. *L. to R.:* Joe Gibbons as Albert, *foreground kneeling:* David Warner as Jim, Peter McEnery as Johnny Hobnails, Henley Thomas as Jeff, Gerry Duggan as Roche, Henry Woolf as Tiny, Timothy West as Ginger.

Peter McEnery as Johnny Hobnails with Henry Woolf as Tiny.

Afore Night Come, Arts Theatre 1962

Paul Dawkins as Spens.

doubt that the RSC have been very much in the forefront of this move towards breaking down conventions in the theatre. They were very opportunist.'[51]

Hall's encouragement and production of controversial plays frequently brought the RSC into headlong confrontation with the Lord Chamberlain, a Court official who, since 1737, had held the office of Dramatic Censor, and to whom all plays to be performed on the British stage had to be submitted for approval.[52]

Hall's war with the Censor began with *The Devils* in 1961, accelerated with *The Representative* in 1963, and came to a head over Clifford Williams' production of *Afore Night Come* at the Aldwych in 1964. The Lord Chamberlain insisted on thirty-four cuts from the printed text (the words he found unspeakable including 'bloody', 'hell', 'Jesus' and 'Christ') and Hall retaliated by announcing that he would make it a future practice to print every cut that the Chamberlain made in company programmes, and that the RSC were determined to 'fight this issue to the end':

'We are not deliberately setting out to bait him, but it is no accident that the plays we are going to present will bring this issue to the front and keep it there. We will focus public attention on our claims ... people should know that between the stage and auditorium hangs a blanket. . . .'[53]

The *Afore Night Come* programme was prefaced by a page, which read in part:

' ... we are obliged to present an emasculated version of *Afore Night Come*, in which the characteristic speech patterns of a particular region are an integral part ... these [cuts] are not totally destructive, but they do jeopardise the play's truth. Moreover, they are often quite arbitrary – the same expletive is allowed on one page and censored on another. . . . The Royal Shakespeare Company is devoted to the production of plays by the bawdiest dramatist in English literature. If Shakespeare had been writing after 1737, the Lord Chamberlain would apply to his plays the same standards he has applied to *Afore Night Come*, and not one of the Histories now in production at Stratford could have been presented in its present form.'[54]

In September 1968 the powers of the Lord Chamberlain as Dramatic Censor were abolished, but this was not before Hall and the RSC had engaged with him on several further occasions. For a performance of *The Rebel*, (a poetry anthology recital at the Aldwych in 1964), the Chamberlain had objected to certain lines in a poem by E.E. Cummings. The RSC printed the poem in full in the programme, and the actor, when he reached the lines, merely paused heavily and the house-lights were brought up to full for the audience to read the 'offending' section to themselves. *Victor* (Aldwych 1964) was cut by the Chamberlain: he objected to a tuba being used to suggest the sound of someone breaking wind, and cut four pages of dialogue from the centre of the play. Hall refused to accept this ruling and insisted that the play would go on uncut or be dropped entirely at a cost of £10,000. On 31st July, five days before opening, the Chamberlain relented and only minor modifications were made. Peter Brook's 1966 production of *US* was seen by the Chamberlain as 'bestial, anti-American and communist', and the RSC were requested to cancel it: Hall, Brook and the Governors objected in the strongest possible terms — with the result that a licence was issued on the proviso that the company made certain cuts.

Some RSC productions like Brook's *Theatre of Cruelty* and the 1962 Arts Theatre Season, had managed to avoid the Censor by using the legal fiction of private or club performances that were not bound by the normal theatre regulations. However Brook's Aldwych production of *Marat-Sade*, together with *Afore Night Come*, finally clashed both with the Censor and with sections of the public and helped to bring about the so-called 'Dirty Plays' controversy of 1964.

In August 1964, Emile Littler, the theatre impresario and a member of the RSC Executive Council, issued a statement to the press, strongly criticizing Hall's policy and publicly dissociating himself from the company's Aldwych programme:

'The London season is a disgrace. As a Governor of the Royal Shakespeare Company and a member of the Executive, I have dissociated myself from the programme of dirty plays at the Aldwych Theatre. These plays do not belong — or should not — to the Royal Shakespeare. They are entirely out of keeping with our public image.... We are depleting our funds by giving the public plays like *Afore Night Come* which they simply do not want to see ... I protested at the last meeting of the Executive Council, because I had to say that we are driving people away ... I don't know what the Arts Council think of these wretched Aldwych plays, but as a taxpayer I resent my money being spent in this manner.'[55]

Sir Fordham Flower, travelling in America, supported Hall:

'Mr Littler's action in giving a press interview as reported to me on the transatlantic telephone, appears to me to be disloyal and incompatible with his membership of the Executive Council ... I and the Executive Council are solidly behind Peter Hall in his direction of the Royal Shakespeare Company. ...'[56]

From these beginnings, the controversy assumed wider proportions, as Peter Cadbury of Keith Prowse Ltd., and Sir Denis Lowson, former Lord Mayor of London and a member of the RSC Governors, gave press interviews in support of Littler's stand. Critics like John Trewin felt that 'it would be unprofitable to defend the Royal Shakespeare's policy',[57] but other critics, including Harold Hobson, Alan Brien, Felix Barker, Bamber Gascoigne, Bernard Levin, Milton Shulman and B.A. Young, forwarded a joint letter to *The Times*:

' ... we are unanimously of the opinion that this company under its present direction is one of the glories of the modern British theatre, and that its work is an absolutely vital ingredient in our theatrical life, and indeed serves a much wider national purpose. ...'[58]

Hall was also supported by the members of his company in an open letter to Sir Fordham Flower, signed by the acting and administrative staff in Stratford and London. The controversy raged in the press for some weeks, with the inevitable exchange of letters and hysterical viewpoints. The final outcome of the Dirty Plays row is best summarized by Sir Fordham Flower:

'What emerges from this welter of print is a tremendous vote of confidence in Peter Hall and the policy in which my Executive Council has interested itself and will continue to pursue ... this attack however leaves some unfortunate aspects. The Aldwych season is now popularly known as "the dirt plays". There is nothing "dirty" in these plays ... I am distressed that major writers of the modern theatre should have been pilloried in this way.'[59]

In the later sixties there were some administrative changes in the RSC. Sir Fordham Flower died in 1966, and L.T.G. (later Sir George) Farmer took his place as Chairman of the Governors.[60] In 1966, Michel St. Denis resigned (through ill health) from the governing triumvirate and was appointed a Consultant Director, and in September 1966 it was announced that Paul Scofield would join Hall and Brook in the Directorate. In 1966, Hall also announced that RSC policy in future would move more in the direction of 'repertoire theatre': 'We are expected to come up with twelve masterpieces a year. This is absurd and we are not going to attempt it in the future. From now on we are not giving you "revivals" — we are offering you redevelopment and restoration of major works. . . .'[61]

Hall directed only one play for the RSC during 1967, and when the 1968 Stratford programme was announced in January, it was also announced that Peter Hall would not be directing that year. This was reported as 'due to his heavy commitments with RSC film work'. On 30th January 1968, an RSC press release announced that Hall would give up his position as Managing Director of the company, but would remain a director with 'special responsibilities'. At the same time, it was announced that Trevor Nunn, a twenty-eight year old Associate Director who had joined the RSC in 1965, would replace Hall in the newly created top position of Artistic Director.[62] A new structure for the RSC. Directorate was proposed, consisting of Trevor Nunn as Artistic Director, with Peter Hall, Peter Brook, Paul Scofield,[63] Peggy Ashcroft and Derek Hornby as his co-Directors, and Michel St. Denis and Peter Daubeny as Consultant Directors. *The Financial Times* wrote:

' . . . whatever influence Mr Brook and Mr Scofield may have had behind the scenes, the voice of authority was always patently Mr Hall's: and this not only in artistic matters but in administrative matters as well. It is therefore good news that the appointment of Trevor Nunn as Artistic Director is accompanied by the appointment of Derek Hornby as Administrative Director. It is wrong to expect an artistic director to have the time, let alone the ability, to look after the business side of an undertaking the size of the RSC . . . We shall be watching Mr Nunn. The RSC has needed a bit

more zing for some time now; there have been torpid
openings at Stratford . . . there have been some dire evenings
at the Aldwych. A new arm at the helm may be what's
needed.'[64]

Peter Hall's 'special responsibilities' were defined as threefold: to
function as a member of the RSC Directorate, to control the
making of films for the RSC, and to supervise the Barbican
Theatre project on behalf of the company. Hall worked with
Trevor Nunn in the Direction of the company until the summer of
1968, and then left Stratford to concentrate on his film work: 'I
have been in the hot-seat for nine years and that is long
enough!'[65]

John Heilpern wrote, in 1970, of Peter Hall's achievement at
Stratford: 'He turned a seasonal theatre into the finest and best
supported company in the world.'[66] And Peter Brook paid a
unique personal tribute to Hall in the RSC *Annual Report* of
1968:

'Peter Hall said, when he asked me to join him in the
Direction of the RSC, "There is a certain quality of work
that we wish to reach nowadays. This quality depends on
certain conditions. My ambition is to create those conditions
and make them available to those who need them". To
achieve this aim Peter Hall's work had to be revolutionary. . . . Peter Hall's leadership meant that at any time,
now or in the future, what he would be handing over would
not be hard and fast. It will never again be run in his uniquely
personal way. What has to be grasped from Peter Hall's
personal tradition is that in new circumstances everything
must be re-examined and new solutions found. Anything is
possible as long as it serves one constant aim: the creating of
conditions which make possible work of a certain quality.'[67]

5. New Concepts
1960-1968

I think everybody recognizes that in the theatre there must
be constant revolution. . . . While working towards a permanent company at Stratford one tended to feel that one was
taking part in something new and adventurous. . . .
Dame Peggy Ashcroft, in an interview with
the author, January 1971.

During the fifties the Memorial Theatre, under the direction of
Anthony Quayle and Glen Byam Shaw, developed and worked
under what came to be known as the star system. The phrase itself
was in use long before the fifties, but Quayle and Shaw established
the practice at Stratford, and yearly Shakespeare seasons centred
around star names and star performances: the Oliviers, Sir John
Gielgud, Dame Peggy Ashcroft, Sir Michael Redgrave, Charles
Laughton, Dame Edith Evans, Sir Ralph Richardson and many
other famous theatre names would head the season's programmes.

These actors came to Stratford and worked for a fraction of the
salary that they could command in the West End, Europe or the
United States, because Stratford offered them the opportunity to
take the great roles in Shakespeare productions at the most
prestigious Shakespeare theatre in the English speaking world. The
Stratford audiences of the fifties came to see the great names of
the theatre at work and a bad season was often reckoned as one
which did not include at least one theatre Sir or Dame in the cast
list.

Within the companies there was a fairly rigid (if unspoken)
hierarchical order: the younger actor and the 'middle-grade' actor
were often seen — from an audience and company view-point — as
satellite attendants on the star performers. However, it should be
emphasized that although the star system is being discussed here in
specific relation to Stratford, it existed almost universally throughout the British commercial theatre of the fifties.

As John Kane pointed out, 'You're talking about a period in the theatre when the actor was really all there was going. Designs and costumes were splendid, but you had these marvellous "power house" actors who took the "star" parts — and people really came to see them. It is undoubtedly true to say that there were certain star actors who chose their supporting cast very carefully ... [and] would also make certain that the moment they made an entrance the lights would be knocked up a notch — so the whole stage would seem to brighten with their presence! And, of course, there have always been the great actors who've *always* been company people, and have *always* loved the play and thought of the play first. . . .'[1]

When Peter Hall began his Directorate at Stratford, his primary aim was the creation of a mainly permanent company of artists: a more long-term goal was the creation of an *ensemble* company of artists — a group of actors, directors, designers, technicians and stage staff who would work together as a unit in pursuit of a common achievement. Hall knew that this latter goal could not be realized overnight; indeed the very implications surrounding the word ensemble suggest a group who have worked together and known each other a reasonable period of time. Hall also realized that it was necessary, particularly in the initial stages of his plan, to import certain artists into the company for specific productions: audiences had to be conditioned to the ensemble idea and the profession had to become accustomed to it.

The three-year contracts laid the foundations of Hall's permanent company, and the open contract he initiated allowed the possibility of highly experienced and talented actors joining his organization without feeling tied down for a three-year period.

It is significant that one of the first artists to join Peter Hall's new company was Dame Peggy Ashcroft, one of the foremost stars in the star system: 'I suppose I'm an exception in one sense. A permanent company has always been an ideal and I have said this on many occasions.'[2]

Hall recognized the popularity — and merits — of the star system, and was aware of the problems involved in creating an ensemble system in its place: 'I believe in stars. Stars exist. . . . Now, the trouble is that I want my cake and want to eat it! . . . but I needed a star who is happy in an ensemble. That *can* exist — and Peggy Ashcroft is the shining example . . . without her, one can almost say that the Royal Shakespeare might not have been created . . . it was a great thing to have a lady of that stature. She's a company person, she's very sensible, and she puts the act of putting on the play before herself.'[3]

The open contract and later scheme of Associate Artists also allowed younger actors who were developing within the company to leave the organization for periods of time — and yet still 'belong' to the RSC: 'The big money and the acclaim of the outside world is something which is attractive to an actor's temperament. It measures his status and is part of his actors' vanity. And a necessary part of being an actor is vanity; and to repress it is dangerous.'[4] Thus, the foundations of the RSC were built on two levels; the backing and artistic support of several internationally famous, highly-experienced, but still comparatively unknown actors. From this latter group, names like Diana Rigg, Ian Holm, David Warner, Ian Richardson, Janet Suzman, and Glenda Jackson can be found in the cast lists (sometimes playing supporting roles) of RSC productions during the first years of the sixties. These actors were Hall's answer to the star system, and on these foundations he hoped to create his ensemble ideal.

The RSC was not the first organization in Britain to envisage an ensemble ideal, nor was Peter Hall the first individual to attempt the bringing together of a permanent group to work in the theatre over a long period. John Gielgud made several attempts to form a group over the thirties and forties — with his seasons at the Haymarket Theatre: 'Gielgud had no subsidy, but as a man of the theatre . . . he wanted to act with his peers and not to be a star surrounded by lesser lights . . . there was unquestionably the feeling of a company. We were, on the whole, a fairly united group. . . .'[5] George Devine's English Stage Company was another outstanding example of theatre vision, in an attempt to create an authors' theatre — a vision very close to some of Hall's own development plans for the RSC. What is unique about the RSC is that it was created from an *existing* organization of major international reputation and importance, and that Peter Hall's vision was so immediately and outstandingly successful. Hall's scheme for the RSC was a creation of conditions whereby the actor could develop to the fullest height of his powers under purely *artistic* conditions and pressures — and to try and remove some of the commercial and success pressures which automatically existed in the English actor's mind. However, the financial pressures on the RSC during its first three years of operation made a certain amount of compromise necessary. Speaking to the company in 1963, Hall said:

> 'A lot of the deficiencies in the organization are due to the fact that we've only just found what we need . . . we're still growing and we still haven't enough money and resources to make it work . . . some of the ideals were undoubtedly buried under the pressures of compromise, improvisation and "keeping the thing going" . . . I hoped, when I began, to create conditions where actors could become artists rather than merely craftsmen . . . we hope that we can create a structure for you in which you know our hopes, our ideas, our pre-occupations; a structure in which you know "what we're at". . . . In the small hours, every actor will tell you that he wants to join a company, and play Hamlet on Monday and the Butler on Tuesday. We have to do no less than create a new system where you can *dare* to play the Butler! And we've begun. . . ."[6]

The basis of Hall's ensemble in which a leading actor could 'dare to play the Butler' was firstly a rejection of the star system as it was known at Stratford in the fifties. Internationally famous actors were still invited to work with the RSC on occasions, but within the permanent company, the star concept was actively discouraged.

This was not an attempt to 'democratize' or 'level off' the company (as some critics have seen it), for Hall recognized and obvious fact that within his company — as in any profession — there were levels and degrees of talent. An extreme over-simplification of Hall's vision would be to state that he was scarching for a 'team spirit' within the structure of the RSC. Writing about the company in 1967, Peter Lewis said:

> 'Life in the Stratford company is monastic, in all but the sexual connotation of the term. . . . Few theatres have such pleasant working conditions — none of the usual cramped squalor backstage, ever-full houses, and a company spirit in which youth predominates, camp is taboo and almost

nobody calls anybody "darling". In some ways it is like
college life. . . ."[7]

This new feeling of company spirit — together with the security of
the long term contract — gave members of the RSC a sense of
family identity, and also did a great deal towards the breaking
down of the old hierarchical barriers within the theatre. Judi
Dench echoed a frequently expressed company sentiment when
she said, 'It's nice to know that you've got a family at your back. I
truthfully don't think there's such a thing as a "leading actor" or
"leading actress" within this company, it is a "sharing out".'[8]

No-one would attempt to pretend that life in the early RSC was
perfect: quarrels, tensions and artistic temperament are everyday
occurrences within any theatre. However, the new regime did alter
the tone of relationships within the theatre, and invited a
frankness and freedom of expression within the acting company.
Ian Richardson commented on this: 'Peter Hall invited open
discussion, and in consequence there was no behind-a-hand-in-the-
corner bitching during his years. All the bitching was in the open.
We all knew exactly where we stood. This tradition (created by
Hall) still exists today. A young actor in the company can openly
come to me and tell me that he would be happier if I did
so-and-so . . . And this sort of thing happens all the time at the
RSC. If you're artistically inclined and not merely ambitious, you
accept all criticism, because it's valuable. . . . What happened when
Peter Hall took control at Stratford was, if you like, a. "quiet
revolution" in the theatre. A stamping out of old traditions. . . .'[9]

As the RSC grew in strength and the early patterns set by Hall
became established, a sense of company style and company
discipline became distinctly recognizable. The company product
which began to emerge was of a type fairly new to the English
theatre: the RSC actor of the mid-sixties was an utterly dedicated
artist who was equally at home in Shakespeare and modern
drama — who could move from the complexity and precision of
Shakespeare verse-speaking to the anarchic lunacy of the
Marat-Sade with equal competence and assurance. Critics began to
comment on the RSC's company style and the feeling of
community identity that was becoming evident through the
productions. Gareth Lloyd Evans, while not in accord with Hall's
methods and motivations (and frequently disliking the production

results), recognized this sense of community:

> 'The most creative feature of this company is its insistence
> upon a democratic ideal of ensemble playing and direction
> ... The Royal Shakespeare Theatre has a strong sense of
> community; mutual criticism and advice is both encouraged
> and given. In a very real sense this theatre is a world within a
> world. All the directors, and many of the actors, believe they
> are justifying a notion that a civilized society cannot exist
> without theatre by themselves creating a kind of society
> within their own theatre. In that society acting becomes a
> part of living. . . '[10]

And Gordon Rogoff, writing for the *Tulane Drama Review*,
commented:

> 'Here, at last, is a theatre in the English speaking world that
> probes not only the rubbish heap of used, misused and
> discarded ideas . . . but also a theatre concerned with formal
> beauty, inner visions, the unexplained sculptural detail, and
> the making of images. One is always made aware of texture as
> well as text. . . . What is astonishing about the Royal
> Shakespeare Theatre is that it is an actor's company willing,
> for the most part, to view the actor not only as an ego, but as
> an instrument, a figure in a design.'[11]

Hall believed that an actor's training should not finish with his
graduation from drama school (as was usual under commercial
theatre conditions), but should be a continuing process of learning
and discovery. From the outset, he took the attitude that an RSC
actor should be in a constant state of training — of mental and
physical preparedness — and this was the idea behind the creation
of the Actors Studio at Stratford. The heavy demands of the
Stratford and London repertoire made continual compromise
necessary, and the Studio was never all that Hall hoped it would
be. But it was a beginning.

During the early years of the sixties, Studio classes under the
direction of Michel St. Denis, John Barton and others were held
on a regular basis, and attendance at these classes were virtually
obligatory (unless prohibited by repertoire commitments) for the
entire acting company. In the first years a heavy emphasis was
placed on learning the techniques of speaking Shakespeare's verse:
'I believe that theatre begins with the word . . . Because without

the word there is no possibility for all the other things in the theatre.'[12] The company were taught about the structure of a line, about rhythm, about end-stopping, about imagery and the meaning of imagery, about alliteration. . . . The approach was analytical, straightforward and intelligent, and the resulting acting style was one of speaking the verse clearly with full regard to *meaning* — and of stripping out all overlay of 'word-music'; of 'singing' or 'declamatory' delivery: ' . . . the "Stratford style" was the realization that there is a rhythm to each speech and a rhythm to each play — find it! Don't put naturalistic crap within the speech — and don't put music and scenic "effects" within the play. . . .'[13]

Studio work also included sessions in movement, mime, fencing, mask-work, improvisation, and general training in many of the theatre techniques that were usually left behind at drama school. In addition to Studio sessions, the RSC actor came to expect pre-rehearsal talks from his director about the background of a particular play; about the social structure of the period in which it was set, about the author, and about the relative importance and position of the various characters when considering the play as a unified whole.

But underlying all the early training, the Studio sessions and the rehearsal procedure, was the word: the verse speaking was always of paramount importance to Hall: 'I think that my greatest achievement in the theatre (if I may be immodest) is to have started a Shakespeare company which conscientiously began to understand what Shakespeare's verse was about, and how to speak it. Because we made a different "noise", everybody said: "They're not speaking the verse!" In fact to my mind *no-one* had been speaking the verse — except great star, idiosyncratic actors who had their own way of making the verse work. That's all gone now and forgotten. We caused a revolution in the speaking of Shakespeare's verse. . . . I would say that's the best thing I've done in my life.'[14]

The true basis of Peter Hall's new company system, was to find a way of exploring rather than exploiting the actor's personality. The long-term contracts gave actors the freedom necessary for exploratory work, and the Studio classes and rehearsal lectures gave a confidence in the text and in the actor's own physical and vocal equipment. Under these almost ideal conditions, certain RSC actors began to emerge within the company. This new star was generally a young actor, but his public image was very different from that of the star of the fifties.

John Kane, a young actor who was prominent among the new generation at Stratford, spoke about the RSC, and his feelings for the company's methods, approach and ideals: 'The RSC evolved a style which is as recognizable and as vital and as exciting as the Berliner Ensemble or the Moscow Art . . . you can sense it when you go to see one of our productions. . . . Obviously I have a kind of romantic attachment to our whole method of work and the way in which we present our plays. I like it. They are very "gutsy" presentations. I like to think that they are also (at their best) productions which start from an intellectual approach and evaluation of the play, and then work up to something theatrical. But they have their feet very firmly rooted in a kind of "collective reality" which the performers share. And they are noted for their general and overall excellence of acting. Sometimes we're bloody awful, but, at our best — we're The Best!'[15]

So the RSC ideal was a theatre in which actors, directors and designers would attempt to work together and in continual relation to each other — instead of the accepted commercial notion of independent entities who came together only during the various stages of rehearsal — if at all. Hall believed that only a theatre community in which all members attempted to have a thorough knowledge of each other — and of each other's working habits — was a true ensemble: 'I don't mean that we're one happy band of brothers, all loving each other. Not a bit of it. But we all know what we hate about each other — which is far more important.'[16]

Under the Hall regime, the individual actor was prepared to submerge much of his personal identity into the community effort. This did not always work, but the new stars of the RSC were (for the most part) dedicated company actors. Those who achieved star status and were then unprepared to accept the company system, generally left the organization for the outside world. The stars who remained part of the RSC structure (often as Associate Artists) were the true products of Peter Hall's 1960 concept.

However, there were critics who saw the RSC's gradual community development as a definite downgrading of the actor, and saw Hall's new breed of star as an insipid shadow of the fifties. During 1969, John Trewin wrote in *Flourish*:

'Today, in Shakespeare particularly, there is a curious reluctance to "give". It is as if an actor or actress were in the ante-room, refusing to go further, refusing to fling the door wide. . . . It is curious, for there are many current actors of high spirit and intelligence. Can it be that they and their directors — who so often have the final word — are intent on interpreting a play to us rather than letting us experience it.'[17]

And Gareth Lloyd Evans, writing in 1970, took up Trewin's point:

' . . . actors and actresses who "make the fire bells ring", have been conspicuous by their absence. Olivier's and Edith Evans' last appearances at Stratford were years ago . . . Gielgud's last appearance (as Othello) was unhappy — a displaced Saturn. Alone, of an older generation, Peggy Ashcroft has held her own with the young Hyperions. . . . The replacement for "giving" actors has been, to use Trewin's words, "interpretation" for "experience". It is as well to be clear, however, whose interpretation we are considering. It is with a shock that we realize, when we consider the Hyperion era at Stratford, that it is much easier to recall directors than actors. Hall, Williams, Barton, Nunn, Brook and *their* histories, comedies, tragedies and what-have-you are remembered more clearly than individual acting interpretations.'[18]

The rise of the directors' theatre in Britain during these years was a subject much discussed and written about. Just as the great star actors seemed to dominate the theatre of the fifties, so the figure of the director seemed to attain an unprecedented prominence and importance over the sixties — perhaps co-incident with the breaking down of the star system and the rise of the subsidized or non-commercial theatre. An actors' star system still exists in the West End of London, but to many critics, the new star in the British theatre of the sixties was the director. Since authors and actor-managers handed over their function as director of plays to a separate individual within the theatre, there have been a succession of great stage directors who could well be termed stars in their own right: men like Stanislavsky, Granville-Barker, Reinhardt, St. Denis, Komisarjevsky, Brecht. However, many of these early directors had their backgrounds firmly rooted in an acting tradition, and viewed their function from the actors' standpoint.

As John Russell Brown points out in his article, *The Study and Practice of Shakespeare Production*[19], the director of the past twenty years has, more often than not, had little or no actual acting experience. Some of the leading English directorial figures of the fifties — Tyrone Guthrie, Peter Brook, and later Tony Richardson, Peter Hall, William Gaskill — were non-actors who entered the professional theatre with the sole purpose of directing plays. Peter Hall is characteristically honest about his beginnings in the theatre: 'I learnt my craft as a director the hard, and silly way — by coming out of Cambridge University . . . and saying loudly to the world, "I can direct plays". It was a monstrous lie, perpetrated by me, and by many of my contemporaries.'[20]

It is therefore probable that many of this new generation of directors began their careers with a somewhat imperfect understanding of the acting process, and this deficiency could well lead to the directorial imposition or interpretation that has so often been criticized. Russell Brown says: ' . . . it would be unfortunate if direction by non-actors should lessen the chances of further innovation from individual, imaginative and skilful exploration of great actors. Special precautions should be taken so that the actor has scope for invention within a general control.'[21]

The RSC under Peter Hall did become a company very largely dominated by the figure of the director — or, more specifically, the five directors mentioned by Lloyd Evans: Peter Hall, Peter Brook, John Barton, Trevor Nunn and Clifford Williams. Other directors were employed by the company, and outside directors were occasionally engaged for particular productions, but it was these five men in the sixties who dominated the RSC public image, and were responsible for the majority of the company's production output. Outstanding RSC productions were often referred to by naming the director, in some cases the leading actor, and then the play. Notable examples include 'Peter Hall's *A Midsummer Night's Dream*'; the 'Brook/Scofield *Lear*'; 'Clifford Williams' *Comedy of Errors*'; 'the Hall/Barton *Wars of the Roses*'; 'Brook's

Marat-Sade'; the 'Hall/Warner *Hamlet*'; 'Trevor Nunn's *Revenger's Tragedy*' — and so on.

It should be stated that the RSC never *publicly* referred to any of its productions in this way — but it is quite usual practice within the company, and also among critics and the general theatre-going public.

Peter Hall agreed that the RSC had become a directors' theatre under his control, but emphatically denied that the director had become the new star: 'That is a judgement from outside. Neither Brook nor I in approaching a play ... say "We must do a play differently' to make sure that we are the star.". ... We do the play as we see it. It's for others to say whether we've drawn attention to ourselves. Certainly it's an expressed opinion. ... I think that if the director is *not* in control of these very intricate texts — whether it be Shakespeare or Pinter — there is trouble! ... there *needs* to be an outside controlling intelligence. That's the director. ... If I had to choose between star actors making mincemeat of the play (and being brilliant themselves), and a director, with less good actors, revealing the play — I would choose the director. That's my position.'[22]

Certain RSC actors voiced their feelings about the company as a specialist theatre — a theatre dominated and controlled by the director and designer. John Kane said: 'I think the RSC is no longer an actors' theatre ... but then the theatre (as a whole) isn't any more ... it's seldom that you get a performance here which stands out as being really "fantastic" and "different" from the rest. Because, I think, that the quality of the rest of the performances are so high. It is against the nature of the RSC actor to "grab the limelight" ... There may be many people who will come to see Peter Hall's productions and (certainly) Peter Brook's productions. I think that Brook *is* an international star, but not the kind that has Afghan hounds and a convertible! He's just an *amazing* wee man!'[23]

Judi Dench, who played Juliet in Franco Zeffirelli's production at the Old Vic in 1960 — before joining the RSC in 1961, commented: 'I resented it terribly when they used to say "Zeffirelli's *Romeo and Juliet*". It's Shakespeare's *Romeo and Juliet*. It's Shakespeare's *A Midsummer Night's Dream*. The balance between directing, designing and performing a play — and

Glenda Jackson as Charlotte Corday and Patrick Magee as de Sade in *The Marat/Sade* directed by Peter Brook at the Aldwych in 1965. Its full title is *The Persecution and Assassination of Marat as performed by the Inmates of the Asylum of Charenton under the direction of the Marquis de Sade.*

Foreground L. to R.: Patrick Magee as de Sade, Glenda Jackson as Charlotte Corday and Ian Richardson as Marat.

THE MARAT/SADE, Aldwych 1965

L. to R.: Jeanette Landis as Rossignol, Jonathan Burn as Polpoch, Hugh Sullivan as Kokol and Freddie Jones as Cucurucu.

being truthful to the author — is a razor-edge really. If it goes over in any way then it's wrong. I'm only suspicious when something goes to extremes: when a director wants to make an effect to the exclusion of the actors — or an actor wants to make an effect to the exclusion of the play.'[24] And Peter Woodthorpe said: 'It [the RSC] *is* a great company, because it has great directors, it has great facilities, and it has some very fine artists. . . . It is *not* an ensemble theatre. We are now living in the age of the directors' theatre — and they call the tune . . . they have more power than anybody else, but this is probably the right thing. It's the conductor's orchestra now isn't it? The conductor is the "star" of the evening — often over the soloist. An actor is bound to resent this slightly.'[25]

Although the RSC director was very much the central figure in the theatre, there were certain 'checks' placed on his activities and powers by the nature of Hall's ensemble scheme: the principles of community effort and mutual criticism and advice did not only apply to the actor. It became an established practice for the company's directors to attend the various rehearsals, run-throughs and dress rehearsals of their colleagues' productions, and then to make constructive (or destructive) criticism to the director concerned. The director was not bound to accept this criticism, but he was bound to listen, and Clifford Williams commented: 'This is always a very painful moment for a director. When his confrères came along and possibly said, "My God this is terrible!".'[26]

A later variation of this practice was Hall's idea of having a second director involved in the production of another: this second director had no actual powers over the production concerned, but it was his function to make progress comments to the play's director — which he could accept or reject as he chose. Both these practices were used fairly consistently during Hall's directorate. It was felt that they would result in a far greater directorial objectivity, and thus be of service to the company's overall aims and ideals.

A further innovation was the principle of joint direction: productions like *The Wars of the Roses*, the 1964 History plays and the 1966 *Henry IV* and *Henry V*, were the result of three (or more) directors working in close collaboration on a single stage presentation. In fact, this was ensemble directing.

Speaking of the practice during the 1966 productions, Clifford Williams said: 'It's a superb discipline for directors. We are proud of our own visions, our particular arrogance, but this makes for balance and tolerance. Theatre is a way of living. The values that, working together, we attempt to choose, amplify, and construct would have validity in society. Three or four years ago I would bridle at any intrusion of my "all-seeing eye" – but I am learning.'[27]

The principle of ensemble direction was by no means unique to the RSC; however, its values to the actor within the RSC structure were obvious. Rehearsal time was greatly multiplied and the minor actor stood in no danger of being under-rehearsed. Nor were the minor scenes neglected – as is sometimes the case when one director is handling a large-scale production. As practised at Stratford, the principle worked on the basis of continuous directorial discussion, and the splitting up of responsibility for various scenes, characters and technical aspects of production.

The problems of overall interpretation, style, and the final putting together of the finished product would seem to be great, but it is reported that such difficulties were rare. Directors made a point of occasionally rehearsing each other's scenes and characters, and one director usually had the final word on any major difference of opinion. John Barton spoke about co-direction: 'There was a risk of confusion. But we carefully talked it out beforehand, and were pretty much agreed about our approach.'[28]

Recognizing the importance of the director within the RSC, it is worthwhile examining certain aspects of the directorial approach and rehearsal methods used – particularly those employed by the five directors already mentioned. Each has a distinct and indivi-dual working style, yet they share a common approach to the aims of the RSC – and, in some respects, have similar views on the function of the theatre as an art form within society. It should be mentioned at this point that any attempt to 'formalize' the art of direction or the process of putting on a play can never be wholly satisfactory. The act of creation in the theatre is essentially ephemeral. The success or failure of a particular production can often swing upon something as elusive as a feeling for the play — or the chemistry between two or more actors, and their director: no two performances in the theatre are identical; no rehearsal period is the same as the last; no good director can approach a play with a set of rules.

To write about Peter Hall's *method* of direction is grossly to over-simplify a process which is constantly changing — constantly demanding fresh approach, new thought, imagination and the application of new knowledge. It also does an injustice to Peter Hall, who has often stated that he sees each new production as an 'unknown quantity' — each rehearsal period as 'an adventure': 'I distrust all methods, and all dogmas. They freeze things. . . . We are searching, and whatever we find today, a new search will be necessary tomorrow. The theatre is a quest, not an acceptance. Accept a theory and you'll by-pass the creative process.'[29] The following pages then, are an attempt to define an intangible, in the course of which some injustices may be perpetrated and some generalizations indulged in. For this, the author makes apology to the directors concerned.

Peter Hall is perhaps the most important, for it was his overall view of the theatre which created the company structure at Stratford and London. In an article, *Directing the Play*[30], Hall wrote about some of his directorial ideas and explained some of his views on the director's responsibility: ' . . . the first thing a director has to say to himself . . . is, "Why in god's name should I do this?" . . . We can. only work on our own impulse, but our responsibility is finally social, simply because I — or any of you who direct plays — have the impudence to collect a group of people together in an auditorium and say, "This thing is worthy of your attention".'[31] In this sense, the controlling factor behind much of Hall's work is an attempt to express his author's intentions in terms that a modern audience can respond to.

However, this desire to express the 'immediate contemporary relevance' of his texts — particularly Shakespeare texts — has brought considerable criticism, both personal and of the RSC in general. There is no doubt that the whole company tended to move towards this approach under Hall's direction. Productions were frequently related to the happenings of the mid-twentieth century; texts were cut, re-arranged, and (very occasionally) re-written; and design and production styles were changed and

adapted to meet these new demands. Many critics felt that Hall
and his fellow-directors were taking dangerous and unwarranted
liberties with Shakespeare texts and interpretation — but Hall
defended his approach quite simply:

> 'If I walk into the Louvre and paint a large black moustache
> on the face of the Mona Lisa, it's there for ever, defaced. But
> if I do *Macbeth* — as I did — in red rugs, I make nobody a
> fool but myself. *Macbeth* is still there at the end — staring at
> me. I have done nothing to *Macbeth*.'[32]

Hall was fully aware of the dangerous nature of his assumptions,
and that such approaches have been used as an excuse for
ignorance, lack of talent — or as a sanction to write happy endings
for *King Lear*. However, he felt that the end justified his means:
'... the risk must be taken if our performances are to have
meaning.'[33] Actors who have worked with Hall are almost
unanimous in stating that the most obvious factor in his approach
to any play is his intelligence. Actors, critics and audiences might
disagree with his particular reading of a piece, but few can justly
claim that it is not intelligent and carefully thought out.

His rehearsal period is generally prefaced by a talk to the cast,
which is used to explain his own reading and interpretation of the
text, and is designed as an introduction to the work of
rehearsal — as a starting point for further exploration and discussion. From this point on, the rehearsal becomes a process of
mutual give-and-take, with Hall (of necessity) as the final arbiter
on any major point of interpretation or production issue.
However, Ian Richardson said: 'He was never a dictator in
rehearsals. He would never settle for any interpretation without
first going into great conversational detail with the actors
concerned.'[34] A Hall rehearsal is generally conducted on an
experimental basis, particularly in the early stages: '... it changes
according to the circumstances in which you all find yourselves
... at the beginning every door must be opened.'[35] The actor is
encouraged to adopt a try anything attitude at the preliminary
rehearsals, in the belief that something positive must emerge from
an intelligent trial-and-error process between actor and director.

For this process to succeed, it is necessary for the actor to leave
his ego outside the rehearsal room — and thus free himself to
experiment in any way at all. Hall considers that one of the most

difficult problems of directing is the breaking down of an actor's automatic defence barrier: he feels that his actors should be able to make utter fools of themselves within a rehearsal, and in doing so, reveal to themselves (and the director) exactly what they can and cannot achieve. Hall does not 'block' moves on any rigid or pre-ordained scheme — in fact, he prefers not to block at all, and to act more in the capacity of editor. Much early rehearsal time is taken up with readings of the play, and Hall encourages his cast to think about the various possibilities for movement. When the time comes to 'put the play on its feet', the actor is then allowed a relative freedom of action within the limits of the setting, and is persuaded to discover a physical life for himself: 'If you can create circumstances in which actors will invent the sort of thing you want to happen, and you then edit it — it's marvellous. As soon as you give the moves, it's like giving people inflexions — they start imitating.'[36]

Hall sees his own role as director as 'part chairman, part doctor, part analyst, part guide, part father, part schoolmaster.'[37] He never attempts to be part actor. In the middle and early stages of rehearsal the actor has comparative freedom, but finally, in Hall's words, ' . . . the director has to move in, and say, "Now I'm the chairman — with the casting vote". He has to edit ruthlessly . . . On the basis of *meaning*, you select, you cut, you change, you economize. And at that time you can do almost anything with an actor . . . You all know what the problems are.'[38]

Most actors who have worked with Hall, comment on the apparent ease with which he conducts his rehearsals, and the thoroughness and sheer professionalism of his approach. Judi Dench, who played Titania in his 1962 revival of *A Midsummer Night's Dream*, said: 'Peter was just marvellous. It was an extraordinarily "professional" feeling. Intellectual — primarily theatrical — but with the intellect "thrown in" at the back . . . he knew *exactly* what he wanted. He knew precisely. I remember *The Dream* rehearsals being exceptionally *easy*. And to be able to say that when playing a big part is phenomenal.'[39]

As previously stated, the modern relevance of a text is a constant source of fascination for Hall, and during the sixties this approach was strongly linked with an interest in the machinations of power-politics. In rehearsal, he will constantly relate an actor's problem of interpretation, action or character to an appropriate modern parallel — to the situation, action or character as it might exist *now*. Ian Richardson has spoken of this approach during the 1967 *Macbeth* rehearsals[40], and John Kane spoke of 'Hall's advice to the players' during the 1965 *Hamlet*: 'When he came to discuss (with those of us who were playing the Players) our entrance into Elsinore, our starting point was *our* reaction as actors to a similar situation. It is the custom for the Players to enter with a flourish, juggling, tumbling — tara-tara etc. Peter suggested that our entrance as players would be little different from the entrance *we* would make ourselves into Windsor Castle for a Royal Command Performance. Of course, we could hardly refrain from making some kind of "entrance" — but it's unlikely that we would come belting through Windsor juggling and doing "Now is the winter of our discontent".'[41]

Hall has always been noted for his versatility as a director. He moves from the handling of large crowd scenes and flamboyant spectacle in Shakespeare and opera, to the protracted silences and dramatic subtleties of Pinter and Albee with equal success. He is always a theatrically exciting director, continually aware of the impact of a sudden brilliant effect on stage and believing that his audience enjoys being occasionally shocked and jolted: ' . . . they'll resist it, but deep down inside they like it'.[42]

This flamboyant streak has not always brought success: his *Macbeth* at Stratford is a notable example of a production where theatrical excitement and impact has been seen as irrelevant excess, best forgotten. He has recently stated his belief that, in the theatre, 'less is more': 'I always take away from actors and singers everything I possibly can — props, furniture, business, moves. . . . The best work I've done is where things have been pared down to such an extent that everything means something.'[43]

Some critics have seized on this statement as the key to the Hall/Pinter successes, and see these productions as the pinnacle of Hall's achievement in the theatre. Actors in the RSC disagree, and Tony Church said: 'I don't believe that he's only good at doing miniatures. I think Peter's sights are bigger. He has the most marvellous way of controlling big forces to a very clearly defined end. His "big" productions are a combination of imagination and thoroughness. . . .'[44] The outstanding success enjoyed by *The Wars of the Roses, Hamlet* and other large scale Hall productions would seem to prove this point. Above all else, Hall's direction and overall philosophy of theatre is centred on a primary belief in the word; in language and the intelligent use of language as the central point of the theatrical experience. In 1963 he stated: 'The primary means of communication in the theatre is words. Those practitioners of "total theatre" — in which music, dance, lights all play a part — generally seem to me to have sent the script writer home. I believe that what distinguishes the theatre from other forms of dramatic communication, is that an actor saying words can communicate to an audience things beyond that which those words actually say.'[45]

Peter Brook has been an innovater since he entered the profession in 1944, and when he joined Peter Hall at Stratford in 1962, his role as the experimentalist of the RSC was clearly accepted. He has always seen the conventions of the theatre as something to be broken down and replaced — 'Yesterday's performance is by now a failure'[46] — and his language of direction is that of the true theatre visionary:

'I want to see a flood of people and events that echo my inner battlefield. I want to see behind this desperate and ravishing confusion an order, a structure, which will relate to my deepest and truest longing for structure and law. I want through this to find the new forms, and through the new forms the new architecture, and through the new architecture the new patterns and the new rituals of the age that is swirling around us.'[47]

To his colleagues, his casts, his critics and his audiences, Brook has always been an enigma: all who know him and all who have worked with him, speak of him in contradictory terms. His excessive demands on the actor's personality and his combat-course rehearsal techniques are now proverbial within the RSC. Some actors quite candidly admit that they would be terrified to work with him, and others, (who have), vow 'never again'. Yet, since 1962, a dedicated 'Brook group' has grown up within the company. These actors complain loudly of the 'punishment' in rehearsal; approach Brook only tentatively and nervously; are infuriated by his constant probing, demanding and questioning technique — and (without exception) say that working with him has been the greatest experience of their theatre lives.

A 'Brook actor' is always glowing in his praise — and contradictory in his language: 'A very great respect grows up. Working with him is an incredible experience — but it's always a love-hate relationship. He makes you sweat blood ... No actor likes to be tortured over his work all day and every day — and half the bloody night as well!'[48] 'He can be disarming, charming, bitter, cruel — and all in a moment! He does not dictate — or even "talk" — to an actor. He makes *you* think it out for yourself ... he throws *all* responsibility squarely on the actor's shoulders. ... To work with Brook is a tremendous and terrifying experience for an actor.'[49] 'He's an autocratic bastard; he's a slave-driver; but he's led me up against myself very firmly! He's made me face myself *all* the time. He's given me the desire to seek for truth and self-integrity; he makes you aware that in your greatest strengths as an actor — there too you'll find your greatest weaknesses. He's the *supreme* director.'[50]

A bare, unadorned stage; harsh, white lighting; a rejection of all the conventional tricks of the theatre; the unusual; the unexpected; these have become the symbols of a Brook production. Since his *Romeo and Juliet* of 1947, Brook has moved more and more in the direction of theatre minus all artifice and decoration: he 'shows his hand' to his audience — and then proceeds to create the experience in an 'empty space', where his own kind of 'magic-time' can happen in the open. In his article, *Plotting with Peter*[51] John Kane writes about some of the many and varied creative processes at a Brook rehearsal — in this case the RSC's revolutionary 1970 production of *A Midsummer Night's Dream*. As always, Brook placed the (apparent) act of creation entirely in the hands of his actors — supplying only a bewildering variety of 'toys' and a continual series of enigmatic comments on the play and the actors' progress:

'He looks at the ceiling or at the floor. His hands become soft pink pincers moulding ideas like pie crust ... in the silences, we sift his unfinished sentences in our minds trying to supply the missing magic word ... that will transform our dullness and re-establish communication. ... Time and time again we would return to a reading of the play during the course of rehearsals . . . again and again Peter would stop us. "Shakespeare didn't write these lines for nothing". I'm still not sure that I understand what it was that he wanted from us at those readings. . . . Every morning began with a "warm up" session. . . . Over the eight-week rehearsal period, the Studio filled up with trapezes, ropes, plastic rods, spinning plates, tennis balls, hoops, paper, string and a variety of musical instruments. For at least half-an-hour every day we exercised with these until they became extensions of ourselves.'[52]

Brook is equally elusive about his own working approach to a text and his creative processes as a director: 'One goes through a whole process of searching rationally, and at some point (if you're on a good "line" and if you have a "feeling" towards the play which is eventually going to take form) suddenly all the complicated thinking that has gone into the planning begins to shrink and crystallize into something rather simple. This becomes, as it were, the "formula" for the play.'[53]

To achieve productions like *Theatre of Cruelty*, *Marat-Sade* and *US*, Brook worked 'on' and 'through' a group of actors from whom he demanded everything: singing, dancing, acrobatics, 'noises', mime, and — above all — total dedication. Maurice Daniels saw a pattern in Brook's progress through the sixties — a progress which produced actors of the calibre of Glenda Jackson and productions as stunningly original as *A Midsummer Night's Dream*: 'These actors let Brook literally "take them apart" (possibly resenting it), yet they also *knew* that he would "put them back together again". . . . Brook has come round full circle from *Lear*: after *Lear* he departed from Shakespeare and "explored" — and then he came back to a Shakespeare text. *The Dream* is the synthesis of all his work. . . .'[54] Since *The Dream*, Brook and a group of actors have formed the International Centre for Theatre Research in Paris[55]. Working with the poet, Ted Hughes, the group are experimenting with sound, music and ritual — and an 'international language' (invented by Hughes) called 'Orghast'. This group gave their first 'work in progress' showing at the 1971 Festival of Arts in Iran. Richard Findlater wrote of the Shiraz performance:

'What does it mean? What did that matter, on the spot? It

was, of its kind, superb . . . also, as a doting American
suggested, "historic" — at least in the annals of Peter Brook.
The debate, and the experiments, will continue.'[56]
The three remaining major directors of the RSC — Barton,
Williams and Nunn — contributed in a highly influential and
individual way to the collective life of the company over the
sixties, and each is, in his own right, a director of major
international standing.

John Barton at one time suffered with the reputation of being
seen as the 'company intellectual',— possibly because of his
academic origins, his extensive textual work, and his almost
exclusive concentration on Shakespeare production. Now Barton
has moved from early productions like *The Taming of the Shrew*
in 1960, to become a director of major power and originality in
the theatre. *The Wars of the Roses*, the *Henry IV* and *Henry V*
productions in 1966, *Coriolanus* (1967), *Troilus and Cressida*
(1968), *Twelfth Night* (1969), *Othello* (1971) and *Richard II*
(1972) with the King and Bolingbroke alternating, have traced a
pattern of increasing assurance and invention in Barton's development as a director: 'I've changed, grown, developed — and I've
become more experienced . . . the main change is probably in how
I put things to actors. One may have the right ideas, but unless one
can find the right and helpful way of expressing it, then it's no
good.'[57]

Barton does not lecture to his cast about a play (although it is
reported that he used to do so during his early years at Stratford):
'My ideas and responses come out of watching the actors and what
they do. . . . I can only express my feelings by *doing* the
production. I'm full of ideas and articulate in the rehearsal room
with the actor, but very inarticulate when anatomizing it critically
outside that context. I think I'm one of the least academic of
people.'[58]

He likes to move the play at the earliest possible opportunity
and the actor is given considerable latitude for individual
expression. However, during rehearsal periods his approach is
primarily textual: ' . . . the intellect is right at the front. John
never looks at you for the first three weeks of rehearsal — he's
looking at the book!'[59] Richard Pasco said of him: 'John Barton
is a very gentle "coaxer". He has given me enormous help by his

scholarship, by his sensitivity, by his ability to "feed" the inner meanings of a text to me like no other director I've ever known. I adore working with John: he's an inspiration to me. . . ."[60]

Among the senior directors at Stratford, Clifford Williams was the only non-university man: he trained as an economist, and then spent his early years in mining, the army, the theatre and in ballet. In 1950, Williams formed Britain's only professional mime company — The Mime Theatre Company — which he directed for three years. From 1953 to 1956, he directed and acted for the National Theatre of South Africa, and on returning to England held a variety of theatre appointments until he became a staff producer at the RSC in 1961. He was later made an Associate Director of the company: 'I was the only one who "came up through the theatre" . . . in a half-humorous (and sometimes half-serious) way in our directorial discussions, they put John in the "academic" chair, Peter in the "political" chair — and me in the "rugby-football" chair.'[61]

Williams' directorial style has always been dynamic, and the product has frequently been highly colourful and exciting: he seems to flourish in the presence of sensational or controversial material, and his productions of *Afore Night Come* (1962/64) and *The Representative* (1963) were among the most talked-about of the sixties. He does, however, need to feel the essential truth of certain plays, and in the case of *The Representative*, he engaged in exhaustive research on the subject matter before giving his full weight to the production: ' . . . a play which seeks to establish by documentary evidence (and a certain amount of speculation) that the head of the Catholic Church was personally responsible for a number of Jewish deaths during the war, was going to cause a considerable amount of upset. There was no way around that . . . I felt that the play *was* truthful. . . .'[62]

Character and the motivation of character are of considerable interest to him, and he talks with his actors at great length about the background to the various characters within a play. In common with his colleagues at the RSC, he also dwells on the general background to a play, the period, and the social relevance of the piece. With rehearsal moves, he tends to leave the actor alone — preferring to be asked rather than to offer advice: 'I think he respects his actors enough to think and believe that they can do it on their own without much help. . . .'[63] His most successful productions for the RSC include the much-revived *Comedy of Errors* (first staged in 1962), his unique 'linked productions' of *The Jew of Malta* and *The Merchant of Venice* in 1964/65, and the two mentioned earlier. Less successful were his *The Meteor* (1966) and *The Tempest* (1963) which he co-directed with Peter Brook.

Outside the RSC he has been responsible for staging successful productions including the revolutionary all-male *As You Like It* for the National Theatre, *Sleuth* and *Oh! Calcutta!* for commercial managements, and he assisted Peter Hall with his controversial *Moses and Aaron* at Covent Garden in 1965.

Trevor Nunn became an Associate Director of the RSC in 1965, having moved to this position by way of Downing College, Cambridge, and a trainee-directorship (later Resident Director) at the Belgrade Theatre, Coventry. In a sense, he entered the RSC as Peter Hall's protégé although he had already shown himself to be a young director of exceptional promise for the future. In 1968, at the age of twenty-eight, Nunn was appointed Artistic Director of the RSC — as Hall's chosen successor: 'I think the clearest way to put it is the way in which Peter framed the offer of my job. He said, "I have been your boss for three years: are you prepared to be my boss?".'[64] During the three years that Hall was boss, Trevor Nunn was responsible for several productions showing a decided flair (including his acclaimed *The Revenger's Tragedy* in 1966 — produced on a shoe string budget): he also developed a philosophy of theatre and a language of direction which was to some extent in the Hall image. Not unnaturally, Nunn's approach to the business of directing is similar to Hall's — yet, at the same time, it is an approach that is very distinctly and uniquely his own. He has Hall's awareness of the dazzling effect, together with Hall's intellectual basis in his approach to the text. It is these two qualities which most actors recognize immediately: 'Trevor, at his best, has a superb intellectual understanding of the play . . . coupled with the most *wonderfully* vulgar love of the theatrical.'[65] 'In many ways, his gifts lie in the Guthrie direction. He has Guthrie's ability to make a "blaze in the theatre" . . .'[66]

Where Nunn differs from Peter Hall is that he is essentially a private person who would rather be a figure in the background than one in the foreground. He sees the director's job in rehearsal as one of diplomacy and discussion. His cast is encouraged to 'suggest and try', but more towards the object of a fully contributing company than the notion of a group working consciously (or unconsciously) on a basic idée-fixe of the director. Nunn's rehearsals are conducted in an atmosphere of privacy — he will admit no observers — but actors report that they are more often fun time than work time: indeed, the majority of RSC actors say that they thoroughly enjoy working with him, and that his productions are more than usually happy ones.

His rehearsal techniques are improvisatory and evolutionary, and often take the form of a 'game' — but a game with a very definite end in view. When he directed *The Taming of the Shrew* (1967), he began rehearsals by asking his actors to kick a fluffy baby's ball around the rehearsal room — and to make absolute fools of themselves in the process. In doing so, the actors' defence barriers (which Peter Hall has spoken of) were broken down: John Kane said: 'It built up an atmosphere whereby no-one was afraid to do something which the others might laugh at. That fluffy ball forged the most happy company I've ever been in. . . .'[67]

The Shrew was conceived as a play-within-a-play, and the cast were seen as a company of Elizabethan players staging the production in the courtyard of an inn. As a further rehearsal game, Nunn encouraged his cast to improvise situations from the everyday life within an Elizabethan acting group each chose for himself the name of an Elizabethan actor, and a series of relationships were improvised within the troupe. Actors were married to other actors — and having affairs with other members of the troupe at the same time: there was a company baby — christened 'Ferdie' — and a spaniel called 'Troilus', and these characters were always present in the play.

It is reported that similar 'games' were played during rehearsals for *The Revenger's Tragedy* and *Hamlet* (1970). In *The Revenger's Tragedy*, Nunn felt that his cast were not getting the sense of the sequence in which the Court searches for the missing Duke, of coming into a chamber and finding the Duke — who had been dead for three days. During rehearsal, Nunn and the actor playing the Duke hid in the theatre, and the entire Court were instructed to search for them: when they were finally found, the 'Court' came running from all parts of the building in response to a call that 'the Duke had been found': 'We were all crowding in there to have a look at the Duke ... Trevor was there, and he said "now remember — he stinks!" ... it was very dark in there and you could hear the sound of people panting from running and exertion. It was an incredible (and invaluable) exercise. That "feeling" was what we used when it came to staging the scene: we remembered the horror and fascination of finding the body.'[68]

As a director, Nunn (like Peter Hall) is intrigued by the possible topicality and immediacy of his texts, and many of his productions reflect this interest. *The Revenger's Tragedy* was to some extent a savage comment on the hypocrisy of our own society; *The Taming of the Shrew* was a study in man/woman relationships from youth's (i.e. 1967) viewpoint; and *The Winter's Tale* (1969) was staged with 'toy box' props, 'hippie' shepherds, rock music and strobe lighting effects: ' . . . the sheepshearing festival became a hug-in, with headbands and beads, much pounding, jerking, twisting and . . . Autolycus bouncing about the stage to the sound of beat music. The shepherds, carters and swineherds, dubbed 'men of hair' in the play, had been transformed into men of *Hair*!'[69]

Another significant feature of Nunn's productions is a highly schematized use of colours and costumes, and the almost consistent use of a box-like chamber setting. In this sense, his productions are very much a work of collaboration with his designer, Christopher Morley, who took over as RSC Head of Design when John Bury left the company in 1968.

The importance and influence of John Bury on design over the sixties cannot be minimized. Working in close association with Peter Hall, Bury revolutionized the entire concept of stage design at Stratford, and with it many of the accepted notions of design in other theatres throughout Britain. Bury was not the sole influence on design during the Hall era: both Ralph Koltai and Sean Kenny provided outstanding and original contributions to the company's development, but it was Bury (as Head of Design) who set the pattern.

During the fifties, stage design was, in general, a fairly

straightforward representational, decorative process: the notable designers at Stratford (with some exceptions) were usually trainees of an art school, and often major painters in their own right. Both Leslie Hurry and Lila de Nobili were painters who designed for the stage in pictorial terms, and the latter designed much of Peter Hall's early Stratford work.

Lila de Nobili's designs in particular were often compared with oil paintings, and the stage picture which she created did sometimes have an 'old master' feeling in visual terms: the *Twelfth Night* which she designed for Hall in 1960 was said to 'echo the dark, rust and gold, dusty Dutch and Flemish painters'.[70] Her costume designs were often stunningly beautiful, and in particular the creations for *A Midsummer Night's Dream* which were intended to complement her romantic settings: ' . . . here were real beings of enchantment, metamorphosed from the twigs, leaves, cobwebs and dew of an English wood.'[71]

Leslie Hurry's design for *Troilus and Cressida* did represent a move towards greater simplicity and selectivity on stage, although his dried blood cyclorama and rich costumes still echoed the painter's hues.

When John Bury joined Peter Hall at Stratford in 1962, he brought with him a process of 'selective realism', and initiated the concept of designing a production from a basic 'image' — an image worked out in discussion between the director and the designer.

Bury had no formal art school or design training: 'All these definitions which are thrown around about nonfigurative and so on mean nothing to me . . . I always think in terms of theatre and function.'[72] He worked as Designer for Joan Littlewood's Theatre Workshop at Stratford East (and on tour) from 1946 to 1961, and within this structure the notion of stage-design in the accepted commercial sense was unknown. With very limited financial resources, designs *had* to be improvisatory and created from the cheapest possible materials: there was no room for the trial-and-error method and a design-budget was almost non-existent. The designing process within the Theatre Workshop was, of necessity, cheap, experimental and 'permanent': because there was no repertoire system (and no resultant set-construction and change-over problems), the Workshop designs were created on the film-set principle. Sets were built on the stage and designed for use throughout the run of a production — then demolished at the end of the season. Under these conditions, sets could be almost totally realistic, and the design process was as much 'set-building' as 'set-designing'.

Bury brought a sense of 'true realism', selectivity and austerity to RSC design — as opposed to the 'romantic realism' of the fifties tradition. In conception (the design 'image') and in his use of authentic (or closely simulated) materials, the Bury style was a triumph of texture as much as form: 'I literally create in terms of scenery, floors, roofs, backwalls . . . one will get one's initial inspiration from the textural image often. One can take a bit of stone in one's hand and say — this is *Hamlet*. . . . It isn't until I begin to create the model in terms of bits of stuff that begin to think at all.'[73] For *The Wars of the Roses, Hamlet* and other major productions of the sixties, Bury worked in terms of textured materials and substances which evolved from the initial design image. *The Wars of the Roses* had a steel image — and the settings and costumes were all created or textured in these terms. The black, glossy formica settings for *Hamlet* were an image of the enclosed, cold, political world of Elsinore as Peter Hall saw it.

Another innovation was Bury's use of sound in theatre design: he felt that a metallic set should not merely *look* like metal but also *sound* like metal. The steel flooring for the Histories was designed to echo the sound of marching feet or the scrape of a broad-sword — and similarly the iron grilles and metallic cages were built to look *and* sound like metal.

Bury also created a substance called 'gunk', with which he textured costumes and scenery to give them that appearance of solidity which characterizes his design style. Gunk was a crude rubber substance which could be sculpted or moulded on to any surface and create an astonishing realism of texture and shapes: the majority of *The Wars of the Roses* costumes were given their richly metallic surfaces through a process of 'gunking'.

The primary feature of Bury's RSC design style was simplicity: in his move away from decoration and embellishment, Bury's designs were highly selective and allowed for nothing extraneous on stage. He saw design as an *aid* to the acting process and the designer's function 'to provide a sounding board for the actor's imagination, to supply him with the basic imagery that he needs'.

© T. F. Holte

David Warner as Hamlet in Peter Hall's production at Stratford in 1965.

HAMLET

Top: Trevor Nunn's production at Stratford in 1970. *Foreground:* Christopher Gable as Laertes, Peter Egan as Osric and Alan Howard as Hamlet. *Bottom:* Peter Wood's production at Stratford in 1961. *Foreground:* Peter McEnery as Laertes and Ian Bannen as Hamlet. *Background:* 2nd from left: Gordon Gostelow as Osric.

Towards the mid-sixties, the design emphasis at Stratford began to move towards still greater simplicity — towards lightness, mobility and space. The settings for the Histories were not entirely satisfactory from a practical or economic point of view, as they created considerable problems for stage staff when it came to changing sets for the varied repertoire requirements. Thus, for practical, economic and aesthetic reasons, Bury's later style moved to what he calls 'the box situation': settings became based on a standard box structure — and all RSC productions were designed to work within this form.

Bury's successor, Christopher Morley, has continued to work within and further develop this style of setting, which is in many ways the mode of design most complementary to the architectural lines and limitations of the Stratford stage — the 'obstinate proscenium stage' that Hall has spoken of.

Bury, together with Peter Hall, has been responsible for the concepts behind the design of the RSC's proposed Barbican theatre, which will have a 'space stage'.

One of the most successful (and least publicized) of Peter Hall's many innovations in the theatre, was his search for a new audience — a search which gradually resulted in a change in the structure of the RSC's audience, at Stratford and (most noticeably) at the Aldwych. Hall has always believed that the ideal theatre audience should be mixed, and that any theatre which caters for a particular type or class of audience is not fulfilling its true social function.

The Stratford audience has always contained a high proportion of tourists, who come to the theatre simply to see a stage presentation there: this audience, by its very nature, tends to be uncritical, to accept most productions readily, and is still an unalterable reality which the RSC must face as part of its 'institutional' function. However, the Stratford audience of the fifties was also predominantly middle-aged, middle-income bracket and middle-brow — a composition and taste very similar to the average fifties audience in the West End of London.

Under the Hall regime, the RSC began to attract a much younger age group into the theatre, and this was perhaps the most immediately recognizable change. The new RSC was a young company with young actors and young directors. The new methods of staging and directing Shakespeare; the varied choice of classical and modern plays at the Aldwych; and the dynamic, forward looking company image projected by Hall and his staff were all reflections of youth and youthful thinking. It was inevitable that this new image would have an immediate and popular appeal to a younger age group — and would result in a dropping off in the support of some of the older or more traditionally inclined playgoers.

These statements are broad generalizations, but it is certain that by 1965 — the year of the Hall/Warner *Hamlet* — there was a distinctly recognizable split in the tastes and opinions of the RSC audience: alongside a youthful, enthusiastic and rapidly growing audience who admired the company's approach, methods and choice of presentation, there was also a smaller (but extremely vocal) element who stood opposed to all that the new RSC image represented. The Dirty Plays controversy of 1964 was only one reflection of this difference in public opinion. In 1965, Peter Hall wrote:

> 'There is now an extraordinary and dangerous division in our audience — between what (roughly speaking) those over 45 and those under 45 want. . . . There is a new generation who do not think of the theatre as a high-brow, intellectual and difficult institution. They only object when it is middle-brow, safe and intellectually specious. So there is a changing audience — an audience not content with pure entertainment . . . it is an audience that is growing and growing fast — as fast as our new universities, as fast as the large sales of LP records and paper-back books. The audience is there — and it is demanding.'[74]

Recognizing the emergence of the new generation of theatregoer, Hall and the RSC made every effort to cater for it, but the company was not only searching for an audience of youth. Theatregoround was an experimental venture designed specifically to take the work of the RSC out, and show it to sections of the population not normally exposed to theatre: the idea was to bring some of these people in to the theatres and in this way to break down some of the class barriers that separated the live theatre from other entertainment media.

The RSC Club was also formed to stimulate new audiences through offers of price reduction on seats and special concessions for block or party bookings. Kaye Flanagan, RSC Club Organizer, reports that there was an overwhelming response from many of the Midlands industrial centres (particularly the British Leyland works in Birmingham) during the early days of the Club. Coach parties of industrial workers would come to Stratford to see Shakespeare productions — an almost inconceivable notion during the fifties.

The company's new Barbican Theatre is architecturally planned to negate some of the social and economic suggestions of discrimination in theatre seating: all seats in the Barbican will be 'good' seats, and there will be an attempt to dispense with the accepted notions of 'stalls, circle and balcony'.

Between 1960 and 1968, Peter Hall found his 'new audience' — an audience that is now an accepted part of the company's life, and (in some ways) influences its production style. Black ties are still to be seen in both RSC theatres on occasions, but more often the audience is casually dressed and seem to view the theatrical experience as much more than simply a social occasion or an entertainment: 'The reasons people walk out into the rain to go to the theatre are at once more positive and more specialized.'[75] Youth undoubtedly predominates in the RSC audience, and this predominance has possibly increased since Trevor Nunn took control of the company. Although there has never been an official audience survey taken in the RSC, a 1964 National Theatre survey reported that 55 per cent of its audience were thirty-five years old — or younger.[76]

Interviewed in 1970, Ian Richardson said: 'The audience of the sixties were the teens, twenties and thirties . . . and still today, the under-thirties form the substantial bulk of RSC audiences. . . . They are now acknowledging the theatre as a true art form — something their parents never really did! The parents saw the theatre as a 'cultural/social' occasion. These kids come for an experience — and they are willing to embrace that experience totally.'[77]

6. Major Productions
1960-1968

The Royal Shakespeare Company must draw on the whole
spectrum of world drama, but this is not their complete
aim. Their work is rooted in Shakespeare, stems from
Shakespeare, and their purpose is to build a strong bridge
between the classical theatre and the truly popular theatre
of our time.

Statement of RSC policy, from the
Royal Shakespeare Company Programmes, 1964.

Between January 1960 and December 1968, the Royal Shakespeare Company under Peter Hall's direction staged over one
hundred separate productions, in Stratford, London, for television
and film, and on tour.[1] A detailed and thorough discussion of
each of these individual productions would be an obvious
impossibility within the scope and definition of this work. It is
therefore proposed to devote this chapter to the discussion of
certain outstanding elements in a series of major RSC productions, and in this way attempt to give some indication of the
pattern of artistic development within the company. Within this
stated aim, the author is constantly aware of the dangers of
over-simplification, omission, and extreme generalization.

In addition there arises the question of selection. What
constitutes a major production? Why should the 1962 production of *King Lear* be discussed to the exclusion of the 1961 *As
You Like It*? The only answer can be that these major productions
have not been selected solely because of their critical,
artistic or box-office success. It is more that each illustrates a
different or continuing aspect of the company's development, and
collectively they represent a reasonable and varied cross-section of
the RSC's scope of activity and achievement over the years in
question.

Peter Hall's production of *A Midsummer Night's Dream* — first
seen at Stratford in 1959 — is interesting in that it remained part

of the RSC repertoire over a period of nearly ten years. The 1959 *Dream* was revived twice on stage (in 1962 at Stratford and 1963 in London), was televised by the NBC network for American television in 1959, and was made into a full-length colour film by the RSC in 1968. This film was also televised in America during 1969. Naturally each revival carried with it certain cast changes, and there were various modifications to setting and action to suit existing conditions,[2] but, in essence, the basic production and design concepts remained virtually unaltered over this ten year period. This production must rank with *The Wars of the Roses* and *Hamlet* as one of Peter Hall's most successful Shakespeare productions. Certainly it was one of the most popular. Hall saw the production as one which would ' . . . take the play back to its beginnings. . . . For me, "Elizabethan" means splendours and conceits'.[3]

Lila de Nobili's setting centred around an Elizabethan court-yard, with a minstrels' gallery and steps to each side in heavily timbered oak. The slightly raked stage floor was covered in straw and parts of the basic permanent setting could be flown out to reveal a woodland setting behind — leafy green and romantic in mood. Kenneth Tynan saw the original 1959 production — with Charles Laughton as Bottom:

'With sound historical justification he [Hall] sees the play as an occasional piece intended for the celebration of a well-bred marriage; accordingly he deploys the action in the great hall of an Elizabethan manor house, which gradually, through the cunning of Lila de Nobili's decor, sprouts greenery and develops into a more or less credible forest. . . . His fairies are closely related to the lost boys of Peter Pan. . . . Admittedly they are clad somewhat like insects and one of them is without doubt a diminutive old lady. . . .'[4]

Gareth Lloyd Evans saw Hall's concept as an attractive but extremely traditional visual approach: 'A very traditional nineteenth century looking woodland. And this is interesting, because I've always felt that Hall had this hankering (visually) for nineteenth century opulent production. I think that is why he's interested in opera. . . . For all his "nowness", every now and then in a Hall production you come across an extraordinary piece of visual traditionalism, and this was certainly true of his *Dream*.'[5]

Tony Church emphatically disagreed with this criticism: 'The wood was a romantic sort of wood — a magic wood. But there were no live rabbits! And what happened in the wood was not at all romantic . . . the ferocity, spitefulness and sexiness of the fairies was something which the nineteenth century would *never* have allowed. Peter was avowedly *against* a nineteenth century sentimental version of *The Dream* . . .'[6]

Certainly there was nothing traditional in Hall's approach to the lovers: he treated them as modern teenagers — awkward, loud, and no respecters of person — much more 'twentieth century adolescent' than 'youngish Elizabethan courtier'. 'This is the point where, I fancy, the doctrinaires are likely to be shocked. For it means putting a modern gloss . . . on a good many of the lines.'[7]

Hall also included many pieces of stage business which represented a deliberate reversal of all the usual conventions: Flute, instead of speaking Thisbe's lines in falsetto, retained a shamefaced baritone, and doubly asserted his masculinity with a heavy pair of boots. Earlier productions had left unanswered the question of how Oberon slipped past the guard on Titania's bower, so Hall disposed of the matter by having one of Oberon's fairies cosh the sentry. During rehearsals for the mechanicals' play, Snug wandered off and started sniffing woodland flowers — only to be brought out of his reverie by the accusing silence of the others. The production placed the emphasis squarely on the comic aspects of the play and much of the stage business was designed to re-enforce this element.

The fairies too were completely unconventional. Hall saw them as ' . . . very sensual. They're sexy and wicked and kinky . . . they aren't pretty creatures hopping about: they have animal senses. I've always tried . . . to make them earthy, so that they're more sensual than the mortals'.[8] The stage fairies were costumed after the manner of Elizabethan courtiers, in beautiful shimmering greens, silvers and golds: but they were also barefoot, tousle-haired, wild-eyed, and slightly tattered in appearance. They were designed to look as if they belonged to, (and were part of), the wood. In Hall's film of *The Dream* he took the fairies a step further: they were almost naked (wearing only strategically-placed 'leaves'), dirty-faced, muddy, and painted all over in slimy, glistening green make-up.

The 1968 film version of Hall's *Dream* did not have the success of the stage production. Filming took place at Compton Verney (near Stratford) — most of it in extremely poor weather conditions — and many of the cast were also engaged in repertoire work in the Stratford theatre at the same time. For these, and a variety of other reasons, the film was an unhappy experience for most concerned with it. Judi Dench, who played Titania in the 1962 stage version and also in the film, said: 'When Peter asked me to do the film I was very excited, but when it actually came to acting in the woods, in mud, in November, in the rain — I found it impossible. I haven't seen that film, because I won't go! . . . although one was nearly naked, I didn't feel nearly as "sensual" as I did in that formal, cobwebby, stiff costume that Lila de Nobili designed . . . the film for me was a kind of hell!'[9]

It met with adverse critical reception when released and as a result received only a very limited distribution in Britain. Hall openly admitted that he was learning his trade as a film director: 'I'm an apprentice film director, I wouldn't presume to call myself more than that. . .'[10] and he also believed that 'the verbal essence of Shakespeare is inescapably non-cinematic'.[11] Much of the film was shot using a hand-held camera, and it also employed a great deal of close-up work — alternating with sudden long-distance shots. Both of these techniques (as Hall used them) resulted in a critical panning, but Hall retorted, ' . . . my first function is to serve the word and not the picture.'[12]

The Peter Hall/John Barton production of *Troilus and Cressida* in 1960 was also something of a revolution: the play had been only infrequently staged at Stratford (the last production was Glen Byam Shaw's in 1954) and it had seldom been particularly successful in theatrical terms. Tyrone Guthrie had directed a well-received, broadly satirical, version at the Old Vic in 1956, but, in general, *Troilus* was not considered to be a playable text. Its extraordinary compression of language and many discordant and contradictory elements had made it a play thought more suited to the study than the stage: 'It belongs, in short, to a period in Shakespeare's development in which the keenness of his apprehension of certain elements of experience . . . was not accompanied by a corresponding sense of order and significance.'[13]

The RSC directors saw the play as a theatrically vivid experience, with particular relevance to the political and moral climate of the early 1960's:

> 'Peter Hall and John Barton have not been satisfied with academic explanations . . . they have found a theatrical basis for it, and so, for perhaps the first time in our history, made *Troilus and Cressida* not merely a collection of beautiful speeches, but a planned, architected, coherent and powerful drama.'[14]

Leslie Hurry's design for *Troilus* was one of the simplest that had been seen at Stratford; the action moved over a huge octagonal shallow box filled with white sand, and the only backcloth was a cyclorama of a vague brown, 'dried-blood' colour. Some critics saw the sandpit as a simple gimmick:

> 'There's nothing basically wrong with playing *Troilus and Cressida*, one of the bitterest, most disenchanted and most potent of Shakespeare's brews in a sandpit, just as there would be nothing basically wrong with producing *Twelfth Night* on roller-skates . . . or *King Lear* in the nude . . . it is *that* sort of production. . . .'[15]

Others found the central sand image extremely powerful:

> 'Cressida ran the sand through her fingers when talking about time . . . and played in it with her feet. When people lay about on rugs it suggested an extraordinarily steamy and erotic mood. Ajax, sulking, made sand-pies, and it then became a child's sandbox. . . . When Hector was killed and dragged off covered in blood, one had a bull-ring image — with Hector as a bloody piece of meat. . . . It was the most powerful design image I've ever seen.'[16]

The simplicity of the *Troilus* design marked the beginnings of a trend which was to become an RSC trademark over the sixties; floor textures, simple images and properties became increasingly important — replacing the elaborate stage 'settings' of the fifties:

'Peter wanted to strip out design as an overlay . . . something that confined or got on top of a production. He wanted simpler, more austere, more selective design.'[17]

Hall and Barton carried this austerity into the production, deliberately ripping any heroic qualities from the play, and playing the text as an expression of the disillusionment of Shakespeare's middle-age. The comic tone was made intensely ironic, and it was played as a savage satire on heroes and romantic love in a world of cynics and egotists. In these terms the play became extremely meaningful to the audiences of 1960, and *Troilus* was one of the first and most obvious examples of Hall's plan to express Shakespeare in terms of twentieth century immediacy — to make his productions speak for 'now'.

One of Peter Hall's earliest policy announcements included the statement that the RSC intended to commission a number of plays from modern dramatists, and to free them from the restrictions and limitations normally imposed by the demands of commercial theatre.

The first play to be commissioned under this policy was John Whiting's *The Devils*: the play was based on Aldous Huxley's novel *The Devils of Loudun*, a story of Urbain Grandier, a curé of Loudun in seventeenth century France, a degenerate libertine — but tragic in that he finally faced humiliation and death at the hands of his enemies on a trumped-up charge of witchcraft and satanic possession of nuns. Whiting was acknowledged in Britain as a dramatist of rare talent, ' . . . the forerunner of a new generation of English playwrights, but dogged by ill luck ever since his emergence ten years ago.'[18] His previous works (including *Saint's Day, A Penny for a Song* and *Marching Song*) had been so severely manhandled by the critics that Whiting had written nothing for the stage in the five years prior to *The Devils*. Peter Hall's admiration for Whiting's work began at Cambridge where, as an undergraduate, he had directed *Saint's Day* and *A Penny for a Song*. Ten years later he commissioned Whiting to write for the RSC:

'I could have written *The Devils* with one set and five characters and put it on in a smaller theatre . . . I hope more plays on this scale can be commissioned. I was given everything I wanted. No compromise whatsoever was made. How many English playwrights in the last three hundred years have been given the kind of opportunity that Peter Hall gave me? . . . there are many playwrights who could write a large scale narrative play if someone offered them a stage and a company. Fashion has moved too far towards the unplotted, un-motivated play — it's restricting the size of the drama.'[19]

Whiting conceived *The Devils* on an epic scale, with the action to be conducted in a series of interlocking short scenes: 'Not one word or one scene is wasted. The language is sober, spare, clean, exact, and it carries us at once into a world where such things can happen.'[20] For the RSC's production at the Aldwych in 1961, Sean Kenny designed an impressionistic arrangement of gauzes, beams and prison bars, and Peter Wood directed his cast through the complex text with an eye to fluidity — one scene overlapping another as the play demanded — and deftly underscoring action and scene change with music and sound-effect. 'It must have presented immense production difficulties, but it is magnificently served by the company, unerringly guided at every stage.'[21] Not all critical response to *The Devils* was favourable:

' . . . one is here unquestionably in the climate of a "great" play . . . [but] . . . this piece of history, for all Mr Whiting's skill and elevation of thought, refuses to bend into a dramatic shape.'[22]

However, most critics recognized the importance of *The Devils* as the beginnings of a new freedom for working playwrights, and were quick to recognize the contribution of the RSC in making the achievement possible:

'Playgoers fortunate enough to attend the first night of *The Devils* enjoyed the rarest of all theatrical experiences — they witnessed the birth of a masterpiece. They saw too, in living terms, the vindication of the idea of a National Theatre, for John Whiting's personal triumph cannot be dissociated from the policy of the Stratford company which created the conditions necessary for its achievement. . . Here was an invitation to write for a large company working together as a permanent team, to write for an unrestricted form of staging that would allow him to give full rein to his imagination, and to write a play on any subject and in any style he chose. This was the answer to the dramatist's prayer. . . .'[23]

The Devils began the RSC's policy of encouraging and presenting the works of new and emergent playwrights. Dramatists including Harold Pinter, Henry Livings, David Rudkin, Giles Cooper and John Arden have had new works premiered by the RSC, the

company's association with Pinter particularly was richly rewarding. Since John Whiting's death in 1963, his plays have achieved
the recognition denied them during his lifetime, and *The Devils*
has recently been made into a highly successful (and controversial)
motion picture.[24] The RSC have also produced further Whiting
plays — *A Penny for a Song* at the Aldwych in 1962, and a revival
of *The Devils* at the Aldwych and on tour.

During 1962, as part of his policy to present both classical and
modern drama side by side, Hall took a lease on the Arts Theatre
in London, intending to use it as a venue for plays of an
experimental nature, and also to try out new playwrights, actors,
directors, production and design ideas. Several important new
works were presented during the season, and two of the Arts
productions, Middleton's Jacobean classic *Women Beware Women*
and David Rudkin's new play *Afore Night Come* were later
included in the main RSC repertoire.[25]

Afore Night Come was the first play to be written by David
Rudkin, a school teacher from Birmingham. In genre, it was
loosely associated with the Theatre of Cruelty phase in British
drama (although written before the actual *Theatre of Cruelty*
seasons by the RSC) and was more strongly associated with a type
of ritualistic theatre. Clifford Williams, who directed the play,
said: 'I think that *Afore Night Come* was interesting in that we (at
the RSC) have always talked about our modern theatre and our
classical theatre being complementary to each other . . . it is a play
which uses language in a classical manner; although it's written in
prose, it's really poetry.'[26]

Set during the harvest season in a Worcestershire pear orchard,
the play explores the build-up and explosion of primitive
emotions — and culminates in a brutal and theatrically terrifying
ritual murder.

'The landscape is peopled by The Group, though they are less
people than an uneasy balance of tensions evolved among the
regular workers on the farm . . . They are joined, and the
balance is disrupted, by the appearance of three Outsiders,
casual workers. There is Larry, the aloof student who is
merely tolerated; Jeff, the city "Ted" who is accepted; and
Roche, the Irish tramp who suffers from laziness and
imagination — both a threat to the life and prejudices of the

Tribe. He provokes first mockery, then a certain pity, and finally uncontrollable hate and murder.'[27]

Roche is decapitated and his head impaled on a pitchfork — to the accompanying sound of a crop-dusting helicopter droning overhead in the darkening sky; the blood-letting is done, and sacrifice made, the foreign element is eradicated, and the Group is purged. Clifford Williams explained the central theme of the play: 'It wasn't really and finally about a group of chaps in a Worchestershire orchard. It went deeper into the blood than that. . . . This sort of operation (which is almost essential for people to preserve their sanity) goes on everywhere. It goes on in rehearsal rooms, it goes on on the factory floor — it went on in that pear orchard. This blood-letting! And letting the blood of the foreign element is simply an element within the human make-up.'[28]

The Lord Chamberlain objected to many of the words to be used in the Aldwych production of the play, but the majority of critics were impressed and enthusiastic about the dramatic power and sheer theatricality of the piece:

'. . . on stage, the severed head of an old tramp, ritually sacrificed on a rubbish dump behind a pear tree, was slowly rolled in a furry ball towards the footlights. . . . Despite some clumsiness of construction, a certain self-conscious bravado of vocabulary, and a great deal of confused incoherence of accent, *Afore Night Come* is a fearsome witches-sabbath of an evening.'[29]

And Kenneth Tynan said, ' . . . not since *Look Back in Anger* has a playwright made a debut more striking than this.'[30]

As a result of the 1962 production of *Afore Night Come*, David Rudkin was named winner of the Evening Standard Drama Award for the most promising playwright of the year. Peter Hall found the 1962 season — and particularly *Afore Night Come* — a useful preliminary experiment which aided his later work on *The Wars of the Roses*: 'I wanted to examine some aspects of man's deep instinctive lusts, even if this took us into the realms of horror. The plays of David Rudkin, Fred Watson, Boris Vian, and also Middleton's *Women Beware Women* — an Elizabethan example — all aided this investigation, and the findings certainly helped me to understand the ritual and violence of Shakespeare's *Henry VI* plays.'[31]

Much has been written about Peter Brook's extraordinary production of *King Lear* (1962), with Paul Scofield in the title role. The production was given extensive press coverage at the time, and numerous articles and exchanges of critical comment appeared in magazines and periodicals for months afterwards: it is still considered to be one of the great productions of this play — and possibly the definitive *Lear* of our time. Tynan said: 'This production brings me closer to Lear than I have ever been; from now on I not only know him, but can place him in his harsh and unforgiving world.'[32] Charles Marowitz, who acted as Brook's assistant director on the production, compiled a progress report of the play in rehearsal, which was later published under the title of *Lear Log*.[33] This unique document provides a first-hand guide to the actual processes involved in the making of the production, and some key to the relationship between Brook and his actors:

'For Brook, *Lear* is a series of intellectual strands which only performance can tie together. Far from being an "unactable" play, he believes its full meaning can only be comprehended existentially — on a stage. He sees it mainly as a play about sight and blindness. . . . In discussing the work of rehearsals, our frame of reference was always Beckettian. The world of this *Lear*, like Beckett's, is in a constant state of decomposition.'[34]

The various interpretative elements which went into the creation of Brook's *Lear* are too numerous and complex to discuss in the space of a few pages. However, there are certain points which are of primary relevance. Later critics of the production have noted the influence of Jan Kott in Brook's *Lear*: it is known that Brook had read (and reportedly been impressed by) *Shakespeare Our Contemporary*[35] before he began the *Lear* rehearsals — although the book had not been published in English at that time. Kott saw certain parallels between tragedy and the grotesque; he related these to *King Lear* and to the work of Samuel Beckett:

'Tragedy is the theatre of priests, grotesque is the theatre of clowns. . . . When established values have been overthrown, and there is no appeal to God, Nature or History from the tortures inflicted by the cruel world, the clown becomes the central figure in the theatre.'[36]

Kott, when discussing *Lear*, also makes frequent reference to the necessity for an empty stage. Brook himself designed the setting for *Lear*: the Stratford stage was surrounded by a series of tall, coarse-textured, off-white screens, and against these were set shapes of metal – rusted, flaking and suggestive of a state of decomposition. The costumes were predominantly leather – textured to suggest long use and wear, and the minimal stage furniture was made in rough, dark wood. One of the most remarkable and effective features of the production was this bare, primitive, setting – and the way in which Brook used it:

> 'I am absolutely incapable of solving a production other than through the scenery. The set is a summing up of everything that one has felt and studied in a production . . . the set is like an "essence" of the play which, if it's wrong, defeats you all the time. The well designed set opens all possibilities . . . I worked on the *Lear* set for about a year, and eventually certain things became clear. . . . It seemed to me absolutely essential that the play should have a contrast between indoors and out. There had to be a feeling of walls, but there also had to be a feeling of space. . . .'[37]

Throughout the production, Brook constantly asked for the audience's imagination, and many critics commented on a marked Brechtian influence in the staging: ' . . . the storm scene stems from the East. Peter Brook lowers three rectangular sheets of metal which tremble in the air, while the actors on the empty stage beneath mime their battle with wind and rain.'[38] These thunder sheets were mechanically operated from backstage; Tony Church has speculated that if Brook were to do *Lear* now, he would probably have these sheets operated by his actors in full view of the audience.[39] Brook used harsh white stage lighting throughout – even during the storm scene – and there was no background music at all, except at the very end when the text actually demands it.

A further Brechtian device was Brook's insistence on the removal of any sympathy or identification which the audience might feel. Immediately following the blinding of Gloucester (and just before the interval) the house-lights were brought up and the action continued in full lighting for some minutes: 'Gloucester is covered with a tattered rag and shoved off in the direction of Dover. Servants clearing the stage collide with the confused blind man and rudely shove him aside.'[40] Brook also cut the exchange of disapproving dialogue between the second and third servants which, in the text, follows and cushions the horror of the blinding.

Paul Scofield's performance was considered more intellectual than emotional: 'Scofield circled Lear like a wary challenger measuring out an unbeaten opponent, and it was apparent from the start that this challenger was a strategist rather than a slugger'.[41] His Lear was not the usual ancient older-than-God king of past productions, but a dominating, rugged figure with grey, close-cropped hair — a man still at the height of his physical and intellectual powers. 'Spurned by his daughters, Lear loses his wits purely in order to punish them: "I shall go mad!" is a threat, not a pathetic prediction.'[42] Tynan saw the Lear of the hovel scene as 'a rustic vagabond: cf. the classless derelicts of Samuel Beckett, and especially the crippled hero of *End-Game*'.[43] Scofield's Lear elicited no pity — merely a sort of condemnation of the man's stupidity: at the conclusion he achieved a wisdom denied him in his sanity; '. . . a Stoic determination, long in the moulding, to endure his going hence. . . .'[44]

The Brook/Scofield *Lear* (together with Clifford Williams' production of *The Comedy of Errors*) toured Europe, the Soviet Union and America during 1964, and was made into a motion picture in 1968/69. This film — much of the shooting done in Denmark using Danish extras and crew — was released in Britain during 1971.[45] The 1962 production of *Lear* is now generally regarded as one of the highest points of RSC achievement over the sixties, and a great deal of the company's later Shakespeare work has been influenced by it.

Tony Church, who played Cornwall in the original production, said: 'Anything that one did on that great bare stage became fantastically selective. This was one of the first really "bare stage" productions that we'd done, and in that sense it was seminal to a great deal of the work that's happened since . . . the text of the play was explored, and worried, and felt, and teased: I believe that *Lear* was the first example at the RSC of really "breaking down" a text and actually "feeling the way" into it. This has now become an RSC trademark. . . . Brook's little mandarin figure sitting there . . . produces an extraordinary concentration. Every line was a minefield . . . one couldn't charge through it. One had to pick out the *exact* meaning of an image and the *exact* meaning of a thought.'[46]

In 1963 the RSC staged *The Wars of the Roses — Henry VI* and *Richard III* adapted to form three plays — and in the following year the history plays from *Richard II* to *Henry V* were added to the repertoire, and the company presented Shakespeare's complete cycle of history plays from *Richard II* to *Richard III* — a feat unique in the history of the English theatre. Each of the seven plays was complete in itself and could be presented in isolation from the rest, but for the first time ever it was possible to see Shakespeare's whole complex scheme from start to finish, and to see clearly and understand the relationship between the component parts: 'Behind immense variety, the themes and characters are continuously developed through the cycle. As Orestes was hunted in Greek drama, so Englishmen fight each other to expunge the curse pronounced upon Bolingbroke's usurpation of the tragically weak Richard II.'[47]

The entire History Cycle was directed by Peter Hall, with John Barton, Clifford Williams, Peter Wood[48] and Frank Evans acting as his co-directors. John Bury designed a unique series of metallic settings for the cycle, using the central steel image: ' . . . surrounding all, the great steel cage of war.'[49] Bury said: 'It was a period of armour and a period of the sword; they were plays about warfare, about power, about danger. . . . And this was the 'image'. We wanted an image rather than a naturalistic surrounding . . . we were trying to make a world; a dangerous world, a terrible world, in which all these happenings would fit.'[50] The metallic image of the English Court changed from king to king, and Bury summarized this development in the 1964 programmes:

Richard II — the overgrown garden of England, the court a tarnished jewel.

Henry IV — the introduction of the steel palace, the countryside grown rusty.

Henry V — the polished steel of England; in France, a golden court and countryside.

Henry VI — a stone saint dominates the English court.

Edward IV — the sun-covered golden drapes in a moment of brief flamboyance, before . . .

Richard III — and the bunker.[51]

Trevor Nunn's production of *The Revenger's Tragedy* at Stratford 1967. *L. to R.:* Ian Richardson as Vendice, Nicholas Selby as the Duke, and Patrick Stewart as Hippolito.

The Jew of Malta directed by Clifford Williams at the Aldwych in 1964, with John Steiner as Mathias and Doris Hare as his mother Katharine.

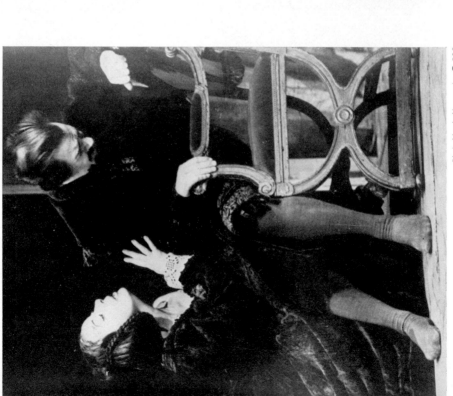

Women Beware Women directed by Anthony Page at the Arts Theatre in 1962. Pauline Jameson as Livia and Trevor Martin as Hippolito.

The stage was floored in steel plate, and on either side of the acting area there were enormous triangular 'periaktoi' towers; these had metallic faces which could be turned to present a different face to the audience, and could also be swung in at different angles to modify the shape of the acting area. To the left of the stage there was a huge metallic wall, in which was set vast double doors. This too could be altered in position to diminish or increase the shape of the acting area, and for the battle scenes the entire set could be swung off to allow a completely bare stage. The metallic theme was carried through to the costumes, and the bright steel of Lancaster and York became rusted and corroded with the passing of years: 'Colour drains and drains from the stage until, among the drying patches of scarlet blood, the black night of England settles on the leather costumes of Richard's thugs.'[52] Bury's designs for *The Wars of the Roses* represented an important step forward in visual development at the RSC: 'Bury, in conception and use of materials opened a new world for us . . . a new sort of realism was achieved. The Histories have influenced much of our design since. . . .'[53]

Peter Hall gave his reasons for wishing to present the complete Histories as mainly political; his article, *Blood Will Have Blood*, printed in the 1964 *Henry VI* programme, sets out his thoughts on the relationship between politics and violence in the plays. Undoubtedly the political situations and manoeuverings within the plays intrigued him, but the productions were also very closely related to his 'Now' policy:

> 'Over the years I became more and more fascinated by the contortions of politicians and by the corrupting seductions experienced by anyone who wields power . . . I realized that the mechanism of power had not changed in centuries. We also were in the middle of a blood-soaked century. I was convinced that a presentation of one of the bloodiest and most hypocritical periods of history would teach many lessons about the present.'[54]

John Kane, who was a junior actor with the company at the time of *The Wars of the Roses*, said: 'You could understand exactly what everybody was doing and why they were doing it, because it was a social and political (very political) production of the plays. You could see the power machine, the emphasis on the Throne, on the Crown, on the conference table in front of the Throne. All that was so beautifully explicit. . . . He [Hall] used big swords, but when those big swords came out they were symbols of power; when Warwick and York met (from either side of the stage) with those enormous swords, you realized that these were the "power men". . . .'[55]

One of the most interesting features of *The Wars of the Roses* and the 1964 Histories was that the finished product was a work of collaboration, and not merely the production of a single director. The joint direction principle was one of Peter Hall's early ideas for the RSC's development, but *The Wars of the Roses* was the first major production in which it was actually practised.'[56] Clifford Williams explained how the principle worked: 'It was an impossible task for one director . . . we knew each other very well, and that meant that we had (long before) accepted our differences in personality, our different ways of talking and our different ways of thinking . . . also there was an overall chairmanship exercised by Peter Hall over the productions. . . . We had talked for a long time about how to split the load in rehearsal.'[57]

In the middle of rehearsals for the 1963 *Wars of the Roses*, Peter Hall was taken ill, and John Barton and Frank Evans took over rehearsals until Hall was able to return to the theatre. In 1964 (with a total of seven plays to work on) the rehearsal load was split between Hall, Barton and Williams, with Evans and Wood assisting. The plays were divided into scenes and each director was responsible for a given set of scenes — or for the overall development of a particular character throughout the cycle. When the time came to put the various plays, scenes and characters together as a whole and finished production, the overall concept was 'chaired' by Peter Hall, and he had the final word on my last-minute differences or difficulties which arose over the completed stage product:

> 'The Hall method of collective direction is exciting. Without such delegation of direction, the development of minor parts, hitherto relegated to satellite attendance on the star, would be impossible. The amount of thought, both about individual performance and the significance of the plays as a whole, is increased by the contribution of creative minds, conducted like an orchestra by Hall himself.'[58]

The Wars of the Roses is considered by most people connected with the RSC, and by many critics and theatre writers, to be the crowning achievement of the company under Hall's direction. Ian Richardson echoed an almost unanimous 'internal' viewpoint when he said: 'The most influential single event in those years was, without doubt, *The Wars of the Roses* cycle of plays. There had been earlier edited versions of this cycle, but it had never before been presented in this way — this revolutionary way. . . . *The Wars of the Roses* was the pinnacle of the RSC's achievement over the sixties — never to be bettered.'[59]

Hall's fascination with politics and political structures was further expounded in his 1965 production of *Hamlet*, which was in many ways, a natural growth out of the pre-occupations of *The Wars of the Roses*.

In a recent interview, Hall said:

'One lives in one's own time and cannot escape it. We don't even know what an Elizabethan interpretation of *Hamlet* was . . . you should approach a classic with the maximum of scholarship you can muster — and then you honestly try to interpret what you think it means to a person living now. . . . Given 1965, the RSC, its audience, all one's knowledge of *Hamlet* — we showed what had to emerge. I saw *Hamlet* as a very political play. . . . Equally, I remembered that in 1965 one thought that the young were very very misunderstood by their elders. We thought them beautiful, tolerant, quiet. They were flower children whose very generosity at times seemed to be apathy. One couldn't get them to react to very much . . . there *is* apathy in *Hamlet* — he feels that the older generation have betrayed him.'[60]

In Hall's production, an 'apathetic' Hamlet was pitted against the Establishment: ' . . . this enormous political machine, Claudius, the super-master politician, surrounded by Polonius and all his advisers. And then Polonius had his own Secretary, and there were Councillors who had secretaries, and the secretaries had secretaries. . . .'[61] Hall's political structure and society were clearly set out in the production, and he spent a great deal of rehearsal time making sure that each actor in the company knew his function within that society.[62] Claudius was represented as a type of modern politician — a thoroughly competent and charming king, albeit a man with his eye to the main chance; Gertrude was seen as, '. . . a big, sexy, mindless creature who couldn't quite comprehend what was going on. . . .'[63] Elizabeth Spriggs, who played the part, said: 'Gertrude was a pawn in the game . . . the same way that Anne in *Richard III* is a pawn. . . . These royal ladies don't have any minds of their own. They're not allowed to have. . . .'[64] Polonius, with the whole Court hierarchy set out beneath him, was an old and knowing politician — '. . . a man who'd sniffed along the corridors of power for years . . .'[65] — and, within Hall's context, a representative of the 'dying generation'. Tony Church, who played Polonius, said: 'I thought that Harold Macmillan was a splendid example of Polonius (and here I thought in terms of 1965) . . . The disease that these sort of people are prone to is being too clever, *not* too stupid. It is a frequent and well-established device of Establishment politicians to laugh at themselves. I worked on the assumption that Polonius was well aware of this. We played a man who was sharp, clever and dangerous. Because these men *are* dangerous — the Establishment is dangerous! Particularly when it's being charming or funny.'[66]

The set was an open, black, shining 'box', with two huge doors opening at the rear, and two inner rooms set off it at either side: 'John Bury's design was enclosed and impervious — a huge black funnel — like the Establishment'.[67] The basic material used was black formica, and the side rooms were decorated with huge fading tapestries — suggesting a vaguely Victorian mood. Costume colours were subdued reds, silvers and blacks, and the entire Court were robed in a pin-striped material, to suggest a world of officialdom. The *Hamlet* costumes were, in a sense, 'timeless'; although the 'line' was Tudor, the 'image' was Victorian-political, and this method of costume design has since come to be associated with many RSC Shakespeare productions — particularly the Ghost: old Hamlet was presented as an armoured 'puppet' figure, almost ten feet high, with huge artificial head, moveable arms, and a long gown which reached the floor to hide the base-platform and wheeling mechanism which supported it. Patrick Magee (playing the Ghost) spoke his lines from a platform inside this figure, while it was moved about by a stagehand underneath.

Claudius, Polonius and the Court were clearly the Establishment, and Hamlet was in rebellion against the Establishment — but at the same time utterly overwhelmed by it and unable to take any effective action against it: 'Hamlet and Ophelia represented that apathy of will that the pressure of the Establishment was causing in the young people of the time. David Warner saw Hamlet as a young man who couldn't get out of the system.'[68]

In casting David Warner as the Prince, Hall (in terms of his declared intention) made an ideal choice. Having achieved considerable critical recognition for his performance as Henry VI in *The Wars of the Roses*, Warner as Hamlet, became an extraordinary symbol of identification for the predominantly young audiences which saw the production. He had an enormous following of young people who would crowd at the stage door to see him and queue all night around the theatre in order to see a performance on the following day. Elizabeth Spriggs said: 'They came rather like they do when they follow pop-singers. . . . He became a cult. . . . At the end of the play they just went mad. Outside the stage door there were hundreds. David used to have to be smuggled out of the theatre. . . .'[69] Tony Church commented: ' . . . they recognized themselves in David. He was one of them and they felt that he was a hero speaking for them. So many very young people told me that for the first time they had understood and felt every word of it.'[70] Warner's Hamlet was tall and gangling, and he wore a long scarf around his neck suggesting a student-type in the angry-young-man image. His interpretation was suggestive of a frightened, bewildered young man who was, more than anything else, affronted by the way in which his elders had let down his generation.

Gareth Lloyd Evans, an avowed critic of this particular production, said: 'Warner's Hamlet appealed terrifically to the teenager of '65. It responded to their sense of — you know — "God's gone!" Warner looked thin and hungry and pockmarked — just like some of the kids that were wandering around at the time. And the mumbling way he talked. . . . It was a production of great theatrical effect which was, to a very great extent, counter to the reality of the play. Part of me says, "God, how awful that Hall should have done this!", and the other part says, "But he managed to get a hell of a lot of teenagers into the theatre who would never otherwise have got there".'[71] Harold Hobson wrote in *The*

Sunday Times: 'If Hamlet is condemned, God is on trial also.'[72], and John Trewin, reviewing the production for *The Birmingham Post*, said:

'Young people in last night's Stratford audience would show by their overwhelming cheers at the close, that David Warner was the Hamlet of their imagination and their heart. Many of their elders, I think, will hesitate ... [But] this contemporary image clearly pleased young play-goers of the decade, whatever their successors may think of it.'[73]

The phrase 'Theatre of Cruelty' was coined by the French poet, play-wright, àctor, director and theatre visionary, Antonin Artaud (1896-1948). Throughout his life, he was obsessed with the feeling that something crucial was missing from life and art in Europe; he believed that in an era of restlessness, only a 'theatre of cruelty', addressing itself to the nerves and senses, could bring men 'back to the real dimension of existence'. In the collection of essays entitled *The Theatre and Its Double*, Artaud sets out his now-famous manifesto of 'cruelty':

' ... I do believe theatre, used in the highest and most difficult sense has the power to affect the appearance and structure of things ... as soon as I said "cruelty" everyone took it to mean "blood". But a "theatre of cruelty" means theatre that is difficult and cruel for myself first of all. And on a performing level it has nothing to do with cruelty we practise on one another, hacking at each other's bodies ... but the far more terrible, essential cruelty objects can practise on us. We are not free and the sky can still fall on our heads. And above all else, theatre is made to teach us this.'[74]

Artaud also believed that words had become over-important in the theatre, and envisaged a theatre 'language' in which non-verbal, physical means of expression took precedence over all other forms. In 1963, Peter Brook and the RSC conducted a series of experiments which found their beginnings in Artaud's doctrines. Jerzy Grotowski, the eminent Polish director who shares many of Brook's ideas on theatre, wrote in *Flourish*:

'We are entering the age of Artaud. The "theatre of cruelty" has been canonised, i.e., made trivial, swapped for trinkets, tortured in various ways. When an eminent creator with an individual style and personality like Peter Brook, turns to Artaud, it's not to hide his own weaknesses or to ape the man. It just happens that at a given point in his development he finds himself in agreement with Artaud, feels the need of a confrontation, tests Artaud, and retains whatever stands up to this test.'[75]

Brook gathered together a group of twelve actors from the RSC, and began to work on his experimental programme — which he named *Theatre of Cruelty*. In the experiment, he was also assisted by various people (including Charles Marowitz) who were interested in experiment and the exploration and re-examination of accepted theatre forms. From the outset, Brook's project was totally subsidized by the RSC which provided enough backing to cover all costs — even if no tickets were sold. Brook believed that the experiment would only be valid if the people involved could work in complete freedom and relaxation, and in this the RSC management supported him: ' . . . because they believe that experiment must be a vital part of the company's work if it is to remain open to all the contemporary influences which should be acting upon it.'[76]

The basic ideas behind the experiment are set out in the pamphlet/programme, *Theatre of Cruelty*, published by the RSC in 1964, and the actual project involved the actors and directors in some months of improvisation, exploratory work with mime, physical and vocal exercises, and testing and re-discovery of various theatrical forms and devices. All this work was carried out under laboratory conditions, and *Theatre of Cruelty* was first presented at the LAMDA Theatre Studio in March 1963 — but the actual experiment was designed to continue in private well beyond this initial public showing. Brook explained why he decided to show the experiment at all:

'Why are we showing this experiment to an audience? Because no theatre experience is complete without that third element, because we need their reactions, we want to see how far we can stir their ideas. We need them to test their reactions just as much as we test our actions. . . . This experimental group is not a shop window for star-spotters, but a team that hopes to be accepted as a team. . . .'[77]

The various techniques, processes and experiments involved in the *Theatre of Cruelty* experiment are set out by Charles Marowitz in *Theatre at Work*.[78] The first public presentation included a twenty minute collage *Hamlet* contributed by Marowitz,[79] part of Genet's *The Screens*, a fragmentary suggestion from Artaud entitled *The Spurt of Blood*, and a series of word-games, acrobatics, mime sequences and experiments in ritual. *Theatre of Cruelty* was shown again at LAMDA in early 1964, and this showing included material from John Arden (a new short play, *Ars Longa Vita Brevis*); Shakespeare (the wooing sequence from *Richard III* — with Richard and Lady Anne communicating only through gesture and facial expression); a piece by Brook called *The Guillotine* (a post-decapitation dialogue between a head and a writhing trunk); some comic scenes from Artaud's career; the recital of a letter from the Lord Chamberlain to the RSC in which he listed cuts for a proposed full-scale Aldwych production of *The Screens*;[80] a series of nonsense-logic duologues which were improvised nightly; and a five minute play called *The Public Bath*, in which a girl stripped and bathed on stage to accompanying dialogue:

> 'The girl in the bath — an unknown 26-year old actress named Glenda Jackson — represents both Christine Keeler and Jacqueline Kennedy. And in the play, devised by Mr Brook, the same phrases — all from *The Times* report of the Keeler trial — are used to refer to both women . . . "an experiment in attitudes showing how the public can, in the same way, make a scapegoat of one woman and a saint of another. An experiment in words — the same words spoken by the same person, can have entirely opposite meanings when applied to different people . . .".'[81]

Reviews for the *Theatre of Cruelty* showings varied from mixed to bad: *The Times* was unenthusiastic, while applauding the RSC's attempt to nourish the 'British avant-garde'; *The Yorkshire Post* headed its review, 'Four Letter Words and Striptease'; and J.L. Styan, reviewing for *Plays and Players* felt that although the ideas behind the experiment had merit, the actual material shown left much to be desired. Yet Styan recognized that which most other critics failed to acknowledge — the fact that Brook had explicitly stated that *Theatre of Cruelty* was *not* intended to be a public performance of an RSC production; it was an experimental showing which anyone — including the critics — who cared to, would be welcome to come and see. Styan said: 'We were privileged eavesdroppers upon the uninhibited, but very right and proper, activities of actors in mock rehearsal.'[82]

The real importance of the 1963 and 1964 *Theatre of Cruelty* showings is that this experiment marked the beginnings of some of the most outstanding and sensational work that the RSC presented during the following years. Brook's original group of actors remained largely together — joined by other members of the RSC — for his production of *Marat-Sade*, and some of the original *Cruelty* group later took part in his *US*. Many of the ideas, concepts, theatrical techniques and acting methods which evolved during the *Cruelty* experiment found their way into later productions — both modern and Shakespeare — by the RSC. Brook's controversial 1964 production of *Marat-Sade* stemmed directly from the *Cruelty* work; indeed this production was in the planning stage during the *Cruelty* experiment, and was the natural conclusion to the group's activities: 'The *Marat-Sade* marked the dissolution of the group, or rather its assimilation into the larger company — the end for which it was intended.'[83] In August 1964, Eric Johns interviewed Peter Brook for *Theatre World*, and Brook (speaking of the *Cruelty* season and the forthcoming *Marat-Sade*) said:

> 'Actors have become masters of words . . . but we want our Royal Shakespeare training to show them how to use their bodies and to make use of other sounds, sounds other than words, of which they have had no experience. In this way, we hope to open up the language of the actor, in readiness for any eventuality . . . our recent performances at LAMDA and Donmar will make it easier for actors to put across the Peter Weiss play.'[84]

Peter Weiss's *Marat-Sade*[85] was undoubtedly the most sensational production staged by the RSC during the sixties: 'Weiss acknowledged Artaud as his mentor. . . . Artaud had played Marat in a film for Abel Gance . . . sound and "happenings" were embedded in the play. . . .'[86] The *Marat-Sade* is written in the form of a play within a play — acted by the lunatic inmates of Charenton Asylum, and directed by the Marquis de Sade.

Confined to Charenton by order of Napoleon, the ageing de Sade devoted his last years to staging productions of his own works, which the inmates performed before the director of the institution and members of the Parisian public. Set in the bath-house of the asylum — with the Director, de Sade, and assorted ladies and gentlemen as 'audience', the play-within-the-play depicts events leading up to the murder of Marat by Charlotte Corday at the height of the Terror during the French Revolution. Weiss intended the content of his play to represent 'the merging of political and psychological action which derives from Europe's experience of the Nazi death camps . . . less about the mechanics of revolution than about the regimes which lead countries into the equivalent of a pornographic dream'.[87]

However, Weiss's didactic purpose seemed of very secondary consideration when compared with the sheer theatricality of the piece, and it was the theatrical possibilities which fascinated Brook:

'This is a play which might have been written for Mr Brook. Everything which he has been doing for the past five years is piled in to brilliant effort. No props are employed, but Marat's hip-bath and the usual paraphernalia of a bath house: from these he has constructed the most tremendous scenes of hysteria, tragedy and violence. . . .'[88]

At times, Brook's stage was a scene of the most complete madness and anarchy: effects included a mass execution complete with buckets of blood; the symbolic whipping of de Sade by Charlotte Corday who used her own hair for the purpose; an anonymous white crowd of madmen surging forward in a berserk frenzy — with seeming intent to assault both stage and actual audience; a trio of deranged singers dressed in the *commedia dell' arte* style; and background musical effects (by Richard Peaslee) which, 'mirrors the grotesque figures of the actors with harsh bell and organ sonorities, and sets bloodthirsty events in the idiom of Lully'.[89] The actual murder of Marat was an exercise in ritual theatre, played before a background of mounting hysteria and screeching lunacy. Reviewing *Marat-Sade*, Bernard Levin said:

'Its breadth, its totality, its breathtakingly rapid and varied use of every imaginable technique, dramatic device, stage picture, form of movement, speech and song, make it as close

as this imperfect world is ever likely to get to the
"Gesamtkunstwerk" of which Richard Wagner dreamed, in
which every element, every force, that the theatre could
provide would fuse in one overwhelming experience."[90]

For Brook's actors, the *Marat-Sade* was an exhausting – and often
personally terrifying – experience. Brook conducted rehearsals in
an atmosphere of complete privacy to allow the actors freedom to
experiment with various forms of madness and lunatic ritual. He
was aware of the dangerous nature of the 'experiment in lunacy'
which he was allowing his group to undergo: during one rehearsal,
a particular actress gave herself what appeared to be an extremely
terrifying (simulated) epileptic fit – so terrifying in fact, that
Brook and others watching felt that she was nearing a very
dangerous stage. Brook immediately stopped the particular experiment and requested the actress never to move into that territory
again. Morgan Sheppard said of the production: 'I would say that
it probably *did* damage certain people. It damaged me in a
way.... It revealed one's psyche to oneself in a way which (for
many of us) came as rather a shock. One wasn't quite able to cope
with one's own inner violences and "nastinesses".... Brook was
enormously concerned with the dangers involved, but, like all
people, he became excited if one was breaking into new
territory...."[91]

Although most reviewers were stunned by the dramatic powers
and stage spectacle of *Marat-Sade*, not all critics found the RSC's
ventures into the realms of cruelty valid:

'Last year the Grand Guignol in Paris closed down, and one
quite understands why. Its functions have been taken over by
institutions of greater repute . . . the emphasis on cruelty is
part of the climate we live in, and nothing is to be gained by
recoiling from it in distaste. But the duty of discrimination
remains. How far is this or that playwright cashing in on the
climate. Is he exploring it; or merely exploiting it?'[92]

Whether by accident or design, nearly every play staged by the
RSC during 1964 was, in some way, influenced by 'cruelty': there
was cruelty, mental and/or physical; violence and/or implied; and
'vulgarity', both Elizabethan and modern. During the year, the
company's productions included the *Richard II* to *Richard III*
history cycle at Stratford; Pinter's *The Birthday Party*, Rudkin's

Afore Night Come, Beckett's *Endgame*, Vitrac's *Victor*, Marlowe's *The Jew of Malta* and Weiss's *Marat-Sade* at the Aldwych; and *Theatre of Cruelty* at LAMDA and *The Screens* at Donmar. One result of the 1964 season was the Dirty Plays controversy. Another result was a year of productions which virtually compelled audiences to leave the theatre with their senses and intelligence jolted and disturbed as never before. Brook, the man primarily responsible for introducing the phrase Theatre of Cruelty to British audiences, said:

> 'Remember Shakespeare went through his middle black period of violence.... Well this is my black period.... Perhaps when I come out on the other side — if I ever do — I will find a new set of values and enter a period of enlightenment where violence wilts and dies.'[93]

Two years after *Marat-Sade*, Brook's experimental work was extended in another RSC project — finally titled *US*. Brook's aim was to 'articulate a world-wide political tragedy in all its aspects, reaching beyond documentary "theatre of fact" to the deeper currents of thought and feeling....'[94] The presentation which he envisaged was originally going to be *Suez* (an examination of the 1956 British débâcle). He decided, however, to treat a subject of more immediate relevance, and settled on the Vietnam war, then in its earlier stages of American involvement and military escalation. Working on source material provided by the company, outside people, the news media, and Brook himself, the *US* experimental project was four months in rehearsal and was finally put together as a showing in October 1966. The script of *US*, together with a full account of the ideas behind the making of the production, has since been published, and provides a detailed reference on all aspects of the presentation:[95]

> 'The birth of *US* was allied to the reaction of a group of us who quite suddenly felt that Vietnam was more powerful, more acute, more insistent a situation than any drama which already existed between covers ... we were interested in a theatre-of-confrontation ... it [*US*] used a contemporary, highly perishable, fun-language to woo and annoy the spectator into joining in the turning over of basically repellent themes.'[96]

Brook was, in effect, asking a British audience of 1966 to feel a direct and personal commitment to the situation existing in Vietnam — a situation in which Britain had no direct political involvement. When it came to choosing a cast for the project, he found that some of his actors were already committed to the ideas behind the presentation, and others weren't. Morgan Sheppard spoke about the first rehearsal: 'Fifteen of us were selected to start work on it, and on the first day of rehearsal we were all asked what we thought about Vietnam. We mostly came out with our various platitudes, but one of the cast — one of the most honest people there — said, "I don't give a damn about Vietnam. Because I'm not there and it's not my problem". And Brook said, "That's an honest statement, so I think that's where we'll start from". . . .'[9 7]

Over the rehearsal period the group worked on improvisatory exercises (in the *Cruelty* vein), evolved sketches and stagings for the source material provided, and trained with acting-technique exercises for two weeks under the direction of Jerzy Grotowski, whom Brook had brought to England to assist with the *US* rehearsals: 'It was like a combat course every morning . . . there were exercises from ten until five in the afternoon — and we were screaming!'[9 8]

The first half of the finished Aldwych presentation consisted of documentary material on the Vietnam war, acted out in styles varying from Chinese symbolism to television journalism, and interspersed with a series of accusatory poems by Adrian Mitchell. The first sequence began with a demonstration of how Buddhist monks burn themselves to death: 'The empty jerrycan is tipped. The token match is struck. We watch how the heat contracts the tendons of the forearms, the fingers, the crossed legs, until the body topples over backwards.'[9 9]   The stage throughout was dominated by a huge, grotesque dummy suspended above the acting area: 'This monster, smothered in American symbols and with a yellow rocket in its belly and a coloured child perched in each of its eye sockets, is war itself.'[1 0 0]

The second half of the presentation was in a very different style to the first, and consisted largely of a dialogue between a man on the point of suicide and an unorthodox liberal girl. Her 'liberal detachment' (taken to represent the audience's own detachment) is finally broken down and she concludes with a screaming demand for an extension of the war into Britain: 'Miss Jackson rises to a prolonged shriek of betrayal and accusation, screaming that she would like to see English babies burnt by napalm, bombs dropped on English households. . . .'[101] *US* ended with the releasing of a boxful of butterflies into the audience, and the burning of a faked one on the stage. Michael Williams explained the origin of this sequence: 'At the very last dress rehearsal, Brook asked us all to assemble on the stage. . . . He'd primed Robert Lloyd, who brought on a table and a black box. Nobody in the cast knew about this. He opened the box and out came all these butterflies; Bob then picked up one — fixed to look real — then he took a cigarette lighter, and the butterfly went whoosh — up in flames. It was one of the most terrifying experiences that I've ever had in the theatre. . . . Brook wanted to give us the absolute emotion one feels when a living creature just goes up in flames. And, of course, we all related our personal feelings to what was going on in Vietnam.'[102]

Critical and audience reaction to *US* ranged from the committed and angered: ' . . . detachment is finally broken down. I have never before experienced this so fully in a theatre . . . [it is] closely in touch with the time we are living in and usually ignore.'[103]; to the apathetic non-response: ' . . . they [the audience] just sat back in their cushioned seats and took it all!'[104]; to the coldly cynical and indignantly angered:

' . . . the answer is a lemon. A coarse answer is the only possible one to this abysmal spectacle, in which the crudity of acting and presentation reflects the cheap, facile ambivalence of the company's attitude to the problems of the war . . . "Vietnam" falls into place, as one among a whole set of current OK catchphrases — Cuba, LSD, homosexuality, plight of women. . . . The Aldwych show is disturbing . . . because of the picture the company present of themselves, of what they choose to call "our own generation": shifty, soft-centred, shallow, self-pitying and self-righteous, above all resentful. . . . The company carries a heavy load of spite to be unburdened on the audience . . we have come to expect this kind of gratuitous punishment from the non-commercial or "dedicated" arm of the theatre — though never anything quite so shiftless. . . .'[105]

In terms of the RSC's development, *US* was the first major British excursion into the field of documentary theatre, and since *US* this type of presentation has achieved an increasing popularity, particularly with the avant garde or fringe wing of the theatre in this country. Certainly, at the time the RSC presented it, *US* conformed to no existing theatrical category. R.B. Marriot wrote:

' . . . the impulse behind it, the ideas, work and dedication that went into the making, transcend *US* simply as the latest production in the Royal Shakespeare's repertory . . . the purpose and effect reach far beyond . . . on any count, *US* is a major landmark in British theatre.'[106]

In June 1965, Peter Hall's production of Harold Pinter's third full-length play, *The Homecoming*,[107] opened at the Aldwych following an extensive pre-London provincial tour. *The Homecoming* stands in the middle of the series of Pinter plays which have been presented by the RSC, and as such is, in a sense, representative of the Pinter/RSC alliance. The RSC had previously staged *The Birthday Party* and *The Collection*, and since *The Homecoming* the company has presented *Landscape* and *Silence*, *Old Times* — Pinter's most recent full-length play — and *Landscape* and *A Slight Ache*. Most of these productions have been directed by Peter Hall, the only exceptions being *The Birthday Party*, which Pinter directed himself, *The Collection* which Hall and Pinter co-directed and *A Slight Ache* directed by Peter James; John Bury has designed all RSC Pinter productions. The RSC/ Hall/Pinter combination is now recognized as one of the most successful relationships of its kind in Britain. It is by no means the first example of a company, director, designer and playwright working together in close and fruitful association,[108] but it is unique in that this particular combination has moved on from strength to strength since its first venture in 1962, and the partnership is now entering its tenth year.

Pinter himself, has moved from the critical failure of *The Birthday Party*'s first London production in 1958, to be regarded as perhaps the most outstanding playwright working in Britain today and to rank among the 'great' dramatists of our time. If the RSC cannot claim to have discovered Harold Pinter, the company — together with the considerable talents of Hall and

Bury – has certainly provided a most admirable vehicle for the presentation of his works. Harold Hobson was one of the first to recognize the potential genius of Pinter. After the 1958 production of *The Birthday Party* at the Lyric Theatre, Hammersmith, had been unanimously damned by his critical colleagues, Hobson wrote in *The Sunday Times*:

> ' . . . Mr Pinter, on the evidence of this work, possesses the most original, disturbing and arresting talent in theatrical London. . . . The early Shaw got bad notices; Ibsen got scandalous notices. Mr Pinter is not only in good company, he is in the very best company. . . . Mr Pinter and *The Birthday Party* will be heard of again. Make a note of their names.'[109]

The Birthday Party was revived in London in 1964 by the RSC, and received admiring notices from many of the same critics who had so roundly dismissed it eight years earlier. During those eight years, *The Caretaker* had been successfully presented in the West End, and the RSC had presented *The Collection* as part of a double bill[110] in 1962. By the time *The Homecoming* was presented in 1965, Pinter was nationally (and internationally) recognized as a dramatist of rare and singular talent. Harold Hobson opened his review of *The Homecoming* by saying: '*The Homecoming* . . . is Harold Pinter's cleverest play. It is so clever, in fact so misleadingly clever, that at a superficial glance it seems to be not clever enough. This is an appearance only . . .'[111]

On a plot level, *The Homecoming* is simple enough: Teddy, who has been some years at an American university and acquired a Ph.D. in the process, returns to visit his family home – a large, squalid residence somewhere in North London. His family consists of Max, the ageing father, Sam, the chauffeur uncle, and Teddy's two brothers Lenny, a pimp, and Joey, a failed boxer. Teddy has left his three children in America, but has with him his wife Ruth, who blatantly and sexually teases both his brothers before agreeing to prostitute herself with and for them. Teddy returns to America alone, leaving Ruth with his family. However, this plot summary inevitably excludes the essence of the play – of most Pinter plays; that indefinable quality of some unknown menace which lurks behind the apparently simple, straightforward plot and simple yet ambiguous dialogue. Pinter has always refused to

A rehearsal for *The Homecoming. Behind the sofa:* Peter Hall (director), Ian Holm on sofa: Terence Rigby and Vivien Merchant.

Ian Hogg, Leon Lissek, Morgan Sheppard, Clifford Rose.

US, directed by Peter Brook, Aldwych 1966

L. to R.: Mike Pratt, Hugh Sullivan, Michael Williams (with microphone), Patrick O'Connell, Barry Stanton and Morgan Sheppard.

elaborate on what his plays mean, and a new Pinter play has come to signal a critical game of hunt-the-symbol. Ronald Bryden provided one of the most interesting comments on *The Homecoming*:

'Pinter's characters have always had an animal instinct for "territory", spatial possession. The strength of his stagecraft is that their obscure warfare, however verbalised, is over the stage itself: for possession of the actual area on which they battle. To have the last word coincides with dominating the stage; the actor who ends upstaging the rest has established his barnyard domination over them like a cock on a dunghill. In *The Birthday Party* and *The Caretaker*, this manoeuvring is implicit. It is flesh and bone of *The Homecoming*. The whole point, structure and joke of the play is that what these actors ... are unfurling is most readily and recognisably described in the language of a zoologist. ...'[112]

Bryden continues to elaborate this explanation, and assigns each of Pinter's characters in *The Homecoming* a different animal role in the 'zoo story mating-game'. Martin Esslin sees *The Homecoming* as: '...a dream image of the fulfilment of all Oedipal wishes...'[113], and parallels the play with *Oedipus* and *King Lear*: '... the desolation of old age and the son's desire for sexual conquest of the mother...'[114] Peter Hall, when asked what *The Homecoming* was 'about', said: 'It is what it is ... What it is, is what happens.'[115] Pinter himself is even more ambiguous about his characters and his plays: 'I don't know what kind of characters my plays will have until they ... well, until they *are*. Until they indicate to me what they are ... once I've got the clues I follow them — that's my job, really, to follow the clues.'[116]

Gareth Lloyd Evans spoke about the Hall/Pinter relationship: 'There is no other director — probably in the world — who understands Pinter like Hall does. I think that their minds go absolutely together. I think that Hall is able to explain Pinter in simple naturalistic terms to his cast, and then give them the freedom (which the lines give them anyway) to develop within that framework ... he makes his stage a total image, and all his props and all the clothes and every gesture becomes an image of what Pinter is doing ... I've never known such complete success as Hall is able to achieve.'[117]

The RSC took *The Homecoming* to the United States in 1967, where it received brilliant critical notices, compared with the mildly favourable reception it had received in Britain. As a result of the USA tour, *The Homecoming* won both the Tony Award and the New York Drama Critics' Award of 1967 for the best play on Broadway, and the Whitbread Anglo-American award for the best British play on Broadway. Peter Hall won the Tony Award as best director for his work on the play.[118] Hall's film version was also acclaimed in America when it was first seen there in November 1973; it had not been screened in England when this book went to press.

Since 1960, it has been part of the RSC's seasonal-planning policy to include, whenever possible, a non-Shakespeare play in the Stratford repertoire. The non-Shakespeare has usually been taken from the works of one of Shakespeare's contemporaries, and the company have produced plays by Marlowe, Ben Jonson, Webster, Middleton and Tourneur. There have also been occasional Aldwych productions of classical plays by writers other than the Elizabethan/Jacobean dramatists. One of the most successful of the RSC's non-Shakespeare presentations at Stratford was Trevor Nunn's 1966 production of *The Revenger's Tragedy*, a play usually attributed to Cyril Tourneur. Revenge tragedy flourished on the English stage during Shakespeare's lifetime:

'The revenge play . . . had in its own day the same kind of universal popularity that the thriller has in ours. . . . The reasons for the revenge genre's popularity were partly social and partly the bringing together of several literary modes. The Elizabethans had translated Seneca's blood-revenge tragedies. Two other traditional modes were at work on Tourneur: the Morality . . . and the Malcontent (now called the Angry Young Man) pouring abuse on social disorders. . . . Tourneur set his play in Machiavelli's Italy, a country then viewed with shocked fascination.'[119]

The Revenger's Tragedy was first published in 1607, and prior to the RSC's production, the only other known professional staging of the play was at the 1965 Pitlochry Festival. The play fascinated Trevor Nunn, and he asked Peter Hall for the chance to stage it at Stratford: 'It was a play that I'd read at university . . . and I was just overwhelmed by it. . . . It seemed to me a play that was

extraordinarily about aspects of our own world . . . where the
relationship between sex, violence and money was becoming
increasingly popular, and expressed through all sorts of things —
spy novels — James Bond. The "good life" — the life of extraordinary opulence and comfort — was also connected with something fundamentally immoral. . . . I was also fascinated by a
society which reviled this development, but could stop talking
about it . . . in all its newspapers, all its magazines, all its radio
programmes, all its television . . . the media were communicating it
more and more, until they became completely enveloped by it.
What fascinated me about the Revenger — about the character
Vendice — was that he was totally schizophrenic; a completely
modern study. He was somebody utterly dedicated to the
destruction of this world, and he was — at the same time — totally
fascinated by it.'[120]

The original 1966 production of *The Revenger's Tragedy* was
staged as a low-budget production to complete the Stratford
season, which was composed almost entirely of revivals from
1965. This was the year of Hall's financial squeeze designed to
gain a higher Arts Council subsidy. 'In order to keep costs down,
they decided to use the *Hamlet* set with a few additional props . . .
also the costumes were made from the cheapest possible material
(actually the linings from other costumes) and these were covered
with a sort of silver glitter dust. . . .'[121] The whole production
was designed by Christopher Morley in terms of blacks and silvers,
and the design was given a formal structure which centred on a
huge silver circle on the black floor of the stage. This circle
imposed a hierarchical order and formalized grouping on the
court: the centre of the circle was the 'centre of the Court' (the
Duke), and the Duke was costumed in bright glittering silver. As
one moved further from this centre, the costumes and stage
became less silver and more black. Trevor Nunn explained: 'We
were involved with positives and negatives: we were involved with
the light which is most brilliant at the centre of a source and
disappears out to the very darkest edges. . . . Does the brightest
necessarily mean the best?'[122] The strong black and white
boldness of *The Revenger's Tragedy* designs represented a complete break from RSC traditions, and during rehearsals some
RSC directors and designers expressed disagreement with the

Nunn/Morley production and design ideas: they felt that 'colour' was needed and that the totally unrelieved study in positives and negatives would not be successful in theatrical terms. To give the production more impact, and to centre its interpretation more closely around his overall concepts, Nunn (with the assistance of John Barton) made quite substantial textual modifications to the printed edition of the play. An examination of the prompt book for the 1966 Stratford production indicates that a considerable amount of new dialogue has been interpolated into the original: the order of scenes has been changed, and the content and setting of certain scenes has been altered. With the exception of one line from *The Atheist's Tragedy*, these textual interpolations and alterations were entirely the work of John Barton.

Despite the spoken doubts of some of his colleagues at the RSC, Trevor Nunn (together with Christopher Morley and the cast) maintained and expressed the fullest confidence in the concepts behind the production. Faced with this total unanimity of belief, the RSC management allowed the production to be staged exactly as planned and designed, and the 1966 *Revenger's Tragedy* proved to be the most successful Stratford presentation of that year. Due to existing repertoire commitments, it was given only a very limited run in 1966 but was revived at Stratford for the 1967 season. In 1969, a revival was mounted at the Aldwych, and the London production was one of the most popular and successful presentations staged by the company for some years. Even in 1966, the critical response was more than favourable; *The Times* headed its review, 'Neglected Classic Now Almost Total Success':

'. . . the Royal Shakespeare Company show once again what can be achieved when their distinctive style is applied to a neglected classic. . . . Where Trevor Nunn's production succeeds so well is in striking the right balance between a stylized and realistic treatment. . . . Visually the play is full of memorable detail. . . .'[123]

And Ronald Bryden, reviewing for *The Observer*, said:

'. . . .*The Revenger's Tragedy* is budgeted on a shoestring. It contains no star names. It is staged on a set from last year's *Hamlet*. Its costumes appear to have been run up out of old oilskins and aluminium paint. It is one of the finest things Peter Hall's regime has accomplished.'[124]

In 1967, Peter Hall staged *Macbeth* at Stratford, with Paul Scofield in the title role. This was Hall's last production as Managing Director of the RSC. In a speech to the company at the first *Macbeth* rehearsal, Hall outlined his interpretation of the play — following a statement that this would be *the* lucky production of 'the unlucky play':

> '*Macbeth* is the play which most uncompromisingly and horribly examines the nature of evil. . . . What Shakespeare is releasing is a sense of evil and a sense of sin, probably unparalleled in dramatic literature . . . it is a worrying and disturbing play which analyses clinically and unsentimentally, the nature of the evil impulses. . . . The play is not about "Should I or should I not do a murder?" The question is never asked. The play is about what happens *when* I do a murder. . . . In a very real sense it is about the metaphysics of evil. The way evil breeds evil, blood breeds blood.'[125]

Macbeth was not a critical success, and it has since been suggested that this was due, in some measure, to a strong difference in opinion between Paul Scofield and Peter Hall over basic interpretation. Clearly, Scofield was not entirely happy in the role, and it was felt by some critics that he was playing a Macbeth which was at odds with the production: ' . . . a thrilling piece of work, but it is limited by a sense of isolation from the rest of the company.'[126]

Hall's interpretation leant strongly towards Christian symbolism, working within a framework of brooding evil and imagery of blood. A year earlier, G.K. Hunter had written: 'Symbolic interpretation of a Shakespearian text which is full of Biblical phrases and images is bound to become explicitly Christian sooner or later, and there is quite a body of modern criticism which has explicitly Christian designs on *Macbeth*. . .'[127] The 1965 *Hamlet* was very much a political production. In the 1967 *Macbeth*, Hall seemed to be moving towards an interest in the religious, and it can perhaps be seen as the beginnings of a personal exploration into the use of religion and religious ritual in the theatre: 'The major difference is Hall's rejection of any modernity-hunting. This *Macbeth* is frankly archaeological . . . here is a Gothic, superstitious Shakespeare, reverting to childhood farm-tales of witches and kings of Christian legend, who bound their realms in the white magic of divine right.'[128] Hall, in his programme notes, said:

> 'Macbeth himself is conscious of damnation in a way in
> which no other Shakespeare hero is. The play was written at
> a very Christian moment, it's the product of a Christian
> society, which ours is not, so we would be doing it a
> disservice if we ignored the Christian references. We have got
> to try to make them not conventionally pious, but concretely
> Christian.'[129]

It is significant to note that following *Macbeth*, Hall moved into
the production of Wagnerian opera, and intended to continue and
extend this interest at Covent Garden.

John Bury's setting and many of the production effects used in
Macbeth were theatrically exciting. The stage floor was entirely
composed of great lengths of blood red carpet; this carpet was
laid in sections and as the play proceeded, various sections were
removed from the stage to reveal 'bone-bleached white' areas
which grew and diminished as the action demanded. The carpet
was said to look 'like heather', or 'like the hide of some great
beast', or — most obviously — an ever-present symbol of blood.
The action moved against rugged backing; ' . . . a geological set,
red granite cliffs like blood-rinsed Old Men of Hoy.'[130] The
opening sequence of the play was a scene of brilliant inventiveness
and effect: ' . . . quite electrifying. There was a "white sheet"
across the stage. Suddenly there was a great crash of
thunder, a flash of lightning and silhouetted against this sheet you
saw the Witches — with a crucifix held upside down. The thunder
crash was followed by a quick blackout — the "sheet" was flown
away — and the Witches were discovered standing on hummocks
of this red carpet, pouring blood down the inverted crucifix and
chanting, "When shall we three . . .". While this scene was going on
the carpet started heaving and moving, and there was a sense of
earthquake — of everything unstable — almost as though the stage
itself was boiling! . . . when the Witches disappear, soldiers — who
had been hiding underneath the carpet — stand up through it,
ready for Duncan's entrance.'[131]

The good versus evil and 'blood will have blood' theme was
carried through the production, and the symbol of the Cross was
prominent throughout. In the England scene (IV.3), Malcolm's
speech about Edward the Confessor and the 'sacred magic of true

kingship' (usually omitted from productions) was included virtually uncut, and was given a central importance. Peter Hall, interviewed a year before his *Macbeth* production said: ' . . . I am being metaphysical. That's why I want to do *Macbeth* . . . I want to move into the late plays of Shakespeare. I'd like now to examine *The Tempest* or *Winter's Tale*. . . . I've been very obsessed for the last two years by the idea of religion, in the broadest sense. I am an agnostic, and have always been, and a couple of years ago I started worrying about it.'[132]

The RSC production of *Macbeth* was dogged by the traditional bad luck that is supposed to surround the play. It was originally scheduled to open on 13th July — which some cast members took as an initial bad omen. Then Hall fell ill with shingles of the left temple, and the production was postponed with a new opening date set for 26th July (a double thirteen). Many actors, who from superstition will not quote *Macbeth* in dressing rooms, saw this new date as a double augury of disaster, and on 28th June it was announced that Hall's illness was severe and that the production would not open until August. In fact, Hall nearly lost the sight of his left eye through this illness. When the production finally opened it was not the highlight of the season that everyone had hoped it would be, and more than one cast member has implied that they knew all would not go well. Peter Hall's illness was undoubtedly a major cause of *Macbeth*'s critical failure, but an interesting sidenote is the story that the production had been offered to Peter Brook, who refused it on the grounds of superstition. Elizabeth Spriggs said: 'Because Brook was superstitious about it, it rather frightened Peter [Hall]. Now he is *not* a superstitious person, but he *was* very, very nervous about it all. . . .'[133]

Macbeth toured the Soviet Union and Finland in 1967, together with John Barton's production of *All's Well That Ends Well*. Ted Valentine, who was on this tour, said: 'The Russians were all very polite about it . . . but I think they were secretly disappointed. They'd been expecting something as exciting as Peter Brook's *Lear*, and that, *Macbeth* clearly wasn't.'[134] Ronald Bryden, reviewing Hall's production for *The Observer*, wrote:

'It's a companion enterprise to his superb Warner *Hamlet* of
    two years ago; a sombre, unhurried, straightforward yet

searching reading of the text for new or neglected meanings. It's a majestic effort, even finer at moments than its predecessor. Only by the standards of that comparison dare one pronounce it on the whole, at present, curiously disappointing.'[135]

And Elizabeth Spriggs, who worked with Peter Hall in several productions over the sixties, said of *Macbeth*: 'This production was just at the time when Peter really came to the end of his tether; his health finally went, and he had to give up running our company. So it's terribly unfair to assess him on his *Macbeth*. I think it was the production of a very tired, sick man. . . .'[136]

At the end of 1967, Peter Hall *was* a desperately tired, ill man. He had been the chief motivating force behind the creation of the RSC and over its eight year record of achievement he made himself responsible for the company product and the company image. It was Hall, more than any other individual, who had fought the battles, exerted the pressures, and made the 'noise' necessary to keep the company alive and moving forward.

His actual illness during 1967 was compounded by a sort of psychological malaise — a growing feeling of apathy towards the company that was the inevitable result of nine years living at tension point. In 1971, Hall spoke about his final year in control of the RSC: 'I was terribly tired. I just didn't want to go on. . . . If a person lives on tension point all the time (like I do), he occasionally goes too far. I've done that. I live very shut off from the theatre now, and not surrounded by theatre people. . . . When I left Stratford it wasn't so much my health, but more the fact that I didn't know what to do next, so I was miserable. I'd created something — and I didn't know what to do next.'[137]

7. The Inheritance
1969-1973

> I have regarded my job for the last three years as fulfilling a
> certain continuity. ... I think one can see a clear and
> continuous development between the previous regime and
> this one. The aims and intentions and policies are still the
> same. But I think there comes a point where having made
> to work — or failed to make work — what one has in-
> herited, one has to actually look at the inheritance. I've
> arrived at the point where I'm examining a lot of the
> precepts and principles of the original Royal Shakespeare
> Company. And I'm beginning to discover that many things
> which held good for the decade of the sixties won't
> necessarily hold good for the seventies.
>
> Trevor Nunn, in an interview with the author,
> 22nd September 1971.

When Peter Hall resigned his position as Managing Director of the
RSC in January 1968, the primary factor stressed in all press
statements and interviews was continuity within the organization.
Trevor Nunn's succession to the leadership and the creation of a
new Directorate to advise on company policy, was seen only as an
internal change in the existing artistic and administrative structure
of the RSC. The official theatre press-release stated: 'In effect,
these changes amount to a re-arrangement amongst the strong
group of artists and executives who already head the RSC. Thus a
continuity of the company's identity, as created by Peter Hall, is
assured. . . .'[1] Hall, Peter Brook and Paul Scofield remained
directors of the company, and the Directorate was further
expanded by the addition of Dame Peggy Ashcroft and Derek
Hornby — a business executive who joined the RSC as General
Manager in 1967. Hornby was appointed to the newly created
position of Administrative Director (immediately below that of
the Artistic Director), RSC Associate Directors John Barton and
Terry Hands were given added responsibilities as Company
Directors of the Stratford and London theatres respectively, and

David Brierley, former assistant to Peter Hall, was appointed General Manager. The new administrative and artistic structure was headed by Trevor Nunn as Artistic Director and Chief Executive — responsible to the Governors. At the age of twenty-eight, Nunn was the youngest ever to have held the senior appointment within the Stratford organization.

Trevor Nunn was educated at the Northgate Grammar School for Boys, and on leaving school he taught for a year, formed the Ipswich Youth Drama Group, and then went on to Downing College, Cambridge. At Cambridge he read English under Dr. Leavis, and also took an active role in university theatre life as an actor and director for the Marlowe Society and at the ADC Theatre. In many ways, his early life shows striking parallels to that of Peter Hall: both were born in Suffolk (Trevor Nunn's father was a cabinet-maker): both studied at Cambridge and were active in theatre life there; and both were approximately the same age when appointed to the position of Director at Stratford.

Nunn's early years in the theatrical profession began with a strong bias towards acting, and he had seriously considered becoming an actor at one stage in his life. However, at Cambridge he discovered that his true métier was directing: 'Once I had started to direct things — at the crudest level, telling other people what do do — the urge to act myself began to diminish and the urge to direct began to grow.'[2]

His early experience and recognized talent as an actor have undoubtedly proved an asset to his career as a director: during his period as an Associate Director of the RSC he was sufficiently competent to be able to take over a leading role in his production of *Tango*, (Aldwych 1966) when an actor fell ill at the last moment. While at Cambridge, Nunn directed over thirty plays, including a Footlights Revue, and formed a touring company which appeared as a fringe event during the 1960 Edinburgh Festival. Also in 1960, he acted with the Marlowe Society in the University Open Air Theatre at Stratford-upon-Avon. In 1962 he was awarded a place under the ABC (TV) Trainee Director Scheme: this scheme (no longer in operation) was designed to train young theatre directors of promise, by seconding them to various major repertory theatres for a two-year 'apprenticeship period'. Nunn had already done some work at the Belgrade

Theatre, Coventry – as an assistant during university vacation periods – and under the ABC scheme he was seconded to the Belgrade as a trainee-director. A year later he was appointed Resident Producer at this theatre, and over a two year period at Coventry he directed plays by Shakespeare, Brecht, Arthur Miller, John Arden and Ibsen: he also acted as Fabian in *Twelfth Night* and as Bob in Shaffer's *The Private Ear*. In 1964, Peter Hall saw Nunn's Belgrade production of *The Caucasian Chalk Circle* and asked him to join the RSC as an assistant director. Nunn declined this original offer, but accepted when invited to become an Associate Director at Stratford in 1965.

Nunn's first year with the RSC was not particularly successful. He assisted David Jones in the direction of an experimental programme, *Expeditions Two*, (Aldwych 1965); directed a children's play, Robert Bolt's *The Thwarting of Baron Bolligrew*, (Aldwych 1966); assisted John Barton and Clifford Williams in the co-direction of the 1966 History Play revivals; and directed *Tango* at the Aldwych. He later said: 'I did a disastrous first year with this company, where literally everything that I touched collapsed – or proved to be a dreadful, dreadful failure! I really was (hourly) expecting my cards. . . . But, for some reason, Peter persevered through until the moment of giving me *The Revenger's Tragedy*.'[3] It was the enormous success of this production which established Trevor Nunn as the most exciting young director in the RSC, and led to his being given *The Taming of the Shrew* (Stratford 1967) and Vanburgh's *The Relapse* (Aldwych 1967). Both these productions proved to be outstanding personal successes, and late in 1967 *The Taming of the Shrew* transferred to the Aldwych following a provincial tour: in January 1968, this production also went to Los Angeles where it was a brilliant success with American critics and audiences. At the end of 1967, Peter Hall suggested Trevor Nunn as his successor and the RSC Board of Governors endorsed his choice: it is also reported that there was spontaneous applause from the company when Hall announced this choice at a specially convened meeting. In a press statement Hall said:

'It would be quite wrong to think that Trevor is my protégé . . . [he] is approved by all – he has grown with the company and in time, I hope someone else will follow him as smoothly. . . . I believe that the theatre has to be inspired by one man and that when the man begins to lag, then it's time to change gear. That man is now Trevor Nunn. I hope he will stamp on the Royal Shakespeare Company what he wants to do.'[4]

Paul Scofield resigned from the company during 1968, and Derek Hornby during 1969, and the RSC Directorate now comprises Ashcroft, Brook, Peter Daubeny, Hall and Nunn. Nunn is — by definition — the final arbiter on any decision. He has defined the Directorate as 'a sounding board for ideas', and speaking of its function he said: 'One must never allow a group such as the Direction to seriously affect one's speed of movement — or the actual flexibility of the organization.'[5] Since his appointment, Trevor Nunn has stamped much of his own personality on the RSC structure; however, this has been most noticeable from an internal company viewpoint. To the average RSC patron, it might appear that there has been no radical change in company policy, and there have been no public announcements to indicate otherwise.

In many ways Trevor Nunn and Peter Hall are alike, particularly in terms of their stage product and their overall philosophy of direction. However, despite their obvious artistic similarities, they are very different people in an administrative sense. Hall thoroughly enjoys the business of running a theatre company, and during his period as Director he was very much the leader and spokesman for the RSC organization. He always combined his artistic talents with a brilliant flair for the work and functions of an impresario and the practical abilities of a top business executive: the Hall image at the RSC was a public one, and the company was *his* organization in every sense of the word — a 'benevolent dictatorship' was enforced.

Trevor Nunn is essentially a private person, and his administration of the RSC has been conducted far more on the basis of a sharing out of responsibility. He is, by his own admission, primarily interested in directing as an art, and not as an administrative function: 'There's a whole side of my job which I'm very tentative about and would frequently prefer to duck: I find the details of manipulation and manoeuvring very pleasant in rehearsal but not in administration.'[6]

The appointment of an Administrative Director in 1968 was one indication of Nunn's reluctance to shoulder both artistic and administrative responsibility, although this appointment only lasted for one year and the RSC's General Manager now functions as the effective administrative head of the organization — answerable to Nunn as the Chief Executive. Nunn rarely gives interviews and there has been surprisingly little publicity attendant on him as an individual since the early announcements surrounding his appointment: he is married to RSC Associate Artist Janet Suzman, although this is not a widely publicized fact. Since his appointment there have been subtle changes in the tone of relationships within the organization — particularly the acting company. Some indication of the nature of Nunn's personality may be seen in the fact that many members of the company report a feeling of informality and community effort that extends beyond the beginnings made under the Hall regime. Peter Ansorge, interviewing Nunn for *Plays and Players*, said:

'He distrusts tape-recorders and confesses to a fear of "formal" interviews. He wants a "dialogue" and it's clear needs to make personal contact with an interviewer. One understands why everyone in the RSC refers to their artistic director by his first name. . . .'[7]

He is often to be seen chatting with the company in the Green Room and makes himself immediately approachable (as Peter Hall did) on any matter concerning his staff. He has stated that he is dedicated to the idea of a theatre's director actually working *with* and living among his actors — as one of them. The point must be re-stated, however, that the organization which Nunn took over in 1968 was an established company of vast international reputation in receipt of considerable government subsidy. The pressures to make, build and finance the RSC which Peter Hall faced in 1960 were not inherited by Trevor Nunn — and there was less necessity for the company's director to become the dominating public and company figure that was Hall in the sixties.

The problems facing Trevor Nunn in 1968 were complex: the problem of making an individual and significant contribution to an existing institution of major standing, while, at the same time, maintaining the continuity that was the essence of RSC company structure and tradition. In this sense, any director who stepped into Peter Hall's shoes in 1968 faced an extraordinarily difficult task. Peter Hall's legacy in 1960 was an outdated Memorial Theatre working within outmoded forms and conventions. Trevor Nunn's legacy was the leadership of a company which was already recognized as one of the most outstanding, dynamic and artistically creative in the world.

Although Nunn has announced no obvious and external changes in company policy since 1968, there have been quite considerable modifications within the internal structure, and a streamlining of the repertoire-revival scheme. In the later years of the Hall directorate, it was becoming an increasingly established practice to transfer one or two Stratford productions to the Aldwych during the early months of the following year. There was an obvious economic basis for the scheme, as it lengthened the life of a production and also made less output demands on the company's resources: as Hall stated in 1967, the notion that the company *had* to produce twelve or so new 'masterpieces' each year was an economic and artistic absurdity. In the early years of the sixties, seasons at Stratford and London would open with a series of major productions at both theatres, and the costs involved in running two large companies were enormous. However, towards the end of the Hall regime, the choice of plays at the Aldwych became largely governed by economic necessity: to hold a large company together in London on a yearly basis was not an economically viable proposition. The result was that the London companies were often recruited on an ad-hoc basis to perform small-cast plays for a season, while the bulk of the permanent RSC acting company was retained at Stratford — transferring to the Aldwych only at the conclusion of the Stratford season for a short London run. Thus the RSC ideal of an actor working in both Shakespeare and modern drama never operated on an entirely satisfactory basis. There are notable examples of RSC actors who worked with the company over a period of years, and during that time were only given the chance to play one or two modern roles.

When Stratford productions transferred to London in December or January, they were usually with a group of actors who had not had the benefit of working on modern texts during that year — nor had the London company any experience in Shakespeare work. Following a brief London season, the major company would return to Stratford to start a new Shakespeare season, leaving a smaller London company to fill-in until the end of the year. This is an extremely broad generalization of the process and there were many exceptions but, in effect, the overall ideology of an RSC actor having simultaneous experience in Shakespeare *and* modern drama was not working in practice. Certain actors had the opportunity to do modern work, but the major proportion of the permanent company were confined to Shakespeare at Stratford — and revivals of Shakespeare at the Aldwych between January and March.

To put right this system — which Hall had already recognized as ineffective — Trevor Nunn instituted what has been termed the 'two-year scheme'. The basis of the scheme was that an actor's 'life' with the RSC should be for a two-year period, and over that period he should be allowed the opportunity to play Shakespeare, tour or do film and TV work, and to take roles in modern or experimental drama. This scheme also signalled the end of the three-year contract that Hall had introduced in 1960, and their replacement by a two-year contract.

Nunn's two-year scheme worked on a simple rotation principle, using two permanent companies very much reduced in size. In this way, he arranged that the RSC actor would have experience in Shakespeare and modern work during his second year of contract, although the first was devoted mainly to Shakespeare in Stratford.

This two-year rotation system has been in successful operation since 1969. Its apparent simplicity should not allow one to forget the immense planning problems which even this simplified system creates, and Maurice Daniels, the RSC's Planning Controller, is continually engaged in the business of co-ordinating and dovetailing the various seasons, tours and special projects with the availability of actors, directors and stage staff. In an organization of the size and complexity of the RSC, no scheme is simple.

One of the more noticeable results of the two-year system has been the choice of plays at the Aldwych since 1969, where there has been a definite concentration on a classic repertoire and 'safe' modern works — with less ventures into experimental projects or the works of new or unknown playwrights. In a recent interview, Trevor Nunn explained the reasons behind his choice of the Aldwych repertoire: 'If you're employing a large company — you've got to give them work! . . . therefore there *has* to be a greater emphasis on the classic repertoire at the Aldwych, but this is something that I did "eyes open" . . . the Aldwych was turning into an ideological centre which wasn't working in practice, and we were starting to play to audiences of 50 per cent average for the modern work. It's a very large theatre for modern work! 1,100 seats (as compared with four-fifty or five hundred at the Royal Court) is a massive total to be filling every night with work which, by definition, is of an experimental nature!'[8]

The two-year scheme also introduced a new concept of ensemble playing to the company — a concept dictated mainly by the very much smaller companies involved. The official RSC policy statement on the new ensemble idea is that it is based solely on artistic considerations. Under Peter Hall, the major Stratford company usually employed fifty or more actors, and the London based company was somewhat smaller. Nunn's two-year scheme is based on a company of approximately thirty five actors at each theatre, and these groups must be fully contributing in every sense. To stage a season of seven or eight major Shakespeare productions with a company of thirty five actors is an impossibility unless *every* member of that company is employed to his fullest capacities. The new ensemble concept was introduced in 1970, and Nunn explained its basis in a press interview:

> 'I've reduced the size of the company, so that everybody plays small parts, understudies and supports his colleagues. We've begun a two-year system of employment and all our actors have a chance of working for a minimum period. In the ensemble all must feel that they're there because they've something to offer; they must be capable of development; there must be a sharing out of opportunities.'[9]

The necessity for each member of the RSC to understudy and take small parts has been received with mixed feelings by the company. Some actors feel that this is true ensemble work, and the system certainly does allow *all* members of the company to play some kind of speaking role during a season. This was not always the case under the earlier system, and there was always a percentage of the

THE WINTER'S TALE
directed by Trevor Nunn.

Right: Stratford, 1969.
Richard Pasco as
Polixenes and Judi Dench
as Perdita.

Below: Aldwych,
1970/71 : after recasting,
costume changes etc.
from Stratford production
1969 : *L. to R.:* Maev
Alexander as Mopsa,
Derek Smith as Autolycus,
and Lisa Harrow as
Dorcas.

Michael Williams as Petruchio and Janet Suzman as Katharina.
The Taming of the Shrew. Directed by Trevor Nunn at Stratford and Aldwych 1967.
L. to R.: Charles Thomas as Tranio, Roy Kinnear as Baptista and John Kane as Biondello.

company which was solely relegated to spear carrying. However, there are members of the RSC who feel that Nunn's ideas have nothing to do with true ensemble, and that it only succeeds in placing an extremely heavy burden on the company's major actors.

An examination of the roles played by lead actors such as Ian Richardson, Judi Dench, Richard Pasco and others since 1969, will indicate excessive seasonal workload — in addition to which, these actors have been expected to take walk-on roles in other productions and understudy their colleagues. During the 1970 season, Ian Richardson played Prospero, Angelo, Proteus and Buckingham, as well as taking the minor walk-on role of Marcellus in *Hamlet* (for part of the season) and being requested to understudy. In the 1971 Stratford repertoire, Judi Dench played Portia, Viola, and the Duchess of Malfi, in addition to a non-speaking role as a Lady in *Much Ado About Nothing*.

These two examples alone show the pressures placed on lead actors during a season of constantly changing repertory, and secondary actors are often required to play in all but one of the season's productions. □ Some members of the RSC also feel that this type of ensemble system negates the whole concept of levels of talent within an organization — a concept which was recognized and allowed for under the Hall regime. Many actors have expressed this opinion in interview, and Richard Pasco echoed a frequent feeling when he said: 'I don't think it works . . . I don't believe that you can have an ensemble company in the truest sense when you have young actors (straight out of drama school) working alongside people who have spent twenty five years in the theatre. You can't just throw these two elements together. . . . This year [1971] I was asked to walk on, and also to understudy a small part — which was *exactly* what I was doing for Tyrone Guthrie at the Old Vic in 1952. . . . I have enormous admiration for Trevor's ideals, and I've done my best to contribute to them. But I don't think it will work. I'm against a star system — but somewhere there must be a compromise between the two.'[10]

During the 1971 season at Stratford, Pasco played Richard II, Orsino, Antonio (in *The Duchess of Malfi*) and Don John: his walk-on role did not eventuate owing to the cancellation of *Timon of Athens*. Interviewed in 1971, Peter Hall supported the view that major artists within the company should not be required to be fully contributing:

'I don't think that Ian Richardson walking on and saying "What ho!" in *Hamlet* is anything to do with the ensemble ideal. ☆ I think it makes Ian Richardson self-conscious (because he knows he's doing the company a favour) and it stops young actors having the chance to say "What ho!" . . . I believe that actors have a certain level of achievement which has got to be respected.'[11]

Trevor Nunn's two-year rotation scheme also creates difficulties for the actor, although it does achieve its primary aim of allowing *all* members of the company to work in a wide variety of roles and types of drama. The problem with the rotation system is that an actor can become 'bound' to a particular production for a two- or even three-year period. ■ John Barton's 1969 production of *Twelfth Night* is an excellent illustration of this point. *Twelfth Night* opened at Stratford and at the conclusion of the season it toured Australia together with *The Winter's Tale*: in June 1970 it opened at the Aldwych for the London season of that year, and in 1971 it was transferred back to Stratford for a second season at the 'home' theatre. Admittedly there were cast changes during the course of this three-year run, but some of the original cast remained with the production for the duration — a situation which is unenviable from any actor's point of view.

In most cases, a 'popular' production can expect to be shown continuously over a two-year period — at Stratford, touring and in London — and the actors involved can well become 'stale' in the process. However, this is one of the necessary compromises between artistic ideals and the 'official'/commercial pressures exerted on the RSC as part of its institutional function.

As part of its national and international role, the RSC now *has* to be a 'factory' in some senses, and there are constant demands on the acting and production staff to keep the product flowing. Peter Hall has said that he believes the greatest single problem facing the RSC's Directorate is that of running a vast institutional and commercial machine — 'the ICI of theatre' — and, at the same time, attempting to retain the company's essential identity, artistic integrity, vigour and excitement. The problem is a very real one.

Since 1969, Trevor Nunn has been searching for solutions, but the basic problem may well remain unsolved while the company operates within its present policies and identity. The search for more workable policies, the re-organization of existing policies, and the possible emergence of a new RSC identity has been the prime motivation behind most of Nunn's internal changes and modifications.

It has been said that during the later years of Hall's directorate and since, the RSC has lacked much of its original drive and energy — and this is perhaps inevitable as the early excitements and challenges of building a structure gave way to permanence and institution. One reflection of the RSC's apparent inertia over recent years is the noticeable fact that it has failed to develop new actors of the Warner, Rigg, Holm, Richardson, Suzman, and Jackson calibre — the products of the new company and the new ideas of the early sixties. There have been notable exceptions such as Alan Howard, Helen Mirren, and John Kane; • but most of the exciting performances since the late sixties have come from actors who 'grew up' with the RSC — or from established artists like Peggy Ashcroft, Paul Scofield, Dorothy Tutin, Judi Dench, and Eric Porter who have been associated with the company's development since its inception.

Another noticeable tendency has been the increasing practice of introducing established actors from outside into the company on a contract basis. These actors are then required to assimilate themselves into the RSC's particular ideals and methods of ensemble playing, which can be difficult as many come from a background of commercial theatre, or from other national companies with entirely different policies and aims. This 'importation' of artists into the company is perhaps a further reflection of the RSC's apparent inability to cast from inside, and indeed, would seem to deny one of the primary aims of the ensemble as Hall envisaged it: a company which would be capable of creating and developing its own talent.

The function and operation of Theatregoround has also undergone changes since Trevor Nunn's appointment. From its beginnings in 1965, Theatregoround has grown into a more or less permanent offshoot of the parent RSC: there have been many minor changes in the composition of Theatregoround personnel

and programmes but it had always been seen as a semi-auton-
omous institution working within the overall company structure.
Until 1970, Theatregoround employed its own Artistic Director
and small staff, and its function (as previously stated) was to take
the work and theatrical ideas of the RSC out to new audiences in
theatres, schools and various community centres throughout
Britain. Theatregoround presentations were originally composed
of fragmentary material, put together in the form of a pastiche
programme of theatre: in the later years of operation, Theatregoround programmes became more selective and artistically aware in
choice of repertoire, and began to conduct ventures into the
realms of experimental theatre. Theatregoround frequently used
actors from the permanent company of the RSC — in conjunction
with its own staff — and it operated under a subsidy from the RSC
Administration.

Theatregoround has never been officially recognized by the Arts
Council as an RSC venture, although the Arts Council know and
approve of the Theatregoround function. The result of this
paradoxical situation is that the RSC's annual grant has never been
specifically extended to allow for Theatregoround work, and any
costs of this operation must be met by the RSC as part of its
overall budget. In 1969, it was estimated that the Theatregoround
activity was costing the company in excess of £17,000 per year to
maintain, and the Governors warned that Theatregoround would
have to be curtailed or dropped if it continued to lose money on
this scale.

In 1970, Trevor Nunn introduced the concept of defining
Theatregoround work as productions which would rehearse 'in
parallel' with the normal repertory work of the RSC, and it was
announced that one Theatregoround performance would be
included in the Stratford repertoire each week. This meant
increasing the number of main house performances from eight to
nine, and the extra performance each week would, in effect,
subsidize the entire Theatregoround operation.

Under this new concept, Theatregoround productions began to
originate in the main house at Stratford as part of the RSC
seasonal programme, and used actors, directors and designers who
were also engaged in all main house work. Gareth Morgan resigned
as Artistic Director of Theatregoround in 1970, and the

operation now functions under an Administrator and small staff who are wholly answerable to the central Administration of the RSC: any artistic direction has become the function of the resident Associate Directors of the company. The 1970 Stratford productions of *King John* and *Dr. Faustus* were designated as TGR productions, as were *Henry V* and *Richard II* productions of the 1971 season.

A Theatregoround production is specifically designed to be less in scale than a normal RSC production: they work with a smaller cast (making considerable use of doubling for roles); they are based on scenic concepts which allow them to be set up in localities of varying size and with differing technical availabilities; they require less in the way of support staff and effects than a Stratford production; and they are required to be as mobile as possible in terms of scenery, props and costumes. In all other respects, Theatregoround productions are identical to RSC house productions. Theatregoround continues to show programmes of an experimental nature from time to time, and has become, in some ways, the 'experimental wing' of the RSC.

Between October and December 1970, the RSC took a lease on The Roundhouse Theatre in London to present a Theatregoround Festival of productions, work-demonstrations and after-play discussions all based on Shakespeare and the Elizabethan theatre. This Theatregoround season also included Studio performances of current Stratford and Aldwych presentations, acted without scenery or costumes ' . . . and given to encourage a creative and close actor/audience relationship'.[12] The major productions at The Roundhouse were *Arden of Faversham* (a new production designed for presentation at the Festival), *King John, Dr. Faustus*, and *When Thou Art King* – a chronological History Cycle adapted for Theatregoround by John Barton from Shakespeare's *Henry IV* plays and *Henry V*. In addition there were Studio performances of *Richard III, Hamlet* and *A Midsummer Night's Dream* from the 1970 Stratford repertoire, and work demonstrations given by RSC directors and associates: these demonstrations were planned to 'show aspects of the company's approach to play production', and they included 'open rehearsals' in which directors and actors re-created the RSC rehearsal situation on stage. The audience were invited to stay and join actors and directors in a critical discussion of various productions at the Festival, and most of the RSC's acting and production staff from both theatres took part.

At the annual meeting of Governors in September 1971, it was announced that the RSC's accounts showed a surplus figure of £6,461 — the first time in ten years that the company had not shown a deficit. It was emphasized however, that this surplus was the result of 'an exceptionally high income from ancillary activities', and it was unlikely that the company could expect to show a continuous surplus in years ahead. The RSC made an overall £82,990 from the proceeds of foreign tours, films and television over the financial year in question, and such sources of revenue are intermittent and limited. The 1970/71 Annual Report shows that box office receipts and attendance records for that year were the highest in the company's history, and that the Aldwych played to an average 82 per cent capacity audience: this figure would appear to support the validity of Nunn's Aldwych repertoire policy.

In September 1971, it was announced that the RSC had taken a short-term lease on a second London Theatre, The Place, a small theatre near Euston that is the headquarters of the Contemporary Dance Theatre. Nunn announced that the RSC would construct an arena stage at The Place for a season of plays, with in-the-round seating for approximately 330 and all tickets priced below £1. It was hoped that The Place would be able to establish 'a far closer actor-audience relationship than is possible at either of the two major theatres'.

The nine-week season beginning in October 1971 showed two London premieres; *Occupations*, a play by Trevor Griffiths dealing with the Italian workers' occupation of the factories in 1920, and *Subject to Fits*, a 'play with music' by Robert Montgomery — loosely based on Dostoyevsky's *The Idiot*. Strindberg's *Miss Julie* made up the three-play repertoire. The RSC's 1971/72 season at The Place was a successful venture — particularly with the younger/student audiences — and there is a possibility that such a season may be presented regularly. A second highly successful RSC season at The Place was presented in 1973.

When attempting an assessment of the RSC's production record over the years 1969 to 1973, there arise the same problems of generalization, selection and relative merit that have already been referred to in the previous chapter. There is, however, one production during this period which stands out as an astonishing coup de théâtre: whatever one's views on the interpretation or validity of the piece, Peter Brook's 1970 production of *A Midsummer Night's Dream* must be recognized as one of the most original and outstanding theatrical experiences of the last decade.

Reviewing the opening night of *A Midsummer Night's Dream* in August 1970, Harold Hobson referred to it as: '. . more than refreshing, magnificent, the sort of thing one sees only once in a generation, and then only from a man of genius.'[13]

Since its Stratford opening the production has toured the United States and played an Aldwych season: over a two year period its popularity and critical acclaim has become so enormous that it has been re-cast and sent on a world tour by the RSC during 1972/73. *The Dream* has been widely written about and discussed, and critical opinion is almost unanimous in stating that it is Brook's finest work to date — one of the greatest achievements of the RSC's twelve-year history. One of the few dissenters was Benedict Nightingale:

'He [Brook] did not reclaim the play; he remoulded it, with the help of Billy Smart, Walt Disney, J.G. Ballard, Meyerhold and several others, including perhaps his own sleeping, dreaming, hallucinating self. . . . It is surely time the Brooks wondered if it is right for external invention to outgrow the internal demands of the text. . . .'[14]

Most writers echoed Hobson, and Clive Barnes, reviewing the Broadway season, stated that Brook's *Dream* was '. . . without any equivocation whatsoever the greatest production of Shakespeare I have seen in my life.'[15] During the 1971 Aldwych season, Ronald Bryden wrote:

'The fame of Peter Brook's production of *A Midsummer Night's Dream* has been rumbling round the world, growing in volume. . . . Everywhere the word was the same. Peter Brook had surpassed his *King Lear*, his *Marat-Sade*, pointed the theatre's nose in a new direction for the next decade, and was one of the greatest, most imaginative directors in the modern theatre.'[16]

Brook's production reportedly found its genesis in two sources. While in Iran during 1969, Brook saw some ancient Persian folk plays in which mime and gesture became of paramount importance: in the same year, with his designer Sally Jacobs, he witnessed a Chinese circus in Paris, and was impressed by the way in which the oriental acrobats differed from their Western counterparts. John Kane, who played Puck in the Brook production, explained the circus influence: 'The Chinese acrobats hid the shape of their bodies with long flowing silk robes and performed their tricks with delicacy and speed, so that it seemed the most natural thing in the world for them to spin plates or walk on stilts.'[17]

Combining the oriental and circus influences, Sally Jacobs set *The Dream* in a bare white box, encircled by an upper gallery some fifteen feet above the lower stage level: the bare stage was hung with ropes, trapezes, swings and ladders, and floored with soft white matting. Her costume designs were the baggy trousers and gaudy-coloured satins of an oriental acrobat, with Puck in vivid yellow satin pantaloons and Titania and Oberon in flowing satin robes. The four fairies (or 'audio-visuals' as Brook referred to them) were dressed alike in drab grey sackcloth material, and their magic was performed with the aid of wire hoops, fishing poles, trapezes and plastic hose-lengths.

In key with the set, the entire production took on the characteristics of a circus, and Brook demanded an exceptional degree of acrobatic and vocal competence from his actors: they were expected to tumble, swing on trapeze, juggle, walk on stilts, climb poles, wrestle, jump in the air, sing — and do full justice to Shakespeare's text and verse. The result was a new kind of theatrical magic — and a new form of theatre ritual. John Kane's article, 'Plotting with Peter',[18] documents some of the varied rehearsal methods employed on *The Dream*, and Brook spoke of the 'hidden play' and the 'new magic' of the production in an interview for *Plays and Players*:

'After a long series of dark, violent, black plays I had a very strong wish to go as deeply as possible into a work of pure celebration of the arts of the theatre ... *The Dream* is a play about magic, spirits, fairies. Today we don't believe in any one of those things and yet, perhaps, we do ... the language

Old Times directed by Peter Hall at the Aldwych, 1971/2. Colin Blakely as Deeley and Vivien Merchant as Anna.

Old Times, Aldwych 1971/2: *L. to R.:* Vivien Merchant as Anna, Dorothy Tutin as Kate and Colin Blakely as Deeley.

Peter Brook's production of *A Midsummer Night's Dream* at Stratford in 1970. *L. to R.:* Alan Howard as Theseus, Sara Kestelman as Hippolyta, Mary Rutherford as Hermia, Christopher Gable as Lysander, John Kane as Philostrate, Frances de la Tour as Helena and Ben Kingsley as Demetrius.

A MIDSUMMER NIGHT'S DREAM

Peter Hall's 1959 production at Stratford. *L. to R.:* Robert Hardy as Oberon, Mary Ure as Titania, Charles Laughton as Bottom and Ian Holm as Puck.

Photo Angus McBean, © *RSC*

Peter Brook's 1970 production at Stratford, Alan Howard as Oberon, John Kane as Puck.

Photo David Farrell, © *RSC*

Sally Jacob's set design for Peter Brook's 1970 production.

A MIDSUMMER NIGHT'S DREAM

Lila de Nobili's setting for the palace scenes, and carpenter's shop scenes using inner stage, in Peter Hall's 1959 Stratford production.

of *The Dream* must be expressed through a very different stage imagery from the one that has served its purpose in the past. We have dropped all pretence of making magic by bluff through stage tricks. . . . We have to start in the open — in fact we begin in a white set and white light. . . .'[19]

Brook's stage product was Shakespeare's text — supported by a series of stunning theatrical effects which were all conducted 'in the open' and all executed through the sheer physical dexterity of his actors. There was little in *The Dream* which could be construed as a behind-the-scenes theatrical trick: the play the audience saw was the play the actors presented, and one was almost totally unaware of the presence of back-stage support staff. The upper gallery encircling the set was used by the entire cast, either as a setting for parts of the action or merely as an observation platform to look down on the performance below.

If a cast member was not required to take part in the action, he was frequently on the gallery 'observing'. The audio-visuals were present on stage almost continuously, to 'interfere', help or take part in the various levels of plot and character. They also acted as a sort of on-stage stage management staff: as the Lovers enacted their woodland chase, the audio-visuals manipulated wire-coil trees from the gallery and made appropriate forest sounds and noises. Puck and Oberon flew on trapezes; Titania's bower was a suspended centrepoint of scarlet ostrich feathers, flanked by audio-visuals who took up yoga positions on trapeze-platforms; the flower-drug 'love in idleness' became a zinc plate spinning on a perspex rod — tossed by Puck and Oberon negligently to each other. The rude mechanicals entered to a cacophony of sawing, rasping sounds, and rehearsed their play in string vests, flat caps, work trousers and braces — a gang of builder's labourers (circus clowns?) at their lunch hour in a white courtyard/wood. Bottom, when refused the role of Lion, downed tools and sulkily walked off-stage up the theatre aisle: in the final scene, Snug, playing Lion over enthusiastically, tumbled into the front row of the stalls and clambered back on stage with profuse apology to the audience.

Throughout the play, the actor-audience relationship was emphasized and strengthened, and Puck's farewell 'Give us your hands' was interpreted literally — with the cast bounding into the auditorium to clasp any hand they could reach. The multitude of effects that the production contained are far too numerous to mention individually, but perhaps the most extraordinary scene was Titania's seduction of Bottom. This became a celebratory ritual of the most complete sexuality — supported by the wild percussion of the two 'musicians' seated on either side of the gallery and the active participation of the entire cast:

> '. . . the zest and barbarity of sound reaches a glorious pagan climax with the meeting of Titania and Bottom. Titania's body arches with desire, she cries out, the fairies carry Bottom in state to her bed, an arm raised through his legs like a giant phallus, with Mendelssohn's "Wedding March" bursting triumphantly on the audience and huge confetti paper plates showering down from the gallery. . . .'[20]

In this scene, Brook appeared to support Kott's view that *The Dream* explores a darker, more powerfully sexual side of love than is normally suggested, although he did not entirely endorse the Kott interpretation: 'Most definitely, Kott wrote very interestingly about the play — though he fell into the trap of turning one aspect of the play into the whole.'[21] Brook's *Dream* was the fusion of many interpretative aspects and technical ideas into a complete theatrical 'experience'. Ronald Bryden, reviewing a Roundhouse studio performance of the production, wrote: 'It resolves in one dazzling synthesis the conflict Brook defined in his book *The Empty Space* between "rough" and "holy" theatre: the popular extrovert tradition of Shakespeare and the intenser ritual one of Greek tragedy, Artaud and Grotowski.'[22] It has been reported that *A Midsummer Night's Dream* will be Brook's final production for the RSC, owing to commitments with his new group based in Paris. If this is so, *The Dream* will prove a fitting climax to a Stratford career which has spanned twenty-five years. It is certain that this production will be written about for years to come.

Peter Hall's world-premiere production of Pinter's *Old Times* opened at the Aldwych in 1971, following a provincial warm-up tour, and has since been re-directed for commercial managements in the United States and Europe. Set in a converted farmhouse somewhere by the sea, the play revolves around three characters engaged in an evening of reminiscences. Deeley, a documentary film-maker, and Kate have been married for twenty years and the third character, their dinner guest Anna, once shared a London room with Kate. The play opens with Deeley interrogating Kate about her early relationship with Anna: he follows this with a wary verbal circling of Anna, which leads finally to a rapid exchange of question and swift evasion between them — with Kate as the silent onlooker.

As the action develops it becomes evident that the characters are engaged in something considerably more important than mere recollection of old times: they are engaged in a progressive battle — an ambiguous battle for 'rights' and 'possessions' unspecified and undefined. Pinter's dialogue is typically evasive — syncopated with pause and silence — as the three are drawn into individual accounts of past events and incidents which do not entirely accord with each other. Truth and fiction become indistinguishable: the more the characters probe and question, the more their minutely differing stories become merged and blended as one. Harold Hobson has suggested that the play concerns '. . . the frightening possibility that the imagination is creative.'[23] What is and what is not, what was and what was not, has no real importance. Ronald Bryden saw *Old Times* as a similar kind of 'war of territorial dominance' to that which underlay *The Homecoming*. Where the plays differ in that *Old Times* is basically a comic text, yet the comic lines are all underpinned with Pinter's characteristic sense of the ominous. Bryden wrote:

> 'You have a wonderful casserole,' says Anna, slightly too warmly. Deeley looks baffled. 'I'm so sorry,' she apologises, blushing and smiling at her Freudian slip. 'I meant wife. You have a wonderful wife. She was always a good cook . . .' Anyone with an ear for Harold Pinter dialogue will recognize the territory. . . . A gauntlet has been thrown down. Battle is engaged. The battle-ground is Kate: which of the two, Deeley or Anna, has possessed more of her? The weapons, as usual, are sex and language: the language of innuendo, cultural discomfiture, the slight verbal excess staking an emotional claim. Truth has nothing to do with it. . . . The winner will be the one who can impose his or her version of the past. . . .'[24]

Hall's direction and John Bury's setting for *Old Times* have both been highly praised and, once again, critics made use of frequent musical analogy to describe the way in which Hall 'translates' Pinter for the stage: 'Peter Hall directs the comedy with a musician's ear for the value of each word and silence which exposes every layer of the text. . . .'[25] During the late sixties, the RSC began to turn towards new American writing, and it has been Hall who directed two of the three Edward Albee plays presented by the company since 1968 – *A Delicate Balance* (1969) and *All Over* (1972).

In 1969, his first year as sole director of the company, Trevor Nunn centred the Stratford season around three of Shakespeare's later plays, *Pericles, The Winter's Tale* and *Henry VIII* – the latter two of which he directed himself. He explained his interest in the late plays in the 1969 programmes: 'Nobody believes any more that Shakespeare's late plays, the romances, are the work of a tired mind or genius gone senile . . . [they] are packed and complex, stylistically they constantly break new ground and old rules. . . . They speak to a time in need of moral certainty.'[26] Together with Christopher Morley, Nunn used the late plays to begin as investigation into the use of a 'chamber setting' for Shakespeare – an enclosed setting in which the private rather than the public lives of characters could be explored. Nunn has declared a greater interest in domestic environments than political ones, and Morley's austere 'white box' became a dominant RSC design style during 1969. Nunn explained his shift of emphasis in a 1970 interview for *Plays and Players*: 'It's being said that the RSC are becoming afraid of throne rooms and courts. I'm sure this is true. In most of our work now we are concerned with the human personalities of a king or queen rather than with their public roles.'[27]

The Winter's Tale became a study of the nervous tensions in Leontes' mind: 'Leontes is in a destructive nightmare "performed" in a "wide gap of time". Spring breaks through the grip of winter, love returns, enabling Leontes to awake his faith and be redeemed.'[28] The concept behind the Nunn/Morley chamber setting was to isolate the actor – the individual – and to make him and his emotions the most important object on stage. The result was a further stripping away of scenic effect and decoration, to enable a greater concentration on a particular human

situation within an enclosed, bare environment. Nunn explained:
'It [the chamber setting] has to work within the scale of the
individual actor — to make his words, thoughts, fantasies and
language seem important . . . what he wears, what he sits on,
possessions directly connected with him, are the next
important point. The middle and far distances are not
important . . . we want the stage to represent earth, (as for
the Elizabethans) and underneath that stage lies hell, the
unknown, the darkly occult. Above it is a canopy, a roof
fretted with golden fire, the gods, heaven, Apollo.'[29]
In fact, the chamber setting created a very simple universe and
placed the individual and his domestic situation at the centre of
that universe. The Nunn/Morley use of highly schematic colour
patterns and colour contrasts further heightened the sense of an
individual in isolation, and Peter Ansorge wrote: 'Nunn is
fascinated by an allegorical presentation of Shakespeare plays —
assessing a character not only in terms of personal psychology, but
also through the costume which is chosen, the tonal significance of
a particular colour.'[30] ▲

Nunn's 1970 *Hamlet* was set in a very different climate from
Peter Hall's 'political' Elsinore of 1965. David Warner's Hamlet
was a young man, spokesman for his generation, at war with the
Establishment: Alan Howard's Hamlet was the study of a mind
almost at breaking point, and the centre of his interpretation was
the shifting balance between real and feigned madness. The 1970
Hamlet was a solitary, unkempt figure in black, set against an
ice-white palace and a white-fur costumed court: ' . . . an intelligent and not insensitive neurotic making a desperate and
ultimately successful bid to come to terms with himself. . . .'[31]
The tone of the tragedy was distinctly domestic and the various
inter-family relationships dominated Nunn's interpretation. The
state of Hamlet's mind was persistently high-lighted by the use of
Christian symbolism: the Prince first appeared wearing a crucifix;
his vow of revenge was taken prostrate before his dagger, dug into
the floor as a symbol of the Cross; the 'To be or not to be'
soliloquy was spoken as a prayer at the altar of a chapel, with
Ophelia seated at a pew and Polonius and Claudius hidden in a
confessional; the Claudius/Hamlet confrontation following the
murder of Polonius was played in front of a statue of the

Virgin — Hamlet held 'crucified' between two courtiers while Claudius beat him; Hamlet visited his mother dressed in the the costume of a friar — 'as much a priest as a son'.

A further interpretative note is the fact that Nunn made this Hamlet a man who was obviously fascinated by the theatre and all things theatrical — a prince dreaming of a career among the players. The players were singled out as the only characters whose coloured costumes differed from the schematic black and white designs, and Hamlet became noticeably 'animated' only when in their presence. His constant use of theatrical tricks and theatrical costume was made into an obvious source of resolution and release — the only escape from his inner turmoil; at one stage he slow hand-clapped himself after an impassioned soliloquy. The RSC programme made note of Anne Righter's comment:

> 'The tragedy is riddled with theatrical language. . . . Through the agency of illusion, the prince has at last separated appearance from reality, hypocrisy from truth. The theatre has been his touchstone.'[32]

John Barton's 1968 production of *Troilus and Cressida* was revived at the Aldwych during 1969, and proved to be an extremely thoughtful and powerful re-thinking of the play, with formal patterns of near-naked warriors set against a bare stage dominated by huge bulls-head symbols. Barton's 1969 *Twelfth Night* at Stratford was set in a wood-slatted box (a variation of the chamber setting), directed in a sombre mood, lit in autumnal tones, and played over the sounds of sea-waves and soft guitar melodies. Hobson called it 'a production drenched in melancholy', and J.W. Lambert wrote: ' . . . Morley has set the play in a long receding wattle tunnel decorated by four flickering candlesticks, but lit from outside. . . . Illyria, like Prospero's isle, is full of sweet sounds that give delight and hurt not. . . . As I recall the innumerable enchantments . . . I beam gratitude to all the players and look forward to more from, I am convinced, a director standing on the threshold of mature greatness.'[33] Lambert was not the only critic who considered *Twelfth Night* to be Barton's finest production, and it has proved to be one of the most popular RSC presentations over recent years.

A Midsummer Night's Dream dominated 1970, but the Stratford season also contained two interesting productions in which the notion of directorial interpretation became a primary influence. Robin Phillips' production of *The Two Gentlemen of Verona* set this early comedy in a twentieth-century idiom and made the subject a modern study of adolescence and puppy-love: younger characters romped about the stage in bikinis and sunglasses, speaking Shakespeare's words interspersed with Beatles' lyrics. Their bored elders watched from the sidelines, and the atmosphere suggested a Mediterranean coastal resort at high summer. Buzz Goodbody's *King John* was directed as a farcical Shakespearian 'comic-book', and John's character was decidedly based on the A.A. Milne conception: 'Politics, war, was reduced to a children's game, and the king to a noisome uppity infant who whooped, leapt, threw pillows at ambassadors, waggled his feet at the nobility, peeped at his courtiers through the lattice of his throne, and finally slid cross-eyed off on to his bottom in the most farcical death scene I can remember having seen.'[34] The 1970 Aldwych season included a production of Boucicault's *London Assurance* (last presented in London during 1890), and Shaw's *Major Barbara*, the first RSC production of a Shaw Play. 1971 was an unexceptional year at Stratford, with John Barton's Victorian *Othello* and Ronald Eyre's *Much Ado About Nothing* as the most interesting new productions of a generally uninteresting season.

During 1971, Trevor Nunn announced the 1972 season at Stratford as a presentation of Shakespeare's Roman Plays — *Coriolanus, Julius Caesar, Antony and Cleopatra* and *Titus Andronicus* — with a 'Plautine production' of *The Comedy of Errors* to complete the repertoire. The cycle ★ would be directed on an ensemble principle, with Nunn in the chair — supported by Buzz Goodbody and Euan Smith as his co-directors. Christopher Morley was to design the entire season, assisted by Ann Curtis. Although there have been Stratford seasons since 1969 which were based on various linking ideas and patterns, the Roman Plays is the first project of this scale to have been attempted by the RSC since *The Wars of the Roses*. The season was based on a single organic idea and a single background notion, and was staged under the collective title of *The Romans*.

In September 1971, Trevor Nunn gave me his reasons for

wishing to direct the plays, and explained the concepts behind the presentation: 'They are not a chronological group: they're not conceived as a group and they bear no special relationship in the dramatist's mind. They do, nevertheless, share a background, and they do share various actions of manners and mores and behaviour and society . . . they share the background of the same State — that went from small tribe, to a city-state, to a republic, to an empire, to something that was overrun by a group of Goths. That development is there within the plays, and (in a sense) there are no textual contradictions to that development. But, obviously, they are separate pieces that one is not even remotely considering approaching in the 'way that *The Wars of the Roses* were treated. . . . It's working with that same group [of actors] over an extended period of time that fascinates me as an artist . . . but, most of all, we're doing these particular plays because three of them are plays which (at this point in time) seem to me to have the most meaning and the most point and the most relevance. . . . They are speaking directly to us now. . . . At the end of that sequence of plays, it is a world teetering on the edge of extinction.'[3 5]

The Stratford stage and auditorium were extensively altered for the season, and the renovations were carried out to Christopher Morley's design. The stage has been re-shaped and thrusts further into the auditorium than before, to suggest a one room, open stage area. Box seating has been added at two levels along the side walls of the auditorium, (some of these boxes overhang the stage), and the stalls seating has been re-arranged to accommodate the new staging requirements. Included in the alterations is the first installation of Rank Strand Electric's new DDM (Digital Dimmer Memory) stage lighting system, which uses a computer to reconcile precise recording with manual improvisation. These architectural and technical modifications can be seen as an attempt to bring the Stratford theatre into line with the proposed staging facilities at the new Barbican Theatre. The concept is certainly based on an open plan and seems designed to bring actors and audience into very close proximity. The new staging at Stratford includes extremely sophisticated stage machinery, intended to make the RST stage one of the most versatile and 'revolutionary' in the world . . . 'an architectural and mechanical marvel.'

The Romans season opened with a spectacularly conceived production of *Coriolanus* — obviously designed to give full play to the stage's new tricks: 'To mark the scene changes walls rise and fall, unexpected flights of steps appear, and even flaming furnaces sprout from nowhere. Or the whole floor tilts forward, while slabs of masonry revolve ... to say nothing of stroboscopic lights, sudden clouds of smoke — and the costumes. ...' *Julius Caesar* was equally effective as stage spectacle, with black-leathered Romans suggesting the Hitlerian SS, and ' ... stage effects that would do credit to a Nuremberg rally.' *Antony and Cleopatra* and *Titus Andronicus* also made considerable use of the stage machinery, while Clifford Williams' production of his much-revived *Comedy of Errors* relied on the simple fixed setting of the original 1962 production. In critical terms, *The Romans* did not receive the almost unqualified approval accorded *The Wars of the Roses* some nine years earlier. *Caesar* and *Coriolanus* were dubbed 'spectacular' and 'impressive' and reviews for *Titus* varied between 'Hollywood vulgarity' and 'spellbinding Grand Guignol'.

Antony and Cleopatra was not the high water mark of the season that was promised, and most reviewers seemed to feel that the production failed to scale the heights. John Barber said: 'All Shakespeare's plays can be effectively acted by a good company of players. But when it comes to *Antony and Cleopatra* something else must be pulled out of the bag. Goodness is not enough.' Janet Suzman's Cleopatra was a technically near-faultless performance, and suggested a woman of vitality and intelligence: ' ... moving from deep feeling to bedroom playfulness in an instant ... in death she gains a real dignity suggesting that she can at last match her dream-image of a superhuman Antony.' It was felt however, that this Cleopatra was *too* clear headed — *too* clever and skilful in the details of political manipulation. 'She tended to rub out the human contradictions of the part.' Richard Johnson's performance as Antony was likewise an intelligent and carefully thought out reading, but not wholly the Antony whose delights were 'dolphin-like': the dissipation of the ageing libertine was somehow missing.

Trevor Nunn's interpretation centered on the cultural contrasts between Rome and Egypt, and (in terms of his over-view of *The Romans* season) gave weight to a world of political intrigue with ' ... a frightening Octavius ... a dictator's fanaticism burning in his eye'. One critic summed-up *Antony and Cleopatra* by calling it a production 'locked by logic' — and this view was echoed when considering *The Romans* season as a whole. Although Nunn had specifically stated that he did not see *The Romans* as a linked cycle of plays, he certainly saw the plays as a political pattern and all programmes carried the note: 'Though each play is complete in itself, together they show the birth, achievement and collapse of a civilization.' In the *Titus* programme, Nunn's article *Shakespeare and Rome* concludes: 'Shakespeare's Elizabethan nightmare has become ours . . . are we already in the convulsion which heralds a fall greater than Rome's?' Most critics commented on the didactic intent of *The Romans*, and there was some feeling that this intent was, on the whole, destructive to the plays as individual entities. It is significant that *The Comedy of Errors* was received with more universal acceptance and critical praise than any other production of the season: *The Comedy of Errors* stood alone . . . 'a world of make-believe!'.

In 1973 *The Romans* transferred to the Aldwych, and critics were able to see them played as a group for the first time. The London staging was considerably altered and 'scaled down': the complicated Stratford sets became a single box set surrounded by high scaffolding, with various drapes and canopies flown in and out to suit the different productions. The Aldwych stage was 'a dark, austere arena, erupting into instantaneous bursts of detailed realism and brilliant colour . . . but always returning to itself'. There were also some cast changes for the London season, most notably the inclusion of Nicol Williamson in the RSC cast list playing the title role in *Coriolanus*. Critical reaction to the Aldwych season was mostly favourable, and it was widely felt that the simpler, less spectacular mode of staging allowed a greater emphasis on individual performance — sometimes marred by the elaborate Stratford mechanics. Williamson's *Coriolanus* received high praise, and John Barber wrote: 'One man alone has given new life and brilliant meaning to the Royal Shakespeare Company. A guest actor, in a troupe which has lately disdained stars, made a nonsense of the whole policy — at least for the Shakespeare heights. . . . Nicol Williamson held the audience breathless.'[36] Summing up the entire *Romans* season, Irving Wardle wrote:

'. . . this is the company's most ambitious group of productions since *The Wars of the Roses* cycle ten years ago . . . as a public event it may lack topical resonance, but in strictly theatrical terms it is a monumental piece of work of a kind that defies the transitory nature of stage performance. . . . At last year's Stratford performances there was a tendency (particularly in the opening tableaux) to bash the plays with a sledge hammer to make them fit the overall pattern. At the Aldwych these schematic underlinings are much muted . . . there is now a continuous Roman world in which the separate plays can lead their own lives.'[37]♦'

There are indications that the next few years may signal far-reaching changes in the entire structure and operation of the RSC. *The Romans* can be seen as the beginnings of a new artistic phase in the company's development, and Trevor Nunn has intimated that there may well be major administrative changes planned for the near future. He has suggested the possibility of a future scheme under which the RSC might be led by 'a group of artists' — with the actual artistic leadership changing hands on a rotation principle every two or three years. Such a scheme would presumably be a logical extension of the Directorate as it now exists, but with each member taking a period of overall responsibility as Chief Executive of the organization. Nunn did not direct any productions during 1971, and stated that he was using the year to conduct a period of review, in which he would examine the overall operation, efficiency and image of the RSC. He said: 'In a sense, what I'm doing is imagining that one could start again completely from scratch — with the experience of the work that Peter did, and also my own experience of running that up to this point. . . . We're learning some very remarkable things . . . [and] These things will amount to considerable structural changes within the organization. . . . It may not appear to be a new image at all: it might be something which goes very smoothly, and nobody from outside will ever realize — because it doesn't show. . . . It might arrive at a point where clearly there is a change in everything — a change of intention — and that will have to be declared!'[38]

Most people connected with the RSC express the feeling that the company is due for re-organization. Views on just what this should entail differ widely, but opinion is unanimous in stating that the structure has become vast and unwieldy, and that the company's function — already institutional — is likely to become more so over the next decade unless changes are made. Hall has recognized that his original creation has become unmanageable, and Nunn appears to be engaged in setting the RSC on a new course for the seventies.

I asked Peter Hall, in December 1971, to speculate on the future role and identity of the Company he founded and directed for nine years. He said:

'I think that the strength of the allegiances that the RSC has built up over the years, and the strength of the direction team, and the strength of the general aesthetic, could probably make it last well for another five years at least. But I wouldn't like to prophesy after that! Nor would I wish to. I think that the theatre is ephemeral and of now. That's part of its "thing"! . . . if I was running the RSC now it would be something quite different. And this isn't any criticism of Trevor — who I admire very much and I think has done a remarkable job. But I'm different to him and he's different to me. . . .'[39]

Afterword
by Trevor Nunn

'As in a theatre, the eyes of men,
After a well grac'd actor leaves the stage,
Are idly bent on him that enters next . . .'
Richard II

Peter Hall is not an easy man to follow. Successful practitioners in the theatre come and go, minutely modifying the achievements of previous generations. The man of genius is rare. He changes our way of thinking. He reconciles opposites. He operates at the outermost frontiers of possibility. He thrives upon uncertainty. He is obsessed.

In the theatre he is usually a writer. Peter Hall is a good writer, but his genius is as an impresario.

The old term has become somewhat debased but I suspect that no other quite serves. The good impresario is the man who has the imagination to conceive of a grand design, extraordinary analytic precision to define its component elements, ruthless will and nerveless determination to resist any deviation from the declared course. He is the man of high diplomacy, political acumen and Machiavellian enthusiasm. But the *great* impresario is only so because of the quality of his vision and his integrity to that vision.

The theatre is, by its collective nature, a place of compromise, between people, and between the polarities of ideals and money. The great impresario achieves his will with people without compromise (or certainly without the appearance of it) and if a choice has to be made between money and an artistic principle, he always, always preserves the principle.

During the ten years from 1959 to 1968, Peter Hall changed the habits and practice of the theatre in the British Isles. He took the 'memorial' out of both the Stratford theatre's title, and approach, he established the idea and the fact of a major permanent national company; he built an empire to contain and promote its tentacular energies, he fought and won the battle for subsidy, he fostered new talent in all fields, and he insisted upon an identifiably hard, unsentimental style of performance and presentation. And he did it all publicly, risking individual censure to achieve a new position and status for his company. He gambled dangerously but with a gambler's faith in himself and his luck.

On a very hot desultory afternoon in Cambridge in the autumn of 1960, I walked past the gates of the Senate House, paused, and took a few steps non-committally towards the open doors beyond, through which came the clear resonance of a lecturer's voice. I entered and stood at the back. A tall imposing young man was delivering his views of the English classic stage, past present and future. There was very little that he did not intend to discard overturn or improve. The lecture was riveting, but it was only at the end that I discovered the name of the lecturer. He was of course the new artistic director of the then Shakespeare Memorial Theatre, Peter Hall. The setting, with its overtones of the young Messiah teaching the elders in the Temple, was sufficiently appropriate to make the whole experience photographically recorded in my memory. And it is uncanny that what he said he would do, he has done.

When I had to follow Peter Hall, at thrilling and daunting short notice, I had just about learned how to run a rehearsal; I hadn't a clue about running anything bigger. I had only ever used somebody else's secretary to type the odd letter, I had never chaired a meeting, I couldn't read a balance sheet, and I was totally unaccustomed to public speaking — so I made no prophetic pronouncements. Continuity was the word. Continuity was the lifeline. Continuity was everything I knew.

Mr Addenbrooke has given his personal view of what has happened to the RSC since I took over the leadership. Perhaps I should add some personal comments, if only to achieve a more balanced picture. (Specific points are noted on pp.314 ff.)

Peter had canvassed the good will and support of all associate artists and permanent members of staff before any announcement was made and to that extent, the vaunted continuity was a reality. Paul Scofield's departure came as the result of a difference between himself and Peter, and a genuine wish to move on. He specially sought me out to explain that his decision had nothing to do with my appointment. I believed that.

However, I also inherited a long list of three year contract artists with many of whom I had no personal acquaintance. Some were in the process of taking 'a year out' from the work of the company. I discovered that 'a year out' usually meant that the associate directors could not offer adequate opportunities for the actor, or they had changed their minds about his potential — he had become 'unpopular'. I was disturbed at the notion of a three year commitment which envisaged that one of the years would be spent elsewhere. I could see its loose pragmatic value, but I could also see how the scheme could be abused by actors and directors alike. In many cases I was unable to persuade individual directors to work again with contract artists who had taken 'a year out'. That meant that at the beginning of my administration, I was attempting to dismantle certain long term arrangements made by Peter, and where I was unable to dismantle, I was forced to uphold the contracts financially. I decided to adapt the system. I offered two year contracts instead of three year contracts, thus rational- izing the two theatre policy and rhythm, and abandoning 'the year out'.

This was in the context of a major financial crisis, which threatened to force the RSC back to Stratford. I had urgent and tense meetings with Lord Goodman, trying to procure from him an unambiguous statement of the Arts Council/Treasury attitude to the RSC, and in particular the RSC's presence in London. We all had the feeling during those months that, since the RSC was weakened by the loss of Peter Hall and since there was not enough subsidy to go round, it would be our company which would go to the wall. While Peter had been able to find each annual shortfall out of the company's reserves, everybody assumed that the crunch would never come. At the first Finance Committee that I attended, I learned that the controlled rundown of the company's reserves was almost complete, and that they would be exhausted within a year. There would then be no money to pay off any deficit that I incurred. The company would be bankrupt.

Against these financial odds, in the five years from 1968-1973 the RSC has achieved a great deal. The late play season in 1969 was publicly and critically amongst the most successful Stratford seasons since the company began, and was a triumph for the smaller company principle. The 1971 London season was the most successful season the company had enjoyed at the Aldwych, and introduced at The Place the new small auditorium policy for certain modern works. The company has regularly broken its own box office records (and all other theatres' box office records) and has, during the period, consistently played to more than a million people, each year. It has managed to reduce its annual deficits drastically and was able to announce a small surplus (after the Arts Council grant) in 1971. But this financial success has owed much to perhaps the most important development over the five years. The RSC has become a truly international company.

Since 1968 we have played all over the world on many occasions, in America (in Los Angeles three times, in San Francisco twice, in New York three times, as well as numerous other cities) in Canada, Japan, Australia and all over Europe in three major tours. Each tour has been a revenue earner which has made all the difference between financial survival and financial disaster.

The last five years have been as secure as a ride on a condemned big dipper. Every plan has been conceived and developed towards survival. The two year plan, the finishing of three year contracts, the change of attitude to the Aldwych, the smaller companies, the transferring of successes, the television and film deals, the international touring have all in some way been responses to the imminent threat of extinction, or at the very least the threat of discontinuing the two theatre organisation. Five years is long enough to fight for such uneasy survival. It is non-productive. It is soul destroying. It is exhausting.

Kenneth Tynan estimated that the collective output of the theatre at any time reached only 2% of the population of this country. Perhaps an up to date survey would put the percentage a bit lower. In the light of such a statistic, what should the function of a subsidized national theatre institution be? Should it be a house of distilled excellence, available to an audience in a defined income bracket? No. I want to be concerned with a theatre that is determined to reach beyond the barriers of income, I want an avowed and committed popular theatre. I want a socially concerned theatre. A politically aware theatre. In reality not in name.

What is subsidy for? For the artist who could not work without it? For the presentation of luxurious mis en scene notions which would remain on the drawing board without financial assistance? Or for audiences, to enable managements to keep admission prices low so that the theatre is not socially divisive? I want to use subsidy more for actors and audiences. I have become disillusioned with luxurious notions. Leonardo da Vinci had them, and presenters of the masque/opera tradition ever since. They misplace emphasis. They indicate that the only significant route of communication is from the director/designer to the critic. I want a theatre which gives back the emphasis to the dramatist, to the actors and to the audience.

The RSC must be the most expert, skilled and distinctive troupe performing the plays of Shakespeare in the world. We *can* be at present, but randomly. The necessary skills can only be achieved with permanence. But an ensemble can only work if there is *one* group, and if there are no hierarchic distinctions within the group. Our money must be spent on the actors and on the audience.

In the 1960's, it was a matter of excitement and curiosity that the RSC was declaring itself to be an ensemble and its short-comings were seen as an understandable part of early development. In the 1970's, the idea of the ensemble is a commonplace; the term is abused, overworked and scorned. 'Every actor is ensemble, but some are more ensemble than others' runs the joke. The cynicism is justified. A mixed economy has meant that the RSC has never got beyond the appearance of 'ensemble' working.

In the 1960's, the sheer size of the RSC generated a popular excitement. In the 1970's the scale of the organisation is taken for granted and its unwieldiness is more noticeable. Recently, the RSC opened twelve productions in ten weeks at three theatres. They included five plays by Shakespeare, a double bill by Pinter, four new plays, and two poetry/documentary programmes. For the most part, the work was received enthusiastically, occasionally ecstatically, and box office records were broken for the period. But the collective achievement went unremarked. That density of output, from one theatre company in a little over two months, was assumed to be the norm. And the truth is, the company has become a grouping of too many people doing too much less well than they are able.

In the 1960's, there was, for the first few years, no National Theatre, presenting a repertoire of representative works, and there was no living connection between new plays in performance and classic plays in performance. Peter Hall changed that with the Aldwych — a theatre taken specially to present seasons of new and classic plays. The theory remains impressive. The actor working with Shakespeare is in danger of atrophy unless he is influenced by contemporary ideas; and the actor working on the new play is deeply in need of a tradition, a framework, a sense of language, to focus his endeavour. The new and the classic must cross fertilize. The same actors must do both. But the theory has never quite worked out in practice. The two year plan got close to it. The percentage of actors working on plays other than Shakespeare (and as well as Shakespeare) was sometimes as high as 50%. In the mid sixties, the new plays had been done by ad-hoc groups of actors joining at the beginning of an Aldwych season, eventually to work in parellel to the Stratford Shakespeare company arriving in London a few months later. The plan I developed implied that new work had to be found to fit the company, not a company to fit the work. And that, for new plays, is the wrong way round. Scripts were turned down because to do them would have meant engaging people from outside the company. It is limiting to try to present new plays with a permanent company. It is highly desirable to present new plays using a pool of artists between whom relationships already exist, and between whom there are certain shared beliefs.

So the RSC must now change again. The associate directors are closely knit. The associate actors are nearly all working for the company at the present time. The base for a new thrust is very strong. The experiences of the last five years have vitally challenged our shared beliefs, adapted and qualified them but in so doing, strengthened them. So we must now re-organize to maintain pre-eminence (relevance and popularity too) in performing the plays of Shakespeare, and we must resist at all costs the possibility of becoming an exclusive coterie theatre for the enjoyment only of those who can afford high prices. The job will be done in time for the opening of our new theatre in Barbican in 1978.

Trevor Nunn
January 1974

Part II

Personal Interviews

PERSONAL INTERVIEWS

While writing this work the following people were interviewed by the author, and full transcripts of those interviews
marked (*) are included here.

Name	Date of Interview
Dame Peggy Ashcroft, * *Director and Associate Artist, RSC*.	January 1971
John Barton, * *Associate Director, RSC*	September 1971

Ronald Bryden,
  Literary Manager, RSC
  Former Theatre Critic
  for 'The Observer'
	February 1972

David Brierley, * *General Manager, RSC*	June 1971 September 1971
E.R. Bosley, *Secretary to the Governors, RSC*	June 1971

John Bury, *
  Associate Designer and
  former Head of Design, RSC
	June 1971

Tony Church,
  Associate Artist, RSC.
  Former Director, Northcott Theatre,
  Exeter
	April 1971
	September 1971

Maurice Daniels, *Planning Controller, RSC*	March 1971

Judi Dench,   November 1971
  Associate Artist, RSC

Tom English,   January 1971
  Former Private Secretary to
  Sir Barry Jackson

Gareth Lloyd Evans,   March 1971
  Department of Extra-Mural Studies   September 1971
  University of Birmingham.

Kaye Flanagan,   October 1971
  RST Club Organizer, RSC

William Gaskill,   April 1972
  (Former RSC Director),
  Artistic Director,
  English Stage Company.

Sir John Gielgud,   April 1972
  Actor

John Goodwin,   April 1971
  Press and Publicity Manager, RSC

Peter Hall, *   December 1971
  Director and former   January 1972
  Managing Director, RSC
  Director, National Theatre
  of Great Britain

Desmond Hall,   June 1971
  Production Manager, RSC

Roger Howells,   December 1971
  General Stage Manager, RSC

Emrys James,   November 1971
  Associate Artist, RSC

John Kane,   October 1971
  Associate Artist, RSC

Trevor Nunn,   September 1971
  Artistic Director, RSC

Anthony Page,   April 1972
  (Former RSC Director)
  Associate Artistic Director
  English Stage Company

Richard Pasco,   October 1971
  Associate Artist, RSC

Ian Richardson,   December 1970
  Associate Artist, RSC

Morgan Sheppard,   October 1971
  Associate Artist, RSC

Elizabeth Spriggs,   November 1971
  Associate Artist, RSC

John Trewin,   January 1971
  Theatre Critic and Historian

Dorothy Tutin,   January 1972
  Actress and Open Contract
    Artist, RSC

Ted Valentine,   September 1971
  Contract Artist, RSC

Clifford Williams, *   June 1971
  Associate Director, RSC

Michael Williams,   June 1971
  Associate Artist, RSC

Peter Woodthorpe,   October 1971
  Contract Artist, RSC.

Trevor Nunn, Artistic Director of Royal Shakespeare Company since 1968.

Dame Peggy Ashcroft.

Dame Peggy Ashcroft

Director and Associate Artist,
Royal Shakespeare Company

January 1971

*In the early sixties Peter Hall talked a great deal about
discovering an acting style for Shakespeare. What did you
understand by this? What was he searching for?*

It's very difficult to pin down exactly. I think that, in a way, Peter
evolved something that could be called a style, but it was an
evolution and not a revolution in style. Throughout my life as an
actor the attitude to the speaking of Shakespeare has changed to a
certain degree. You see, I think that what we do now basically
goes back to William Poel, who I suppose was the first anti-
romantic, anti-singing style Shakespearian. He gave first attention
to the meaning, in the belief that if you follow the sense and
punctuation of Shakespeare, you speak the verse. It is not
necessary to put 'verse' up in inverted commas. Of course you
have to observe the fact that it *is* verse and not prose, but I have
never felt that this has to be a conscious effort.

Shakespeare's verse is so powerful that (in some senses) you
have to fight it, so there will not be too much verse and not
enough sense. I do think that when I began in the theatre there
was probably a more poeticized attitude to speaking Shakespeare, certainly a more romantic attitude than now exists. Edith
Evans (who I worked with when I was young — in *Romeo and
Juliet* and other plays), had been a student of William Poel. She
had his attitude to Shakespeare very strongly. Olivier and I (in
Romeo and Juliet) were fighting all the time to keep to the
'truth' — and in those days Olivier was accused of not being able
to speak verse. He was so engrossed in portraying character and
the actual content of the scene, and he didn't wish to make the
verse flowery in any way. He fought against this, and was
criticized for it. — Now of course this is completely accepted. But

that is going back a long way! What you're really interested in is
the fifties and sixties.

It has been said that the late fifties and early sixties was a
period in which it was fashionable to have a rough or
provincial accent for Shakespeare. Do you agree?

Of course, with the various social changes the actor has changed
too. I agree that there was a tendency in the fifties and sixties for
actors to feel that it was necessary to have a regional accent of
some kind to be O.K. It was a sort of inverted snobbery. But I
think that has gone now, though I don't think that people mind
when actors have regional accents, and I think the language would
be very much poorer if we didn't have them. On the other hand, I
feel that the job of an actor is to interpret character, in every way.
If you are playing the Prince of Denmark then you should speak
like a prince, if an American or Yorkshireman you assume the
accent required of you. As an actor, one should be able to speak in
whatever accent is required.

Do you think that Peter Hall evolved a peculiarly RSC style of
acting and speaking . . . a Stratford style?

I would say two things about Peter. He had an academic's
understanding of what Shakespearian verse is and he was anxious
to have this verse spoken correctly and precisely. But he was also
deeply concerned (and this is what distinguishes him from most
other directors of Shakespeare) with what he believed was the
overall conception of the play. Peter was very much interested in
the political aspects of the plays, in *The Wars of the Roses* there
was *so* much that was political. Peter had the ability to impress on
his actors, that the chief interest in a production was the meaning
of the play rather than a series of splendid individual performances. In *The Wars of the Roses* we were encouraged to look at our
parts from an epic or chronicle point of view. We were telling a
story, a story of history, and we should not develop too many
complexities within the characters. Of course one can so easily do
this with Shakespeare, the characters are so marvellously and fully
written. Peter wanted the characters to be rather plainer and
simpler statements of broad aspects. It was the sweep of the plays
and the story that they told that was his chief interest.

'The Wars of the Roses' has been described as the most brilliant achievement of Hall's career. Would you agree with this view?

What, in your view, made this particular presentation unique?
Well, *The Wars of the Roses* was unique because the *Henry VI*'s have so seldom been done in our theatre, rarely in my lifetime. I know that the Birmingham Rep. and the Old Vic have done them, but the number of people who saw these productions was probably rather small. At Stratford, Peter took the bold step of abridging them, a step which (on the whole) didn't cause too many objections from Shakespeare scholars. The adaptation enabled one to see this whole sequence (from *Henry VI* to *Richard III*) in a very short time. This is normally very difficult to do, and the *Henry VI*'s in their uncut form are pretty heavy going.

Do you think that John Barton's actual 'creation' of Shakespearian verse, used as linking passages, was justifiable?
Yes, I think it was. It was openly admitted that this had been done. There were certain passages where John got carried away, and those were eliminated from the final text. There was one magnificent death scene John wrote – I'm trying to remember –

Winchester?
Yes, have you read it? I don't remember the exact lines because we didn't play it, it was cut. But it was *magnificent*!

There have been some objections to 'The Wars of the Roses' adaptation particularly the danger that some of this 'Shakespeare' will find its way into anthologies. Some scholars feel that the RSC has moved into a new (and dangerous) phase of adaptation of Shakespeare.
I would rather question that. I am against adapting Shakespeare and I think that this is something that one shouldn't lend oneself to. I really don't think that the RSC make a practice of it. There are of course certain things that one does. I have interpolated two lines into Katherine (in *Henry VIII*), but only on the grounds that they are in Holinshed, and the whole of Katherine is in Holinshed: Shakespeare couldn't have included them at the time of writing, for political reasons.

Can you talk a little about Peter Hall's other work?

Yes. His *Wars of the Roses* was an innovation, a landmark. I think Peter will always be remembered for that. And also for his historical cycle the following year, when we did the plays from *Richard II* to *Richard III*. But I think that his production of *Hamlet* was just as remarkable and I would.say perhaps on an even higher plane than *The Wars of the Roses*. Of course it showed another aspect. *Hamlet* was Shakespeare in depth and *The Wars of the Roses* was really a tremendous chronicle. His production of *Twelfth Night* and his *Troilus and Cressida* were very much tops for me. It's really very difficult to judge a production that you are in in the same way as a production that you see from the front.

You were quoted as saying (in an interview for 'Nova') that Peter Hall is 'the man of the most vision and daring that the English theatre has produced in my time'. Would you still agree with that comment?

Did I say that? Yes, I think I *would* say that. And I think that I would also say that he arrived on the scene at the right time. I think that George Devine, in one sense, had as much vision — and as much daring. But his canvas was a very different one — it was a completely different vision. It was the vision of the author's place in the theatre rather than the place of a company and actors in the theatre.

In the fifties, Anthony Quayle rejected the idea of a permanent company for Stratford on the grounds that the great West End stars would never join such an organization. Why did you agree to join the RSC as a long-term contract artist?

Well, I suppose I'm an exception in one sense. My whole life has been spent seeking to be part of a permanent company. A permanent company has always been my ideal and I have said this on many occasions. I think it should be remembered that Gielgud was the first person in this country to try the idea of a permanent company. Gielgud had no subsidy, but as a man of the theatre — as an actor he wanted to create his own theatre. And he wanted always to act with his peers, and not to be a star surrounded by lesser lights. In 1934, 35 and 36, and later in 44 and 45 at the Haymarket, he came very near to this ideal. He formed a group around him and although none of us could be given contracts for more than a season there was, unquestionably, the feeling of a company. We were, on the whole, a fairly united group. We stayed together, we were a permanent company. I think it is very sad that John is not a part of either of the two great companies but I think he reached a point where he didn't want it any more.

Of course Glen and Tony were correct in thinking that they wouldn't get actors of any standing or reputation to form a permanent *Shakespeare* Company. One simply cannot do Shakespeare year in and year out. Peter's vision and daring was in convincing the Governors at Stratford that we had to have *two* theatres. And here one has to thank Fordham Flower, who accepted that vision and fought Peter's battles with the economy and the Governors. Taking on the Aldwych was the biggest battle, the greatest hurdle; the presentation of modern plays as well as Shakespeare. Peter has been often castigated by critics who say 'if you had only stayed in Stratford there wouldn't be money difficulties. Stratford had always paid its way, you wouldn't be needing subsidies', and so on. But, without the Aldwych, we wouldn't have the company that we have today. Our company can play Shakespeare as full-bloodedly and whole-heartedly as they do only because they are *not* committed to playing Shakespeare for the whole of their lives, or for three years on end.

The restrictions of serving only one author must pose many difficulties. I think of Ian Richardson who really hasn't had much modern work . . .
He's fared rather unfortunately. He's had mostly Shakespeare, and this *has* happened to some of the actors. But I think Ian is rather an exception, because he was making such tremendous headway in Shakespeare and developing so strongly. I do think he found great satisfaction in what he achieved and agree that it's now time that he should be able to concentrate on the moderns.

Will you talk a little about the star system of the fifties at Stratford?
Star system is a very old phrase. It has always been used of the commercial theatre, anyone talking of the commercial theatre

talks about a star system. In reference to Stratford, I suppose that
Barry Jackson, and then Quayle and Shaw brought the star system
to the Memorial Theatre as opposed to the Shakespeare repertory
company that had existed under Bridges Adams. And of course
there was an enormous renaissance at Stratford because of this;
the audiences enlarged and certainly the standard improved.
Before Barry Jackson came to Stratford, each Shakespeare play
received only one week's rehearsal. It was a very good thing that
someone finally came along who wouldn't stand for this. If you
talk about the 'bad old days' at Stratford it really means that
actors were subjected to this sort of thing, this terrible one week's
rehearsal. Actually the companies were wonderful, there were
marvellous Shakespeare actors like Dorothy Green . . . one could
go on. And there were many very fine productions. I will always
remember the Komisarjevsky *Lear* as one of the finest productions
of *Lear* that I've ever seen! A director could only have done that
sort of thing with superbly equipped, confident Shakespeare
actors, actors who could give a first-rate performance on a week's
rehearsal.

*It has been said that Hall brought an 'anti-star' system to
Stratford. Do you have any comment on that?*
I think 'anti-star system' suggests something too positive and
excluding. What the RSC wants — and what company doesn't? —
is all the very best actors they can find, but who are also actors
interested in ensemble acting whether they are stars or not . . . to
name four, Gielgud and Scofield, Edith Evans and Irene Worth, are
all stars who share this attitude and have played for the RSC.

*Is there a danger of complacency stemming from the security
that an actor is offered by a company system? Does a company
system have any disadvantages?*
I don't think that the security has any disadvantages, because if a
young actor has signed on for three years, he then knows he has
the financial security of three years full employment. But he also
knows that it's up to him. It depends on how he improves
himself as an actor whether he advances in the company and gets
better parts during those three years. There is no allocation of
named parts. Actors at Stratford play as cast, that is if you are a

'playing as cast' member of the company. I don't think there is any complacency, I don't think there can ever be complacency in the theatre. I think that the three years are important. This is a different system from the National Theatres on the Continent who have companies that are there ad infinitum and there is very little room for a young actor to move upwards. These are static companies. With a three year contract this could not happen. But there's no magic attached to three — once the permanence has been found the system allows actors to come in and go out of the company.

Has the Studio been an influence on the development of actors at Stratford? Or is the Studio the way to promotion in the RSC? This has been suggested to me.

Yes, that is true. One of the difficulties with the Studio, and one which we've seen very clearly, is that there is a tendency and a danger that young actors will be forced into feeling that the Studio is a sort of shop window, that the Studio is a place where they must prove themselves. This attitude negates the whole reason for having a Studio. It isn't there so that directors can come and say 'that actor is rather good, we'll give him so-and-so'. On the whole we have tried to fight this attitude as much as possible. If this attitude holds then the relaxation of working in a Studio and experimenting is absolutely destroyed.

To what extent do you think Peter Brook and Michel St. Denis have influenced the development of the RSC?

I think that St. Denis' influence was, in the main, on Peter [Hall], and I think that Peter would agree with this. Michel came and did only two productions, *The Cherry Orchard* and then the Brecht [*Puntila*]. But his association with Peter was invaluable; he was there for Peter to talk to, and discuss attitudes to the company and to productions. Peter has always maintained that this was of enormous value to him. Michel also did important work in the Studio, and gave advice on the Studio classes.

He was, then, primarily a teacher of the theatre?

Yes. He was indeed. He was, from my point of view, the most instructive director that I have ever worked with, but his form of direction is, in a sense, one hesitates to say 'of the past', but it isn't the way in which actors are now used to working in the theatre. With Michel, it was the direction of a master. Because he was a brilliant director he knew how to treat each actor, and he made the actors feel that they were contributing of course. He worked on the system that the director has planned his whole production from A to Z. And one knew that *he* knew what the whole was supposed to be. And this is marvellous, in one way. On the other side, if you take Peter Hall, or Peter Brook, I think they would say that a play is an adventure, an experiment, an unknown — and we'll discover it together.

To my generation, Peter Brook is possibly the most 'exciting' director to have worked at Stratford over the sixties . . .
Without question. I, alas, have never worked with Peter. It's really very sad.

How do you think Brook has influenced the RSC?
It's very difficult to say what influences a company. If a director influences a large number of actors, then he influences the company. Of course Peter's productions of *Marat-Sade* and *US* were unique in the history of our company. I know that there are certain actors in the company who say 'I couldn't work like that' and lots don't work with him. But there are others who become totally indoctrinated by Brook's methods. I would say that he has been an enormously creative and invigorating influence on the company. I think that every actor who works with him develops an attitude of questioning, an attitude of 'truth' towards what he's doing. And this is very valuable.

Have the audiences changed over the years you have worked at Stratford? Is the RSC today a theatre-of-youth?
You know, they say that the sign of real old age is when the policemen start to look so young. To me, the audiences seem very much younger than when I was young. Of course there have always been young audiences at Stratford, we've inevitably attracted students and schools. When I sit in the audience at Stratford I don't really know that I find it so very different from when I used to sit there in the fifties. I feel that the Aldwych

Theatre has, in some ways, seen more change, the Aldwych is
rather more remarkable for its youth. I think I would always
(reluctantly) admit that the Stratford audience is too indulgent,
too uncritical. They come to a festival they come to see the
absolute 'what's it' of Shakespeare done by the company who
should be doing it. And they simply accept it; I think far too
readily. Stratford is like a shrine, but then it always has been.

*How do you think staging and design have changed over the last
twenty years?*

John Bury has been a tremendous influence, scenically, on
Shakespeare production, his architectural attitude to style. I think
that designs are probably simpler now than they were. Of
course, during the fifties we had the principle of the continuous
running of a play, one scene had to be moved into another
without pause, even then. I find it a little difficult to pinpoint
exact differences between Bury and say Motley. Bury came into
his own with *The Wars of the Roses,* it was such an enormous
problem to deal with. He invented this extraordinary setting,
moving walls which adapted to the scene. One still tends to think
of his work in terms of vast, moving walls! But of course he has
done such a variety of other productions. One thinks of his
Delicate Balance, again working with Peter. I think there is a
tremendous precision about Bury's work, there is never anything
extraneous on the stage. Everything is there for a specific purpose.
In much the same way, I think that part of Peter's style is a very
classical attitude. He wants no movement just for movement's
sake. Any move that Peter directs must have a very definite
dramatic purpose, otherwise he would rather the actor remained
still. Bury's designs are, in a sense, made to match this attitude of
Peter's. I think it's something they share. It is very 'pure' —
undecorated.

*The sixties then, were a complete rejection of the more
romantic designs and costumes of the fifties. Some of the
flamboyance was gone?*

Yes. People say to me, 'Why do you always do everything at
Stratford in blacks and browns?' They ask 'Why can't we have
some colour?' But we *do* have colour — though not for colour's
sake.

*In what direction do you think the RSC has moved since Peter
Hall left in 1968?*

It's a very difficult heritage for Trevor to shoulder, and I suppose
his major innovation has been an organizational one. We had got
ourselves into an extremely complicated and expensive pattern,
which was to have an A/B company at Stratford and an A/B at the
Aldwych. It was designed so that B could go out into the
provinces while A could come in to Stratford, or A could come in
to the Aldwych. It wasn't really very workable. We were also
tending to do productions at the Aldwych which didn't use our
manpower economically, because if you have a large company,
and then continually put on plays with very small casts, this
proves to be a rather expensive pattern. Also, we had to take into
consideration the fact that Shakespeare was wanted in London. If
you have the RSC at the Aldwych then you have to give the public
a certain amount of Shakespeare. So Trevor came to the
conclusion that the principle we must work towards was to have
two companies, one for Stratford and one for the Aldwych. He
tried this out, and I think this scheme was justified. When one
company is finished at Stratford they would come to the
Aldwych, and the Aldwych would come to Stratford, a round-the-
clock system. And there is the opportunity to tour with the
Stratford company before they come into the Aldwych. This is, in
a sense, a simplification, but it has its dangers in that actors are on
a conveyor belt. I mean, *Twelfth Night* came from Stratford to the
Aldwych, and now this year *Twelfth Night* goes back into the
Stratford repertoire. There *has* to be some latitude for letting
actors off this conveyor belt, and there are difficulties because it
means you have to re-cast the plays. But this is an 'inside' problem
and perhaps not really of great interest. These are some of the
things that Trevor has tried to deal with and he is still evolving
new patterns to solve the problems.

*Do you find that the style of productions has changed much
over the past three years?*

I think everybody recognizes that in the theatre there must be
constant revolution. You can develop a style (which Hall did) but
that style must not remain static, or you will become the Comédie
Française. A theatre must develop. I think it's really too soon to

see in which way Trevor's style is going to develop. Also, I think that we all recognize that we're in a very critical situation artistically. Out of the success of the company there arise demands, mechanical demands, on the organization, to produce — more productions have *got* to be done. So, as Trevor put it, the tail is wagging the dog. I think that we must find a way, it may be through a reduction in the number of productions that we do, to get back more inside ourselves and examine in which direction we are going . . . and in which direction we ought to go.

Your own career at Stratford has spanned twenty years. Which role do you remember with the most affection?

I don't really like talking about myself, but I'll try. I think I remember Beth in *Landscape* with most affection. One has a different attitude to classical and modern roles, you can't help it. If one has played a great number of classical roles there is such a hunger to do something new . . . and one's attitude towards it is bound to be more — grateful. Of the Shakespeare roles at Stratford I most enjoyed Katherine in *The Taming of the Shrew*, which I have never played before, and came to play for the first time when I was fifty-four. A very stimulating, and rather dangerous adventure! But it was intensely enjoyable because it is a very enjoyable part. Enjoy with a capital E! I suppose I get less chance to play comedy than I do tragedy so one enjoys it all the more. Margaret in *The Wars of the Roses* certainly, because that was a new part. It was really like doing a new play. It was a marathon part, and an unsympathetic part, which I always rather enjoy. I rather like slightly nasty women, having been overfed with ingenues in my youth. If one were to say which part, of all parts, has given me the most satisfaction, I suppose it would be Cleopatra in Glen Byam Shaw's, to me, most memorable production since my youth — and Michel St. Denis. One is just very lucky to have had the chance to play it.

Which director has influenced you most?

Peter! Peter Hall. The word 'influenced' is difficult. I would rather say, I think, 'received the most from'. But of course I've worked with him more than other directors and that is very important. When a director and an actor work constantly together this is when you really get tremendous understanding. I always have great confidence when I play with Peter. I know that Peter knows all my weaknesses and all my dangers, and my potential too I hope. We can communicate very easily.

How do you see the RSC's role in the future . . . as a national and international theatre force?

It is so difficult to see where the world is going as of this moment. And because one can't see where the world is going, it is very hard to see where the theatre is going. While working towards a permanent company at Stratford one tended to feel that one was taking part in something new and adventurous. We have now become Establishment! One doesn't like that particularly, so we have to re-create and find new ways. I don't mean that our own attitude to what we do is Establishment, but I think that to many of the young we are! To a lot of the young who work in the theatre. I think we have to maintain the standard we have reached, but we must also see that we don't repeat ourselves. We must have a fresh look at everything — which doesn't mean that we resort to gimmickry or to playing a 'fashionable' or 'modern' way. I think that we must provide a reflection of the times we live in. That, in a sense, is what Peter Hall did in his time. He was looking at Shakespeare, and the plays, and the theatre from the viewpoint of his generation — but now that attitude is no longer valid. I wouldn't like to say where we are going. I hope we shall go on!

John Barton

Associate Director
Royal Shakespeare Company

September 1971

In the early sixties there was much talk about a company style at Stratford, and a need to improve the standard of verse speaking. What did you see as the major need when Peter Hall took control at Stratford in 1960?

To get some sort of continuity. It's very difficult for an actor to be at ease in Shakespeare — and on top of the verse — unless he has experience in playing it. Although actors in the fifties had come back for more than one year, the company was mainly formed ad hoc each season. Good actors, experienced in modern theatre or television or film work, are often out of their depth when confronted with a Shakespeare text. It takes time to become easy and proficient with Elizabethan verse, and can rarely be picked up in the course of rehearsing one particular play.

You were responsible for much of this early training. Was this, in fact, the beginnings of The Studio?

No, Michel St. Denis started the Studio and ran it for two or three years. I took over the bulk of the work when he became ill. We wanted the studio partly for experiment, and partly because many of the actors didn't get sufficient opportunities to develop in the work of the main house.

In 1960, you and Peter Hall jointly directed 'Troilus and Cressida'. Can you talk a little about this production — particularly the sandpit image?

There was a great deal of talk about what the floor texture should be. I don't remember whose idea the sandpit was. We think that the floor is often the most important element of design. The sandpit gave the right 'Mediterranean-heat-epic' quality, and everyone responded to it.

The sandpit was quite a revolutionary breakthrough: a break away from the Motley/de Nobili designs which seemed to dominate the late fifties. It wasn't the style of 'The Wars of the Roses' and later design — but it seemed to be a move in that direction.

It was a part of Peter's thinking to simplify design, so that it wasn't something elaborate that got on top of the play and the acting. He wished to make design more austere and more selective — to give the fullest possible focus to the actor. The key part of the design often became the props, which were more important perhaps than the 'setting' in the old sense of the word.

There has been quite a deal written about the rehearsal problems surrounding year 1960 production of 'The Taming of the Shrew'. What actually went wrong with this production?

Ultimately, nothing went wrong with it. It was one of our successes in the early years, and it played through the next year at the Aldwych.

Is there any truth in the reports that you and Peter Hall 'fell out' due to his taking over this production?

No, I don't think that we fell out over it. I think that it took me a bit of time to adjust to the RSC. The bulk of my theatre work at Cambridge was with amateurs, and working with professional actors is a quite different experience, as I slowly learnt through trial and error. The situation was one which has come up a number of times. If a group of actors are very unhappy with a particular director then they go to the director of the theatre. He may take the production over — or someone else may do so. Peter was under that kind of pressure . . . but there was no particular disagreement about how the play should be done.

How was the idea for 'The Wars of the Roses' originally conceived? Hall has said that you dreamed of a definitive production of Henry VI's at Cambridge.

Peter and I had talked a lot over the years about the *Henry VI's* as he explains in his introduction to the book [*The Wars of the Roses*, BBC publication, 1970]. He reckoned that to do four plays (all three *Henry VI's* and *Richard III*) was perilous from a box-office point of view, as three of the plays are not popular ones. We both agreed that the three *Henry VI* plays should be cut and re-staged to form two only. But we soon found out that mere cutting didn't solve the problem of how each of these plays could stand dramatically by itself. This led us to knock the text about much more than we had at first envisaged.

'The Wars of the Roses' was handled by three directors. How did the ensemble direction principle work in practice?
Very well. The only danger lay in possible inconsistency between what two directors might say to a given actor or about a given scene: there was a risk of confusion. But we carefully talked it out beforehand, and were pretty much agreed about our approach. We also divided up the scenes so that a particular director was chiefly responsible for a particular actor. Clifford [Williams] took all the scenes which concerned King Henry IV; I took the Hotspur and Shallow scenes and Peter took the Falstaff scenes. Of course, Falstaff meets Shallow at a given moment, but it was understood that the final word about Falstaff should come from Peter. When we revived them later (in 1966), I was in the chair, Clifford continued by doing the Henry IV scenes and Trevor [Nunn] did the Hotspur/Shallow scenes. Doing *The Wars of the Roses* meant rehearsing three plays at once, which would be more than one director could handle by himself. Peter had the final word on everything, but there were some scenes which he didn't get near until the play was run, and then he would say what needed doing with them. One of the great advantages of having a group of directors is that it gives more rehearsal time on individual scenes.

But one can't do this with any play. It wouldn't work, for instance, in one with a small group of characters which are all continually involved with one another.

How did the co-direction principle work for 'Troilus and Cressida' in 1960?
I only worked on the battle sequences and the text, which is a particularly difficult one. Peter took the main responsibility for the production.

Can I digress a little here? How did you originally get your reputation for staging brilliant fight-scenes? Have you had any training?

No. But I found myself (in my acting days) doing stage fights and continually getting minor injuries. So, I evolved a technique of making everything *look* as dangerous as possible, while at the same time ensuring the maximum of safety. I've never had a fencing lesson in my life, and know nothing at all about proper fencing. I worked out a form of fighting which can (I hope) be more theatrical and exciting than the real thing. The latter can be dull to watch because the movements are often minor and not theatrically vivid.

Some critics have expressed the view that the linking passages used in 'The Wars of the Roses' — the pastiche Elizabethan verse — is an extremely dangerous practice, moving into territory as questionable as Tate's re-write of 'Lear'.

I agree. I wouldn't approve of it normally at all. I wouldn't dream, for instance, of trying to write bits into *Lear*. It would be quite impossible to copy Shakespeare's mature style. But, as I argued in the Introduction to *The Wars of the Roses*, the *Henry VI* plays seemed to me a special case.

What influence did you and Peter Hall have over the TV version? I believe that you 'sat in' on the actual filming. . . .

Yes, I was there virtually the whole time. We had a lot of discussion beforehand with the television directors about the style in which it should be shot. Peter laid out the approach and we made a lot of comments during the course of shooting.

Were you both happy with the TV version? Was it faithful to the stage original?

Television is a different medium and we had to try to turn the production into something which works for that medium. We didn't want to lose the quality of the originals, yet we knew that stylistically they had to change. I thought that each section (we shot it in nine sections — each play divided into three) got better than the one before. *Richard III* was done first, and I thought it was the least good. Then came *Henry VI* and then *Edward IV*. I

John Bury.

John Barton.

Twelfth Night directed by John Barton at Stratford in 1969 with Judi Dench as Viola and Charles Thomas as Orsino.

Left: Troilus and Cressida directed by John Barton at Stratford in 1968 with Michael Williams as Troilus and Helen Mirren as Cressida. *Right:* Ian Hogg as Coriolanus and Patrick Stewart as Tullus Aufidius in the Stratford production of the four plays in *The Romans* directed by Trevor Nunn with John Barton, Buzz Goodbody and Euan Smith.

think *Edward* was without doubt the best of the three: we and the television directors had got to know each other's language, and we had found a style. But it all comes back to the basic problem of how to film Shakespeare, which I doubt has ever been fully solved. I'm not sure whether it's actually possible to translate Shakespeare successfully into another medium.

Where do you think the RSC company image has moved since Hall relinquished control in 1968? I've heard it said that the company style had become more slanted towards youth and youthful thinking.

It's not easy to generalize bout this. You could say it about a given production, but I don't think you could do so about the productions as a whole. There's been more continuity than change. The company's become that much more permanent and continuous each year. I suppose design has become somewhat more austere. Individual actors develop and individual directors develop, and everyone tries to find the right style for a given play. I don't think that we have a particular way of tackling everything. We do different kinds of production according to the needs of a particular play.

Over the sixties the RSC became known as a specialists theatre — a theatre dominated by the director and designer. Would you agree with this view?

On the whole I think this is true: in the forties and fifties the interest in a Shakespeare production was more focused on a star actor. With the RSC the focus has been more on the play as a whole, and I believe that the overall standard of playing *throughout* a cast has improved. I think that a director's scrutinizing and examining of every moment in a play does make for stronger ensemble playing. The supporting parts and the play as a whole become much better served than they were, say, in Wolfit's companies — when he tended to be the centre, with nothing much going on around him. The plays were consequently given an unbalanced showing.

I don't believe in talking about 'directors' theatre' or an 'actors' theatre'. Most of the productions that Peter Hall or Peter Brook have done have brought unknown actors to the fore, and the number of actors who have grown from the ranks in the RSC over the years is pretty considerable. I can think of very few productions of which one could say they were basically the director's. Peter Hall did a famous *Hamlet* — but it was also a famous David Warner *Hamlet*, with very fine performances from everyone else. I thought that *Hamlet* had the best Polonius, Gertrude and Claudius that I've ever seen. . . .

Can I move to a personal level. What made you leave an academic career to take on a life in the professional theatre?
The knowledge that I was totally unsuited for an academic career. I'd done specialist research on very limited academic subjects (about what went on in the Elizabethan Theatre and the translation of Anglo-Saxon poetry) — and I knew about these things. But I wasn't academic in the true sense. For instance, I had read very little — because I was always acting or directing. I came to feel more and more like a fish out of water — and I was very relieved to leave Cambridge and come here when Peter invited me.

You haven't done much work outside the RSC since 1960, and have concentrated almost exclusively on Shakespeare production. Is there any reason for this?
I get more satisfaction out of doing a Shakespeare play than anything else. I'm interested to see a modern play, but there's very few that I'd like to direct. The sheer work and involvement in bringing Shakespeare alive on the stage is challenging, increasingly difficult, and yet very satisfying and rewarding. I would, in fact, like to do a Greek play — or a Chekhov — or a Restoration piece. But my main interest is in trying to do justice to Shakespeare. He is *so* rich and complicated that I find him an unfathomable mine. I've worked on some of his plays a number of times, and each time I come back to them they appear more rich and complex.

How do you, as a director, approach the rehearsal process and early thinking for a new production?
I read the play a great deal, steeping myself in it and getting to know it as well as I possibly can. But I never find my way very far before I start rehearsing. I can't exposit a play, and never give a long talk to the company before I begin. I like to put it on its feet

in rehearsal. My ideas and responses come out of watching the actors and what they do. This is something I feel very strongly about. I can't lecture on a play. I can only express my feelings by *doing* the production. I'm full of ideas and articulate in the rehearsal room with the actors, but very inarticulate when anatomizing it critically outside that context. I think I'm one of the least academic of people: it was a peculiar quirk of fortune that I was offered a Fellowship on those particular subjects. Even now I will never lecture on a play, but I will only answer questions about it. I can only explain a play by doing it. I can discuss details with anybody — but I find it very hard to conceptualize or to sum a play up.

Has your directing style and rehearsal method changed much over the years?

I've changed, grown, developed — and I've become more experienced. But the change is hard to put into words. It's a matter of many details. I'm probably more catholic in my taste now. The main change is probably in how I put things to actors. It's not enough to have the right idea; unless one can find the right and helpful way of expressing it, then the idea is valueless. I've perhaps learnt how to help actors, and to be flexible in approach. The way in which I work on the text has, for instance, changed over the years. It, of course, also changes from play to play. *Richard II* is a highly formal rhetorical text, and most of *Othello* is highly naturalistic. Consequently I did more text work on *Richard* than on *Othello*. A lot depends on the play.

How did you approach 'Othello' [1971 Stratford season]? Can you talk a little about your production ideas?

I don't want to. I'd rather say that what I think should reveal itself in the production.

Well, can you tell me a little about the concept of a period setting. I find the idea of a Victorian 'Othello' very interesting. Did this idea stem from your designer?

No, it was entirely my idea. In fact, Julia Trevelyan Oman initially wanted to set it in the Renaissance, partly because she herself had done so much work with a nineteenth century setting. It was an exceptional idea for me because on the whole I don't approve of changing the period for Shakespeare, and have only done it once before. I think that it is often apt to distort the play — and to turn it into something else. But it seemed to me that in this particular case, there were many things that could be gained, and little lost. The whole military background is very difficult to define if one tries to express it in Renaissance terms. The extraordinariness of Desdemona's marriage makes much more sense if set in a period where she would appear as a nineteenth century girl who becomes liberated from her background. And I felt that Othello himself, who is a half mystical figure, alien to the age he lives in, would be better seen to be so by giving the production a detailed and particular social background.

I also believed that the more naturalistic and the more rooted in reality I made the production, the more the basic difficulty of believing in the improbabilities of the plot might be solved. I also had a hunch that, after doing so many Elizabethan productions, I could work more imaginatively and richly by taking a different context. But perhaps most important of all, I realised that the period change could be made with virtually no textual anachronism.

John Bury

Associate Designer and former Head of Design
Royal Shakespeare Company

June 1971

*'The Wars of the Roses' marked the beginning of a completely
new style of design at the RSC . . . it was a complete break from
the Leslie Hurry and Lila de Nobili designs which dominated
the late fifties and early sixties. What was 'revolutionary' about
'The Wars of the Roses' design?*

We tend to work in terms of the physical environment in which
the play takes place, so this means that we open up two things: we
open up the whole question of the shape of the stage. And when
you start to talk about the shape of the acting area then you also
start to talk about the shape of the auditorium. And here
relationships and things like that become the most important
things. That's the volume side of things.

The other point is what you make the surfaces out of, and this
is where the environment of the action becomes exciting, because
one has a whole realm of building. One builds one's scenery, one
also builds in space — with different materials. We took a very
striking image for *The Wars of the Roses*, because we built
everything out of steel, or simulated steel. We used copper foil for
most of it (the stuff you wrap around boilers). You see, one's got
to get one's image, and then having the image one's got to go back
to the business of 'how can I get it on the stage? How can the
stage-staff handle it?' and all the rest of it. If one is making a film
then you simply get the men with blow torches in and put it up.
And when you've finished with it you can just take a bulldozer
and knock it down.

This method of scene building wasn't new to me, because I'd
worked for fifteen years in experimental theatre (for Joan
Littlewood at Stratford East) where we literally built up all our
scenery on this theory. We never simulated anything at all; it was

always totally real. We worked on a sort of film-set solution . . .
we used to drag knocked-down houses and bits of ships and things
on to our stage, put them up and then knock them down again.
And of course this was easy under experimental conditions,
because you don't have repertoire set-change problems — you're
going to play a play for so long as it runs, and if you want six
truckloads of builder's scaffolding and two loads of sand on the
stage you can build wherever you want to build. And at the end of
the run you take it all down. Here (at the RSC) it was a matter of
wedding the technique I'd worked on as a young man, to the
requirements of what one calls 'professional repertoire theatre'.

*Can you elaborate a little on the use of steel as an image for
'The Wars of the Roses?'*
Well, I think it's fairly self-evident. It was a period of armour and a
period of the sword: they were plays about warfare, about power,
about danger. One spent one's time either in armour, or piercing
someone's armour — or being pierced. And this was the image of
the plays. We wanted an image rather than a naturalistic
surrounding . . . we were trying to make a world: a dangerous
world, a terrible world, in which all these happenings fit.

*I didn't see the stage production, but from what I remember of
the television version (which I saw in Australia), the image
seemed to move strongly into leather for 'Richard III' . . . 'the
black leather of Richard's thugs . . .'*
No. But we did use leather a lot. We used blackness for *Richard*.
You see, once you decide to design in metal, then you have to
consider the function of differentiating one's characters. If you're
doing it in paint then you make everybody who's on the 'white'
side have white tabards and everybody on the 'red' side have red
tabards. And when the French arrive they wear blue and gold
tabards. That's very easy. But if you don't use paint and
everything's metallic, then you must make the costume look like
they have degrees of rust, or they must be textured or hard. So
one didn't introduce any 'soft' elements, one had to do the job
within the language of working in metals. One then said that iron
rust will give the red blood and the red roses of Lancaster, and the
hard white steel will give us York, gold will be France, and copper

will be something else. Just like a metalsmith doing a sculpture.
We used very hard black enamel for *Richard III*.

How do you and the director (say, Peter Hall) set about the
preliminary planning for a production? How do director and
designer function together at this stage?

The trouble is you see, that all good relationships in the
theatre — between actor and director or director and designer —
are very long term things . . . so one doesn't really begin in a
formal way. Peter and I are probably talking about two productions ahead (in shorthand) while we're working on another one. So
then, when the time comes, it's very difficult to say who thought
of this or that. I'm terribly influenced by Peter: he's got a very
keen visual imagination and he knows what he wants and what he
wants to say. On the other hand he obviously finds that I help him
a lot, because he will give me an idea and I process the idea in a
way which he likes. There's no doubt that the initial imagery will
come from Peter's way of doing something . . . which is as it
should be.

The problem of design is really what you are going to design.
You don't design the text. You shove Hamlet at me and I read
it . . . and then what choices do I make? As a professional designer
I can possibly tell you (off-the-cuff) some twenty five different
methods of designing *Hamlet*, depending on what you want to get
out of it. All of them are equally valuable, because there is no one
way to design *Hamlet*. But there *is* one way to design a particular
production of *Hamlet*: Peter Hall has a definite idea of a
production of *Hamlet*, what he wants *Hamlet* to say, what he
wants to get out of his production, and there is a definite way of
designing that. And this is the thing that you've got to find out if
you don't know a director.

This is what makes the RSC (and other important repertoire
theatres) different from the run of the mill. Where you have
designers who design in a very specific style; who have their way
of doing things . . . and if you want a set done that way say 'we'll
have Leslie Hurry or John Bury because he always does his designs
this way and we want one of those . . .'. In just the same way one
might buy a Rubens because that's the sort of painting that you
want to get. But if one is working in a situation like this (at the

RSC) one is after something entirely different. One is trying to write a 'language' for each production, one isn't buying a design off the peg. And, as such, one's got to decide what the production is. The more one works with a director the more one starts reading the clues, and when one talks about clues one really begins to pick up very small things. Peter will say 'steel' — and you go away and think what that means and then comeback to him.

What we do together in the early stages is to try to find the image which will express what he [Peter] wants to say. Having got that image we can split it up quite a lot . . . I will go away and produce various projects and bring them back to him. There's no point in wasting two weeks hammering on a model bench unless you know exactly what you're at.

You would see this type of relationship between the director and designer as the most essential factor.
Oh ·yes, because this is when one really knows what one's talking about. Peter doesn't have to explain his whole aesthetic to me, nor do I to him. When one goes to work with a strange director he then has to spend days telling you how he likes his shows done and what he thinks about the particular piece. We use our own shorthand. We've got now some ten years experience of each other, so we can say things fairly simply — and we can also say the sort of things we really feel.

The other very important point about working in repertoire theatre is working under contract. Because if you get a designer working on a fee, and you say to him 'Come and design my *Hamlet*' . . . and he's given three months to do it in and £500. And then, half way through, you say 'start again. . . .' This sort of thing is awfully hard on the freelance chap.

Do you see any dangers in the rise of the specialist theatre? A theatre dominated by Directors and Designers?
Everything is dangerous isn't it? And the more you risk in creation, the more danger you're letting yourself in for. It's very easy to continue in a laissez-faire situation. The more you stick your neck out, and to reach higher things you must stick it out more and more, the greater your danger of having it chopped off. Obviously if things go wrong they will go wrong in a bigger way.

Once you start putting your whole theatre under conscious, positive direction you can create a very great theatre, because all the great European theatres are those that have been put under conscious direction. They've all had periods of flowering and they've all had periods of decline. Where they've been tied to one person, the cycle is pretty controllable. Nobody spends more than ten years doing their best work in one particular field. They will build something up, and then it will start collapsing as the people who control it get interested in other things.

With the RSC one hopes that the situation is self-perpetuating. Directors will come and go, but the torch will be handed on, so one can reach a whole series of peaks as Hall gives way to Nunn and so on. When Peter went, Trevor took over and we needed to have new designers and we needed to have new actors. We cannot have the Comédie Française situation whereby I sit here until I have a long grey beard and when the twenty third director comes along he still has me as 'Chef of Design', and he can't shift anything until I retire, and there's someone else of fifty waiting to take over from me. It's right that we should all be loose, and go. Trevor has had to create his own team, and his successor must create the next one.

You and Peter Hall together created a house style of direction and design during the sixties. In which direction do you think the house style of the RSC has moved since 1968?

Oh it's moved quite a lot hasn't it? I mean, one's own individual style changes over the years. The house style that you mention started over the two years of the Histories ('63 and '64). This was the first time at Stratford that one designer really did an appreciable amount of work. Over those two years I did literally everything, and this was unique in this country. At Stratford we produced a house style only for this history period, but as soon as we'd done it we tended to break it up again. The style of design came about because of practical considerations — allied to what we felt was artistically important. One wasn't being 'simple' consciously for the sake of simplicity. When one has a limited amount of resources then the important place to put these resources is with the actor and on the actor ... and not peripherally.

So, after the Histories, when we broke up again and had a group of designers working, I wanted to find some method of keeping a sort of unity of design, without doing it all myself. This obviously depended — to a certain extent — on finding designers who are like minded. We can never be same minded about anything, and we didn't want to create a German situation of a hierarchy, where we would have a lot of people doing imitation Bury's — with him sitting on top with a stamp. We wanted to feel in different directions — but we did not want to have stagehands changing scenery every night and building different shape stages etc. So, we started to create the 'box situation', the grey box with standard floor and standard rake, in which everybody had to work. This did of course limit designers to some extent, and some people kicked against it and didn't like it. Some critics attacked it, 'that dreary old box again!'

> *Peter Hall once described the Stratford theatre as having 'an obstinate proscenium stage'. What are some of the problems with this stage?*

The sight line is fairly limited, because it's a wide auditorium and a narrow proscenium arch — so in fact, you can't use a lot of the stage for acting in. We built the apron, but it's so difficult to get rid of the frontal feeling of that frame . . . although we tend to disguise it by making it look like part of the box.

> *Can you talk a little about the Barbican project — the early planning and some of your ideas for the new Barbican stage? How will the new stage differ from the existing Stratford stage?*

Well, it hasn't got the remains of a proscenium arch . . . it's a very wide angle. You see, the wider the angle of your audience, the more the sense of inclusion of the acting area with the auditorium. On the other hand we felt there was a point where you could get too wide. For very large audiences, theatre-in-the-round doesn't seem to be the answer. If you're sitting three rows deep around an acting area then I'll go a long way with the theories of theatre-in-the-round, but once you start talking about 1500 people the actors have to project, and nobody projects with the back of their head. You have to hear them and you have to see them.

And also there were our theories about the nature of production, how extrovert, how introvert, how epic, because the pendulum is swinging back towards an epic style of theatre. This will not work in the round. So we didn't want a wider angle than the angle that an audience can command. And this was variously defined by various people — Olivier said it was from where you were standing centre stage and the audience could see both your eyes. Peter described it as a gesture, so that an actor could turn to the audience, and the audience could be encompassed at a glance without any bodily turning. And this made us turn our backs on any peninsular or thrust or three quarter stages.

We wanted to create a stage which was as open and as one-room as possible, so that the actor worked in the midst of and with his audience, and not behind an illusionist frame. At the same time it had to be an audience he could deal with. So, we produced what we called the 'wide fan shape'.

The other thing we're very keen on is that we wanted to continue with our theory that a production needs its own amount of scenery, and nobody else's amount. By which I mean that the problem of a conventional stage is that if you want to do a production — say a Beckett — or something which needs a chair and dustbin and nothing else — then you have to create an enormous amount of scenery to hide the lighting battens and stage manager and all the rest of it. It costs just as much to put on this low budget production as it does a high budget production, because of the huge volume of stage that has to be filled. We wanted to create the same advantages that an in-the-round theatre has . . . in that you have an acting area which is just in space. So our auditorium wall (in the fan) continues right round the back of the acting area.

So, although we have a big theatre we can in fact do very cheap, very experimental productions in it at very little cost. Because if you've got all the shutters down you can put a hearth rug, one chair and a potted palm, and that will be the *total* set, a *total* statement. From that chair onwards, our sets can expand 'in space', so that we're not really defining where the acting area begins and where the stage ends.

And this is what you call a 'Space Stage'?
Yes, one tends to make up terms as one goes along. The term

space stage has been used before to define stages which are not fixed, and in which you define your own spaces for scenery, lights etc. It is basically an architectural shape which has to be filled.

Peter Hall has spoken about differences between working in the theatre and working in opera. Are there any different requirements when you design for opera?
It's much more of a practical problem really, because I don't really see why we shouldn't design them in the same way. What I am saying is that designing for the requirements of an opera house is very different from the requirements of designing for a repertoire theatre. The stages are totally different in nature and the repertoire system is of a totally different nature . . . and the rehearsal patterns are different. So, working at the Opera House is very different from working here. The problem lies in the actual system of control more than anything else. The actual designing is much the same. But, the period of most operas is right in the middle of the period of romantic illusionist designing. Here there is a different problem. Shakespeare was written for epic, non-illusionist staging, whereas Wagner wasn't. So one can't really say that what one does for Shakespeare one can do for opera.

You brought a new style to Shakespeare design. Your style with opera designs would be bound more by convention?
Yes, I think it has to be.

Peter Hall has talked of a new concept in opera production. Do you have any similar plans for opera design?
No . . . one hopes that some new concepts will arise in the course of doing it. One hopes that if one does design opera for some five years at the Opera House, one will not leave opera design in exactly the same place as where you picked it up. We haven't any conscious ploys or plots or systems which we intend to hoik on the Opera House. One is tending to feel at the moment that the Opera House is a pretty immovable beast, and although you may set out to do battle with it, it has a way of winning. It's so bound by traditions and probably rightly so.

Peter Hall

Director and former Managing Director
Royal Shakespeare Company.
Director National Theatre of Great Britain.
Associate Professor of Drama, University of Warwick
First Interview
December 1971

I've spoken to several people who worked with you at Cambridge, and you were described as a 'somewhat shy' person . . .

Yes. I was trying not to have anything to do with the theatre. I suddenly got scared. I'd always wanted to do what, in fact, I did — but I didn't have any money; I thought I was going to get married; and I decided I'd better stop all this nonsense about the theatre and become a teacher, or take a job which was dependable. So, I tried for my first two years at Cambridge not to have anything to do with the theatre. But the autumn I went up — having made that decision — I booked the ADC for the autumn two years ahead, to do a production in case I changed my mind. So I was rather ambivalent about the theatre for two years, and I hung about the fringes of university drama — and tried not to make my way in it.

What interests me is how the 'somewhat shy' person of Cambridge days became the public figure heading the RSC. You have been described (in print) as ruthless, ambitious, you've been compared with Machiavelli, you have been spoken of as a man with a 'public mask of affability and charm — disguising a driving ambition' —. I suppose what I'm really asking is, 'What is the real Peter Hall?'

I've absolutely no idea of the answer to that question. I certainly have a public mask: I certainly have a mask as a director. I don't think it's possible to be a director unless you do. It doesn't drive a ruthless ambition. I'm not as ambitious as I have made out . . . or as others have made me out to be. I like winning! But I don't like winning if I'm hurting other people. I really don't. I wouldn't accept that about myself.

During your years in control at the RSC, certainly your productions reflected a deep interest in power (and particularly power-politics). Would you say you were 'ruthlessly ambitious' at that stage?

I ~~think I'm~~ ambitious: I don't think there's anything wrong with being ambitious. ~~I was~~ ambitious in the Stratford years for something that I'm not ambitious for now. If you get the chance at the age of twenty nine to have a lot of power — and to try to realize a dream in the theatre — then you do perhaps fall in love with power. And I think I did. But I'm not in love with it any more. That's because I'm forty-one now, and different I suppose. One changes. I still enjoy power. I *love* committees! I love meeting what seem insuperable odds. Those are all fairly childish things in a sense. I don't like power when it means that you've got to fire somebody, or take a production away from a director, or take a part away from an actor —

Although you did all these things over the sixties. You were quoted (in 'Nova') as saying: 'I see each production about two weeks before opening and I have three choices — cancel, change the director for another or take over myself.' If productions were looking bad you did these things at the RSC —

That is true. That is also true of Trevor Nunn or Laurence Olivier . . . or anybody who is putting on a play.

You also said (in 'Nova') that you saw each actor once a year and told him exactly *what you thought of his work —*

I tried the soft let down for some years, saying, 'Yes, you're very good and I'm sure that you'll develop beautifully — but we don't want you'. And they didn't believe me. I think it's much better to say, 'I may be completely wrong about you, but I don't think you're good enough to stay in the company'. There's no avoiding the fact that if you're running a theatre you have to hire and fire people. Hiring is pleasurable — firing is very unpleasant!

You talked earlier about a 'dream' at the age of twenty nine —

I regret to say that I had this dream at fourteen and a half . . .

From my research it appears that its basis was a true ensemble company working in England under full state subsidy.

Yes. A company, and a state subsidy certainly, which would give conditions of work which no other theatre had. But it started on a much cruder level, which was going to Stratford with a school party to see *Love's Labour's Lost* — and saying 'I want to run that theatre!' —

That story is true —
Absolutely true.

And the model railway station which you transformed into a toy theatre?
Well, all children play with toy theatres. . . .

I believe you were very influenced during your time in Germany under National Service, seeing the state subsidized arts in operation.
Very poor though they were, because it was just after the war. But even so, although there wasn't enough to eat and drink, they still had their theatres and opera houses.

Was your International Playwrights Theatre an early attempt to create the dream?
Yes. It was in a way. There was a tremendously generous American, Roger Stevens. He subsidized Harold Pinter — when Harold Pinter was a man who had written one play which ran for four nights at the Lyric Theatre Hammersmith. And he also gave me money to do things in the West End that I wanted to do. And he was really behind it.

Why did the venture fold eventually?
We didn't have enough money. You can't work in a commercial situation with un-commercial products. It's just that. We didn't get very far. The idea of trying to form a company I actually started at the Arts Theatre.

Dame Peggy has told me that the three-year contract was really the thing which made the company idea work. She feels that

Gielgud's earlier attempts also failed through lack of money —
Yes. I saw, in Gielgud's attempts at the Haymarket — and in
Olivier's seasons at the New — what *could* be produced by a
continuity within a group. It had a great effect on me. I think the
problem now is that the companies are so big that they cease to be
groups.

> *This is perhaps a personal view, but I feel that the ensemble
> ideal never really worked until a year or so back, when Trevor
> Nunn actually had actors like Ian Richardson walking on and
> saying 'What ho!' in 'Hamlet'.*

I don't think that Ian Richardson walking on and saying 'What
ho!' in *Hamlet* is anything to do with the ensemble ideal. I think it
makes Ian Richardson self-conscious (because he knows he's doing
the company a favour) and it stops young actors having the chance
to say 'What ho!' I believe that actors have a certain level of
achievement which has got to be respected. They may play *smaller*
parts than they normally would — but I don't believe in this
walking on, bit-parts and understudying.

> *Trevor Nunn does believe in this as an 'ensemble ideal' — or so
> he said to me —*

I know he does — or did. But I don't believe it works. *When* it
works, I think it introduces a certain self-consciousness into the
proceedings . . . and I think if you ask Trevor about this in some
years time, he may tell you the same.

> *I realize I'm trying to formalize something which defies
> formalization, but I see your own pattern of development as a
> director moving out of the power phase of 'The Wars of the
> Roses' and 'Hamlet', into something which could be called, I
> suppose, 'religious ritual', 'magic' — I'm thinking of a pattern
> from 'Moses and Aaron' — through 'Macbeth' into Wagnerian
> opera. . . .*

Yes, these are the things that interest me, at this moment. I'm not
actually conscious of it — I can only see patterns in my own work
after they've occurred. Because I don't think one can make
patterns. But, in general terms, I think you're correct. I think my
attraction towards opera has always been very deep, because I

spent much of my youth in music. And the attraction to work in opera was something to do with the larger size — the larger ambiguity of music as opposed to words.

You have stated that you are a radical by political conviction. Does this still hold true?
Yes.

Are you an agnostic?
Yes. But I'm being increasingly disturbed about it.

One of your stated reasons for relinquishing control of the RSC in 1968 was a desire to devote more time to exploring the techniques of cinema. What is the attraction now? I still think of you as primarily a man of the dramatic theatre —
I've always been very interested in the cinema ... right from schoolboy days — the Cambridge Film Society. I've always wanted to make films — but I didn't want to make films as much as I wanted to run a theatre company. So I began to run a theatre company — and became (in some sense) a bit famous — and then people started to ask me to make films. Which I then couldn't do. But now at forty I feel that I've been lucky enough to learn to make films by *making* them! I feel I can direct a film now.

Your film which primarily concerns my work is 'The Dream'. It was a critical 'failure': the actors who appeared in it were not particularly happy when making it. Looking back what do you think was wrong with it?
Well, I was trying an experiment to see if you could film all Shakespeare's text.

Do you think that Shakespeare is filmable?
The only Shakespeare film I've seen that really worked was *Throne of Blood* — because it didn't have any language in it. I'm not sure Shakespeare is filmable — and I thought this at the time of *The Dream*. I wanted to see — in my terms of 'verbal rhythms' — if he was. So I did it quite uncompromisingly (I really did) — and consciously.

You were panned mainly for your use of technique —
That's right.

And the actors were unhappy?
They were very happy at the time! The actors were unhappy
afterwards because it was a failure. Which I well understand. But it
was some recompence that it was a great success in America. . . .

Was this for TV?
Yes, and it received an Emmy nomination, and got some very
good reviews.

*A very general question. What production do you consider to be
the pinnacle of your achievement at the RSC?*
The period of *The Wars of the Roses, The Homecoming, Moses
and Aaron* at Covent Garden, *Hamlet . . .*

*Any particular production? Would 'The Wars of the Roses'
qualify?*
Yes.

*This was a period of immense personal strain for you. You were
reported as having suffered a form of nervous breakdown and
your first marriage was breaking.*
I don't think it's quite accurate to say I had a nervous breakdown.
I was told that I couldn't work for six months, and I, in fact,
didn't work for three weeks. I went back and did *The Wars of the
Roses.* Peter Brook was the person mainly responsible for getting
me back to work — and for getting the doctors' advice ignored. I
was exhausted. I had great personal problems.

*You were quoted as saying that you 'went down with deep
depression and loss of faith in your talents'. Again last year you
spoke of a 'dream in which you'd failed as a theatre director'.
Do you still feel insecure?*
I had this dream again last week — because I was giving a lecture at
Cambridge on Sunday. Certainly I'm insecure: one has always got
to prove oneself anew. Each piece of work you do is up for public
scrutiny. You can never afford to say: 'Well, I'm all right now!'

At the age of forty you've already held two of the most influencial and coveted positions in world theatre. You founded and directed the RSC over a period of nine years, and you have held the position of Director-designate of the Royal Opera House. Where does one go at forty with this achievement behind you?

I don't know. I think I will have to write some more: whether it's a sort of boring theoretical book about the theatre (which I'm afraid I shall write!) or perhaps film scripts. I *must* do some more films. But these are only actually subsidiaries to what I *know* I shall have to do sooner or later – which is to run a theatre company again.

You are obviously aware that it is being widely speculated that you have been (or will be) offered the Directorate of the National Theatre. Should the leadership of the National be offered, would you consider it?

I would consider it. But there are many questions that I would wish to have answered in myself. The RSC's blood and my life-blood are commingled – even at this moment.

But do you think that the RSC (as it exists today) is still the organization you created.

No, it's not. It's what Trevor has created since. But it's still organically part of me and part of my life. And I feel part of it.

You have been quoted as saying that once you do something, then you tend to lose interest in it . . .

Yes, but I haven't lost interest in the RSC because it's Trevor's and not mine. The reason I left Stratford was because I was beginning to lose interest: I thought it was a routine. I thought: 'Oh God, we've done that play at Stratford already in my time' . . . No, I'm wholeheartedly behind the RSC in Trevor's image. I'm still very much part of the company and part of Trevor's councils. I still do a lot of work for them, and I feel very involved with them. No, to go back to your earlier question . . . another theatrical appointment would have to be . . . I have a quite different personal aesthetic at this moment than the one that the RSC *is*. I mean if someone said to me, 'Here's a theatre and here's unlimited money — create a company', I would do something (at this moment) quite different. Because I'm different. Times have changed. I happen to know what that would be — and sooner or later I would like to do that. Whether it's a National Theatre or not. I'd like the actors to be a group who (by the demands that are made of them) are at the top of their bent as professionals. I'd like them to have ideal conditions and very good pay, and then we could really set out to discover a play together. And, like the Berliner Ensemble, in its better days, you would rehearse for two months, you dress rehearse, you preview — and you then say, 'these are the areas that we're going to change', And you don't open until you're ready. And that *is* a dream. But that's what I would like to do.

During the sixties you and Peter Brook seemed poles apart in directorial terms and areas of interest. Would you now like to move into something like Brook's search for a new theatre language?

I'm not sure that that's true. Brook is my greatest friend. (Whether I'm his greatest friend I don't know — but I feel he's mine.) We're both very close, and we've done a lot to each other over the years. Perhaps in some way we complement each other. I don't find myself at variance with his basic approach to the theatre at all. I must believe in the search for a new language, because the death of any form of theatre at any time is when convention and accepted practice fall upon it. But I *don't* believe that the theatre exists without the word! And I think Peter, at the moment, is struggling to prove that it can exist without the word. I believe that he will find that it doesn't and can't.

So you essentially re-state what you declared in '59 — the idea of putting the word foremost —

I believe that theatre *begins* with the word. In the beginning there is the word. Absolutely! Because, without the word there is little possibility for all the other things of the theatre. If the theatre is *only* word then it's literary and boring and thin and academic. But I know that a silence on the stage means nothing — unless it's surrounded with the most marvellous words. The more marvellous the words are, the better the silence. Or the better the physical activity — or whatever.

The Hall/Pinter relationship comes in here —
Yes, certainly it does. Doing Pinter has been very important in my
life — and still is.

Gareth Lloyd Evans (a severe critic of your work at Stratford)
feels that you are the world's greatest exponent of Pinter. He
feels that your work with Pinter texts represent the peak of
your achievement. Would you agree with this?
I don't actually. It has been very important for me (obviously) —
and Pinter happens, in his aesthetic of theatre, to correspond with
a lot of things in me. Whatever it may be: whether it's words or
action or colour or costume or lights, you've got to select that
which really means something. And Pinter does that very well.· I
think that my greatest achievement in the theatre (if I may be
immodest) is to have started a Shakespeare company which
conscientiously began to understand what Shakespeare's verse was
about and how to speak it. But because we made a different
'noise', everybody said: 'They're not speaking the verse!' In fact to
my mind *no-one* had been speaking the verse before — except
great star, idiosyncratic actors who had their own way of making
the verse work. That's all now gone and forgotten. We caused a
revolution in the speaking of Shakespeare's verse. And, at the gate
of heaven, if I was asked to justify myself, I would say that is the
best thing I've done in my life. Although that is, in fact,
unrecognized.

Was your declared 'search for a distinctive Stratford style' a part
of this? Was the style the end-product of your early concen-
tration on verse speaking?
No, because style comes from 'doing' — and a group of people —
and a particular way of regarding the plays. I think the Stratford
style was the realization that there is a rhythm to each speech and
a rhythm to each play — find it! Don't put naturalistic crap within
the speech — and don't put music and scenic effects within the
play —

The new actor at Stratford. You appeared to make a conscious
effort to stamp out the old star system, and some of your critics
felt that you were attempting to 'socialize', to level off the

acting at Stratford, an anti-star system if you like —
I think that a 'star' exists because of what he presents on the stage.
I believe in stars. Stars exist. They are fact. But it seems to me that
a star who is capable of disrupting the company, is just not worth
it, however great his talent. Because I know you cannot create a
play with him — in my terms. Now, the trouble is that I want my
cake and want to eat it. The great star roles need stars. But I
needed a star who is happy in an ensemble. That *can* exist — and
Peggy Ashcroft is the shining example. She was the first actor I
asked to take a three-year contract and she said yes. And she's
never wavered. And without her, I think one can almost say that
the Royal Shakespeare might not have been created. I mean, it was
a great thing to have a lady of that stature. She's a company
person, she's very sensible, and she puts the act of putting on the
play before herself.

You did appear to create your own brand of star at Stratford —
David Warner, Ian Holm, Diana Rigg . . . How did this RSC
company product differ from the star of the fifties?
I don't think it differed in any public way at all. I mean, the
people who had star quality, the public made into stars. When I
went to Stratford as a visiting director you couldn't ask an actor
to improvise. You couldn't ask him to do something that he
couldn't do, because he would expose himself. Nor indeed could
you ask him to observe the rules of Shakespeare's verse. That
would have been considered an imposition on his self expression.
And that changed with this new generation of people.

Were you trying to achieve something of the same revolution at
the Opera House. Kenneth Pearson's article suggests that you
and Davis wanted to move the Opera House towards a
'twentieth century commitment' . . . was this the problem
there?
Yes, but it's the best of its kind in the world, and I've got a lot of
time for it. But, you see, I don't believe that an Opera House
which does fine productions which only have an audience for six
or eight performances is really justifying its subsidy. The audience
at Covent Garden are about twenty thousand opera buffs who go
to everything . . . and often go to everything two or three times.

The ordinary public can't get in, so the ordinary public don't go. I was horrified at *Tristan* to see the same people there night after night. I think that if the opera was able to create a proper ensemble of stars (or people who become stars) — we've produced a lot of opera stars over the last few years — then it would be able to have performances of its productions twenty or thirty times — instead of only six or eight.

The chief reason I left the Opera House was that having gone through months of work on a production — and achieved it in some measure with a cast — when it comes back, it's with a different cast, with maybe eight days rehearsal. If we did this in the theatre we'd be booed off the stage. But, because the music is a kind of 'varnish' which makes everything acceptable, nonsenses are permitted in the repertory system of the opera houses around the world — which *could not* be permitted in the theatre. As I discovered that I could not change it, I thought that it wasn't profitable to remain there. I would have been haunted with the ghosts of my own productions. And there would have been no time to give them life again.

Two of the principles which you introduced at Stratford are of great interest to me. First the principle of co-direction — of directorial collaboration on a production — and secondly the idea of actually talking to a cast on the background and meaning of a particular play. (This — many actors tell me — was completely new to them.) Why co-direction?

Well, I just think that direction is a very lonely business, and like all lonely positions you can get entrenched in your own opinions, so that they become dogmas. You cease to be open to yourself, or to the play, or to the actors . . . One of the greatest advantages of the RSC was — and is — that a play done there will have the benefit (if not in actual co-direction terms on the floor) in its later stages of people like Trevor Nunn, Peter Brook, John Barton coming in and telling you if they think it's going adrift —

The triumvirate at Stratford of yourself, Peter Brook, and Michel St. Denis was obviously designed to relieve you from the loneliness that you've spoken of.

Yes, and also I needed wisdom. Michel St. Denis, historically, didn't do (at that point in his life) a great deal for the company, and he would be one of the first to admit that. But he did a hell of a lot for me.

He was there for you to talk with?
Oh he was! And he was a great, great man.

You were quoted at one stage as saying that you were seeking a new audience for Shakespeare, and more particularly an audience of young people. I saw your first season at Stratford (as a schoolboy in 1960), and on returning to England ten years later, I was astounded to see the difference in the composition of the Stratford audience. There were kids with bare feet and wearing jeans, mingling with ladies in evening dress and black-tied gentlemen. What were you seeking in your audience, your new audience?
I think the great thing about any audience is that it should be mixed. If you said to me that it is a working-class theatre or a young-peoples' theatre, or a ten-pounds-and-over-upper-class theatre, I would say that I don't want to work there. A real audience is mixed. What worried me about the early Stratford audience was that it wasn't mixed enough. So I wanted to get more young people in.

I know that your 'Hamlet' brought young people in droves. How else? Theatregoround, the RSC Club?
Yes, the Club, concessions, and I think also the general image that we presented to the world.

Were you in fact the direct instigator of Theatregoround?
I was behind it absolutely. But like most things we did at the RSC in those early years, we weren't really ready to do it. But if we'd waited until we were ready to do things, we wouldn't have done anything at all.

Were you hoping in late '60 and '61 that the RSC would become the National Theatre?
No. . . .

The company seemed to be striving for this sort of recognition and there was considerable press comment and speculation at the time about it.

The truth of the National Theatre position (let it be on record now — it hasn't been before) is that in 1959, Sir Laurence (who was working with me at the time) said to me: 'I'm going to have a go at making the National Theatre — will you join me as number two?' And I said: 'I'm very flattered Larry, I'd love to . . . but I'm going to make my own as number one' . . . and I went to Stratford! There was then a move in the early sixties to amalgamate the Royal Shakespeare and the Old Vic to form the National Theatre. A move which I finally resisted. During the early years of the National, I certainly did use the fact that the National was getting a lot of money from the word go — to point out the fact that we weren't. I didn't try to demonstrate that we were better than the National — or that we *were* the National.

Somebody once called the RSC the Hovercraft to the National Theatre's Rolls Royce . . .

Well yes. We were two very different institutions, but I think that Larry would be the first person to admit that what happened at the RSC in 1960 and '61 and '62, paved the way and helped in the formation of the National Theatre. We *were* the first company in this country in those sort of terms.

Another very general question. What do you consider your greatest mistake during your years at Stratford — '60 to '68? If you could go back, what would you not do?

In 1966, the Arts Council and Lord Goodman said: 'There's no more money — you can't have an increase!' And we did a season of revivals at Stratford — with only one new production — in order to try and mark time. You *can't* mark time in the theatre. That was my biggest mistake. It's when my heart went out of it. I just saw it as a never ending battle for subsidy. I thought it would go on for ever; that we would never be accepted. You see, nobody *asked* us to be the RSC. Now everybody says: 'Oh yes, the RSC' . . . but even eight years ago people were asking why the RSC should be in London. So, from the word go, I was trying to get a new theatre built in London which was ours.

This is why I was so keen to get the Barbican off the ground. I began that very early on. In those days I disliked Lord Goodman more than I can say; he seemed to me the 'villain' of my scenario! He was putting us up against the wall and seeing what we were made of. He was seeing if we had the strength to remain in London. Otherwise, we should go back to Stratford. And I made the mistake of compromising — when I should *not* have compromised. I should have announced a season of new productions.

I feel fairly strongly that the RSC (over the sixties) became more and more a theatre of directors and designers. Do you have any comment on this?
Yes it did. And I don't see any problem in that.

Is the director/designer the new star?
No he's certainly not the new star. Certainly not.

The Peter Hall/David Warner 'Hamlet', Brook's 'Lear', Brook's 'Dream' . . . this sort of thing . . .
That is a judgement from outside. Neither Brook nor I in approaching a play, say: 'We must do a play "differently" to make sure that we are the star'. We do the play as we see it. It's for *others* to say whether we've drawn attention to ourselves.

You would agree that it is a fairly frequently expressed opinion?
Certainly it's an expressed opinion. It usually means that people don't like it. I've never yet heard anybody say: 'The director is the star — it's disgraceful. God I loved that production!' They will say — about an evening with a great star actor — 'I loved him; what a star!' I don't think the director has become the star at all. I do think that if the director is *not* in control of these very intricate texts — whether it be Shakespeare or Pinter — there is trouble. We're not dealing with something that is put on by a group of actors together . . . there *needs* to be an outside controlling intelligence. That's the director. If he does it well — he will allow the actors to function. And the better the actors are the better the play is. If I had to choose between star actors making mincemeat of the play (and being brilliant themselves) and a director with less

good actors revealing the play — I would choose the director. That's my position.

Elizabeth Spriggs told me that Peter Brook was superstitious of 'Macbeth' — and that he refused to do it at Stratford. Is there any truth in this?

I had asked Peter to do *Macbeth* repeatedly during my time at Stratford — as indeed I asked him to do *The Wars of the Roses*. Peter has always said that he will never do *Macbeth* and that he will never do *La Forza del Destino*, because they are unlucky works in the theatre. And Peter happens to be (for all his rational calm) a highly superstitious person.

Did the superstition surrounding 'Macbeth' worry you at all? The production was dogged with ill-luck, you were very ill at the time.

I had shingles and nearly lost the sight in my left eye. I'm not a superstitious person . . . but it worries my wife when I say: 'I must do *Macbeth* again.'

Why did 'Macbeth' fail? I feel that it did — for a variety of reasons.

Looking back on it, I hadn't got my conceptions to a full point. The set wasn't right, the staging wasn't right. I don't think the chemistry of Scofield and Merchant worked at all . . . and I thought it would.

Where do you think the RSC has moved since you relinquished control? Trevor Nunn has said that the tail is wagging the dog . . .

I think the strength of the allegiances that the RSC has built up over the years, and the strength of the direction team, and the strength of the general aesthetic, could probably make it last well for another five years at least. But I wouldn't like to prophesy after that. Nor would I wish to. I think that theatre is ephemeral and of now. That's part of its thing. Which is why I say to you, that if I was running the RSC now it would be something quite different. And this isn't any criticism of Trevor — whom I admire very much and I think has done a remarkable job. But I'm

different to him and he's different to me — although we're very
alike and linked in all sorts of intricate ways. I'm just saying that if
I were running a theatre company now it would be something
different — because I'm different.

Peter Hall

Director and former Managing Director
Royal Shakespeare Company.
Director National Theatre of Great Britain.
Associate Professor of Drama, University of Warwick
Second interview
January 1972

I'd like to go back to the subject of controversy. Throughout your life you seem to have been involved in various public controversies. For instance, the Dirty Plays row. I've read all the press at the time — but is there any inside story to this one? It seems to me the controversies began with your earlier fights with the Lord Chamberlain... even as far back as 'The Devils'...

Oh it started years earlier. My first brushes with the Chamberlain go back to the year 1954 and '55 ... when I first began in theatre. I was doing plays like *The Immoralist* (an adaptation of the Gide book) and *South* by Julian Green, which was about a homosexual and was banned. And then when we transferred *Godot* we weren't allowed to say 'Christ' — and we weren't allowed to say 'bastard', it was ridiculous, because we *were* allowed to do it at the Arts. In those days if you were a member of a theatre club, then you were allowed to have your morals corrupted without anybody worrying about it. Then I was involved with *Endgame* — and the Chamberlain said that Beckett couldn't have the line 'God — the bastard. He doesn't exist!' I think the whole set-up with the Chamberlain was dangerous and awful. And I did (in common with many of my colleagues) mock the Lord Chamberlain's office in the press; and speak about it as loudly as possible and as often as possible.

You wrote a scathing preface to the 'Afore Night Come' programme...

Indeed yes. And we did a poetry anthology in which we weren't allowed to say a line —

The E.E. Cummings thing?

Yes . . . so we asked the audience to read it to themselves, and brought the house-lights up so that they could. They were allowed to read it (and be corrupted) but they weren't allowed to hear it read.

Is it true that you felt that the whole Dirty Plays row came about because Emile Littler wasn't pleased with your repeated attacks on the Chamberlain. Was this the real story, or was there more?

What happened was that the BBC (on *Not so Much a Programme — More a Way of Life*) did a song — purporting to be sung by Emile Littler — saying 'I don't like other people's dirty plays, I only like my own'. (He was, at that moment, presenting a controversial play in London). Anyway, Emile sued the BBC and there was a long and expensive case which was settled in his favour. I was in the witness box with two others over that one. The cross-examination against me rested on the fact that I had not told people that *Afore Night Come* was not suitable for children. Unfortunately they hadn't checked the print on the leaflet — because it *did* say 'This play is not suitable for children'. The inside story of it was this: I'm sure that Emile Littler was honestly disgusted by certain tendencies in the theatre. He represents a certain kind of West End family entertainment — and I think he felt that this was threatened by the kind of plays that were being done (subversive and dirty from his point of view) and thought that I (and the Chairman) of the RSC, and others, were getting away with murder by doing them.

Because of the position you held at Stratford, I feel that you were one of the people most responsible for the final abolition of the Chamberlain as dramatic censor —

I don't think *I* played a crucial role. . . .

You, in your capacity as Director of the RSC.

I think one helped by making noise. And I gave very long evidence to the Commission on the Lord Chamberlain. There was a Royal Commission on whether or not the Lord Chamberlain should exist. A lot of people gave evidence. Tynan, myself . . . I hope that

I helped. I think that we shall all have to be vigilant to see that it never returns.

Can you talk a little about your relationship with the RSC. Board of Governors — and particularly with Sir Fordham Flower?

My relationship with the Board of Governors was really pretty marvellous. They were often worried sick — and had every right to be — by the speed with which we were building the organization and the risks we took. But they really gave me an enormous amount of scope — they counselled prudence on occasions — but, on the whole, they gambled on me. I don't believe that a committee is capable of gambling by its very nature: a committee has to take the safe and considered and consensus view. That is, unless the committee is led by a man of vision (if he succeeds) — and rashness (if he fails)! And, in the case of the RSC, that man was Fordham Flower. Why he decided to back me in 1958, all goes back to the Stratford tour of Russia. In 1958 we went to Leningrad and Moscow — and I had by then been appointed and had sketched out (in some detail) what I wanted and hoped to do.

But the real moment when I felt that Fordham Flower would go through fire for me, was in the Astoria Hotel, Leningrad. We sat up all night, and I told him why I thought we had to get a London theatre, and why we had to make contracts, and why we had to have an ensemble, and what I thought continuity meant — the whole embryonic policy. It varied in detail, but from 1958 on I never changed it. We were always aiming for these things. And Fordham Flower said, 'All right. I don't know whether we can do it: I don't necessarily think we can. But I'll back you through thick and thin.' And he kept his word to me. He was fantastic. He was also capable of saying to me, 'You'll never get *this* through — it's too far; too quick; too much . . .' He was very good at that. He really was an enormous stabilizing influence — and without him I could not have done it.

I think the relationship between the Chief Executive of a theatre and the Chairman is really the nub of the matter. And that has been seen in this country many times — when it hasn't quite worked! Fordham Flower was superb, and it was a great sadness for me that he died the way he did and so early. When I look back, the freedom that the Governors gave me in choice of plays; in choice of repertory; and in overall planning was amazing. I suppose the rashest act of my life had come off when, at the end of the first year at the Aldwych, I realized that it could work and that it was going to work. It might have its ups and downs — but as an idea it was going to work. Now a company of this size had to have an arena in which it could bring on new talent to feed these two vast theatres. We still had no grant and we were still living on our savings: we were still gambling for our future. And the Governors let me take the Arts Theatre for an experimental season.

So you then had three theatres, two on lease, and no subsidy . . .

No subsidy was the point. No-one was prepared to give us a subsidy because we were, in fact, creating a National Theatre — and we hadn't been asked to be a National Theatre. This area of history perhaps will never be written, but it goes back to the time when I was directing Sir Laurence in *Coriolanus*, and he said that he was going to make a National Theatre work somehow — and invited me to join him as number two. And I told him that I'd just accepted the Stratford offer — and no, I wouldn't join him. I would have loved to work with him — and one of the sadnesses of my career is that, because of the polarization between the RSC and the National, I haven't worked with Larry again. *Coriolanus* was a very creative thing for me, and I would have liked to work with him again. We are very friendly and we have a close relationship . . . but it just hasn't ever worked out — because of what we each represented during the years when the National was growing and the RSC was growing.

But during that time I was *scared stiff* that the National Theatre was going to get a heavy subsidy and we weren't. There was a moment when it looked as if we were going to be bled out by not getting any subsidy. We would then have collapsed and gone back to Stratford. It very nearly occurred — but we just managed to whisk around that one.

What interests me, is the report that the money which you used to subsidize yourselves in the early years, came from the

Janet Suzman as Cleopatra in the third of the four plays in *The Romans* at Stratford in 1972. Directed by Trevor Nunn with John Barton, Buzz Goodbody and Euan Smith.

Right: Janet Suzman.

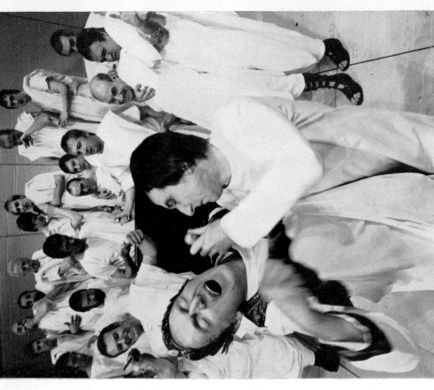

The Assassination from *Julius Caesar*, second of the four plays in *The Romans*, at Stratford 1972. Brutus, John Wood. Julius Caesar, Mark Dignam.

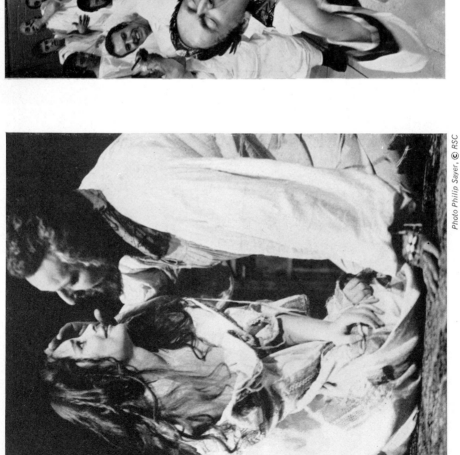

Lisa Harrow as Desdemona and Brewster Mason as Othello in John Barton's production at Stratford in 1971.

Surplus Funds Account — the proceeds of Australasian tours — and that this amounted to well over £100,000 . . .

When I went to Stratford there was a considerable sum of money (which included the Australian tour money) which was the theatre's saving back to 1879. And it amounted to quite a nest-egg. Now, while the theatre had that it would never get subsidy. On the other hand — how improvident to spend it! But it was this money that financed the policy but not all of it.

To go back some time, can you tell me a little about the Elizabethan Theatre Company and your work for them. When you were Director of Productions at the Oxford Playhouse, was this for the Elizabethan Theatre Company?

No. It was for a man called Thane Parker of the London Masque Theatre — who had taken a lease on the Oxford Playhouse for a short period. He was also one of the leading lights in the forming of the Elizabethan Theatre Company . . . there was a tie-up between him and some of the people involved . . .

Colin George and John Barton were the main figures —

And Peter Wood, Toby Robertson, Tony Church . . .

Did you get your early professional Shakespeare production experience through the Elizabethan Theatre Company?

Yes, the first Shakespeare production that I did which you could call professional (although I hardly would) was *Twelfth Night* — and then *The Merchant of Venice* — for the Elizabethan Theatre Company in the autumn after I left Cambridge. But, as so many of the people involved were ex-Cambridge people, it wasn't really very different from the Marlowe Society going on tour.

Your life has been very largely bound up with Cambridge associations hasn't it?

Yes, very much so. Stratford at this moment is full of Cambridge people. It's *so* Cambridge; Trevor, David Jones, John Barton, Guy Woolfenden, David Brierley, it's unending. It is a rather alarming thought from one point of view I suppose!

When Brook was appointed to the RSC triumvirate in 1962, his

declared function within the company was that of the experi-
mentalist, the innovator. Was this your notion when you invited
Brook to join you?

It was the main area in which he was going to work — because
that's what he is. That's what his interest in theatre is. I hoped
that Michel's links with the past and the European tradition of
theatre, and his knowledge of teaching and development of actors,
and Peter's experimental and very modern thinking, would make a
marvellous balance. And I think it did.

'The Theatre of Cruelty' was essentially a private experiment,
but 'US' was a public one — and it received mixed notices. As
Director of the company, what did you see as the validity of
showing a programme like 'US'. It was, I know, the first
documentary production of that scale ever mounted in
Britain . . .

Yes it was. Peter felt that this subject wanted bringing into the
theatre, and I absolutely agreed with him. And there was
something burningly important about Vietnam that ought to be in
the theatre *now*. No-one was writing a play about Vietnam — and
you can't really go up to a writer and ask him to write one. Also,
Peter had developed so many new techniques which were in·search
of material to prove their validity. The first half of 'US' had the
gloss and efficiency of a political review, with (perhaps) very much
bite. The second half, I think, dug deeper. This changed the tone
of the piece — and it also gave it weight. I don't think 'US' would
have worked without Dennis Cannan's contribution. But Dennis
couldn't have made that contribution unless there had been all the
work. I was interested in it on two fronts. In those days (no longer
now), it seemed important for the theatre to claim freedom to
discuss important contemporary subjects. At that time this was
the province of the newspapers, television and radio. But because
of the Lord Chamberlain, the theatre did not — could not.
Everybody was scared stiff that we were about to commit some
terrible political blunder.

Are you aware of your place in the theatre history of Britain?
That's for others. I'm concerned about what I'm doing *today* — I
truly am. My wife occasionally tries to keep clippings — and I

actually do go around destroying them. I cannot bear it. It's like that whole showbiz thing of one's 'track record' — One's 'credits'. I really find all that beside the point. It seems to me that there is a sediment — a deposit — of what you've done and the influence you've had. And that exists. People argue about whether you did this or that — right or wrong. I sometimes feel I've learnt no lessons from what's been written about me. I've just learnt a lot of deep and burning lessons from my colleagues and from myself. I hope therefore, that one changes. I also have a very strong feeling about criticism, and about what's written about one. That's another reason why I don't keep clippings. I try to keep it at arm's length. It's also why I *pretend* not to regard it.

This is the public mask we talked about last time?
Yes. Too many people in the theatre believe what's written about them. And you *mustn't* believe what's written about you. Whether it's good or bad. It is a viewpoint from a person outside of yourself . . . and it's extremely muddling — and at its most dangerous when you believe it. I've seen actors who believe that they are geniuses because of the notices they've been given. We all begin every job from scratch. We are all liable to fail on everything. Totally liable to fail . . . and we must remember that.

Your first marriage was attended by enormous publicity — with both you and your wife as major showbusiness figures. You seem to have retreated into more of an enclosed private life now. You do, in fact, keep your theatre life completely apart from your home/private life?
I'm quite secret in some ways.

You once said that you have very few friends (real friends) . . . in '66 you said that your friends were Brook and two teachers. Does this still hold true?
John Barton's a real friend. Trevor Nunn is now — he wasn't in my life then. I think I've got half-a-dozen friends now . . . so it's better. Peggy Ashcroft is a real friend. But I'm very bad with friends . . . very bad! I don't take care of my friends. That's part of being private . . . and also part of just working too hard.

Why do you work so hard?
I've honestly no idea. I like working hard.

You've driven yourself all your life. I believe that you worked a seventeen-hour day at Stratford?
Yes, I did. I can only assume that I like it. It goes back to being a child, and the pressures that I put on myself as a child. The pressures to 'get on'. I *cannot* be idle. I really can't. I get terribly uptight if I've got nothing to do.

Do you suffer from tenseness, tensions, because of the pace you live at?
Yes, I do. I get terribly tense, but I usually release it by getting uptight about something else. It is fairly idiotic actually that I'm sitting here talking to you now. I was up until two this morning with Edward Albee and Trevor Nunn, discussing a new production; I started telephoning at eight this morning – the designer, the costume designer, and each of the actors. And I've been giving notes on the 'phone up until you arrived at 11.30. We are going to talk for an hour or so. I'm having lunch with Angela Lansbury to give her notes. Then I start rehearsing at two. I'm auditioning at 5.30, and then I have an *All Over* preview tonight. It's idiotic – but I know that if I see you and talk to you today, it will actually 'feed' my day's work . . .

It will break the pattern?
Break the pattern and keep up the pressure. I work best under pressure. The way I rehearse is that I always start well; it's always very exciting and stimulating. Then, after about a week, a great 'nothing' develops. Nothing happens at all. And until things are desperate, my adrenaline doesn't start to flow. Sometimes I misjudge that. Actors who know me very well watch out to see what sort of 'crisis' I will manufacture if there isn't one. On myself – or on them! This *must* be why I work so hard. It must be.

I'd like to talk about your rehearsal technique. Your own words are that you 'avoid a method'. It has been suggested that you allow your actors comparative freedom and then in the last

*week you move in — cutting, editing — and being The Director
in the fullest sense . . . It's also been suggested to me, that with
your extraordinary skill and delicacy as a director, you can get
your actors to do what you want. Yet you don't start rehearsals
with a fixed idea —*

No, I don't. I start with whatever the object is that I'm trying to
find. The play, the opera — whatever. And I set out to find an
expression of it. It depends on the people that you're finding it
with.

*I spoke with Dorothy Tutin last night about the difference in
rehearsing Pinter and Shakespeare. Your Shakespeare rehearsals
were often prefaced by a talk — whereas the Pinter is a process
of mutual discovery . . .*

You know, I think now that if Dorothy and I were to do a
Shakespeare together, that (providing I had long enough) the
Shakespeare would be very like the Pinter rehearsals. Unfortu-
nately, if it takes five weeks to find an hour and fifteen minutes of
Pinter — how long does it take to find three-and-a-half hours of
Shakespeare? Given the fact that the language is different. We're
not plugged in to Shakespeare. I've never in my life had enough
time to do a Shakespeare production. One day I hope I will!

*What do you consider to be 'enough' time? You worked on a
five week schedule of rehearsal at Stratford (speaking generally).*

Yes. When I went there it was three. I got it up to five. Now it's
six. I'd like ten. I'd really like ten weeks!

*Talking about Lord Goodman last time we met, you referred to
him as 'the villain of my scenario' during the RSC years —*

Now he's not, and we like and see a lot of each other.

*Your health was generally very poor when you left the RSC in
'68 —*

I had shingles . . . and I was terribly tired I just didn't want to go
on.

Is your health good now?

Marvellous. I've got more energy now than ever. Certainly much more than when I left the RSC. If a person lives on tension point all the time (like I do), he occasionally goes too far. I've done that.

How do you relax? I know that you used to play the piano a lot – do you have any other recreation?

I live very shut off from the theatre now, and not surrounded by theatre people. I've got a splendid home and a marvellous wife and children. I fish a bit . . . and I walk a bit . . . If it sounds as though I spend two or three days meditating over a fish – I don't! If I don't catch a fish I stop fishing! Yes, I do still play the piano; I play records a lot . . . and I read obsessively – all the time. How do I relax? I don't think I do. I seem to fill any relaxation time with a great deal of activity – always. This relaxation thing you know, I think is one of the modern myths. I'm sure that primitive man didn't relax. I think he got on with whatever he was interested in – hunting, eating, making love, running, building something . . . or he went to sleep. In a primitive state, man built something because he needed it . . . and therefore there was satisfaction in doing it. He killed an animal because he was hungry – and for the satisfaction of the act.

I believe ·the concept of relaxation comes from the fact that now most people spend their lives doing things they don't want to do, in order to get some money to buy things that they're not sure they want. And they buy things which are supposed to divert them, or amuse them, or relax them. I mean, the whole concept of 'going on holiday' is a very modern one . . . simply because it's only necessary if you admit that most of your life is bloody rubbish! I love holidays . . . but I like holidays when I've got something to do. My idea of a holiday is something with an objective in mind. To go somewhere because I want to see something . . . or want to write something.

Last time we met, we talked about your future, and you talked of running a theatre company again. Since then it's been announced that you and others have formed Script Development Limited. Can you tell me more about this scheme?

Oh, that's a very simple hope on the part of a number of writers and directors to make original subjects financeable as pictures. Script Development is not going to make films, it's going to make scripts. And then help get those scripts backed. The awful thing at the moment is to get any development money . . . to actually get a script written is almost impossible. You're either supposed to do it for nothing, or in exchange for the small sum of money you're given to write it, you give up everything . . . artistic control, percentage points . . . everything. You give the picture away. And then if the company who financed it read the script and don't like it (and decide not to make it), you can't get the bloody thing back. Script Developments is fairly modest . . . it should be a little ginger group. . . .

It's not your future then?
No. It's very secondary. It's to help me (and a few of my mates) get a bit more muscle in the film industry.

What does money mean to you today? You started your life with very little, and at the age of forty-one you are a fairly wealthy man —
I'm not wealthy.

You have the trappings of wealth.
Oh I have the trappings of wealth — yes. But my only actual wealth is the house I live in. I have no savings; I don't play the stock-market; I'm reasonably well insured because of my family; and I believe that I will continue to earn enough money to live by my work. And if I was struck down very ill — then I'm insured. I think money is to be spent. And I find people who live their lives in order to 'put money by' — to leave it for their children to quarrel over — simply ludicrous. I don't understand that type at all. Money, to me, is something that I get for an activity that I'm engaged in. And if I can buy something which I enjoy, like a picture, or a piece of sculpture, or a lot of records, or books, or a car — then I'll spend the money. And if I can't — then that's too bad. It wouldn't actually hurt me very much now if my standard of living crashed. I wouldn't like it — but it wouldn't hurt me. I'd get on to the next job. I don't do *anything* for money.

Can I return to the subject of 'nowness'. Just looking around this room, — and having seen pictures of your home — it seems to reflect 'now' very much, the present tense.

I like modern design. I'm very interested in modern architecture and modern furniture.and objects. I like surrounding myself with modern objects. I either want to live in a room in which *everything* is something I endorse — or I want to live in a room which is just a higgledy-piggledy mess . . . and I'll shut my eyes and won't notice. I'm a bit of a perfectionist in my own home.

Dorothy Tutin used an interesting musical analogy when she said that you 'conduct' a rehearsal, she spoke of you 'conducting' the cast, you 'talk' with your hands—

I'd love to be a conductor, and I have a great envy of conductors. And I would also like to have been a man who could make a film so obsessive and personal that he 'writes' with film. That's the only kind of film worth making. I'd love to be all those things, but, if I am able to choose what I have to do, then there's no doubt. I will go back to running a theatre.

Running a theatre company is still a 'must'?

I'm sure of it. There's no doubt about it. That is, if anyone wants me to. It's all very well for me to say 'I must go back'. Somebody has to ask me. But I know that I can't avoid it. I'm perfectly sure that's what I am — a theatre director. And an impresario. Clowns want to play Hamlet, and I would like to be (sometimes) a writer: that's my biggest envy. Sometimes a conductor — because I'm a bit of a musician — but I *am* a theatre director.

Clifford Williams

Associate Director
Royal Shakespeare Company

June 1971

During the sixties, the RSC often used a principle of joint direction — where two or more directors collaborated in the staging of a particular play. How did this principle work in practice?

First of all, it wasn't really a principle. One of the first examples of collaboration at the RSC within the years you're talking about was when I directed *The Tempest* with Peter Brook — in association. When it was decided that I would do the play, he said 'Look, I've done the thing several times before, and if I'm around can I help you do some work on it?' And so we hit on this formula whereby I was completely responsible for the end product, but he worked 'in association' with me. But this was not exactly a half-and-half share . . . I had the major responsibility. The production wasn't very successful as a matter of fact . . .

Why was that do you think?

Oh, a number of reasons. I think actually that it wasn't bad in many ways, but it was far too far in advance of what people could take at that time. In the same way I think that Peter Brook's *Dream* would have been booed out of court in 1962 or 63. I may be wrong here . . . one can only speculate. But many of the things that were turned down in that *Tempest*, bits of stage practice, have been subsequently accepted by audiences and critics. Also, because there were a number of directors here (resident directors) it became normal practice — as one got near to the opening of a production — for the other directors to come and view rehearsals, run-throughs, dress rehearsals, and to make comments of a constructive (and sometimes of a destructive) nature about what they saw. And I think that this was always a very dangerous moment for the director. When his confrères came along and possibly said 'My God this is terrible! . . . what's all this about?' etc. etc.

I don't think any director is very secure . . . I've never met a secure director. It was very easy to lose what you had through listening too much to other views. But, in general we found that despite the danger, despite the embarrassment — and sometimes the anger that one felt at being met with a lambasting from one's fellow directors — that because we were all working here together (and because everyone got their turn at shooting down everyone else) we did begin to make the process of mutual self-criticism a very valuable one. We listened without letting the hackles rise.

Did Peter Hall institute this procedure at Stratford?
No, I think it just happened, because there were a lot of directors here on the spot. I don't think that any formal pronouncement ever went out about it. Later on there were attempts to formalize it, but in the early days when a director did a show, then we would naturally expect Peter (as Managing Director of the Company) to come to the run through or dress rehearsal and make his comments. Towards the end of Peter's time here — when he was getting very tied up in other work — there was an actual attempt to institute a system whereby there was a second director tied to each production.

For instance, John Barton did *All's Well*, and I (although I was only free for a week or so at that time) was tied to it as second director. It was my agreed job to watch it and to say things in John's ear . . . which he could accept or not accept as he chose. Then, of course, there was *The Wars of the Roses* and the '64 History Cycle . . . and the reason that was shared was because we agreed that it was an impossible task for one director. It couldn't be done by one man, two might quarrel — so we decided to have three!

The three directors who worked on the Histories are of very different temperament, and certainly work in very different ways. How did you make this particular joint production gel as a unified whole?
Again there was no problem, because we gelled as people in any

case . . . we knew each other very well . . . and that meant that we had (long before) accepted our differences in personality, our different ways of talking and our different ways of thinking. We knew all that. I mean, I knew what was different between John and myself, but I also knew what we had in common. Also, there was an overall chairmanship exercised by Peter Hall over the productions. On the other hand, John Barton had been very instrumental in formulating the concepts and the ideas . . . But acted often as a . . . how can I put it . . . a 'contrary spirit'.

Sometimes I felt that they were going too far in pursuing a particular idea, and I would say 'Now I think that's crazy . . .' and let them beat the idea against my stone wall for a while to see what came out of that. But there was none of the disruption or dissension that one might have expected. We had talked for a long time about how to split the load of rehearsal . . . was John going to take two plays, me two and Peter three? Or would John take all the Falstaff scenes and me all the Hal scenes . . .? And what would happen when these two characters came together . . .? All this had to be argued out in advance. We tried (whenever possible) to watch each other's scenes being rehearsed. We also – from time to time – let the other two directors direct the scenes of the third one. In other words, if I'd done a scene involving Falstaff – then this scene was basically my responsibility.

But from time to time Peter would come and have a look at the scene, throw in an idea or two, ask what I was doing with it, and he might actually rehearse that scene. Then I could come back to it and say 'Christ, what the hell have you all been doing with it. . .'.

How did this work at the later stages of rehearsal, when the whole had to be pulled together for performance?
I don't recall that very distinctly, but there was no trouble. That was the extraordinary thing – because we all expected trouble. I think that some of the actors on stage might have felt more troubled than we did sitting in the stalls. Peter was very much the chairman, John dealt with technical staging and I busied myself a great deal with the visual side in terms of lighting (which I enjoy very much). I think that was how we split our load at the later stages of rehearsal.

You have the reputation (in Australia anyway) of being the 'theatrical' (as distinct from the 'academic') director at the RSC. You have been responsible for much of the purely 'theatrical' excitement in this theatre over the past ten years . . . plays like 'Afore Night Come', 'The Representative', 'The Jew of Malta'. . . Do you have any comment on this?

I was the only one who 'came up through the theatre'. I started as a call boy and went on to ASM: I spent three years doing stage management. I became an actor, I became a dancer, I wrote mime plays and I ran several repertory companies. The others entered the theatre from university. I guess that in a half-humorous (and sometimes half-serious) way in our directorial discussions, they put John in the 'academic' chair, Peter in the 'political' chair — and me in the 'rugby football' chair.

What prompted you to join an organization like the RSC? What were your motives in joining, and what has made you stay part of the Company for ten years?

Constantly doing ad hoc work (which can be very exciting) only fulfils one aspect of oneself. One does feel the need (and the more it isn't there the more one feels it) of being part of an organization. Also — and this was very important to me when I joined the RSC in 1961 — there was the economic situation. It wasn't just an artistic need . . . I joined because I was getting a permanent salary. I was fed up with never knowing when I was going to do my next work. I joined as a staff producer, not a director . . . I joined in a very menial way. But because I had done a lot of directing work elsewhere I felt that if I joined I would sooner or later direct . . . which it transpired I did. One is able to do more work within a company than if one is waiting to do freelance work outside. So . . . it's a mixture of 'I'd like to be part of the RSC because everyone says they're the best . . .', and simply 'If I am part of this organization, then thank God, I've got a certain amount of economic security for a while.'

Your productions have often been surrounded by controversy. There was 'Afore Night Come', and 'The Representative'. . . Can you talk a little about some of these productions?

Afore Night Come was interesting in that we've (at the RSC) always talked about our modern theatre and our classical theatre being complementary to each other .,. .

The extraordinary thing about *Afore Night Come* is that it uses language in a classical manner — although it is written in prose, it is really poetry, a 'happening' (before the word 'happening' had been coined). I remember saying to the actors at the time that it was like taking in a deep breath and letting it out again . . . and that was all. The play was just a cycle . . . a spasm . . . a very long (a couple of hours) spasm. The play was very specific in one sense . . . set among those trees, with Worcestershire 'peasants' and chaps down from Birmingham doing casual work. But the play was talking about the way in which people, out of fear — of the unknown, of the strange — or from resentment (which may be based on a number of factors), will quite ruthlessly eradicate the foreign element in their midst. And really not realise that they've done it.

This sort of action in the play (and you suddenly realize it at the end) is repeated like a yearly sacrifice. At the end they don't realize that they have done it . . . but they are purged in some way. This sort of operation (which is almost essential for people to preserve their sanity) goes on everywhere. It goes on in rehearsal rooms — it goes on on the factory floor . . . it went on in that pear orchard. This 'blood letting'! And letting the blood of the foreign element is simply an element within the human makeup. You can't even take a moral attitude to it. It's organic.

During 'Afore Night Come', the RSC was involved in a row with the Lord Chamberlain over certain cuts in the text. Hall prefaced the 'Afore Night Come' programme with an article attacking censorship. To what extent were the Chamberlain's cuts actually destructive? Did they destroy the meaning of the play?

No. It was 'politics'. In those days if the Chamberlain said cut something then you cut it. But I guess the Chamberlain wasn't out front every night . . . so how did he enforce it? This was one of the absurdities of the situation. If he said 'Cut the word "fuck" ' then you cut it, but you could still go on and say it!

So the Dirty Plays row was more political than based on a real grievance?

No . . . Hall played the situation politically, but the grievance was genuine. We were capable of censoring ourselves . . . as capable, certainly, (as to what the theatre could and could not do) as a civil service office.

What about 'The Representative'? This production also aroused a great deal of controversy, and (I believe) caused offence to the Catholic Church?

This was the first play (as I recall) in which we started to have discussions and debates on stage after performances . . . in which the audience stayed behind, and we had speakers on stage. These were not only people associated with the show, but people from the outside as well. I remember that we had a Jewish Rabbi, and a priest from The Society of Jesus, and a number of others. All would argue the toss after performances, and the audience would chip in and make impassioned speeches. This was the first time that we did this sort of thing at the RSC. It was clear that a play which sought to establish by documentary evidence (and a certain amount of speculation) that the head of the Catholic Church was personally responsible for a number of Jewish deaths during the war, was going to cause a considerable amount of upset. There was no way around that. My own feeling then (and it still remains) is that although some of Hochhuth's evidence is tenuous, in general I felt that the play *was* truthful. It can be argued that this sort of semi-documentary play doesn't have to be truthful . . . but that's another point. I did feel, in fact, that this one *was* truthful.

I read a tremendous lot about the subject and talked to people about the subject — and I didn't ever hear a convincing refutation from the Catholic side of Hochhuth's accusations. In any case, Hochhuth's main point (it seemed to me) was not to hit the Pope over the head. On the contrary, it was to present the Pope like other people in an influential position, as caught in a sort of crisis of conscience, in which he didn't know which way to turn. The pity of it was (in Hochhuth's opinion) that the Pope turned the wrong way. When there were certain decisions he could have taken to help the Jews he didn't. Hochhuth argued that this was for primarily economic considerations, and here I think was where I found the evidence tenuous. But that the Pope did not take the steps which other much lowlier priests did take, I found absolutely proven in the play. And therefore I felt no moral compunction about putting my full weight behind it.

Do you, as a director, need to feel the essential 'truth' of what you're doing?

In terms of that sort of play, yes! I've been through this same sort of problem with Hochhuth's second play, *Soldiers*, the play about Churchill. *Soldiers* was a very different sort of play from *The Representative*. *Soldiers* was really a sort of 'poetic' play, with Hochhuth using Churchill much more as a symbol than was the case with Pius in *The Representative*. But, in general, when one is doing a play which is dealing with living people (or recently living people) and is possibly being very critical of them, I think one needs to be persuaded, not necessarily that the things said are true, but that the playwright's methods and intentions are sincere not malicious and make sense.

Did you plan 'The Jew of Malta' and 'The Merchant of Venice' productions as two plays to be presented together, or was this a sheer coincidence?

Both. We didn't do *The Jew* at Stratford initially, we did it in London ... and because it did go so very well, we decided to take it to Stratford. And so we thought it would be a good idea to twin it with *The Merchant* ... but when *Jew of Malta* was first staged we had no intention of doing *The Merchant*.

I've seen some pictures of these productions, and the sets look quite unusual ... they looked as though they were made in polystyrene. Wasn't this somewhat unusual for the time?

Yes, at the time they were unusual (and they were polystyrene). It was an extraordinary set that Koltai did for *The Jew of Malta* — and I think it started quite a lot of trends.

You staged 'Comedy of Errors' very quickly — as a sort of stop gap measure for Brook's 'Lear' — and it was an extraordinary success. Why do you think that this particular production was so successful?

Well, it was put on very, very quickly. We only had about three weeks . . . but it is a very short play. Actually what happened, was that Brook was going to do *Lear* and Scofield fell ill, so *Lear* had to be postponed. The management didn't know whether to pad out by doing more performances of the other plays in the season, or to put on an extra play. Ultimately they decided to do *Comedy of Errors*. This was the first play that I did at Stratford . . . I arrived rather quaking. But we had fun, and it worked. I think it was successful because it is a very, very straightforward play. And, in practical terms, the audience laughed a hell of a lot, so they enjoyed themselves. It had moments of sentiment, and little bits of decent theology thrown in — and it also had a very handsome cast. They were an extremely strong cast. I think that audienes were surprised and delighted to find that there was such a jolly play within the Shakespeare canon . . . (it hadn't been done at Stratford for some years). It became a sort of 'monster' pursuing me around . . . The production was revived some seven or eight times over a period of four years. And it was revived again in 1972.

Some years ago, 'Nova' carried a long article on the RSC, in which you were quoted as saying, 'We all have a sort of love-hate relationship with Peter Hall'. Why do you think he sets up this dual reaction in people? Many people I've spoken to have expressed a love-hate feeling towards him.

Peter had an ability to make everyone feel that they were very important. And, of course, this was splendid when you really felt that you — perhaps of all the people around — were the most important person in his eye. Then, inevitably, you perceived that this was not the case. And it was your own fault, not Peter's. To him, *everyone* was important. And I guess that this sometimes set up feelings of disappointment and even jealousy of other people. One became very attached to Peter, and one liked to be 'in the sun'. If you suspected that there was a shadow falling on you, then you got very hurt about it. This perhaps explains the 'hate' side of that remark . . . Perhaps, also, I personally used to think that he complicated situations simply because of his own interest in complicated situations. He's a gamesman, he likes Chinese puzzles. Sometimes, rather than going directly to the crux of a problem,

Sir Fordham Flower.

Photo Nev's Cameron, © RSC

Clifford Williams.

John Wood as Brutus (*foreground*) and Richard Johnson as Mark Antony in *Julius Caesar* at Stratford in 1972.

Right: Richard Johnson.

he would discover some novel approach . . . because that was more fun, more complex. And this used to irritate me. But this was just a question of difference in nature.

Do you think it is a fair statement to say that during the sixties the RSC became a specialist theatre a theatre of directors and designers?

No.

But the director did become a very powerful figure over the sixties. We saw the emergence of things like 'Peter Hall's production of . . .' or 'Peter Brook's production of . . .' and so on.

That is true. A great deal of journalistic and reviewers' comment centred on the directors involved in the company's work. I suppose the directors were not over-modest in that situation. One did not go out of one's way to turn away publicity which could not fail to help the company generally. But I cannot remember any director (including myself, I hope) who sought power and publicity for his own sake. I think we are all imbued with a 'company' spirit, and that was what we cared about.

Are there planning meetings with the Artistic Director or other directors prior to the start of rehearsals?

Yes. Often brief, depending on the Artistic Director's own commitments. But there is usually some exchange of ideas over a given play.

Does the director have complete artistic freedom in the handling of his production?

Yes. Subject to the fact that he must, in general, select his cast from whoever is available in the company, and the production must be designed so as to fit into the repertoire system.

David Brierley

The Head of Design, the Literary Manager and the Music Director.
Royal Shakespeare Company

September 1971

*Can you tell me the nature of the relationship between the RSC
and the Arts Council?*

The Arts Council is a national agency. It receives its funds each
year from the Treasury — through the Department of Education
and Science. Each year we have to submit to the Arts Council our
estimate of the next year's budget. We have to forecast the
revenue we estimate our organization will be able to derive from
all sources other than the Arts Council — and to estimate the cost
of the whole operation. We ask for a grant which will make up the
difference.

Do you overestimate in your request for a grant?

No. But we have never yet reached the situation with the Arts
Council where they have given us a grant which has a reasonable
chance of actually balancing costs and revenue. There is a certain
area for haggle. But this is very narrow . . . because we are in
agreement with the Arts Council about what the cost of our work
is, and we are in agreement about what the grant *ought* to be. The
problem *is* that they keep saying 'We can't afford to give you that
grant! . . .

It is then the responsibility of the Governors of the RSC to
decide how we go into a particular year, and how we finance that
year with the grant we are given.

*Do the Arts Council 'police' your activities in any way? Do they
have a representative on the policy making committees of the
RSC?*

An Arts Council assessor is entitled to be present at all meetings of
the Governors and of the Executive Council.

In what ways do you operate with the British Council?
Only per project. The British Council is interested in promoting an image of British culture abroad, and of exporting British cultural products. Therefore, when there is a place in the world to which they would like to export British culture (in the form of the RSC) they come to us and say, 'Can you go there?' Alternatively, a prospective foreign host may come to us and request a visit. If we find that the finances don't fit, we then go hand-in-hand to the British Council and request subsidy.

Then the British Council would subsidize most of your international touring?
They subsidize our international touring which cannot otherwise pay for itself. The States tours are not subsidized by the British Council.

What about DALTA? I find this body somewhat confusing?
DALTA started off by being a voluntary meeting-together of the four big state-supported companies. The Royal Shakespeare Company, The National Theatre, Covent Garden and Sadler's Wells. It started in 1966 as a purely voluntary thing: we all decided that because we were all big and all supported by the Arts Council, then there must be areas in which all our interests were as one. So we formed ourselves into an association called The Dramatic and Lyric Theatres Association — and we attempted to reveal to ourselves those areas of common ground ... such as negotiating together with unions; reviewing workshop accommodation (the possibility of having common workshop facilities); the idea of touring together; seasons together; and in fact general liaison with each other. But it has changed since then. Hardly any of the common ground theories turned out to be well founded. We all work in *such* different ways. There were some DALTA Seasons which grew out of the early negotiations. Instead of each of us undertaking individual provincial tours, we all went together and offered to provide a touring programme of drama, opera and ballet. This worked for a little while, but we found that our attempts to bend our timetables to match each other were breaking the back of all of us. Also, in 1968, the RSC could no longer afford to tour. The money just wouldn't run to it.

What exists in DALTA today grew out of these beginnings. Over later years, a number of new companies have become attached to DALTA – companies whose activities are much more based on touring than ours are and there are now many more DALTA members.

A logical development of DALTA might be a sort of 'sub agency' of the Arts Council. In *The Theatre Today* report* there is a recommendation that there should be a national touring agency, so that when the Arts Council encourages its beneficiary companies to tour it should not include touring costs as part of its head grant to the companies. We should be able to ask a central agency for specific funds for this purpose. This is the direction in which DALTA is moving at the moment.

It seems that the RSC has almost dropped the regional touring concept entirely –
It's become more and more difficult for us to take our large productions out. Occasionally we do something rather special, like taking *Old Times* on a four-week preview tour of the regions . . . But Theatregoround do the greater part of our touring, and it is through them that we now maintain an RSC presence in the provinces.

How far abroad from Stratford does Theatregoround venture?
It has been down as far as Penzançe and up as far as Newcastle. In general, however, there are proscriptions on its movement. We are *far* from abandoning touring as a concept. We thoroughly support all that can possibly be said about how desirable it would be for the RSC to show itself through the country. The principles are something we very much wanted to pursue, but the practices are difficult. There is no money for it, and also (a very important point) many of the regional theatres are now quite unsuitable to receive the sort of work we have to offer. They're the wrong shape; they have the wrong staff. Our work does not really transfer to other theatres satisfactorily. In a sense, the RSC has outgrown the chain of theatres into which we could go . . .

The Theatre Today in England and Wales: the Report of the Arts Council Theatre Enquiry, 1970, published by The Arts Council of Great Britain, 1970.

Can you briefly outline the structure and the chain of responsibility within the RSC administration?

I'll give you the two responsibility trees that we have drawn up and most of it is self-explanatory. I'll run through the major points. ... The only appointment which you don't see on these charts is that of Production Controller. He will be an executive who has responsibility for co-ordinating production and stage functions. This appointment will be made shortly. ... Let's look at the Administrative Responsibility Tree first. The Governors, Executive Council and Finance Committee head the organization and the function of the first two is self-evident. The Finance Committee is a non-constitutional body of Governors – an 'inner caucus' which has no statutory or constitutional identity. It meets more regularly than Executive Council and it is more closely in touch with management functions than Executive Council. At each Council meeting a report of the Finance Committee is presented, in which their doings, observations and recommendations are set out. The recommendations are particularly important, because it is very unusual for Executive Council to act against a recommendation of the Finance Committee, although it *is* at liberty to do so.

Who comprises the Finance Committee? Are there any 'outsiders'?

No. It's purely internal. It's self-elective from within the Council, and its Chairman is also Chairman of Council.

Following the Finance Committee on the chart is the office of Artistic Director and Chief Executive. This title (Chief Executive) is the title by which Trevor is contracted, and the title by which he is recognized in the Schedule of Approvals and Authorities and in his Terms of Reference issued by the Governors. Beneath this position there are two advisory bodies: the Direction (Ashcroft, Brook, Hall and Nunn – with Nunn as Artistic Director), and the Planning Committee. The Planning Committee is a meeting together of any people who at a given time can make a contribution to the resolution of any problem. If one tries to be a little more precise, it would normally include a group of executives such as the Artistic Director, the General Manager, the Planning Controller, the Head of Publicity and Publications, the

Financial Controller — and (in the future) the new appointment the Production Controller. The Planning Committee will also comprise the resident Associate Directors of the Company, the Head of Design, the Literary Manager and the Music Director.

Where will the office of Production Controller exist on the Administrative Responsibility Tree?

In the positions where the General Stage Manager and Production Manager are now seen. The Production Controller will 'control' both these areas, and the Stage Management and Production Management will be answerable to him . . . instead of reporting direct to me. . . .

The General Stage Managers are the immediate Management representative in the areas of rehearsal and performance. Under the General Stage Manager's control comes the day-by-day organization of the company: . . .

The Stratford Manager is the Manager of the Royal Shakespeare Theatre, Stratford-upon-Avon. He has control over the House Manager, the Box Office Manager and he also has responsibilities for catering; properties belonging to the theatre (and their maintenance); the Picture Gallery; and also for the Library — which now exists at the Shakespeare Centre.

The Stratford Manager also has responsibility for the Winter Season. The London Manager has responsibility for our relations with our Landlord at the Aldwych.

The Planning Controller is the 'control centre' for all productions and acting staff availability. A sort of 'operations room'. . . .

Ronald Bryden, formerly theatre critic for *The Observer*, will be joining the Royal Shakespeare Company as Literary Manager next January, and this title appears on the Artistic Responsibility Tree.

The Financial Controller is a key figure within the organization. In the crudest possible sense, he is an 'accountant'. He is responsible for all matters of cash throughout the organization; he is responsible for settling debtors' and creditors' accounts; he is responsible for all financial transactions which we are engaged in. But he also has a much more important administrative responsibility in a creative sense, and this is to do with the marshalling, quick processing, and feeding back to management of the

financial implications of whatever artistic action we are taking. He
reports to Governors and Management on a regular monthly basis
on *exactly* how we stand in a financial sense. The production
department submit figures to him on a day-to-day basis, so we
then know exactly how much we are spending as a production
moves through rehearsal and staging. He accumulates the
company's financial information daily, and he then makes it
meaningful to us (in the form of reports). In this way, we can see
the overall picture — the whole span of operations.

The Financial Controller also does the spade work for the
annual budget, and he also carries out investigations into any areas
in which I suspect there may be a lack of financial control. . . .
He's got a very wide ranging and very influential job. Part of it is
run of the mill accounting, but another part is much more closely
integrated with the whole artistic working of the operation. We
need financial and statistical information to effectively monitor
the artistic functions of the company. Since we created the position
of Financial Controller in 1967 our whole grasp of the immediacy
of our financial 'plight' has improved out of all recognition. We are
now in much better financial control of ourselves, and we are
therefore able to be much more efficient artistically.

The Artistic Responsibility Tree defines functional artistic
responsibility, and some of the people who appear on this chart
appear with a somewhat different apparent responsibility on the
Administrative Responsibility Tree. What we are stating by the
Artistic Responsibility Tree, is that the Artistic Director is the
man who finally holds responsibility for the success of our artistic
product; and this chart sets out the relative ways in which the
contributions towards the success of the artistic product go back
to him as the co-ordinator and the ultimate 'can-carrier' for the
whole operation.

Part III

Appendices

GOVERNORS

Executive Council

Finance Committee

Artistic Director and Chief Executive

Planning Committee

Direction

General Manager

General Stage Manager
Stratford or London
— Company
— Stage Management
— Band
— Maint. Ward. & Wigs
— Electricians
— Stage Staff

Stratford Manager
— House Manager
— Box Office
— Catering
— Properties and Gardens
— Picture Gallery
— Library
— Winter Season

Planning Controller
— Music Director
— Casting
— Company

Head Publicity/Publications
— Stratford
— London

TGR Administrator

Club Organiser
— Mailing
— Departments

Financial Controller
— Stratford
— London

London Manager
— House Manager
— Box Office
— WTS
— Landlord

Production Manager
— Scene Shop
— Prop Shop
— Paint Shop
— Production
— Wardrobe
— Production Wigs
— Hire Department

ROYAL SHAKESPEARE COMPANY   APRIL 1971   ADMINISTRATIVE RESPONSIBILITY TREE

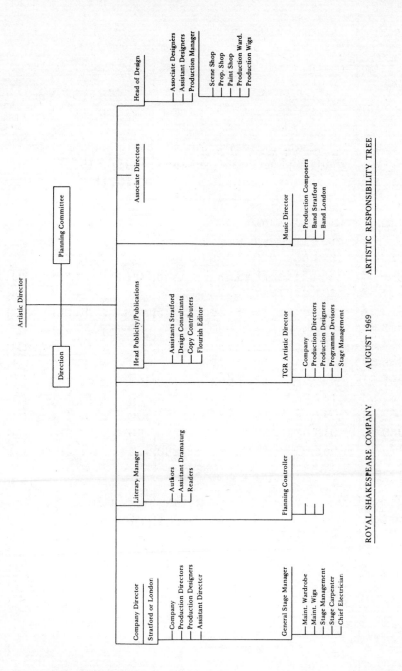

Artistic Director

Direction

Planning Committee

Company Director — Stratford or London
- Company
- Production Directors
- Production Designers
- Assistant Director

General Stage Manager
- Maint. Wardrobe
- Maint. Wigs
- Stage Management
- Stage Carpenter
- Chief Electrician

Literary Manager
- Authors
- Assitant Dramaturg
- Readers

Planning Controller

Head Publicity/Publications
- Assistants Stratford
- Design Consultants
- Copy Contributers
- Flourish Editor

TGR Artistic Director
- Company
- Production Directors
- Production Designers
- Programme Devisors
- Stage Management

Associate Directors

Music Director
- Production Composers
- Band Stratford
- Band London

Head of Design
- Associate Designers
- Assistant Designers
- Production Manager
  - Scene Shop
  - Prop. Shop
  - Paint Shop
  - Production Ward.
  - Production Wigs

ROYAL SHAKESPEARE COMPANY   AUGUST 1969   ARTISTIC RESPONSIBILITY TREE

**Audience totals, box office receipts,
grants, and accounts over the year 1960-1971.
(from Annual Reports 1960-1971)**

Year	Audience totals	Box Office receipts	Total grants	Accounts*	
1959-60	384,539	£247,426	nil	£ 1,498	(S)
1960-61	382,244	£318,087	£ 5,000	£ 12,369	(D)
1961-62	391,872	£479,870	£ 5,000	£ 29,023	(D)
1962-63	no figures	£503,784	£ 15,000	£ 38,066	(D)
1963-64	no figures	£479,080	£ 57,000	£ 45,196	(D)
1964-65	no figures	£469,786	£ 85,000	£ 65,643	(D)
1965-66	1,003,340	£559,177	£ 95,000	£ 23,107	(D)
1966-67	955,039	£568,693	£152,500	£ 444	(D)
1967-68	1,187,787	£598,395	£205,000	£ 32,536	(D)
1968-69	1,048,386	£614,287	£226,500	£161,126	(D)
1969-70	1,013,583	£778,269	£236,450	£ 71,307	(D)
1970-71	1,043,033	£842,747	£280,670	£ 6,461	(S)

*These figures indicate the overall Surplus or Deficit shown over the year.

Appendix 4

Schedule of Terms and Conditions
of the Long Term Contract

A.   The Manager may call upon the Artist to perform anywhere in the world, but the conditions of the following standard contracts shall apply in the following circumstances on any point on which those conditions are more favourable to the Artist than those of this contract and on any point on which this contract is silent.

(a) In Stratford-upon-Avon, at the Aldwych Theatre, or any other London theatre leased by the Manager for a repertoire season, and on tour in the United Kingdom of Great Britain and Northern Ireland — the Royal Shakespeare Theatre contract as approved from time to time by British Actors' Equity Association.

(b) In the West End of London in the event of a special season — the Esher Standard Contract for London Straight Plays as approved from time to time by the London Theatre Council, except that the provisions thereof relating to salary shall not apply.

(c) Elsewhere in the world — the Equity/V.A.F. Standard Contract for Overseas Engagements, special attention being drawn to Clause 18 of that contract, which reads as follows: 'When this contract is used in respect of an engagement in the United States of America, or in another country in which an appropriate union of Artists has an Agreement with British Equity or the Variety Artistes' Federation, the terms of the contract approved by the appropriate union in the country concerned shall apply on any point on which the terms of that contract are more favourable to the Artist than the terms of this contract'.

B.   Salary
The Manager agrees to review the salary paid to the Artist at the end of each period of 12 months during the engagement and may at his discretion increase the salary having regard to the parts to be played by the Artist. It does not necessarily follow that there will be an annual increase of salary throughout the period of the contract. An exception to this, however, is made in the case of an Artist whose weekly salary is £25 or less: in this event, if the Manager shall not have notified the Artist of an increase of salary of at least £3 three

months before the end of the first year, the Artist shall acquire the right to terminate this this agreement by giving three months' notice in writing. Such notice may take effect only at the end of a season of plays in which the Artist is appearing, or to which he is committed. A season of plays is understood to be (a) the Shakespeare season in Stratford from approximately April to November, or (b) the Aldwych season of plays from approximately May in one year to March the following year, or (c) the last four months of the Aldwych season in the case of an Artist transferring to the Aldwych in a production from Stratford.

C. Exclusive Services

The Artist shall be engaged exclusively by the Manager and during the period of this contract shall not perform or exercise his talent for the benefit of any other Company, institution or person without the prior written consent of the Manager which shall not be unreasonably withheld.

When the Artist is performing for any management other than the Royal Shakespeare Company there will at all times be a 'credit' to read: 'Mr or Miss . . . is a member of the Royal Shakespeare Company', and such credits to appear as follows:

Theatre
In the published programme.

Television
1. In the published programmes, i.e. Radio Times or TV Times etc.
2. After the Cast List shown at the beginning or end of the transmission.
3. Vocally, by the announcer, if no cast list is shown.

Radio
1. In the published programmes, i.e. Radio Times or TV Times etc.
2. Vocally, by the announcer.

Films
After the Cast List shown at the beginning or end of the Film.

D. Suspension of Contract

(a) The Artist is entitled, by giving not less than four months' notice, to suspend his employment under this contract for the purpose of undertaking professional employment elsewhere. Consent to a period of suspension shall not be unreasonably withheld by the Manager if requested on less than 4 months notice. Notice may not be given under this clause except to terminate at the end of a season of plays in which the Artist is appearing or a season of plays to which he is committed. The aggregate of such periods of suspension shall not exceed 9 months during the three years of the engagement except by special arrangement with the Managing Director.

If the Artist wishes to extend an agreed period of suspension he must apply to the Manager at least 4 weeks before the end of the period of suspension. If the Artist has not applied for an extension he will be on first call to the Manager.

(b) If, during a period of suspension, the Manager offers a part to the Artist in an RSC production and the Artist accepts, the Manager will pay the Artist his non-playing salary from the date of the acceptance until the Artist starts rehearsals. During this period Clause E paragraphs (c) and (d) will apply.

(c) No salary shall be payable to the Artist under this contract during any period of suspension under this paragraph, but such period of suspension shall be regarded as part of the three years of the engagement of the Artist.

E.   Non-Playing Periods

(a) During periods when there is no casting for the Artist with the Royal Shakespeare Company and, as a consequence, he is neither rehearsing nor performing, the Manager will pay 75% of his playing salary. The aggregate of non-playing periods shall not exceed 9 months during the three years of the engagement. The non-playing salary will not apply to holiday periods and will be subject to the Manager giving written notice to the Artist as follows:

(1) A minimum of one month's notice of non-playing periods of four weeks or less.

(2) A minimum of three months' notice of non-playing periods of more than four weeks.

(b) If, during a season of plays, there are periods when the productions in which the Artist is appearing are temporarily withdrawn from the repertoire, such periods — up to a maximum of one month each — will not be considered as non-playing periods and the Artist will be entitled to his full playing salary. All or part or any such period may, at the discretion of the Manager, be considered as holiday due to the Artist under Clause F(b).

(c) During a non-playing period the Artist is entitled to accept professional employment elsewhere subject to the written consent of the Manager which shall not be unreasonably withheld.

(d) When the Artist is engaged in professional employment elsewhere his non-playing salary will be suspended. This applies to the specific period during which his is working for another management, but is subject to the following qualifications:

(i) During a non-playing period if the Artist's total earnings from professional employment elsewhere are less than the total amount on non-playing salary due to him, the manager will pay to the artist the difference between the two total amounts.

(ii) During a non-playing period if the Artist's total earnings from employment elsewhere exceed the total of his current playing salary with the RSC for the whole of the non-playing period, then the non-playing salary due to the artist for periods when he is not working will be reduced by a percentage on a sliding scale; this percentage reduction will be equal to the percentage by which the Artist's outside earnings exceed the total of his current playing salary with the RSC for the whole of the non-playing period.

F.   Holidays
(a) The Artist shall be entitled to:
> (i) One week's holiday with pay in respect of each 26 weeks' service.
> (ii) One week's holiday for each 52 weeks' continuous service.

(b) The Manager undertakes to release the Artist from all rehearsal and performance commitments for a minimum period of two consecutive weeks each year so that he can take that part of the holiday due to him as specified in (i) above and making a total of three weeks holiday each year. The date for these holidays will be appointed by the Manager and a month's notice in writing will be given to the Artist.

(c) Periods of suspension of this contract under Clause D shall not be considered as periods of service in relation to the length of holiday due to an Artist.

G.   Touring Expenses
(a) The Manager shall provide the Artist's transport to and from London and/or Stratford-upon-Avon and from place to place where the plays are performed during the engagement. The Manager shall not be liable for any fares through the termination of the engagement by the Artist. The Artist shall in all cases travel by the train or conveyance appointed by the Manager and in the compartment assigned to him when a coach is reserved. The Artist shall be allowed to have conveyed at the expense and cost of the Manager on trains, boats or other means of conveyance, one travelling basket or trunk not exceeding one hundred pounds in weight, but the Artist shall pay all expenses to and from stations and places of the Artist's residence. The Artist shall be deemed to consent to the signing of any consignment note by the Manager whether at 'owner's Risk' or otherwise for the purpose of such transport and be a party thereto.

(b) When the Artist is required to appear outside the London area and Stratford-upon-Avon, a touring allowance of 20% of the playing salary will be paid, subject to a minimum of £6 per week.

H.   Commuting Expenses
An Artist required to appear in the same season in Stratford-upon-Avon and London and/or elsewhere during the period of this engagement, in addition to fares, will be paid cost of reasonable accommodation and other out-of-pocket expenses. Payment under this clause would not apply to an Artist who is receiving payment under Clause G.

I.   Accommodation Allowance
If the Artist's normal residence is elsewhere than in Stratford-upon-Avon and he is engaged for all or part of a season in Stratford-upon-Avon, but not required to travel between the two theatres, he will receive an accommodation allowance of 10% of his playing salary with a minimum of £4 per week when required to take up residence in Stratford-upon-Avon. The same terms

will apply to Artists if their normal place of residence is Stratford-upon-Avon when they are required to play in London.

J. Discontinuation

If the Manager shall terminate the continuous presentation of plays in London by discontinuing the Lease of a Theatre in London or otherwise then the Manager may terminate this agreement by giving to the Artist at least three months' notice in writing under this clause. Notice given under this clause shall not expire prior to the termination of the presentation of plays in accordance with this clause.

K. Illness

The provisions of Paragraph D of Schedule 1 to the Royal Shakespeare Theatre contract shall apply to this contract, except that the Manager will pay in any one year of the engagement not less than three weeks' full salary and a further three weeks' half salary in the case of absence due to certified illness.

L. Equity

Only full members of British Actors' Equity Association may be engaged on the terms of this contract and the Artist shall be required to work only with full or probationary members of the Association or with members of such other organizations of Artists as may be approved by the British Actors' Equity Association, but notwithstanding this proviso the Artist shall take no action to impede or endanger the production or run of the tour or season and shall continue to fulfil the terms of this Agreement unless otherwise instructed by the Council of the British Actors' Equity Association.

M. Arbitration

Any dispute and questions whatsoever which shall arise between the parties hereto or their respective representatives touching this Agreement or the construction or application of any clause or thing herein contained in any way relating to this Agreement or the affairs dealt with herein or hereunder or the rights, duties or liabilities of the parties to this Agreement shall if the parties are unable to agree be referred to the Provincial Theatre Council for consideration and recommendation. If either party shall be unwilling to accept such recommendation the question shall be referred to two arbitrators, one to be appointed by each party in accordance with and subject to the provisions of the Arbitration Act 1950 or any statutory modification thereof for the time being in force. One Arbitrator shall be nominated by the Manager and the other Arbitrator (to be appointed by the Artist) shall be nominated by the British Actors' Equity Association. Provided that this clause shall not in any way affect or restrict the right of either party to this Agreement to apply to the Courts for relief by way of injunction.

RSC Stage Productions, 1960-1971

Note: As the Stratford and Aldwych seasons do not run concurrently, the productions listed below have been divided into Stratford and Aldwych seasons, and they are listed under the calendar year in which they occurred. The symbol (R) following a production indicates a revival or a transferred production. Occasional seasons (e.g. The Arts Theatre) follow the two major lists.

STRATFORD PRODUCTIONS

Production and Year	Director	Designer
1960		
The Two Gentlemen of Verona	Peter Hall	Lila de Nobili
The Merchant of Venice	Michael Langham	Desmond Heeley
Twelfth Night	Peter Hall	Lila de Nobili
The Taming of the Shrew	John Barton	Alix Stone
Troilus and Cressida	Peter Hall and John Barton	Leslie Hurry
The Winter's Tale	Peter Wood	Jaques Noel
1961		
Much Ado About Nothing	Michael Langham	Desmond Heeley
Hamlet	Peter Wood	Leslie Hurry
Richard III	William Gaskill	Jocelyn Herbert
As You Like It	Michael Elliott	Richard Negri
Romeo and Juliet	Peter Hall	Sean Kenny
Othello	Franco Zeffirelli	Franco Zeffirelli, Peter J. Hall (costumes)
1962		
Measure for Measure	John Blatchley	John Bury
A Midsummer Night's Dream [first produced 1959]	Peter Hall Maurice Daniels	Lila de Nobili Alix Stone
The Taming of the Shrew (R)	Donald McWhinnie	John Bury
Macbeth	William Gaskill	René Allio
Cymbeline		

The Comedy of Errors	Clifford Williams	John Wyckham and Clifford Williams, Anthony Powell (costumes)
King Lear	Peter Brook	Peter Brook

1963

The Tempest	Clifford Williams and Peter Brook	Farrah
Julius Caesar	John Blatchley	John Bury
The Comedy of Errors (R)	Clifford Williams	John Wyckham, and Clifford Williams; Anthony Powell (costumes)
'The Wars of the Roses' *Henry VI* *Edward IV* *Richard III*	Peter Hall, John Barton and Frank Evans	John Bury; Ann Curtis (costumes)

1964

Richard II *Henry IV: parts 1 and 2* *Henry V* *Henry VI* (R) *Edward IV* (R) *Richard III* (R)	Peter Hall, John Barton and Clifford Williams	John Bury; Ann Curtis (costumes)

1965

Love's Labour's Lost	John Barton	Sally Jacobs
The Jew of Malta (R)	Clifford Williams	Ralph Koltai
The Merchant of Venice	Clifford Williams	Ralph Koltai
The Comedy of Errors (R)	Clifford Williams	John Wyckham and Clifford Williams; Anthony Powell (costumes)
Timon of Athens	John Schlesinger	Ralph Koltai
Hamlet	Peter Hall	John Bury; Ann Curtis (costumes)

1966

Henry IV: parts 1 and 2 (R)	John Barton, Clifford Williams and Trevor Nunn	John Bury; Ann Curtis (costumes)
Henry V (R)	John Barton and Trevor Nunn	John Bury; Ann Curtis (costumes)
Hamlet (R)	Peter Hall	John Bury; Ann Curtis (costumes)
Twelfth Night	Clifford Williams	Sally Jacobs
The Revenger's Tragedy	Trevor Nunn	Christopher Morley

1967

The Taming of the Shrew	Trevor Nunn	Christopher Morley
Coriolanus	John Barton	John Bury; Ann Curtis (costumes)
The Revenger's Tragedy (R)	Trevor Nunn	Christopher Morley

All's Well That Ends Well	John Barton	Timothy O'Brien
As You Like It	David Jones	Timothy O'Brien
Macbeth	Peter Hall	John Bury; Ann Curtis (costumes)
Romeo and Juliet	Karolos Koun	Timothy O'Brien

1968

Julius Caesar	John Barton	John Gunter; Ann Curtis (costumes)
King Lear	Trevor Nunn	Christopher Morley
The Merry Wives of Windsor	Terry Hands	Timothy O'Brien
As You Like It (R)	David Jones	Timothy O'Brien
Dr. Faustus	Clifford Williams	Farrah
Troilus and Cressida	John Barton	Timothy O'Brien
Much Ado About Nothing	Trevor Nunn	Christopher Morley

1969

Pericles	Terry Hands	Timothy O'Brien
The Merry Wives of Windsor (R)	Terry Hands	Timothy O'Brien
The Winter's Tale	Trevor Nunn	Christopher Morley
Women Beware Women	Terry Hands	Timothy O'Brien
Twelfth Night	John Barton	Christopher Morley Stephanie Howard (costumes)
Henry VIII	Trevor Nunn	John Bury

1970

Measure for Measure	John Barton	Timothy O'Brien
Richard III	Terry Hands	Farrah
Dr Faustus (TGR)	Gareth Morgan	Stephanie Howard
Hamlet	Trevor Nunn	Christopher Morley
King John (TGR)	Buzz Goodbody	Christopher Morley and Andrew Sanders
The Two Gentlemen of Verona	Robin Phillips	Daphne Dare
A Midsummer Night's Dream	Peter Brook	Sally Jacobs
The Tempest	John Barton	Christopher Morley and Ann Curtis

1971

The Merchant of Venice	Terry Hands	Timothy O'Brien; costumes with Tazeena Fir
Twelfth Night (R)	John Barton	Christopher Morley Stephanie Howard (costumes)
Richard II (TGR)	John Barton	Ann Curtis
Henry V (TGR)	John Barton	Ann Curtis
Much Ado About Nothing	Ronald Eyre	Voytek
The Duchess of Malfi	Clifford Williams	Farrah
Othello	John Barton	Julia Trevelyan Oman

1972

Toad of Toad Hall	Euan Smith	Adrian Vaux
The Romans		
Coriolanus	Trevor Nunn, with Buzz Goodbody	Christopher Morley and Ann Curtis
Julius Caesar	Trevor Nunn with Buzz Goodbody and Euan Smith	
Comedy of Errors (R)	Clifford Williams	John Wyckham and Clifford Williams Anthony Powell (costumes)
Antony and Cleopatra	Trevor Nunn, with Buzz Goodbody	Christopher Morley and
Titus Andronicus	and Euan Smith	Ann Curtis

1973

A Midsummer Night's Dream (R)	Peter Brook	Sally Jacobs
Romeo and Juliet	Terry Hands	Farrah
Richard II	John Barton	Timothy O'Brien and Tazeena Firth
As You Like It	Buzz Goodbody	Christopher Morley
Love's Labour's Lost	David Jones	Timothy O'Brien and Tazeena Firth
The Taming of the Shrew	Clifford Williams	Farrah
Toad of Toad Hall (R)	Euan Smith	Adrian Vaux

ALDWYCH PRODUCTIONS

Production and Year and Author	Director	Designer
1961		
The Duchess of Malfi John Webster	Donald McWhinnie	Leslie Hurry
Twelfth Night(R) William Shakespeare	Peter Hall	Lila de Nobili
Ondine Jean Giraudoux	Peter Hall	Tanya Moiseiwitsch
The Devils John Whiting	Peter Wood	Sean Kenny; Desmond Heeley (costumes)
The Hollow Crown (R)	John Barton	Devised by John Barton
Becket Jean Anouilh	Peter Hall	Leslie Hurry
The Taming of the Shrew (R) William Shakespeare	Maurice Daniels	Alix Stone
The Cherry Orchard Anton Chekhov	Michel St. Denis	Farrah
1962		
As You Like It (R) William Shakespeare	Michael Elliott	Richard Negri

The Art of Seduction	John Barton	adapted by John Barton from Laclos' Les Liaisons Dangereuses
The Caucasian Chalk Circle Bertolt Brecht	William Gaskill	Ralph Koltai
The Collection Harold Pinter	Peter Hall and Harold Pinter	John Bury
Playing with Fire August Strindberg	John Blatchley	John Bury; Motley (costumes)
A Penny for a Song John Whiting	Colin Graham	Alix Stone
Curtmantle Christopher Fry	Stuart Burge	Farrah
Troilus and Cressida (R) William Shakespeare	Peter Hall	Leslie Hurry
The Devils (R) John Whiting	Peter Wood	Sean Kenny; Desmond Heeley (costume

1963

The Physicists Friedrich Dürrenmatt	Peter Brook	John Bury
King Lear (R) William Shakespeare	Peter Brook	Peter Brook
The Comedy of Errors (R) William Shakespeare	Clifford Williams	John Wyckham and Clifford Williams
The Beggars Opera John Gay	Peter Wood	Sean Kenny; Leslie Hurry (costumes)
A Midsummer Night's Dream (R) William Shakespeare	Peter Hall	Lila de Nobili
The Representative Rolf Hochhuth	Clifford Williams	Ralph Koltai
The Hollow Crown (R)	John Barton	Devised by John Barton

1964

'The Wars of the Roses' (R) William Shakespeare	Peter Hall, John Barton, and Frank Evans	John Bury; Ann Curtis (costumes)
The Rebel Devised by Patrick Garland	Patrick Garland	Stuart Durant
The Birthday Party Harold Pinter	Harold Pinter	Ralph Koltai
Afore Night Come (R) David Rudkin	Clifford Williams	John Bury
Endgame Samuel Beckett	Donald McWhinnie	Ralph Koltai
Expeditions One James Saunders Jean Tardieu Fernando Arrabal John Whiting Samuel Beckett	Elsa Bolam, Robin Midgley, Garry O'Connor and John Schlesinger	

Victor Roger Vitrac	Robin Midgley	Barry Kay
Marat-Sade Peter Weiss	Peter Brook	Sally Jacobs; Gunilla Palmstierna-Weiss (costumes)
Eh? Henry Livings	Peter Hall	John Bury
The Jew of Malta Christopher Marlowe	Clifford Williams	Ralph Koltai
The Merry Wives of Windsor William Shakespeare	John Blatchley	André François

1965

Expeditions Two Charles Wood Johnny Speight Irene Coates David Mercer	David Jones and Trevor Nunn	John Collins
The Comedy of Errors (R) William Shakespeare	Clifford Williams	John Wyckham and Clifford Williams
Henry V (R) William Shakespeare	John Barton, Trevor Nunn	John Bury; Ann Curtis (costumes)
The Homecoming Harold Pinter	Peter Hall	John Bury
Puntila Bertolt Brecht	Michel St. Denis	Farrah
The Hollow Crown (R)	John Barton	Devised by John Barton
Marat-Sade (R) Peter Weiss	Peter Brook	Sally Jacobs; Gunilla Palmstierna-Weiss (costumes)
Hamlet (R) William Shakespeare	Peter Hall	John Bury
The Thwarting of Baron Bolligrew Robert Bolt	Trevor Nunn	Elizabeth Duffield; Ann Curtis (costumes)

1966

The Government Inspector Nikolai Gogol	Peter Hall	John Bury; Ann Curtis (costumes)
The Investigation (R) Peter Weiss	Peter Brook and David Jones	
Tango Slowomir Mrozek	Trevor Nunn	Timothy O'Brien
Days in the Trees Marguerite Duras	John Schlesinger	Timothy O'Brien
The Meteor Friedrich Dürrenmatt	Clifford Williams	John Bury
Staircase Charles Dyer	Peter Hall	Timothy O'Brien
US	Peter Brook	Sally Jacobs

Belcher's Luck David Mercer	David Jones	Alan Tagg
The Thwarting of Baron *Bolligrew* (R)	Trevor Nunn	Elizabeth Duffield Ann Curtis (costumes)

1967
Ghosts Henrik Ibsen	Alan Bridges	Jocelyn Herbert
Little Murders Jules Feiffer	Christopher Morahan	Ralph Koltai
As You Like It (R) William Shakespeare	David Jones	Timothy O'Brien
The Taming of the Shrew (R) William Shakespeare	Trevor Nunn	Christopher Morley
The Relapse Sir John Vanbrugh	Trevor Nunn	Christopher Morley
The Criminals José Triana	Terry Hands	John Bury
The Hollow Crown	John Barton	Devised by John Barton

1968
Macbeth (R) William Shakespeare	Peter Hall	John Bury; Ann Curtis (costumes)
All's Well That Ends Well (R) William Shakespeare	John Barton	Timothy O'Brien
Under Milk Wood (TGR) Dylan Thomas ·	Terry Hands	Gordon Melhuish
Indians Arthur Kopit	Jack Gelber	John Bury; Ann Curtis (costumes)
The Merry Wives of Windsor (R) William Shakespeare	Terry Hands	Timothy O'Brien
The Relapse (R) Sir John Vanbrugh	Trevor Nunn	Christopher Morley
The Latent Heterosexual Paddy Chayefsky	Terry Hands	Timothy O'Brien
God Bless Jules Feiffer	Geoffrey Reeves	John Gunter
Julius Caesar (R) William Shakespeare	John Barton	John Gunter; Ann Curtis (costumes)

1969
A Delicate Balance Edward Albee	Peter Hall	John Bury; Beatrice Dawson (costumes
A Dutch Uncle Simon Gray	Peter Hall	John Bury
The Hollow Crown	John Barton	Devised by John Barton
Troilus and Cressida (R) William Shakespeare	John Barton	Timothy O'Brien
Landscape and *Silence* Harold Pinter	Peter Hall	John Bury; Beatrice Dawson (costumes

Much Ado About Nothing (R) William Shakespeare	Trevor Nunn	Christopher Morley
Silver Tassie Sean O'Casey	David Jones	John Bury
Bartholomew Fair Ben Jonson	Terry Hands	Timothy O'Brien
The Revenger's Tragedy (R) Cyril Tourneur	Trevor Nunn	Christopher Morley
Tiny Alice Edward Albee	Robin Phillips	Farrah
After Haggerty David Mercer	David Jones	Alan Tagg

1970

London Assurance Dion Boucicault	Ronald Eyre	Alan Tagg
The Winter's Tale (R) William Shakespeare	Trevor Nunn	Christopher Morley
The Plebeians Rehearse the Uprising Günter Grass	David Jones	Farrah
Twelfth Night (R) William Shakespeare	John Barton	Christopher Morley; Stephanie Howard (costumes)
When Thou Art King (R) Adapted by John Barton from William Shakespeare	John Barton	Ann Curtis
Major Barbara George Bernard Shaw	Clifford Williams	Ralph Koltai
Henry VIII (R) William Shakespeare	Trevor Nunn	John Bury
The Two Gentlemen of Verona (R) William Shakespeare	Robin Phillips	Daphne Dare

1971

Old Times Harold Pinter	Peter Hall	John Bury
A Midsummer Night's Dream (R) William Shakespeare	Peter Brook	Sally Jacobs
Enemies Maxim Gorki	David Jones	Timothy O'Brien
The Man of Mode Sir George Etherege	Terry Hands	Timothy O'Brien
The Balcony Jean Genet	Terry Hands	Farrah
Exiles James Joyce	Harold Pinter	Eileen Diss; Robin Fraser Paye (costumes)
Much Ado About Nothing (R) William Shakespeare	Ronald Eyre	Voytek

1972

All Over	Peter Hall	John Bury;
Edward Albee		Beatrice Dawson
		(costumes)
The Oz Trial	Buzz Goodbody	—
prepared from court transcripts by		
David Illingworth and Geoffrey Robertson		
The Merchant of Venice (R)	Terry Hands	Timothy O'Brien and
William Shakespeare		Tazeena Firth
The Lower Depths	David Jones	Timothy O'Brien and
Maxim Gorki		Tazeena Firth
Othello (R)	John Barton	Julia Trevelyan Oman
William Shakespeare		
A Midsummer Night's Dream (R)	Peter Brook	Sally Jacobs
William Shakespeare		
Murder in the Cathedral	Terry Hands	Farrah
T.S. Eliot		
The Island of the Mighty	David Jones	Timothy O'Brien and
John Arden and		Tazeena Firth
Margaretta D'Arcy		

1973

Susanna Andler	Howard Sackler	Berkeley Sutcliffe
Marguerite Duras		
Landscape (R)	Peter Hall	John Bury
Harold Pinter		
A Slight Ache	Peter James	John Bury
Harold Pinter		
Coriolanus (R)	Trevor Nunn, with	Christopher Morley and
Julius Caesar (R)	Buzz Goodbody	Ann Curtis
Antony and Cleopatra (R)	and Euan Smith	
Titus Andronicus (R)		
William Shakespeare		
Midwinter Spring		
Nicol Williamson	Nicol Williamson	—

OCCASIONAL SEASONS

(A)   ARTS THEATRE SEASON, 1962

Production, and Author	*Director*	*Designer*
Everything in the Garden	Donald McWhinnie	Henry Bardon
Giles Cooper		
Nil Carborundum	Anthony Page	Michael Knight
Henry Livings		
The Lower Depths	Toby Robertson	Hutchinson Scott
Maxim Gorki		
Afore Night Come	Clifford Williams	John Bury
David Rudkin		
Women Beware Women	Anthony Page	Sally Jacobs
Thomas Middleton		

The Empire Builders Boris Vian	David Jones	Sally Jacobs
Infanticide in the House of *Fred Ginger* Fred Watson	William Gaskill	Stephen Doncaster

(B)   1964 SEASON AT LAMDA AND THE DONMAR REHEARSAL
       THEATRE

Theatre of Cruelty	Peter Brook and Charles Marowitz
The Screens	Peter Brook and Charles Marowitz

(C)   THEATREGOROUND FESTIVAL AT THE ROUNDHOUSE,
       1970

When Thou Art King (R)	John Barton with Gareth Morgan	Ann Curtis
Arden of Faversham	Buzz Goodbody	Annena Stubbs
King John (R)	Buzz Goodbody	Christopher Morley and Andrew Sanders
Dr. Faustus (R)	Gareth Morgan	Stephanie Howard
A Midsummer Night's Dream (R)	(studio) Peter Brook	Sally Jacobs
Richard III (R)	performances) Terry Hands	Farrah
Hamlet (R)	Trevor Nunn	Christopher Morley

(D)   RSC AT 'THE PLACE', 1971

Occupations Trevor Griffiths	Buzz Goodbody	Tazeena Firth
Subject to Fits Robert Montgomery	A.J. Antoon	Leo Yoshimura
Miss Julie August Strindberg	Robin Phillips	Daphne Dare

Note: These lists do not include Theatregoround productions, unless such productions originated — or were later included — as part of the main house repertoire at Stratford or the Aldwych. The RSC has given occasional 'commercial' seasons of particularly successful productions, and these seasons are not included in the lists.

RSC Films and Television Productions, 1960-71

Note: Not all the following presentations have been 'made' (in a financial or contractual sense) by the RSC, although all are claimed as company credits.

FILMS

1967   *Marat-Sade*, directed by Peter Brook.
1967   *Tell Me Lies*, directed by Peter Brook from the 1966 Aldwych production of *US*.

1969   *A Midsummer Night's Dream*, directed by Peter Hall
1969   *King Lear*, directed by Peter Brook

TELEVISION PRODUCTIONS

The following programmes were made under the RSC/BBC contract:

1962 (April)   *The Cherry Orchard*
1963 (March)   *As You Like It*
1964 (January)   *The Comedy of Errors*
1965 (April)   *The Wars of the Roses*. This programme was repeated on BBC 2 between January and March, 1966. It was also shown by television networks in The United States, Canada and Australia.
1967 (March)   *Days in the Trees*
1969 (June)   *All's Well That Ends Well*. This was the first colour television presentation of an RSC production. It was repeated in February 1970.

The following programmes were shown under independent agreements:

1965   *The Hollow Crown* was shown on American Television.
1969   Peter Hall's film of *A Midsummer Night's Dream* was televised 'coast-to-coast' by the CBS Television Network in the United States, and was seen by an estimated 30 million viewers.
1969   A programme based on Trevor Nunn's 1969 production of *The Winter's Tale* was produced for ATV's 'Opening Night' series.
1971   The BBC's 'Review' programme in January 1971 was devoted to the work of Peter Brook, and excerpts from his RSC productions of *A Midsummer Night's Dream*, *Marat-Sade*, and *US* were included.

In addition to the above, segments and excerpts from various RSC stage productions have been shown on different television programmes — generally within a broader context or as part of studies on British theatre.

Appendix 6

International and
Provincial Tours since 1913

Note: These lists have been compiled from the catalogues at the Shakespeare Centre Library, Stratford-upon-Avon, and include only the major touring projects undertaken by the companies involved. Early Theatreground projects and Theatreground short tours from the home theatres have not been included.

INTERNATIONAL TOURS

Year	Countries and/or Cities	Productions
1913/14	(Stratford-upon-Avon Players led by F.R. Benson) Canada and U.S.	Sixteen plays
1913/14	(Stratford-upon-Avon Players led by Henry Herbert) South Africa	Numerous plays
1922	Sweden (Christiania)	*Much Ado About Nothing* *Twelfth Night* *The Taming of the Shrew*
1928/29	Canada and U.S.	Eight plays
1929/30	Canada and U.S.	Nine plays
1931/32	U.S. and Canada	Nine plays
1949/50	Australia (Melbourne, Sydney, Brisbane, Adelaide)	*Much Ado About Nothing* *Macbeth*
1950	Germany (Berlin, Hamburg, Wiesbaden, Düsseldorf)	*Measure for Measure*
1953	New Zealand (Auckland, Christchurch, Dunedin, Wellington) Australia (Sydney, Brisbane, Melbourne, Hobart, Launceston, Adelaide, Perth)	*Henry IV (i)* *Othello*
1953/54	The Continent (The Hague, Amsterdam, Antwerp, Brussels, Paris)	*Antony and Cleopatra*

1955	The Continent (Vienna, Zürich, The Hague, Amsterdam, Rotterdam, Berlin, Copenhagen, Hanover, Oslo, Bremen, Hamburg)	*Much Ado About Nothing* *King Lear*
1957	The Continent (Paris, Vienna, Venice, Belgrade, Zagreb, Warsaw)	*Titus Andronicus*
1958/59	U.S.S.R. (Leningrad, Moscow)	*Romeo and Juliet* *Twelfth Night*
1962	The Continent (Zürich, Geneva, Amsterdam, Utrecht, The Hague, Rotterdam, Tilburg, Arnhem, Paris)	*The Hollow Crown*
1963	U.S. (Washington, Boston, New York, Los Angeles)	*The Hollow Crown*
1963	France (Paris)	*King Lear*
1963/64	U.S. and Canada (Bus and truck tour of 33 towns and cities)	*The Hollow Crown*
1964	Eastern Europe (Berlin, Prague, Budapest, Belgrade, Bucharest, Warsaw, Helsinki, Leningrad, Moscow)	*King Lear* *The Comedy of Errors*
1964	U.S. (Washington, Boston, Philadelphia, New York)	*King Lear* *The Comedy of Errors*
1965/66	U.S. (New York)	*Marat-Sade*
1966/67	U.S. (Boston, New York) The New York season ran for six months with a RSC cast, and followed a fortnights touring run in Boston.	*The Homecoming*
1967	European Tour (Helsinki, Leningrad, Moscow)	*Macbeth* *All's Well That Ends Well*
1968	U.S. (Los Angeles)	*The Taming of the Shrew* *As You Like It*
1968	France (Paris)	*All's Well That Ends Well*
1969	U.S. (Los Angeles, San Francisco, Detroit, Baltimore, New Haven)	*Much Ado About Nothing* *Dr. Faustus*
1969	The Continent (Switzerland, Germany, Holland)	*Troilus and Cressida*
1970	Japan (Tokyo, Fukuoka, Osaka, Nagoya)	*The Winter's Tale* *The Merry Wives of Windsor*
1970	Australia (Melbourne, Sydney, Adelaide)	*The Winter's Tale* *Twelfth Night*
1971	U.S. (New York) The New York run was followed by a four-week tour of Chicago, Boston, Toronto, Philadelphia.	*A Midsummer Night's Dream*
1964	In November 1964, the RSC gave a special presentation of sonnets and scenes from Shakespeare in Rome for Pope Paul.	

PROVINCIAL TOURS (SINCE 1960)

Year	Cities or Towns	Productions
1962	Edinburgh (The Edinburgh Festival)	*Troilus and Cressida*
	Newcastle, Leeds, Manchester,	*The Devils*
	Liverpool	*Curtmantle*
1962	Coventry, Cambridge	*The Hollow Crown*
1963	Edinburgh, Newcastle, Bradford,	*A Midsummer Night's Dream*
	Manchester	*The Physicists*
1965	Cardiff, Manchester, Sunderland,	*The Homecoming*
	Liverpool, Cambridge, Brighton	*The Comedy of Errors*
1966	Brighton	*Staircase*
1967	Glasgow, Edinburgh	*As You Like It*
		The Taming of the Shrew
1967	Liverpool	*Ghosts*
		As You Like It
1967	Manchester	*As You Like It*
		Ghosts
		The Relapse
		The Taming of the Shrew
1967	Bristol, Cardiff	*Ghosts*
		As You Like It
1968	Belfast (followed by a tour	*The Hollow Crown* (TGR)
	of schools)	*Under Milk Wood* (TGR)
1968	Liverpool, Norwich, Newcastle,	*Julius Caesar*
	Manchester, Glasgow	*The Merry Wives of Windsor*
1971	Oxford, Cambridge, Guildford,	*Old Times*
	Nottingham	

Appendix 7

Administration and Staff List 1960

Peter Hall	Director
John Barton	Assistant Director
Patrick Donnell	General Manager

The Company

Peggy Ashcroft	Donald Layne-Smith	Christopher Cruise
Harry Andrews	Dinsdale Landen	Don Webster
Dorothy Tutin	Susan Maryott	Gloria Dolskie
Denholm Elliot	Mavis Edwards	Maroussia Frank
Elizabeth Sellars	Tony Church	Wendy Clifford
Max Adrian	Peter Jeffrey	Mandy Miller
Eric Porter	Barbara Barnett	Julian Battersby
Peter O'Toole	Michel Dotrice	Walter Brown
Patrick Wymark	Ian Richardson	Donald Douglas
Derek Godfrey	Clifford Rose	James Kerry
Jack MacGowran	Roy Dotrice	David Sumner
Paul Hardwick	David Buck	Clive Swift
Patrick Allen	Dave Thomas	Philip Voss
Frances Cuka	Stephen Thorne	William Wallis
Ian Holm	Roger Bizley	James Langley
James Bree	Diana Rigg	Dennis Waterman

The Staff

House	John Jolley	Manager and Licensee
	Leonard James	House Manager
	Edoardo Milano	Catering Manager
	Peter Hampson	Box Office Manager
	John Goodwin	Press and Publicity
	Vincent Pearmain	Press and Publicity

Production	Desmond Hall	Production Manager
	Fred Jenkins	Construction Carpenter
	Gerry Watts	Property Master
	John Collins	Scenic Artist
Stage	Maurice Daniels	Stage Director
	Alisoun Browne	Deputy Stage Director
	Colin McIntyre	Stage Manager
	Eddie Golding	Stage Carpenter
	John Bradley	Chief Electrician
	Audrey Sellman	Wardrobe Mistress
	John Roberts	London General Manager
	Raymond Leppard	Music Adviser
	Brian Priestman	Music Director

Administration and Staff List 1973

Peggy Ashcroft, Peter Brook and Trevor Nunn, *Direction*; Trevor Nunn, *Artistic Director*; Peter Daubeny, Peter Hall, *Consultant Directors*; David Brierley, *General Manager*; Maurice Daniels, *Planning Controller*; John Goodwin, *Head Publicity/Publications*; Christopher Morley, *Head of Design*; James Sargant, *Production Controller*; William Wilkinson, *Financial Controller;* Desmond Hall, *General Production Manager*; Rosalinde Hatton, *Scenic Artist*; Fred Jenkins, *Construction Shop Manager*; William Lockwood, *Property Shop Manager*; Genista McIntosh, *Casting*; David Perry, *Costume Administrator*; Peter Pullinger, *Technical Co-ordinator*; Hal Rogers, *Overseas Tours Manager*; Michael Tubbs, *Deputy Music Director*; Irene Weerdmeester, *Head of Wigs*; Guy Woolfenden, *Music Director*

Publicity and Publications
William Allan, Peter Harlock and Vincent Pearmain *Press Representatives*

Theatregoround
Peter Kemp *Administrator*

RSC Club (Aldwych)
Kaye Flanagan *Organiser*

Advisers and Consultants
Jeremy Brooks, *Plays*; Joe Clark *Costume Cutting*; John Collins, *Scenic Art*; Andrew Downie, *Singing*; Kenneth Lintott, *Wigs and Make-up*; George Mayhew, *Graphic Design*; John Moore, *Sound*

ASSOCIATE ARTISTS

Actors
Peggy Ashcroft, Colin Blakely, Brenda Bruce, Tony Church, Patience Collier, Jeffery Dench, Judi Dench, Susan Fleetwood, Peter Geddis, Ian Holm, Alan Howard, Geoffrey Hutchings, Emrys James, Richard Johnson, John Kane, Ben Kingsley, Estelle Kohler, Bernard Lloyd, Brewster Mason, Helen Mirren, Richard Pasco, Eric Porter, Roger Rees, Ian Richardson, Diana Rigg, Norman Rodway, Paul Rogers, Sebastian Shaw, Morgan Sheppard, Donald Sinden, Derek Smith, Elizabeth Spriggs, Patrick Stewart, Janet Suzman, David Waller, David Warner, Michael Williams, John Wood

Directors
John Barton, Peter Brook, Peter Hall, Terry Hands, David Jones, Trevor Nunn, Clifford Williams

Designers
John Bury, Farrah, Christopher Morley, Timothy O'Brien

Movement
John Broome

Music
Guy Woolfenden

Play Adviser
Ronald Bryden

Voice
Cicely Berry

The Company: Royal Shakespeare Theatre

John Abbot	Michael Ensign	Clement McCallin
Ray Armstrong	Susan Fleetwood	Lloyd McGuire
Robert Ashby	Brian Glover	Peter Machin
Eileen Atkins	Nickolas Grace	Colin Mayes
Annette Badland	Wilfred Grove	Richard Mayes
Alan Bates	Denis Holmes	Richard Pasco

Sydney Bromley
Brenda Bruce
Gavin Campbell
Janet Chappell
Tony Church
Timothy Dalton
Jeffery Dench

Louise Jameson
Charles Keating
Catherine Kessler
Estelle Kohler
Beatrix Lehmann
Maureen Lipman
Bernard Lloyd

Anthony Pedley
Ian Richardson
Sebastian Shaw
Derek Smith
David Suchet
Leon Tanner
Janet Whiteside

The Company: Aldwych Theatre

Wendy Allnutt
Darien Angadi
Peggy Ashcroft
Madeline Bellamy
Colin Blakely
John Bott
Walter Brown
Loftus Burton
Joseph Charles
Mark Dignam
Michael Egan
Edwina Ford
Paul Gaymon
Judy Geeson
Patrick Godfrey
Gareth Hunt
Geoffrey Hutchings

Oscar James
Christopher Jenkinson
Richard Johnson
Malcolm Kaye
Jonathan Kent
Jill Lidstone
Sidney Livingstone
Philip Locke
Rosemary McHale
Joe Marcell
Martin Milman
Gerard Murphy
John Nettleton
Robert Oates
Tony Osoba
Lennard Pearce
Tim Pigott-Smith

Emlyn Price
Corin Redgrave
Mary Rutherford
Peter Schofield
Nicholas Selby
Morgan Sheppard
Mark Sheridan
Patrick Stewart
Desmond Stokes
Janet Suzman
Keith Taylor
Margaret Tyzack
David Waller
Margaret Whiting
Arthur Whybrow
Nicol Williamson
John Wood

Staff at the Royal Shakespeare Theatre:

Julian Beech, *Sound Technician*; John Bradley, *Lighting Engineer*; Eddie Golding, *Master Carpenter*; Roger Howells, *General Stage Manager*; Bob Leedham, *Property Master*; Leslie Mitchell, *Box Office Manager*; Audrey Sellman, *Maintenance Wardrobe*; Robert Vaughan, *Manager and Licensee*; Judith Vickers, *House Manager*; Brian Harris and Clive Morris, *Lighting Assistants*

Staff at the Aldwych Theatre:
Lucy Coghlan, *Wig Manager*; Alf Davies, *Chief Stage Technician*:
Terry Diamond, *Property Master*; Gordon Kember, *London Music
Director*; David Kitchenham, *Wardrobe Master*; Michael Lansdale,
Chief Lighting Operator; Frances Roe, *Wardrobe Supervisor*;
Maggie Roy, *Production Assistant*; Peter Skinner, *Box Office
Manager*; Frank Stevens, *General Stage Manager*; Sama
Swaminathan, *House Manager*

Statement of RSC Policy, 1973

The Royal Shakespeare Company are divided between the country and the capital, playing concurrently at two theatres for most of each year. They appear at their Stratford-upon-Avon home, the Royal Shakespeare Theatre, from April to December; and at their London home, the Aldwych Theatre, from July to March.

The RSC are formed round a core of artists under long-term contract. By working constantly together in a varied repertoire the company aim to be a flexible ensemble with a distinctive character.

Shakespeare is the RSC's central concern; the company are responsible for most of the major Shakespeare productions seen in this country. Five or more Shakespeare plays (with occasionally a non-Shakespeare) compose each year's Stratford season.

The RSC's annual Aldwych season complements the company's Shakespeare work by consisting of some modern plays as well as Shakespeare and other classics. This bridge between Shakespeare and the contemporary theatre keeps the RSC's Shakespeare productions in touch with modern thought.

RSC Theatregoround productions, as well as playing in the company's Stratford and London theatres, are taken out to theatres, schools, colleges, and community centres throughout Great Britain.

The RSC occasionally give short experimental seasons in which they challenge accepted forms of acting, writing and directing.

Last year a total of well over $1\frac{1}{3}$ million people visited the RSC's two theatres and saw their productions on tour. This figure is believed to be a world record. But no theatre company working in repertoire can recoup expenditure. Giving the public a wide choice of plays, staged concurrently and continually changing, is an expensive system. Even with year-round full houses, subsidy is necessary. This year's Arts Council subsidy is £365,000: less than one quarter of the company's costs, the rest being met from the box office.

The Corporation of the City of London is building the RSC a new London theatre in the Barbican Arts Centre. This will be ready by 1977/8 and the company move there from the Aldwych.

In 1969 the RSC's first colour film *A Midsummer Night's Dream* was shown on CBS television network in America, and released for world-wide cinema distribution. In 1971, a screen version of Peter Brook's RSC production of *King Lear*, with Paul Scofield, was also released.

Of the members of the RSC Direction (Peggy Ashcroft, Peter Brook and Trevor Nunn), Trevor Nunn holds the top post of Artistic Director. He is responsible to the Board of Governors of the Royal Shakespeare Theatre whose President is the Earl of Harewood, Chairman Sir George Farmer, and Vice-Chairman Dennis L Flower.

RSC Consultant Directors are Peter Daubeny, and Peter Hall who founded the company in 1960 and was Managing Director until 1968.

Of the RSC's two theatres the parent, the Royal Shakespeare Theatre, was called the Shakespeare Memorial Theatre from 1879, when it was founded, to 1961. Its founder was Charles Flower whose family — notably Sir Archibald and more recently, Sir Fordham — have supported and guided the theatre throughout its long history. It was gutted by fire in 1926 to be replaced six years later by the present building. Incorporated under Royal Charter and state-subsidised, with the Queen as Patron, it virtually belongs to the nation.

RSC Awards since 1960

1960 **Evening Standard Drama Awards**
BEST ACTRESS: Dorothy Tutin as *Viola* in *Twelfth Night*
Printing World National Letterpress Awards
HIGH MERIT CERTIFICATE: Souvenir Programmes

1961 **Evening Standard Drama Awards**
BEST PLAY: *Becket* by Jean Anouilh
BEST ACTOR: Christopher Plummer as *Henry II* in *Becket*
BEST ACTRESS: Vanessa Redgrave as *Katharina* in *The Taming of the Shrew*

1962 **Evening Standard Drama Awards**
BEST PLAY: *The Caucasian Chalk Circle* by Bertolt Brecht
BEST ACTOR: Paul Scofield as *King Lear*
MOST PROMISING NEW PLAYWRIGHT: David Rudkin for *Afore Night Come*
Paris Festival Theatre des Nations Awards
BEST ACTRESS: Dame Peggy Ashcroft in *The Hollow Crown*
Printing World National Letterpress Awards
HIGH MERIT CERTIFICATE: Souvenir Programmes

1963 **Paris Festival Theatre des Nations Awards**
GRAND PRIX FOR BEST PRODUCTION: Peter Brook's *King Lear*
French Critics' Circle Awards
BEST DIRECTOR: Peter Brook for *King Lear*
Plays and Players London Theatre Critics' Awards
BEST DIRECTOR: Peter Hall for *The Wars of the Roses*
BEST NEW ACTOR: David Warner as *Henry VI* in *The Wars of the Roses*

1964 **Evening Standard Drama Awards**
BEST ACTRESS: Dame Peggy Ashcroft as *Queen Margaret* in *The Wars of the Roses*
Variety Club of Great Britain Awards
BEST STAGE ACTRESS: Dame Peggy Ashcroft as *Queen Margaret* in *The Wars of the Roses*
Plays and Players London Theatre Critics' Awards
BEST DIRECTOR: Peter Brook for *The Marat/Sade*

1965 **Evening Standard Drama Awards**
BEST ACTOR: Ian Holm as *Henry V*, and as *Lenny* in *The Homecoming*
MOST PROMISING NEW PLAYWRIGHT: David Mercer for *Ride a Cock Horse* (not an RSC production) and *The Governor's Lady*
New York Drama Critics' Awards
BEST PLAY: *The Marat/Sade* by Peter Weiss
Variety's New York Drama Critics' Awards
BEST DIRECTOR: Peter Brook for *The Marat/Sade*
MOST PROMISING NEW ACTRESS: Glenda Jackson as *Charlotte Corday* in *The Marat/Sade*
Plays and Players London Theatre Critics' Awards
BEST ACTOR: Paul Scofield as *Timon of Athens*
BEST DIRECTOR: Peter Hall for *Hamlet* and *The Homecoming*

1966 **New York Tony Awards**
BEST PLAY: *The Marat/Sade* by Peter Weiss
BEST DIRECTOR: Peter Brook for *The Marat/Sade*
BEST SUPPORTING ACTOR: Patrick Magee as *de Sade* in *The Marat/Sade*
BEST COSTUME DESIGNER: Gunilla Palmstierna Weiss for *The Marat/Sade*
Plays and Players London Theatre Critics' Awards
BEST ACTOR: Paul Scofield as *Khlestakov* in *The Government Inspector* and as *Charles Dyer* in *Staircase*
BEST PRODUCTION: Peter Brook's *US*

1967 **Variety Club of Great Britain Awards**
BEST STAGE ACTOR: David Warner as *Hamlet*
Plays and Players London Theatre Critics' Awards
BEST NEW ACTRESS: Estelle Kohler as *Juliet*

BEST DESIGNER: Ralph Koltai for *As You Like It* (a National Theatre, not an RSC production) and *Little Murders*

New York Tony Awards
BEST PLAY: *The Homecoming* by Harold Pinter
BEST DIRECTOR: Peter Hall for *The Homecoming*
BEST DRAMATIC ACTOR: Paul Rogers as *Max* in *The Homecoming*
BEST SUPPORTING ACTOR: Ian Holm as *Lenny* in *The Homecoming*
New York Drama Critics' Awards
BEST PLAY: *The Homecoming* by Harold Pinter
British Poster Design Awards
AWARD CERTIFICATE: *Henry V* poster

1968 **FVS Foundation (Hamburg University) Awards**
SHAKESPEARE PRIZE: Peter Hall
International Screen Printing Competition
FIRST PRIZE: *Macbeth* poster

1969 **Clarence Derwent Awards**
BEST SUPPORTING ACTRESS: Elizabeth Spriggs as *Claire* in *A Delicate Balance*
Variety's London Critics' Awards
BEST SUPPORTING ACTRESS: Elizabeth Spriggs as *Claire* in *A Delicate Balance*
Plays and Players London Theatre Critics' Awards
BEST DIRECTOR: Trevor Nunn for *The Revenger's Tragedy* and *The Winter's Tale*
BEST ACTRESS: Dame Peggy Ashcroft as *Agnes* in *A Delicate Balance* and *Beth* in *Landscape*
BEST DESIGNER: John Bury for *Silence*
MOST PROMISING ACTOR: Alan Howard as *Achilles* in *Troilus and Cressida* and *Lussurioso* in *The Revenger's Tragedy*

1970 **Plays and Players London Theatre Critics' Awards**
BEST DIRECTOR: Peter Brook for *A Midsummer Night's Dream*
BEST DESIGNER: Sally Jacobs for *A Midsummer Night's Dream*

British Poster Design Awards
AWARD CERTIFICATE: *The Winter's Tale* poster
AWARD CERTIFICATE: *Henry VIII* poster
New York Tony Awards
BEST DIRECTOR: Peter Brook for *A Midsummer Night's Dream*

1971 **Plays and Players London Theatre Critics' Awards**
BEST PLAY: *Old Times* by Harold Pinter
BEST ACTRESS: Dame Peggy Ashcroft as *Claire Lannes* in *The Lovers of Viorne (not an RSC production)* and *Katharine* in *Henry VIII*
BEST DESIGNER: Farrah for *The Balcony*
BREAKTHROUGH ACTRESS: Heather Canning as *Polya* in *Occupations* and *Christine* in *Miss Julie*
Clarence Derwent Awards
BEST SUPPORTING ACTRESS: Heather Canning as *Christine* in *Miss Julie*

1972 **Paris Drama Critics' Awards**
MEILLEUR SPECTACLE DE L'ANNEE: Comedie Francaise in *Richard IIII* director Terry Hands, designer Farrah composer Guy Woolfenden — all RSC Associate Artists
National Screen Printing Awards
FIRST PRIZE: *Murder in the Cathedral* poster

1973 **FVS Foundation (Hamburg University) Awards**
SHAKESPEARE PRIZE: Peter Brook
Evening Standard Drama Awards
SPECIAL AWARD: Sir Peter Daubeny for his services to world theatre

Notes to the Text

CHAPTER 1

The Background Years

1. *Council Books of the Corporation of Stratford-on-Avon*, February 1611-1612, Volume B, p. 220.

2. *Borough of Stratford-on-Avon Chamberlain's Accounts*, 1622-1647, p. 3.

3. Undated Shakespeare Memorial Theatre pamphlet, *Shakespeare Memorial Theatre, 'General Boxes'*, Ref. P 71.2 (Gen.).

4. J.C. Trewin and T.C. Kemp, *The Stratford Festival*, (Cornish Bros., 1953), gives an account of early Stratford Festivals.

5. J.C. Trewin, *Benson and the Bensonians*, (Barrie and Rockliff, 1960), gives an account of the 'Benson years' at Stratford.

6. J.C. Trewin and M.C. Day, *Shakespeare Memorial Theatre*, (Dent and Sons, 1932), p. 184. This work sets out the history of the Memorial Theatre until 1932. A further history of the theatre is given in Ruth Ellis, *Shakespeare Memorial Theatre*, (Winchester, 1948).

7. Notes from *Shakespeare Memorial Theatre, 'General Boxes'*, Ibid. (3) above.

8. J.C. Trewin, *The Birmingham Repertory Theatre 1913-1963*, (Barrie and Rockliff, 1963), gives a full account of Sir Barry Jackson's work at Birmingham.

9. Sir Barry Jackson, 'The New Idea at Stratford', *Theatre World*, April, 1946, pp. 29-30. This article contains an almost complete statement of early Jackson policy.

10. Ibid.

11. *The Huddersfield Examiner*, 23rd July 1947.

12. Peter Brook's early career is discussed in some detail in Chapter 3, below.

13. *The Recorder*, 10th October 1947.

14. Norman Marshall, *The Other Theatre*, (Lehmann, 1947), p. 186.

15. J.C. Trewin, *The Birmingham Repertory Theatre 1913-1963*, Ibid. (8) above.

16. *The Wolverhampton Express*, 2nd July 1947.

17. *The Manchester Guardian*, 7th January 1948.

18. *The Birmingham Mail*, Editorial, 7th January 1948.

19. John Trewin, Theatre Critic and Historian, in an interview with the author, 15th January 1971.

20. Tom English, former Private Secretary to Sir Barry Jackson, in an interview with the author, 22nd January 1971. Tom English was Press Officer at Stratford during Sir

Barry's directorate, and became Sir Barry's private secretary at a later date.

He held this position until Sir Barry's death in 1961.

21. J.C. Trewin, *Shakespeare on the English Stage 1900-1964*, (Barrie and Rockliff, 1964), p. 211.

22. *The Stratford Herald*, 11th June 1948.

23. T.C. Kemp, *The Birmingham Post*, 5th August 1948.

24. *The Times*, 11th June 1948.

25. Two novels based on his wartime experiences: *Eight Hours from England* and *On Such a Night*.

26. The first international tour by a company from the Shakespeare Memorial Theatre was in 1913, when Frank Benson sent two companies abroad — under the name of the Stratford-upon-Avon Players. A list of SMT international tours since is included in Appendix 6.

27. *The Scotsman*, 4th August 1950.

28. *The Stage*, 7th September 1956.

29. Anthony Quayle and Ivor Brown, *Shakespeare Memorial Theatre 1948-1950*, (Reinhardt, 1950), p. 14.

30. E.M.W. Tillyard, *Shakespeare's History Plays*, (Chatto and Windus, 1944).

31. Anthony Quayle, 'Introduction', J. Dover Wilson and T.C. Worsley, *Shakespeare's Histories at Stratford, 1951*, (Reinhardt, 1952), p. vii. This work gives a detailed account of the 1951 season, together with critical commentary on the productions.

32. Ibid.

33. Kenneth Tynan, *Curtains*, (Longmans, 1961), p. 35.

34. *Plays and Players*, August 1954.

35. Anthony Quayle, reported in *The Daily Telegraph*, 20th December 1952.

36. Anthony Quayle, reported in *The Birmingham Gazette*, 4th February 1954.

37. *The Birmingham Gazette*, 5th February 1954.

38. T.C. Kemp, *The Birmingham Post*, 10th February 1954.

39. Sir Laurence Olivier appeared as Katherine in a schoolboy production of *The Taming of the Shrew* in 1922. As part of the Birthday celebrations of that year, this production was staged as a special matinee at the Memorial Theatre.

40. Ruth Ellis, *The Stratford Herald*, 28th January 1955.

41. *Titus Andronicus* had been considered as the Birthday Play of 1929, but was rejected in favour of *Much Ado About Nothing*. Ruth Ellis in *Shakespeare Memorial Theatre*, wrote: '... the certainty that this gory play would not be popular probably deterred the Director.'

42. This production is discussed in Chapter 3, below.

43. *Plays and Players*, July 1956.

44. Peter Hall's career is discussed in some detail in Chapter 2, below.

45. *The Stage*, 7th September 1956.

46. Anthony Quayle, reported in *The Birmingham Mail*, 17th September 1956.

47. Both at the Royal Court Theatre for the English Stage Company.

49. Peter Hall, reported in *The Birmingham Post*, 15th November 1958.

Chapter 2

1. Peter Lewis, 'Peter Uses You . . .', *Nova Magazine*, August 1967.

2. Peter Hall, 'Theatre for Me', *The Sunday Telegraph*, 24th July 1966. This article was published as a series, running over three weekly parts.

3. Ibid.

4. Ibid.

5. Ibid.

6. Ibid.

7. Tony Church, RSC Associate Artist, in an interview with the author, 29th March 1971.

8. Peter Hall, 'Theatre for Me', *The Sunday Telegraph*, 24th July 1966.

9. Peter Hall, 'Theatre for Me', *The Sunday Telegraph*, 17th July 1966.

10. Atticus, 'Hamlet When a Student', *The Sunday Times*, 22nd August 1965.

11. Peter Hall, 'Theatre for Me', *The Sunday Telegraph*, 24th July 1966.

12. Ibid.

13. Peter Hall, RSC Director and former Managing Director, in an interview with the author, 3rd December 1971.

14. Tony Church, Ibid. (7) above.

15. Peter Hall, 'Theatre for Me', *The Sunday Telegraph*, 31st July 1966.

16. Ibid.

17. Ibid.

18. Tony Church, Ibid. (7) above.

19. Peter Hall, 'Theatre for Me', *The Sunday Telegraph*, 31st July 1966.

20. Tony Church, Ibid. (7) above.

21. Peter Hall, Ibid. (13) above.

22. Tony Church, Ibid. (7) above.

23. Peter Hall, 'Introduction', John Barton and Peter Hall, *The Wars of the Roses*, (BBC Publication, 1971), p. ix.

24. During the fifties and earlier, there were two major theatrical touring circuits in Britain. The number one circuit was to cover a series of large major theatres in provincial cities, and the number two circuit covered smaller towns and theatres. The system no longer exists in this form.

25. Peter Hall, 'Theatre for Me', *The Sunday Telegraph*, 31st July 1966.

26. Tony Church, Ibid. (7) above.

27. Peter Woodthorpe, RSC Contract Artist, in an interview with the author, 13th October 1971.

28. John Trewin, 'The Young Director', *The Birmingham Post*, 29th October 1958.

29. This production is discussed in Chapter 6, below.

30. Tony Church, Ibid. (7) above.

31. John Goodwin, RSC's Head of Publicity and Publications, in an interview with the author, 14th April 1971.

32. Peter Hall, Ibid. (13) above.

33. Peter Hall, reported in *The Daily Express*, 22nd March 1965.

34. Ibid. (1) above.

35. Clifford Williams, RSC Associate Director, in an interview with the author, 22nd June 1971.

36. Ian Richardson, RSC Associate Artist, in an interview with the author, 11th December 1970.

37. John Kane, RSC Associate Artist, in an interview with the author, 23rd October 1971.

38. Peter Lewis, 'Peter Uses You . . .', Ibid. (1) above.

39. Ibid.

40. Ibid.

41. Peter Hall, 'Theatre for Me', *The Sunday Telegraph*, 31st July 1966.

42. Peter Hall, Ibid. (13) above.

43. Peter Lewis, 'Peter Uses You . . .', Ibid. (1) above.

44. Peter Hall, reported in *The Daily Mail*, 5th June 1963.

45. Peter Lewis, 'Peter Uses You . . .', Ibid. (1) above.

46. The University of Warwick's scheme of Associate Professorships is designed to encourage and strengthen the University's relationships with industry and other organizations. An Associate Professor is not a full-time staff member, but acts in an 'honorary' capacity — taking an interest in the University's activities and delivering occasional lectures on topics of interest.

47. Gordon Gow, 'In Search of a Revolution', *Films and Filming*, September 1969.

48. Ibid.

49. Peter Woodthorpe, Ibid. (27) above.

50. Michael McNay, 'Producing Pinter', *The Guardian*, 1st June 1971.

51. A realistically staged 'orgy' sequence in this production aroused considerable press comment at the time.

52. John Heilpern, 'The Showman', *The Observer*, 29th November 1970.

53. Peter Hall, 'Shouts and Murmurs', *The Observer*, 14th March 1971.

54. Martin Cooper, *The Daily Telegraph*, 3rd December 1970.

55. Peter Heyworth, *The Observer*, 20th June 1971.

56. John Bury, RSC Associate Designer and former Head of Design, in an interview with the author, 21st June 1971.

57. Peter Hall, reported in *The Evening Standard*, 8th July 1971.

58. Kenneth Pearson, 'Why Peter Hall Left Covent Garden', *The Sunday Times*, 11th July 1971.

59. Peter Hall, Ibid. (13) above.

60. Trevor Nunn, RSC Artistic Director, in an interview with the author 22nd September 1971.

61. Peter Hall, Ibid. (13) above.

Chapter 3

1. Peter Hall, 'A New Way With Shakespeare', *The Sunday Times*, 22nd November 1959.

2. Peter Hall, reported in *The Birmingham Post*, 14th January 1960.

3. Peter Hall, 'Speech to the Company', January 1963, *Royal Shakespeare Theatre Tapes*. Shakespeare Centre Library, Stratford-upon-Avon.

4. Peter Hall, 'A New Way With Shakespeare', Ibid. (1) above.

5. Peter Hall, reported in *The Daily Mail*, 9th November 1961.

6. *Shakespeare Memorial Theatre Press Release*, 8th March 1960, from the personal files of John Goodwin, RSC's Head of Publicity and Publications.

7. Ibid.

8. An example of the initial RSC long-term contract is included in the Appendix.

9. Shakespeare Memorial Theatre Press Release, 16th October 1960, from the personal files of John Goodwin, RSC's Head of Publicity and Publications.

10. Ibid.

11. Peter Hall, reported in *The Manchester Guardian*, 9th March 1960.

12. Peter Brook, 'Peter Hall by Peter Brook', *RSC Annual Report*, 1968.

13. Sir Fordham Flower, RSC Chairman of Governors, 'The Policy of the Royal Shakespeare Theatre', an article written in 1965 — and presumed unpublished. From the personal files of John Goodwin, RSC's Head of Publicity and Publications.

14. Peter Hall, 'Speech to the Company', January 1963, Ibid. (3) above.

15. Peter Hall, reported in *The Birmingham Post*, 27th June 1962.

16. Peter Hall, reported in *The Birmingham Post*, 23rd November 1961.

17. Peter Hall, reported in *The Birmingham Post*, 27th July 1962.

18. *The Observer*, Editorial, 8th July 1962.

19. Peter Hall, 'Avoiding a Method', *Crucial Years*, RSC booklet, (Reinhardt, 1963), p. 5.

20. *The Times*, 14th January 1960.

21. T.C. Worsley, *The Financial Times*, 6th April 1960.

22. Peter Hall, 'Shakespeare and the Modern Director', *Royal Shakespeare Theatre Company 1960-1963*, (Reinhardt, 1964), p. 44.

23. Ian Richardson, RSC Associate Artist, in an interview with the author, 11th December 1970.

24. *RSC Press Release*, 12th April 1962, from the personal files of John Goodwin, RSC's Head of Publicity and Publications.

25. Peter Hall, 'Avoiding a Method', Ibid. (19) above.

26. Michel St. Denis died in London during 1971. At the time of his death, he held the position of Consultant Director to the RSC.

27. Ian Richardson, Ibid. (23) above.

28. Michel St. Denis, 'A Studio for Experiment and Training', *Crucial Years*, RSC booklet, (Reinhardt, 1963), p. 24. Many of St. Denis' ideas on theatre and the responsibilities of the profession are set out in Michel St. Denis, *Theatre: The Rediscovery of Style*, (Heinemann, 1960).

29. John Kane, RSC Associate Artist, in an interview with the author, 23rd October 1971. (*See* Appendix A.)

30. *The Observer*, 16th October 1966.

31. 'Backstage Prodigy', *John Bull*, 13th August 1949.

32. Ibid.

33. John Trewin, Theatre Critic.

and Historian, in an interview with the author, 15th January 1971. At the time of this interview, John Trewin was completing a biography of Peter Brook — later published in December 1971: J.C. Trewin, *Peter Brook — A Biography*, (Macdonald, 1971).

34. Ibid.

35. *The Birmingham Post*, 7th April 1947.

36. *The Coventry Evening Telegraph*, 7th April 1947.

37. John Trewin, Ibid. (33) above.

38. Peter Brook, 'Notes', *Titus Andronicus Programme*, 1957 season, Stoll Theatre, London.

39. *The Daily Mail*, 15th August 1955.

40. Kenneth Tynan, 'Hall and Brook Ltd.', *The Observer*, 3rd July 1957.

41. *The Observer*, 16th October 1966.

42. Penelope Gilliatt, 'Peter Hall's First Stratford Season', *Shakespeare Memorial Theatre Season Programme*, 1960.

43. Ibid.

44. *The Yorkshire Post*, 16th December 1960.

45. The script of this production, illustrated and with some comment on the anthology, was published in 1971: John Barton and Joy Law, *The Hollow Crown*, (Hamish Hamilton, 1971).

46. Kenneth Tynan, *The Observer*, 15th October 1961.

47. Bernard Levin, 'An Independent View', *RSC Season Programme*, 1962.

48. Ibid.

49. Statistics from John Goodwin, RSC's Head of Publicity and Publications.

50. Roger Gellert, 'The Plays — An Impression', *Crucial Years*, RSC booklet, (Reinhardt, 1963), p. 8.

51. Peter Hall, 'Introduction', John Barton and Peter Hall, *The Wars of the Roses*, (BBC Publication, 1970), p. vii. This text gives a complete account of the making of the adaptation and includes a copy of Shakespeare's text — with Barton's modifications clearly set out.

52. The three parts of *Henry VI* were staged as a continuous sequence at the Birmingham Repertory Theatre in 1953, and this production transferred to the Old Vic in the same year. The Old Vic staged *Henry VI* in 1957 and 1958.

53. Peter Hall, 'The Director and the Permanent Company', Charles Marowitz and Simon Trussler, *Theatre at Work*, (Methuen, 1967), p. 151.

54. John Barton and Peter Hall, *The Wars of the Roses*, p. xxiv, Ibid. (54) above.

55. *Henry VI*, RSC Programme, 1964.

56. The RSC's production of *The Wars of the Roses* and the later RSC/BBC television production, is further discussed in Chapters 4 and 6 below.

57. Bernard Levin, *The Daily Mail*, 21st August 1963.

Chapter 4

1. Peter Hall speaks about the overall problems involved in directing the RSC in an interview, 'The Director and the Permanent Company', Charles Marowitz and Simon Trus-

sler, *Theatre at Work*, (Methuen, 1967), pp. 148-159. More specific views about Shakespearian actors and acting are in Peter Hall, 'Avoiding a Method', *Crucial Years*, RSC booklet, (Reinhardt, 1963), pp. 15-16.

2. Peter Hall, reported in *The Birmingham Post*, 21st March 1964.

3. Peter Hall, 'Speech to the Company', January 1963, *Royal Shakespeare Theatre Tapes*, Shakespeare Centre Library, Stratford-upon-Avon.

4. Peter Hall, 'Shakespeare and the Modern Director', *Royal Shakespeare Theatre Company 1960-1963*, (Reinhardt, 1964), p. 44.

5. Maurice Daniels, RSC Planning Controller, in an interview with the author, 9th March 1971. A list of RSC Associate Artists appears in the Appendix.

6. The final wording of this amended contract was not formally approved by Equity until April 1967, although the contracts were in use by the RSC from 1965.

7. Maurice Daniels, Ibid. (5) above.

8. Peter Hall, 'The Director and the Permanent Company', Ibid. (1) above, p. 153.

9. Peter Lewis, 'Peter Uses You . . .', *Nova Magazine*, August 1967.

10. Gareth Lloyd Evans, Department of Extramural Studies, University of Birmingham and theatre critic for *The Guardian*, in an interview with the author, 29th March 1971.

11. Ibid.

12. Peter Hall, reported in *The Stratford Herald*, 4th March 1966.

13. *RSC Programmes* (Stratford), 1964 to 1965.

14. This production is discussed in Chapter 6, below.

15. Dr. Lloyd Evans has criticized this particular aspect of RSC policy on more than one occasion. An article, 'Shakespeare, The Twentieth Century and "Behaviourism"', *Shakespeare Survey 20*, (Cambridge University Press, 1967), pp. 133-142, discusses RSC productions of the History plays and *Hamlet* (1965), and a recent lecture entitled 'Shakespeare Now', is to be published in *Stratford Papers*: Stratford Seminar, edited by Professor Berners Jackson, McMaster University, Ontario, Canada.

16. Ibid. *Shakespeare Survey 20*, p. 142.

17. *Flourish* (RSC Newspaper), Editorial, June 1964.

18. *Flourish*, July 1965.

19. *Plays and Players*, January 1966.

20. TGR is the common abbreviation for Theatregoround used within the company.

21. *Flourish*, April 1966.

22. Undated Theatreground Programme, (possibly 1966), from the author's own collection.

23. See text of interview with John Bury, p. 216-7.

24. Peter Hall, reported in *The Birmingham Post*, 10th February 1965.

25. Royal Shakespeare Theatre's Twenty Fourth Summr School on Shakespeare, *Programme*, 1971.

26. These publications continued into the early sixties, the last in the series being, *Royal Shakespeare Theatre Company 1960-1963*. A complete list of these publications appears in the reference section of this work.

27. John Goodwin, RSC's Head of

Publicity and Publications, in an interview with the author, 14th April 1971.

28. R.B. Marriot, 'Flourish — For the Actor and the Public', *The Stage*, 2nd July 1964.

29. *Crucial Years*, RSC booklet, (Reinhardt, 1963).
Theatre of Cruelty, RSC pamphlet/programme, 1964.

30. John Goodwin, Ibid. (27) above.

31. *RSC Annual Report*, 1963.

32. Peter Hall, RSC Director and former Managing Director, in an interview with the author, 3rd December 1971.

33. John Harrison, 'The Public Patron', *The Stage*, 5th June 1964.

34. A brief finance table including all grants made to the RSC over the period 1960-1971, appears in the Appendix.

35. Ian Richardson, RSC Associate Artist, in an interview with the author, 11th December 1970.

36. John Goodwin, Ibid. (27) above.

37. Peter Hall, 'Speech to the Company', January 1963, Ibid. (3) above.

38. A complete list of RSC provincial and international tours over the period 1960-1971, appears in the Appendix.

39. A complete list of RSC films and television productions over the period 1960-1971, appears in the Appendix.

40. Sydney Newman, reported in *The Stage*, 11th June 1964.

41. John Barton, RSC Associate Director, in an interview with the author, 18th September 1971.

42. The TV production of *The Wars of the Roses* is further discussed in John Barton and Peter Hall, *The Wars of the Roses*, (BBC Publication, 1970), and a full cast list is given.

43. David Brierley, RSC General Manager, in an interview with the author, 22nd September 1971.

44. Roger Manvell, *Shakespeare and the Film*, (Dent and Sons, 1971), contains chapters on Hall's film of *A Midsummer Night's Dream* and Brook's *King Lear*.

45. David Brierley, Ibid. (43) above.

46. Peter Hall, reported in *The New Daily*, 14th March 1964.

47. Some background to the World Theatre Seasons is contained in Peter Daubeny's autobiography, *My World of Theatre*, (Jonathan Cape, 1971).

48. Peter Daubeny, *Plays and Players*, April 1966.

49. Kenneth Tynan, *Tynan Right and Left*, (Longmans, 1967), p. 167.

50. *The Daily Telegraph*, 15th January 1964.

51. Gareth Lloyd Evans, Ibid. (10) above.

52. In 1737, the Lord Chamberlain's prerogative powers received statutory recognition, and his function in the theatre was clearly defined in Sections 1 and 2, *Geo. II*, C.28. A detailed account of the Lord Chamberlain's office and powers, the history of dramatic censorship in Britain, and examples of censorship over the sixties, are contained in Richard Findlater, *Banned: A Review of Theatrical Censorship in Britain*, (Macgibbon and Kee, 1967).

53. Peter Hall, reported in *The Daily Herald*, 26th June 1964.

54. *Afore Night Come*, Aldwych

Theatre programme, 1964.

55. Emile Littler, reported in *The Daily Telegraph*, 24th August 1964.

56. Sir Fordham Flower, reported in *The Daily Telegraph*, 28th August 1964.

57. John Trewin,*The Birmingham Post*, 26th August 1964.

58. *The Times*, 1st September 1964.

59. Sir Fordham Flower, reported in *The Birmingham Post*, 31st August 1964.

60. Sir George Farmer's appointment was the first time that a member of the Flower family had not held the senior position at the Stratford theatre, although members of the family still serve on the Board of Governors.

61. Peter Hall, reported in *The Stage*, 24th March 1966.

62. Trevor Nunn's early career is discussed in Chapter 7, below.

63. In April 1968, Paul Scofield resigned from the Directorate of the RSC for 'personal reasons'. He also resigned from the company. In 1971, he joined the Directorate of the National Theatre.

64. 'New Blood at Stratford', *The Financial Times*, 3rd February 1968.

65. Peter Hall, reported in *The Daily Telegraph*, 31st January 1968.

66. John Heilpern, 'The Showman', *The Observer*, 29th November 1970.

67. Peter Brook, 'Peter Hall by Peter Brook', *RSC Annual Report*, 1968.

Chapter 5

1. John Kane, RSC Associate Artist, in an interview with the author, 23rd October 1971.

2. Dame Peggy Ashcroft, RSC Director and Associate Artist, in an interview with the author, 16th January 1971.

3. Peter Hall, RSC Director and former Managing Director, in an interview with the author, 3rd December 1971.

4. Peter Hall, 'The Director and the Permanent Company', Charles Marowitz and Simon Trussler, *Theatre at Work*, (Methuen, 1967), p. 154.

5. Dame Peggy Ashcroft, Ibid. (2) above.

6. Peter Hall, 'Speech to the Company', January 1963, *Royal Shakespeare Theatre Tapes*, Shakespeare Centre Library, Stratford-upon-Avon.

7. Peter Lewis, 'Peter Uses You . . .', *Nova Magazine*, August 1967.

8. Judi Dench, RSC Associate Artist, in an interview with the author, 11th November 1971.

9. Ian Richardson, RSC Associate Artist, in an interview with the author, 11th December 1970.

10. Gareth Lloyd Evans, 'Shakespeare, The Twentieth Century and ''Behaviourism'' ', *Shakespeare Survey 20*, (Cambridge University Press, 1968), p. 133.

11. Gordon Rogoff, 'Richard's Himself Again', *Tulane Drama Review, (T34)*, Tulane University, 1966, p. 37.

12. Peter Hall, Ibid. (3) above.

13. Ibid.

14.   Peter Hall, Ibid. (3) above.

15.   John Kane, Ibid. (1) above.

16.   Peter Hall, 'Directing the Play', *Amateur Stage*, January 1970, p. 18.

17.   J.C. Trewin, 'Acting With a Flourish', *Flourish*, Summer 1969.

18.   Gareth Lloyd Evans, 'Interpretation or Experience? Shakespeare at Stratford', *Shakespeare Survey 23*, (Cambridge University Press, 1970), pp. 131-132.

19.   John Russell Brown, 'The Study and Practice of Shakespeare Production', *Shakespeare Survey 18*, (Cambridge University Press, 1965), p. 67.

20.   Peter Hall, 'Directing the Play', *Amateur Stage*, December 1969, p. 17.

21.   John Russell Brown, 'The Study and Practice of Shakespeare Production', Ibid. (19) above.

22.   Peter Hall, Ibid. (3) above.

23.   John Kane, Ibid. (1) above.

24.   Judi Dench, Ibid. (8) above.

25.   Peter Woodthorpe, RSC Contract Artist, in an interview with the author, 13th October 1971.

26.   Clifford Williams, RSC Associate Director, in an interview with the author, 22nd June 1971.

27.   Clifford Williams, reported in *The Guardian*, 21st April 1966.

28.   John Barton, RSC Associate Director, in an interview with the author, 18th September 1971.

29.   Peter Hall, 'Avoiding a Method', *Crucial Years*, RSC booklet, (Reinhardt, 1963), p. 14.

30.   Peter Hall, 'Directing the Play', *Amateur Stage*, December 1969, January 1970.

31.   Ibid. December 1969, p. 18.

32.   Ibid, p. 17.

33.   Peter Hall, 'Shakespeare and the Modern Director', *Royal Shakespeare Theatre Company, 1960-1963*, (Reinhart, 1964), p. 41.

34.   Ian Richardson, Ibid. (9) above.

35.   Peter Hall, 'Directing the Play', *Amateur Stage*, January 1970, p. 16.

36.   Ibid, p. 18.

37.   Ibid.

38.   Ibid, p. 19.

39.   Judi Dench, Ibid. (8) above.

40.   Ian Richardson, Ibid. (9) above.

41.   John Kane, Ibid. (1) above.

42.   Peter Hall, reported in *The Birmingham Post*, 14th November 1970.

43.   Peter Hall, 'Director in Interview', *Plays and Players*, July 1970.

44.   Tony Church, RSC Associate Artist, in an interview with the author, 25th September 1971.

45.   Peter Hall, 'Speech to the Company', January 1963, Ibid. (6) above.

46.   Peter Brook, 'False Gods', *Flourish*, Winter, 1965.

47.   Peter Brook, 'A Search for a Hunger', *Encore*, July-August 1961.

48.   Michael Williams, RSC Associate Artist, in an interview with the author, 15th June 1971

49.   Ian Richardson, Ibid. (9) above.

50.   Morgan Sheppard, RSC Associate Artist, in an interview with the author, 23rd October 1971.

51. John Kane, 'Plotting With Peter', *Flourish*, Summer 1971.

52. Ibid.

53. Peter Brook, 'Speech to O.U.D.S.', 15th November 1962, *Royal Shakespeare Theatre Tapes*, Shakespeare Centre Library, Stratford-upon-Avon.

54. Maurice Daniels, RSC Planning Controller, in an interview with the author, 9th March 1971.

55. Peter Brook set up the International Centre for Theatre Research in 1968, and the project is partially subsidized by the French and Persian Governments. The group consists of Brook (as Director), and between ten and sixteen actors of various nationalities. They work in a disused tapestry factory in Paris, and are not committed to give performances at any time, seeing their work as 'mainly experimental'.

56. Richard Findlater, 'Myth and Magic Among the Persians', *The Observer*, 12th September 1971.

57. John Barton, Ibid. (28) above.

58. Ibid.

59. Judi Dench, Ibid. (8) above.

60. Richard Pasco, RSC Associate Artist, in an interview with the author, 6th October 1971.

61. Clifford Williams, Ibid. (26) above.

62. Ibid.

63. Richard Pasco, Ibid. (60) above.

64. Trevor Nunn, reported in *The Birmingham Post*, 28th March 1968.

65. John Kane, Ibid. (1) above.

66. Richard Pasco, Ibid. (60) above.

67. John Kane, Ibid. (1) above.

68. Ibid.

69. Benedict Nightingale, 'Shakespeare is as Shakespeare's Done', *Theatre 71*, (Hutchinson, 1971), p. 156.

70. *Studio*, November 1960.

71. Ibid.

72. John Bury, reported in *The Guardian*, 19th August 1965.

73. John Bury, reported in *The Guardian*, 19th August 1965.

74. Peter Hall, 'The New Theatre and the Amateur', *Amateur Stage*, March 1965.

75. Dennis Barker, 'Why do People Go to the Theatre?', *The Wolverhampton Express and Star*, 14th October 1963.

76. This survey was taken during the National Theatre's production of *Andorra* in 1964, and the results are reported by Kenneth Tynan in *Tynan Right and Left*, (Longmans, 1967), p. 171.

77. Ian Richardson, Ibid. (9) above.

Chapter 6

1. A complete list of RSC productions, 1960-1971, appears in the Appendix.

2. The setting was altered somewhat when the production transferred to the Aldwych, to fit the specifications of the stage and to accommodate the difficult sight-lines of this theatre.

3. Peter Hall, reported in *The Daily Express*, 3rd June 1959.

4. Kenneth Tynan, *Curtains*, (Longmans, 1961), pp. 238-239.

5. Gareth Lloyd Evans, Department of Extramural Studies, University of Birmingham and theatre critic for *The Guardian*, in an interview with the author, 24th September 1971.

6. Tony Church, RSC Associate Artist, in an interview with the author, 25th September 1971.

7. T.C. Worsley, *The Financial Times*, 14th June 1963.

8. Peter Hall, interviewed by Gordon Gow, 'In Search of a Revolution', *Films and Filming*, September 1969.

9. Judi Dench, RSC Associate Artist, in an interview with the author, 11th November 1971.

10. Peter Hall, 'In Search of a Revolution', Ibid. (8) above.

11. Ibid.

12. Ibid.

13. D.A. Traversi, *An Approach to Shakespeare*, (Sands and Co., 1938), p. 64.

14. *The Sunday Times*, 31st July 1960.

15. *The Daily Mail*, 27th July 1960.

16. Tony Church, Ibid. (6) above.

17. John Barton, RSC Associate Director, in an interview with the author, September 1971.

18. *The Manchester Guardian*, 21st February 1961.

19. John Whiting, interviewed by *Time and Tide*, 9th March 1961. A further interview with Whiting, together with a brief biography, appears in Charles Marowitz and Simon Trussler, *Theatre at Work*, (Methuen, 1967), pp. 21-35.

20. *The Financial Times*, 21st February 1961.

21. Mary Holland, *RSC Season Programme*, 1961.

22. *The Manchester Guardian*, 22nd February 1961.

23. Frank Granville Barker, *Plays and Players*, April 1961.

24. *The Devils*, directed by Ken Russell. Released in Britain by Warner Bros. Distributors Ltd. in 1971.

25. *Afore Night Come* was revived at the Aldwych in 1964, and *Women Beware Women* was given an entirely new production in 1969.

26. Clifford Williams, RSC Associate Director, in an interview with the author, 22nd June 1971.

27. *The Observer*, 28th June 1964.

28. Clifford Williams, Ibid. (26) above.

29. Alan Brien, *The Sunday Telegraph*, 10th June 1962.

30. Kenneth Tynan, *The Observer*, 10th June 1962.

31. Peter Hall, 'Shakespeare and the Modern Director', *Royal Shakespeare Theatre Company 1960-1963*, (Reinhardt, 1964), p. 46.

32. Kenneth Tynan, *The Observer*, 11th November 1962.

33. Charles Marowitz, 'Lear Log', Charles Marowitz and Simon Trussler, *Theatre at Work*, (Methuen, 1967), pp. 133-147.

34. Ibid., pp. 133-134.

35. Jan Kott, *Shakespeare Our Contemporary*, (Methuen, 1965).

36. Ibid., 'King Lear or Endgame', p. 112.

37. Peter Brook, 'Speech to

O.U.D.S.', 15th November 1962, *Royal Shakespeare Theatre Tapes*, Shakespeare Centre Library, Stratford-upon-Avon.

38.   'A Lear of the Head', *The Spectator*, 16th November 1962.

39.   Tony Church, Ibid. (6) above.

40.   Charles Marowitz, 'Lear Log', Ibid. (33) above, p. 142.

41.   Ibid., pp. 135-136.

42.   Kenneth Tynan, *The Observer*, 11th November 1962.

43.   Ibid.

44.   Ibid.

45.   Roger Manvell, *Shakespeare and the Film*, (Dent and Sons, 1971), devotes a chapter to a discussion of Brook's film of *King Lear*.

46.   Tony Church, Ibid. (6) above.

47.   *Richard II*, RSC Programme, 1964.

48.   Although Peter Wood assisted in the direction of the 1964 Histories, his name does not appear in the credits. At the time he was working with the National Theatre, and his assistance at Stratford was on an 'unofficial' basis. He worked mainly on the production of *Richard II*.

49.   John Bury, 'The Set', John Barton and Peter Hall, *The Wars of the Roses*, (BBC Publications 1970), p. 237.

50.   John Bury, RSC Associate Designer and former Head of Design, in an interview with the author, 21st June 1971.

51.   *Henry VI*, RSC Programme, 1964.

52.   John Bury, 'The Set', Ibid. (49) above.

53.   Maurice Daniels, RSC Planning Controller, in an interview with the author, 9th March 1971.

54.   Peter Hall, 'Introduction', *The Wars of the Roses*, (BBC Publication, 1970), pp. x-xi.

55.   John Kane, RSC Associate Artist, in an interview with the author, 23rd October 1971.

56.   The 1960 production of *Troilus and Cressida* was actually directed by Peter Hall, although it was credited as a joint production. John Barton took responsibility for the textual work involved and for staging the fight scenes.

57.   Clifford Williams, Ibid. (26) above. In this extract, Williams is speaking of the 1964 season.

58.   Arthur Calder-Marshall, *The Listener*, 18th June 1964.

59.   Ian Richardson, RSC Associate Artist, in an interview with the author, 11th December 1970.

60.   Peter Hall, 'Director in Interview', *Plays and Players*, June 1970. An interesting note is the continuation of this quotation: 'So what is *Hamlet* now? The flower-children of yesterday have produced a new generation who want to shout down all opposing opinions. The Shakespeare play I'd like to do most is *The Tempest* because it's about wisdom, understanding and also resignation — the experience of power at one remove.'

61.   John Kane, Ibid. (55) above.

62.   A condensation of Hall's 'talk' to the *Hamlet* company, appears in Charles Marowitz and Simon Trussler, *Theatre at Work*, (Methuen, 1967), pp. 160-163.

63.   Gareth Lloyd Evans, Ibid. (5) above.

64.   Elizabeth Spriggs, RSC Associ-

ate Artist, in an interview with the author, 13th November 1971. Elizabeth Spriggs played Gertrude in the 1965 *Hamlet*.

65. Gareth Lloyd Evans, Ibid. (5) above.

66. Tony Church, Ibid. (6) above.

67. Ibid.

68. Ibid.

69. Elizabeth Spriggs, Ibid. (64) above.

70. Tony Church, Ibid. (6) above.

71. Gareth Lloyd Evans, Ibid. (5) above.

72. Harold Hobson, *The Sunday Times*, 22nd August 1965.

73. John Trewin, *The Birmingham Post*, 20th August 1965.

74. Antonin Artaud, *The Theatre and Its Double*, (Calder and Boyars, 1970), pp. 59-60.

75. Jerzy Grotowski, *Flourish*, August 1967.

76. *Theatre of Cruelty*, RSC pamphlet/programme, 1964.

77. Ibid.

78. Charles Marowitz, 'Notes on the Theatre of Cruelty', Charles Marowitz and Simon Trussler, *Theatre at Work*, (Meuthuen, 1967), pp. 164-185.

79. This was later published in an expanded form as *The Marowitz Hamlet*, (Penguin, 1968).

80. *The Screens* was finally staged at the Donmar Rehearsal Theatre in London for a week during May 1964. Performances were free and the audiences were invited — mostly made up of actors, playwrights and other members of the profession.

81. *The Daily Mail*, 10th January 1964.

82. J.L. Styan, *Plays and Players*, March 1963.

83. Charles Marowitz, 'Notes on the Theatres of Cruelty', Ibid. (78) above, p. 183.

84. Eric Johns, 'A New Theatre Language', *Theatre World*, August 1964.

85. The full title of Weiss's play (abbreviated to *Marat-Sade*) is *The Persecution and Assassination of Marat as Performed by the Inmates of the Asylum of Charenton under the Direction of the Marquis de Sade*.

86. Charles Marowitz, 'Notes on the Theatre of Cruelty', Ibid. (78) above.

87. *The Times*, 21st August 1964. A short biography of Weiss, together with an interview in which he discusses the themes of *Marat-Sade* is in Walter Wager, *The Playwrights Speak*, (Longmans, 1967), pp. 150-168.

88. *The Financial Times*, 21st August 1964.

89. *The Times*, 21st August 1964.

90. Bernard Levin, *The Daily Mail*, 21st August 1964.

91. Morgan Sheppard, RSC Associate Artist, in an interview with the author, 23rd October 1971. Morgan Sheppard was a member of Brook's Cruelty group, and also worked in *Marat-Sade* and *US*.

92. Laurence Kitchin, *Drama in the Sixties*, (Faber, 1966), p. 22.

93. Peter Evans, 'Peter Brook and the Theatre of Blood', *The Daily Express*, 25th August 1964.

94. *US*, Playscript 9, (Calder and Boyars, 1968), p. i.

95. Ibid.

96. Ibid. Peter Brook, 'Introduction', pp. 10-11.

97.   Morgan Sheppard, Ibid. (91) above.

98.   Ibid. Grotowski's technique-exercises (some of which were used by the *US* group) are set out in his 'acting manifesto', *Towards a Poor Theatre*, (Methuen, 1969).

99.   *The Daily Mail*, 14th October 1966.

100.   *The Times*, 14th October 1966.

101.   Hilary Spurling, 'Mr Brook's Lemon', *The Spectator*, 21st October 1966.

102.   Michael Williams, RSC Associate Artis, in an interview with the author, 15th June 1971. Michael Williams also worked with Brook on *King Lear* and *Marat-Sade*.

103.   *The Times*, 14th October 1966.

104.   Morgan Sheppard, Ibid. (91) above.

105   Hilary Spurling, 'Mr Brook's Lemon', Ibid. (101) above.

106.   R.B. Marriot, *The Stage and Television today*, 20th October 1966.

107.   Pinter's first two full-length plays were *The Birthday Party* (1957) and *The Caretaker* (1959).

108.   The English Stage Company and Joan Littlewood's Theatre Workshop both provided outstanding examples of this kind of relationship.

109.   Harold Hobson, *The Sunday Times*, 25th May 1958.

110.   *The Collection* was presented on a double-bill with *Playing With Fire*, directed by John Blatchley.

111.   Harold Hobson, *The Sunday Times*, 6th June 1965.

112.   Ronald Bryden, 'A Stink of Pinter', *The New Statesman*, 11th June 1965.

113.   Martin Esslin, *The Peopled Wound*, (Methuen, 1970), p. 155. This work is a comprehensive critical study of Pinter and his works, and contains reference to all plays staged by the RSC — with the exception of *Old Times* (1971).

114.   Ibid. p. 153.

115.   Peter Hall, reported in *The Cambridge News*, 22nd April 1965.

116.   Harold Pinter, interviewed by Walter Wager, *The Playwrights Speak*, (Longmans, 1967), p. 149.

117.   Gareth Lloyd Evans, Ibid. (5) above.

118.   In Britain, Ian Holm won the 1965 Evening Standard Drama Award for his roles as Henry V, and Lenny in *The Homecoming*. Peter Hall won the Plays and Players Award of the same year for his work on *Hamlet* and *The Homecoming*.

119.   *The Revenger's Tragedy*, RSC Programme, 1969. The G. Salgado edition, *Three Jacobean Tragedies*, (Penguin, 1965) was the basic text used for the RSC production, and the introduction gives some background to the period and the play.

120.   Trevor Nunn, RSC Artistic Director, in an interview with the author, 22nd September 1971.

121.   Ted Valentine, RSC Contract Artist, in an interview with the author, 24th September 1971.

122.   Trevor Nunn, Ibid. (120) above.

123.   *The Times*, 6th October 1966.

124.   Ronald Bryden, 'Villains in a Vicious Circus',*The Observer*, 9th October 1966.

125.   Peter Hall, 'Speech to the

Macbeth Company', July 1967, *Royal Shakespeare Theatre Tapes*, Shakespeare Centre Library, Stratford-upon-Avon.

126. *The Times*, 17th August 1967.

127. G.K. Hunter, 'Macbeth in the Twentieth Century', *Shakespeare Survey 19*, (Cambridge University Press, 1966), p. 7. The RSC used the G.K. Hunter edition of *Macbeth* (New Penguin Shakespeare, 1967) for the 1967 production.

128. Ronald Bryden, *The Observer*, 20th August 1967.

129. *Macbeth*, RSC Programme, 1967.

130. Alan Brien, *The Sunday Telegraph*, 20th August 1967.

131. Ted Valentine, Ibid. (121) above. Ted Valentine played Lennox in *Macbeth*.

132. Peter Hall, 'The Director and the Permanent Company', Charles Marowitz and Simon Trussler, *Theatre at Work*, (Methuen, 1967), p. 155.

133. Elizabeth Spriggs, Ibid. (64) above. Elizabeth Spriggs played the first Witch in *Macbeth*.

134. Ted Valentine, Ibid. (121) above.

135. Ronald Bryden, *The Observer*, 20th August 1967.

136. Elizabeth Spriggs, Ibid. (64) above.

137. Peter Hall, in an interview with the author, 28th January 1972.

Chapter 7

1. *RSC Press Release*, 29th January 1968, from the personal files of John Goodwin, RSC's Head of Publicity and Publications.

2. Trevor Nunn, reported in *The Birmingham Post*, 28th March 1968.

3. Trevor Nunn, RSC Artistic Director, in an interview with the author, 22nd September 1971

4. Peter Hall, reported in *The Birmingham Post*, 31st January 1968.

5. Trevor Nunn, Ibid. (3) above.

6. Trevor Nunn, 'Director in Interview', *Plays and Players*, September 1970.

7. Ibid.

8. Trevor Nunn, Ibid. (3) above.

9. Trevor Nunn, reported in *The Guardian*, 18th December 1970.

10. Richard Pasco, RSC Associate Artist, in an interview with the author, 6th October 1971.

11. Peter Hall, RSC Director and former Managing Director, in an interview with the author, 3rd December 1971.

12. *RSC in the Roundhouse: Theatre-go-round Festival*, RSC pamphlet, 1970.

13. Harold Hobson, *The Sunday Times*, 30th August 1970.

14. Benedict Nightingale, 'Shakespeare is as Shakespeare's Done', *Theatre 71*, (Hutchinson, 1971), pp. 167-168.

15. Clive Barnes, reported in *The Observer Magazine*, 13th June 1971.

16. Ronald Bryden, 'Dream in a Persian Market', *The Observer Magazine*, 13th June 1971.

17. John Kane, 'When My Cue Comes Call Me, And I Will Answer', *The Sunday Times*, 13th June 1971.

18. John Kane, 'Plotting With Peter', *Flourish*, Summer 1971.

19. Peter Brook, 'Director in Interview', *Plays and Players*, October 1970.

20. 'Spotlight', *Vogue Magazine*, June 1971.

21. Peter Brook, 'Director in Interview', Ibid. (19) above.

22. Ronald Bryden, *The Observer*, 6th December 1970.

23. Harold Hobson, 'Remembrance of Things Past', *The Sunday Times*, 6th June 1971.

24. Ronald Bryden, 'Pinter's New Pacemaker', *The Observer*, 6th June 1971.

25. Ibid.

26. *The Winter's Tale*, RSC Programme, 1969.

27. Trevor Nunn, 'Director in Interview', Ibid. (6) above.

28. Trevor Nunn, 'Notes', *The Winter's Tale*, RSC Programme, 1969.

29. Trevor Nunn, 'Director in Interview', Ibid. (6) above.

30. Peter Ansorge, *Plays and Players*, September 1970.

31. Peter Roberts, *Plays and Players*, July 1970.

32. Anne Righter, *Shakespeare and the Idea of the Play*, (Penguin, 1967), pp. 143-146.

33. J.W. Lambert, 'The Wind and the Rain', *The Sunday Times*, 24th August 1969.

34. Benedict Nightingale, 'Shakespeare is as Shakespeare's Done', Ibid. (14) above, p. 165.

35. Trevor Nunn, Ibid. (3) above.

36. *The Daily Telegraph*, 24th October 1973.

37. *The Times*, 25th October, 1973.

38. Trevor Nunn, Ibid (3) above.

39. Peter Hall, Ibid. (11) above.

TREVOR NUNN
Notes to Chapter 7
taken from a letter from Trevor Nunn to the author dated 9th January 1974.

○ Since I took over the control of the company, we have presented fourteen new plays and recent Aldwych seasons have included plays never previously presented in this country or neglected since the turn of the century. By what criterion is *The Silver Tassie* safe, or *Enemies* by Gorki, or *The Balcony* by Genet; (as far as one could gather, nobody previously knew of the existence of *London Assurance*)? After changing to the two year plan, the company presented *The Plebians Rehearse the Uprising* by Gunter Grass, *After Haggerty* by David Mercer, *Tiny Alice*, *A Delicate Balance*, and *All Over* by Edward Albee, *Landscape*, *Silence*, and *Old Times* by Harold Pinter, *The Island of the Mighty* by John Arden, and we are about to open *Duck Song* by David Mercer, *Section Nine* by Philip Magdalany and *The Bewitched* by Peter Barnes. The 1964 Aldwych season was a high point in the RSC's policy of presenting new plays. It included *The Birthday Party* (revival of a play previously seen in London), *Endgame* (revival of a play previously seen in London), *Victor* (production of neglected twentieth century minor classic), *Afore Night Come* (transfer of new play from small auditorium season), *The*

Marat-Sade (new play), *Eh!* (new play) and *The Jew of Malta* (little-done classic). The season we are currently presenting includes *Landscape* and *A Slight Ache* (revivals of plays previously seen in London), *Duck Song* (new play), *Section Nine* (transfer of new play from small auditorium season), *The Bewitched* (new play), *Travesties* (new play), *Summer Folk* by Gorki (never performed before in England) and *Sherlock Holmes* (production of neglected twentieth century minor classic).

Clearly all seasons have not been so rich in new work. For example the 1967 season, the last of the seasons organized by Peter Hall. The company presented *Ghosts* (a safe classic play?), *Little Murders* (new play), *The Taming of the Shrew*, *As You Like It*, *The Relapse* (a safe classic play?), *All's Well That Ends Well* and *Macbeth*. In the following year, I organised a season which included *Indians* (new play), *God Bless* (new play), *The Latent Heterosexual* (new play), *Julius Caesar*, *The Merry Wives of Windsor* and *The Relapse*.

It seems to me, in comparisons of this nature, it is vital not to generalize. Therefore the extent to which there has been a 'definite concentration on a classic repertoire' needs to be clarified, and the term 'safe' is demonstrably inapplicable.

□ The work load that you describe is not unusual, in the RSC, the National Theatre or any other repertoire theatre, and the situation did not change between 1967 and 1969. Research will show you that many leading performers have appeared in four plays in a season, and that for most actors, 'a play out' is all that they expect, and even that is not a contractual obligation. Eric Porter played Malvolio, Ulysses and Leontes while rehearsing Ferdinand in *The Duchess of Malfi*, in the 1960 season. Does this example alone show the pressures placed on lead actors when the company was first formed? How many actors had more than one play out during *The Wars of the Roses* — or the great histories season of 1964. I think you should compare apples with apples, and establish whether the individual work load has changed over the last ten years. To my certain knowledge it has not.

☆ This remark is perfectly reasonable in the context of Peter Hall's interview. But in this context, it takes on a quite different meaning. You use it as an argument in support of Richard Pasco's statement, and therefore it purports to offer a considered criticism of the system I was instituting. But we both know that it does not actually offer a considered criticism. The quotation indicates that actors were being asked to make token appearances, and it ridicules that idea. But since that was not the case, and since Ian Richardson was not asked to 'walk on and say "What ho" ', I think the sentence is misleading and ill-judged. By the way, you say earlier that Ian Richardson played 'the minor walk on role of Marcellus'. Surely the accurate description is 'small part'. Minor indicates that the part is insignificant, but what he has to say about the bird of dawning belies that. 'Walk on' indicates that the part is speechless. But Marcellus has 69 lines. In the same season Alan Howard undertook the very difficult task of playing the goddess Juno, in the masque in *The Tempest*. Is Ceres also a 'minor walk on role'? It is only 25 lines, but I trust you would agree they are lines of some significance. You don't mention how the understudy system worked that year — how for the first time all our work was covered at a very high level. Nevertheless, I think the comment from the actors is absolutely fair, and accurate.

■ Since the aim and object of a serious theatre company such as the RSC must be to develop its work over a period of time, I find I just cannot comprehend your objection to a 'two or even three year period'. However I think you are talking about the natural concomitant of any repertoire company system, and not what you describe as 'the rotation system'. For example, David Warner, Elizabeth Spriggs, Brewster Mason and Tony Church played Hamlet, Gertrude, Claudius and Polonius in Peter Hall's production. Ian Holm played Henry V for three years during the 1964/65 and 66 seasons.

In the production of *Twelfth Night*, only Judi Dench, Emrys James, Lisa Harrow and Gordon Reid remained constant through the three versions. Malvolio was played by Donald Sinden, Derek Godfrey and Tony Pedley. Sir Toby was played by Bill Fraser, Leslie Sands and Tony Church. Aguecheek was played by Barrie Ingham and Jeffery Dench, Maria by Brenda Bruce, Elizabeth Spriggs and Janet Whiteside, Orsino by Charles Thomas and Richard Pasco, Fabian by Peter Geddis and Alton Kumalo, Antonio by Antony Langdon and Morgan Sheppard, The Sea Captain by Don Henderson and Sydney Bromley, etc. etc. During the period that *Twelfth Night* was retained, Judi Dench also played Hermione, Perdita, Major Barbara, Portia, the Duchess of Malfi and Grace in *London Assurance*, so there was not exactly the danger of staleness.

No other production performed for three consecutive seasons. The actors who played in all three versions were not under long term contract and did so at their choice. What therefore is *Twelfth Night* an illustration of? *The Revenger's Tragedy* was mounted three times. Before the two year plan. *The Comedy of Errors* four times. Before the two year plan. What is 'unenviable from any actors' point of view'? I just don't think you have a point here.

● I am not sure of your criteria here. Why is David Waller excluded from the notable exceptions list, or Ben Kingsley, or Estelle Kohler, or Patrick Stewart, or Susan Fleetwood? Which performance of Paul Scofield in the seventies were you thinking of? Which performance of Eric Porter were you thinking of since the late sixties. Is there any fundamental distinction between the periods of time that John Gielgud, Edith Evans, Ian Bannen, Christopher Plummer, Paul Rogers and Barbara Jefford have spent with the company and those that Nicol Williamson, Angela Lansbury and Alan Bates have recently. Except of course Nicol Williamson was a member of the company in 1963 and was not sufficiently promoted to stay — one of the home grown stars to slip through the net. A number of attempts were made during the past ten years to involve John Wood with the RSC. Fortunately that has now happened. He has been with the company for three years and is now entering his next period of work. Is his position substantially different from Eric Porter's ten years ago? Is your contention that the present artistic director should not admire certain actors (not associated with the previous administration) and wish to involve them in the company?

What I am trying to establish is that actors are promoted through the company with the same regularity, and actors from outside the company join with the same regularity. Aren't you really saying that you don't like the new people as much as the old?

▲ You quote enthusiastic reviews of *A Midsummer Night's Dream*. You quote enthusiastic reviews of *Old Times*. You are silent about *The Winter's Tale*. Why? It was called variously, the best thing the RSC had achieved since *The Wars of the Roses* and one of the finest productions of a Shakespeare play during the post war era. That is, a lot of the theory you quote actually worked in practice. It played with constant success in Stratford, Japan, Australia and London. Nobody could be aware of this from your account. Perhaps you saw the production and didn't like it. Fair enough. But surely you should acknowledge that the critical response was different from your own.

★ Since I insisted throughout the two years of presenting the Roman plays that they were not 'a cycle', I think it's misleading for you to use the term.

♦ The statement you quote is accurate. Undeniably I said it. Equally undeniably it is a vague and unfocused comment (for which perhaps we can all be forgiven once or twice in our lives). I have stated the thinking behind the Roman seasons with clarity and accuracy elsewhere, in programme notes, and the like. If you would like to publish a clear paragraph of my intentions, then I suggest this:

The plays are not a chronological cycle. They weren't conceived as a group. Nevertheless Shakespeare did return on four separate occasions to the same background — a state that developed from tribe to city to republic to empire, and was finally overrun by barbarous tribes. He uses that background to conduct a less inhibited examination of political motives and social organization than was possible when he was dealing with English history.

Working with the same group of actors over an extended period fascinates me — and given time, we may discover how much relationships the plays *do* have to each other.

♦ Clearly my personal feelings are involved here, and though I could challenge your factual accuracy in the use of such phrases as 'most reviewers' and 'mostly favourable' and 'there was some feeling', my main reaction is of anguished impotence as a victim of injustice. You quote a long section of a review about the failure of Janet Suzman's Cleopatra. You don't qualify this when you talk of the presentation of the plays at the Aldwych. Yet you know that her performance was hailed as the best Cleopatra that had as yet been seen, and this response was almost unanimous. The critical reaction to Richard Johnson went through a similar transformation. You don't mention it. You don't report the extraordinary diversity of critical comment with reviewers all recommending one of the plays as the best, and not to be missed, but each recommending a different play. You don't acknowledge that the productions of *Coriolanus, Julius Caesar* and *Antony and Cleopatra* are the most successful productions of these individual plays that have been done in England for a very long time (certainly since the RSC came into being).

Reference Section

The nature of the source materials available for a comprehensive study of the Royal Shakespeare Company makes a neatly documented reference section difficult. There is an abundance of raw material in the form of newspapers, pamphlets, programmes, advertising matter, press releases and various documents and letters concerning the artistic and administrative functions of the company; however, there is a lack of detailed historical studies of the development of the RSC, and of the many different aspects of the company's work. Much of the reference material for this work has been taken from the sources already mentioned, and also from tape-recorded interviews and speeches, theatre prompt books, letters and conversations with members of the RSC — past and present — over a two year period.

In view of these difficulties, this reference section has been divided into three parts. The first section lists books which have been of value for general reference; the second lists play texts and editions which have been specifically referred to; and the third lists the various source materials which have been made available through the Shakespeare Centre Library, Stratford-upon-Avon. It would be impossible to catalogue the many informal conversations with members of the RSC which have been of great assistance to this work. A list of recorded interviews with the author appears at the beginning of Part II.

I would like to thank all those who have allowed me to quote from material within their copyright: *The Daily Telegraph* and *Sunday Telegraph, The Sunday Times, The Observer, The Financial Times, The New Statesman, The Daily Mail, The Guardian, The Spectator, Amateur Stage, The Stratford-upon-Avon Herald, Nova, The Birmingham Evening Mail, The Stage, Tribune,* MacDonald & Janes, The Cambridge University Press, Max Reinhardt Ltd., Faber & Faber, Mr. Kenneth Tynan and Mr.

Gordon Gow; the quotations from *The Times* are reproduced with the kind permission of *The Times*, those from *The Birmingham Post* by courtesy of the *Birmingham Post* and the extract from *Tynan Right and Left* by Kenneth Tynan is reproduced by permission of Penguin Books Ltd.

The following books and articles have been used for general reference in the course of this work:

Artaud, A., *The Theatre and Its Double*, Calder and Boyars, 1970

Barton, J. and Hall, P., *The Wars of the Roses*, BBC Publication, 1970

Brook, P., *The Empty Space*, Macgibbon and Kee, 1968

Brown, I., *Shakespeare Memorial Theatre 1951-1953*, Reinhardt, 1953

Brown, I., *Shakespeare Memorial Theatre 1954-1956*, Reinhardt, 1956

Brown, I., *Shakespeare Memorial Theatre 1957-1959*, Reinhardt, 1959

Brown, I. and Quayle, A., *Shakespeare Memorial Theatre 1948-1950*, Reinhardt, 1950

Brown, J.R., 'The Study and Practice of Shakespeare Production', *Shakespeare Survey 18*, (Nicoll, A., *ed.*), Cambridge University Press, 1965

Brown, J.R., *Effective Theatre*, Heinemann, 1969

Brown, J.R., *Shakespeare's Plays in Performance*, Penguin, 1969

Brustein, R., *The Third Theatre*, Jonathan Cape, 1970

Clunes, A., *The British Theatre*, Cassell, 1964

Daubeny, P., *My World of Theatre*, Jonathan Cape, 1971

Day, M.C. and Trewin, J.C., *Shakespeare Memorial Theatre*, Dent, 1932

Dover Wilson, J. and Worsley, T.C., *Shakespeare's Histories at Stratford 1951*, Reinhardt, 1952

Ellis, R., *Shakespeare Memorial Theatre*, Winchester, 1948

Esslin, M., *The Peopled Wound: The Plays of Harold Pinter*, Methuen, 1970

Findlater, R., *Banned: A Review of Theatrical Censorship in Britain*, Macgibbon and Kee, 1967

Gay, F., *ed. Who's Who in the Theatre*, (14th edition), Pitman, 1967

Goodwin, J., *ed. Royal Shakespeare Theatre Company 1960-1963*, Reinhardt, 1964

Grotowski, J., *Towards A Poor Theatre*, Methuen, 1969

Hale, O., *and others, ed. The Encore Reader*, Methuen, 1965

Hartnoll, P., *ed. The Oxford Companion to the Theatre* (2nd edition), Oxford University Press, 1957

Hunt, H., *The Live Theatre*, Oxford University Press, 1962

Hunter, G.K., 'Macbeth in the Twentieth Century', *Shakespeare Survey 19*, (Muir, K., *ed.*) Cambridge University Press, 1966

Kemp, T.C. and Trewin, J.C., *The Stratford Festival*, Cornish, 1953

Kitchin, L., *Mid-Century Drama*, Faber, 1960

Kitchin, L., *Drama in the Sixties*, Faber, 1966

Kott, J., *Shakespeare Our Contemporary*, Methuen, 1964

Lloyd Evans, G., 'Shakespeare, The Twentieth Century and "Behaviourism" ', *Shakespeare Survey 20*, (Muir, K., *ed.*), Cambridge University Press, 1967

Lloyd Evans, G., 'Interpretation or Experience? Shakespeare at Stratford', *Shakespeare Survey 23*, (Muir, K. *ed.*), Cambridge University Press, 1970

Manvell, R., *Shakespeare and the Film*, Dent, 1971

Marowitz, C. and Trussler, S., *ed.*, Theatre at Work, Methuen, 1967

Marshall, N., *The Other Theatre*, Lehmann, 1947

Morley, S., *ed. Theatre 71*, Hutchinson, 1971

Nicoll, A., *The Development of the Theatre*, (5th edition), Harrap, 1966

Righter, A., *Shakespeare and the Idea of the Play*, Penguin, 1967

Rogoff, G., 'Richard's Himself Again', *Tulane Drama Review (T 34)*, Tulane University, 1966

St. Denis, M., *Theatre: The Rediscovery of Style*, Heinemann, 1960

Sprague, A.C. and Trewin, J.C., *Shakespeare's Plays Today*, Sidgwick and Jackson, 1970

Sweeting, E., *Theatre Administration*, Pitman, 1969

Tillyard, E.M.W., *Shakespeare's History Plays*, Chatto and Windus, 1944

Traversi, D.A., *An Approach to Shakespeare*, Sands, 1938

Trewin, J.C., *Shakespeare on the English Stage 1900-1964*, Barrie and Rockliff, 1964

Trewin, J.C., *The Birmingham Repertory Theatre 1913-1963*, Barrie and Rockliff, 1963

Trewin, J.C., *Benson and the Bensonians*, Barrie and Rockliff, 1960

Trewin, J.C., *Peter Brook: A biography*, Macdonald, 1971

Trewin, J.C., *Drama in Britain 1951-1964*, Longmans, 1965

Tynan, K., *Curtains*, Longmans, 1962

Tynan, K., *Tynan Right and Left*, Longmans, 1967

Wager, W., *ed. The Playwrights Speak*, Longmans, 1967

(B)

The following texts and editions of plays have been specifically referred to in the course of this work. For SMT and RSC Prompt Books see Section (C) below.

Barton, J., and Hall, P., *The Wars of the Roses*, BBC Publications, 1970

Marowitz, C., *The Marowitz Hamlet*, Penguin, 1968

Pinter, H., *The Homecoming*, Methuen, 1965

Pinter, H., *Old Times*, Methuen, 1971

Royal Shakespeare Company, *US* (Playscript 9), Calder & Boyars, 1968

Rudkin, D., *Afore Night Come*, (New English Dramatists 8), Penguin, 1963

Shakespeare, W., *Complete Works*, Craig, W.J., *ed.* (Oxford Standard Authors), Oxford University Press, 1905

Shakespeare, W., *Macbeth*, Hunter, G.K., *ed.* (New Penguin Shakespeare), Penguine, 1967

Tourneur, C., *The Revenger's Tragedy*, in *Three Jacobean Tragedies*, Salgado, G., *ed.*, Penguin, 1965

Weiss, P., *Marat-Sade*, Calder & Boyars, 1965

(C)

Much of the material used in this work has been made available through the collections held at the Shakespeare Centre Library,

Stratford-upon-Avon. The following is a list of the collections within which the relevant material is contained:

1. Shakespeare Memorial Theatre – Royal Shakespeare Company, Theatre Records, Volume 35 to Volume 80.
These volumes contain articles and extracts from newspapers and periodicals that are of relevance to the activities of the SMT and RSC over the years 1946 to 1971. They also contain programmes and pamphlets published by the theatre, and certain advertising material which was sometimes published separately from the normal production programmes.

All press quotations included in this work have been drawn from this source, and may be referred to by quoting the date and name of publication in which the article or review appeared. In some cases, the titles of newspaper reviews do not appear in the *Theatre Records*, but when available, they have been included in the footnotes.

2. Shakespeare Memorial Theatre – Royal Shakespeare Company, Annual Reports of the Board of Governors.
These reports are not available on general request, but only through personal application to the General Manager, Royal Shakespeare Company. All financial information and most statistical information included in this work has been taken from this source.

3. Royal Shakespeare Theatre, Tapes.
This collection consists of tape-recordings of various speeches and rehearsal talks given by Peter Hall and other members of the RSC between 1960 and 1968. These tapes are not available on general request, but only through personal application to the General Manager, Royal Shakespeare Company.

4. Shakespeare Memorial Theatre – Royal Shakespeare Company, Prompt Books.
Prompt Books of all SMT/RSC productions over the years 1960 to 1968.

5. Shakespeare Memorial Theatre — Royal Shakespeare Company, Programmes, 1946 to 1971.

6. Shakespeare Memorial Theatre — Royal Shakespeare Company, Production Photographs.

7. Shakespeare Memorial Theatre, General Boxes (from 1926).
These boxes contain collections of letters and documents that are of relevance to the activities of the Shakespeare Memorial Theatre.

Index